MAKING
THE BEST
OF IT

MAKING THE BEST OF IT

FOLLOWING CHRIST IN THE REAL WORLD

JOHN G. STACKHOUSE, JR.

OXFORD
UNIVERSITY PRESS

OXFORD
UNIVERSITY PRESS

Oxford University Press, Inc., publishes works that further
Oxford University's objective of excellence
in research, scholarship, and education.

Oxford   New York
Auckland   Cape Town   Dar es Salaam   Hong Kong   Karachi
Kuala Lumpur   Madrid   Melbourne   Mexico City   Nairobi
New Delhi   Shanghai   Taipei   Toronto

With offices in
Argentina   Austria   Brazil   Chile   Czech Republic   France   Greece
Guatemala   Hungary   Italy   Japan   Poland   Portugal   Singapore
South Korea   Switzerland   Thailand   Turkey   Ukraine   Vietnam

Published by Oxford University Press, Inc.
198 Madison Avenue, New York, NY 10016
www.oup.com

First issued as an Oxford University Press paperback, 2011

Oxford is a registered trademark of Oxford University Press

Library of Congress Cataloging-in-Publication Data
Stackhouse, John Gordon.
Making the best of it: following Christ in the real world
/ John G. Stackhouse.
p.   cm.
Includes bibliographical references and index.
ISBN 978-0-19-517358-1 (hardcover); 978-0-19-984394-7 (paperback)
1. Christianity and culture.   I. Title.
BR115.C8S7185 2008
261—dc22
2007034724

1 3 5 7 9 8 6 4 2

Printed in the United States of America
on acid-free paper

To the memory of
my beloved father
and best man,
John G. Stackhouse
(1935–2006),
who *always*
made the best of it

CONTENTS

ACKNOWLEDGMENTS

Even though this is a big, academic book, it is also in the nature of the case a highly individual one. For on this largest of all topics, Christian discipleship in the world, one can hope only to offer an individual vision—as informed and as careful a vision as possible, of course, but still necessarily individual.

Yet many people have contributed to the outlook expressed in this book. I am grateful for the Christians of Bethel Gospel Chapel in North Bay, Ontario, as I am for the Christian Brethren movement in Canada, of which it was a part. They provided a church family for me throughout my youth that manifested a serious, sectarian discipleship that marks me still.

I am grateful for the InterVarsity Christian Fellowship, which brought me out of my denominational enclave and into my first ecumenical contacts in high school and university. Its fine press likewise brought me Francis Schaeffer and others who introduced me to the bracing "world-transformative Christianity" of the Reformed tradition. Years at Wheaton College and Northwestern College deepened my acquaintance and regard for this vision, as did reading and contributing to the late, lamented *Reformed Journal*—with the voices of Rich Mouw and Nick Wolterstorff probably the most impressive to my ears on these matters.

Finally, I am glad that one of those Wheaton College/*Reformed Journal* stalwarts, a young professor named Mark Noll, mildly suggested in my graduate-student days that the Lutheran tradition, strange as it was to us, might have some important things to say that neither the sectarian sort nor the Reformed sort of evangelicalism was saying. From his tutelage, then, I went on to study under a couple of Lutherans: Jerald Brauer and Martin Marty. And Marty's influence upon my thinking in this sphere is best described as simply fundamental. I won't quote him much on the pages that follow, but the thousands of pages of his writing I have read and the hundreds of hours I have spent in his company have formed my outlook more than has any other source.

David Martin, however, has also shaped my thinking deeply on these matters. And I am grateful to David for his generous encouragement of several of my recent efforts, and this one in particular. To know that this book meets with his approval, if not complete agreement, is greatly reassuring, particularly given the vast fields I only sketchily and vulnerably survey in what follows. Likewise, I am thankful for the sharp eyes and kind nudges of Alan Jacobs, Robin Lovin, Craig Slane, and Jonathan Wilson, who read sections dealing with subjects on which they are truly expert. Hans Boersma and Gerry McDermott provided me with readings of the entire manuscript that were so perspicacious and wise that the book simply cannot meet their standards! But it is much the better for their many suggestions.

In the latter stages of research for this book, Regent College generously offered me time in a half-year sabbatical and the Association of Theological Schools generously provided me money in a Faculty Research Grant. Doug Harink and Jonathan Wilson guided me valuably in research zones unfamiliar to me, although I am sure they wish I had read more of, and been persuaded more by, the books they suggested.

My research assistant, Elaine Yu, simply does all things well. She has made this large project much easier from start to finish. (I mean that quite literally, as, among other things, she ably compiled the index.) Also from start to finish, I have enjoyed the support of editor Cynthia Read, whose patience on this project was tested, alas, and yet was found kindly sufficient. It is an honor to work with her again.

My sons, Trevor, Joshua, and Devon, have admirably stayed out of Papa's way when he was upstairs reading and writing. As they are now young men, I hope this book will soon help them at least a little through the vicissitudes they will face in the decades to come. My wife, Kari, has endured a number of vicissitudes already in the company of her husband, and for her record of making the best of it I am grateful from the heart.

While I was writing this book, my father shocked us all by passing away just after his seventy-first birthday; he was in such apparent good health that death came while he was pausing between racquetball games at his sports club. With the rest of our family I mourn the loss of someone who was, as Irenaeus put it, truly "the glory of God...a man fully alive."

MAKING
THE BEST
OF IT

INTRODUCTION

"Who is Jesus Christ, for us, today?" This question, posed by Dietrich Bonhoeffer in the middle of the last century, continues to guide Christian ethical thinking as it focuses our attention on the essential matter of the Christian religion, the person of Jesus Christ.[1] The Christian faith is both *faith in* Jesus of Nazareth, the Christ (Messiah) of God, and also *faithfulness to* Jesus Christ. (This double meaning is in both the Hebrew and Greek words for "faith" in the Bible.) Christian faith simply is discipleship to Jesus Christ.

Who is it, then, who has this faith and practices this faithfulness? We do. Christians do. But not only Christians in general—*we ourselves* both as particular individuals and as particular groups in a particular moment, in this place and time, today. Thus the "us" of Bonhoeffer's question whom I hope both to represent and to address in the present volume must be recognized as a particular kind of Christian: those living in North America, and then by extension those who live in similar modern, pluralistic societies—whether citizens of Frankfurt, Marseille, Edinburgh, Sydney, or Hong Kong. I expect this book will be of some use to Christians elsewhere, too, but I want to recognize that I cannot speak to everyone, for theology should not presume to speak timelessly and universally, but only as helpfully as possible in a particular context. So I aim to be useful to those who share important aspects of my own situation here in Vancouver, Canada.

---

1. Only Bonhoeffer aficionados will care, but I will observe that this question does not actually appear where it is always said to appear, namely, in Bonhoeffer's famous letter to Eberhard Bethge of 30 April 1944 (*Letters and Papers from Prison,* ed. Eberhard Bethge, trans. Reginald Fuller, Frank Clarke, and John Bowden [New York: Macmillan, 1962 (1953)], 279). Indeed, I have not found this exact locution anywhere in my reading in Bonhoeffer, nor have I found any citation to it, other than this one, among the secondary literature I have read (even though Larry Rasmussen, an expert on Bonhoeffer, claims that "Bonhoeffer frequently puts it" in this form [Larry Rasmussen, "The Ethics of Responsible Action," in *The Cambridge Companion to Dietrich Bonhoeffer,* ed. John W. de Gruchy (Cambridge, UK: Cambridge University Press, 1999), 219]). Bonhoeffer, in fact, writes thus: "What is bothering me incessantly is the question what Christianity really is, or indeed who Christ really is, for us today."

So Bonhoeffer starts where we all should start: with Jesus Christ, whose identity and mission constitute the heart of *our* identity and mission. And as we consider Christ, and then the whole Bible's testimony to God's work in the world, we confront a second, corollary question that I suggest also lies at the heart of the Christian religion: *Who are we, for Jesus Christ, today?*[2]

Answering this second question is the task of this book. The question is that of ethos, the character or nature of something or someone. We have come to think of ethics in terms of morality, of right and wrong. But following Jesus is not just a matter of discerning and practicing what is morally good, just as ethics derives from a more fundamental concept, the concept of essence, of what it is to *be* this or that. Thus medical ethics, at least traditionally, goes beyond bioethics to questions even of dress (lab coat or not), etiquette, advertising of services, and so on—what is proper to the profession of medicine in its several modes. Christian ethics, then, is not primarily about what to do rightly or wrongly, but fundamentally about what it is to *be Christian in the world,* what is proper to the profession and practice of Christian faith. Being Christian in the world is an identity, a motive, an agenda, and a posture, all of which lead into action. As Glenn Tinder puts it, albeit with the word "political" pointing toward the broader character of "cultural" in this phrase, "I believe that the primary political requirement of Christianity is not a certain kind of society or a particular program of action but rather an attitude, a way of facing society and of undertaking programs of action."[3]

Dietrich Bonhoeffer's own discussion of this matter is therefore entitled *Ethik*.[4] His countryman Paul Tillich is usually credited with inventing the term "theology of culture" for what in fact "ethics" used to denote in English and *Ethik* still denoted in German in the middle of the twentieth century: a comprehensive theological understanding of the world and of the Christian role in it.[5] So this book is an ethics in the older sense and thus a theology of culture: a theology of

---

2. Bonhoeffer gives his own version of this question, albeit not quite the same one, on the opening page of *The Cost of Discipleship:* "What we want to know is...what Jesus Christ himself wants of us" (trans. R. H. Fuller [New York: Simon and Schuster, 1995 [1937]).

3. Glenn Tinder, *The Political Meaning of Christianity: An Interpretation* (Baton Rouge: Louisiana State University Press, 1989), 8.

4. See Dietrich Bonhoeffer, *Dietrich Bonhoeffer Works,* vol. 6: *Ethics,* ed. Clifford Green, trans. Reinhard Krauss, Charles West, and Douglas Stott (Minneapolis: Augsburg Fortress, 2005).

5. William Schweiker explains: "In various writings on the theology of culture, Paul Tillich noted that it is actually a contemporary version of what Friedrich Schleiermacher...meant by 'ethics.' According to Schleiermacher, ethics is the comprehensive and normative examination of culture and history aimed at providing orientation of life.... By the time Tillich was writing, that capacious conception of ethics had been lost to the focus on moral imperatives and generalized duties.... Insofar as that was the case, what should we call an analysis of human world-making and self-formation, especially if one is attentive to the religious

cultivation, of human activity on earth, of living out the primeval command of God to human beings: "Till the earth" (Gen. 2:15).[6]

This book is, indeed, a book of theology, as long as "theology" is here broadly understood. The word "theology" can mean at least four things: (1) the doctrine of God itself within the various topics of systematic theology: for example, the doctrine of Christ (Christology), the doctrine of salvation (soteriology), the doctrine of the church (ecclesiology), and so on—and therefore what theologians sometimes call "theology proper"; (2) any systematic account of some teachings on spiritual subjects: for example, the theology of the Book of Isaiah, the theology of Paul's epistles, the theology of Augustine, the theology of the Roman Catholic Church; (3) the discipline of systematic, or sometimes "dogmatic," theology, which integrates the various other disciplines of theological study (such as Biblical theology, philosophical theology, and historical theology) into a contemporary statement of Christian confession; and (4) reflection on any subject that is conducted with primary reference to the special revelation given to us in the person of Christ and in the Scriptures: thus one can speak of a theology of work, or a theology of art, or a theology of the family.

Theology of culture, therefore, is theology in the fourth, broadest sense: a God-centered understanding of culture shaped by what God has revealed to us about it. Whatever its level of sophistication, theology of culture asks simply this: What is the world? What is our identity and mission in the world? What, in short, is our vocation? *Who are we, for Jesus Christ, today?*

I have written this book because Christians in North America, but also in Britain, Europe, Australia, New Zealand, and other modern societies, typically encounter one or both of only two models of serious Christian engagement with the world and I think we need another—or, at least, most of us do. The one extant option is the option of cultural transformation, of totally reshaping society according to Christian values. This is the option espoused by the American

---

character of these activities? Tillich called it the theology of culture" ("Having@Toomuch. com: Property, Possession, and the Theology of Culture," *Criterion* 39 [spring 2000]: 27).

6. Langdon Gilkey, a student of both Paul Tillich and Reinhold Niebuhr, comments from a different angle, that of the definition of "theology" rather than "ethics": "The task of theology is no longer merely the elucidation of 'doctrines' from the sources of scripture and tradition, nor merely the effort to prove by reason the validity of Christian affirmations. It is now even more the interpretation of the mystery and travail of human existence, social history and personal history, by means of the symbols of Christian faith, to show that it is these symbols, and these alone, that make sense of the confusions of ordinary life. These theological changes, therefore, provide the ground not only of an innovative theological analysis of the entire scope of human existence, but of a new discipline as well, the theology of culture, or, better for Niebuhr, the theology of society" (*On Niebuhr: A Theological Study* [Chicago: University of Chicago Press, 2001], 26). As different as Tillich or Niebuhr is from me theologically, we share this interest in theologically interpreting the world, the human place in it, and the role of the church in God's economy.

religious right—and left. It is also expressed in the more refined accents of neo-
Calvinism, the "world-formative" or "transformational" agenda of the tradition
descending from Abraham Kuyper and Herman Bavinck in the Netherlands of
the late nineteenth century and extended into the twentieth century via Herman
Dooyeweerd, D. H. Th. Vollenhoven, and Hans Rookmaaker. A similar movement is the approach of conservative Roman Catholicism, which seeks in its own
way to influence culture along Christian lines and ideally to transform it into
a thoroughly Christian enterprise. Journals such as *First Things,* writers such as
George Weigel and Richard John Neuhaus, and, indeed, popes John Paul II and
Benedict XVI have articulated a Catholic agenda of pervading and ultimately
dominating culture—with the help and guidance of the Holy Spirit.[7] And liberation theologies, beginning with Gustavo Gutiérrez and James Cone, articulate
their respective social-transformationalist visions.

The main alternative on offer is the response of holy distinctness, of a definite
Christian community living in contradistinction to the rest of society and thus
offering the beneficial example and influence of an alternative way of life. In
popular religious culture this shows up in Protestant sectarianism, whether in the
enclaves of fundamentalism, the burgeoning but self-consciously marginal congregations of Pentecostalism, or the traditional communities of Mennonites, Amish,
and Hutterites. This option also has its sophisticated versions, particularly in the
community of thought arising out of the writing of the Anabaptist ethicist John
Howard Yoder and his Methodist epigone Stanley Hauerwas, and more recently
out of the movement known as Radical Orthodoxy, identified with John Milbank,
Catherine Pickstock, and others. Disgust with the religious right, and particularly
with the comfortable alliance between evangelical Christianity and conservative
politics, drives these Christians away from dubious cultural entanglements into
fellowships of the dedicated that shine like cities on a hill above a plain on which
Matthew Arnold's confused armies war by night. From these places of integrity
they offer what help they can to their neighbors while refusing any activity that
would compromise their radical testimony to the gospel of new life.

One cannot help being impressed by the zeal, vision, and integrity of many
Christians in one or another of these various traditions. Any auditor or reader
who does not opt for one of them, however—whether "take it over" or "refuse all
entanglements"—can be prompted by partisans to feel guilt over his compromise,
to feel shame over her capitulation. *Serious* Christians, so we have been told, elect
one of these and pursue it with single-minded confidence.

---

7. An epitome of such thinking can be found in George Weigel, "World Order: What Catholics
Forgot," *First Things* 143 (May 2004): 31–38.

We must acknowledge immediately that the Bible itself can seem to focus on extremes, rather than on negotiated intermediate positions. David Martin, himself a professed Niebuhrian realist, remarks that "Christian language is of little help in the resolution of conflict, because it moves necessarily between the poles of alienation and reconciliation, loss and retrieval, ex-communication and communication, rather than political compromise and reasoned negotiation."[8]

I think David Martin is right about most things, but I hope he is wrong about this assertion, because most of us live in a world that is grayer than these black-and-white options, and some of us earnestly want Biblical guidance for such living. Indeed, most of us make our way in a world in which success means asking for ten, hoping for eight, and settling for six. We experience compromise, disappointment, unexpected impediments, and unintended consequences.

When we garden (to draw on an ancient Biblical image), we industriously prepare the soil, select the plants, tend and protect them as best we can, and expect a harvest of flowers or fruit. But we know that pests will return, that some plants will not thrive, and that drought or flood might wipe out a year's work in a week. Still, we don't then withdraw into a hydroponic alternative in a nice, safe greenhouse. Likewise, when we build a dwelling, we plan carefully, budget appropriately, hire the most reputable workers we can find, and lay in the best materials we can afford. We set to work and something good comes of it, even though we inevitably encounter labor problems, cost overruns, defective materials, perhaps an earthquake. We don't give up building or gardening, even though we know we will not achieve anything like the ideal.

So is there a theology to undergird and direct such life in the real world? Is there a legitimate, even commendable, theology—not of cultural conquest nor of cultural withdrawal, but of cultural *persistence*—that can inspire Christian vocation? There have been indeed such theologies, upon which we still can draw. And it is my hope to provide such a theology to help us answer both realistically and hopefully this central question: *Who are we, for Jesus Christ, today?*

This book comes in three parts. The first provides basic categories in which to consider the matters related to being Christian in the world today. After defining such fundamental terms as "church," "world," "Kingdom of God," and "culture," it proceeds to an exposition of H. Richard Niebuhr's now-classic categories of "Christ" and "culture." Niebuhr's typology has not always been well understood, and it has been soundly criticized. It endures, however, as the touchstone for everyone discussing these things. And I believe it can be improved in several ways—none of which is more important than the rehabilitation of the "Christ in

---

8. David Martin, *Christian Language in the Secular City* (Aldershot, UK: Ashgate, 2002), 13.

paradox with culture" type that is clearly the option least well presented by Niebuhr and also the option with which I am most in sympathy in this book. I cheerfully recommend, however, that those readers not interested in this definitional discussion should proceed directly to the substantive parts of the book that follow.

From these preliminary matters, then, we turn in Part Two to examine three mid-twentieth-century figures from whom I have particularly profited in thinking about these things: C. S. Lewis, Reinhold Niebuhr, and Dietrich Bonhoeffer. I look at both their writings and their lives for clues—both positive and negative—about what it can mean to be Christian in our day. I do not hereby mean to imply that these three white, well-educated, middle-class, Western Christian men say all there is to say about these matters. Dorothy Day, Karl Barth, Martin Luther King Jr., Gustavo Gutiérrez, James Cone, Mother Teresa, Bob Goudzwaard, Vladimir Soloviev, Simone Weil, John Paul II, Jacques Maritain, Nikolai Berdyaev, Hans Urs von Balthasar, Jacques Ellul, and Wendell Berry represent just some of the diversity in the modern Christian conversation on these matters. And as globalization and modernization proceed apace, we will want to hear voices more varied still. I have been educated in the mainstream North American academy, however, and so I offer simply what I have found most valuable in formulating what I myself want to contribute to this conversation.

Moreover, George Steiner avers that "the best readings of art are art" rather than criticism per se.[9] Inspired by that bon mot, albeit with gratitude to the many scholars from whose criticism I have indeed profited, I offer a reading of the ethical work of Lewis, Niebuhr, Bonhoeffer, and others, particularly by producing some of my own. In this light, I will not pause in the rest of the book to keep quoting Lewis, Niebuhr, or Bonhoeffer. I could do so indefinitely, but the book is not, after all, about them. It is instead about broad themes that they suggestively addressed and that I myself take up in Part Three.

In the third part, therefore, I offer a set of basic theological and ethical considerations. I begin by establishing the folly of relying on mere slogans in ethics and thus the need for theory that is both sound and sufficiently complicated for the subject matter. I then set out some methodological reflections on how to construct ethics in our time. I proceed to discuss the value of locating ourselves properly along the time line of the great Biblical narrative, and the dangers of mistaking our place on it. Then we will explore the nature of God's mission in the world, and ours, and go on to trace out our callings, as humans and as Christians, in their multifold complexity. A series of principles and practices will emerge from, and

---

9. George Steiner, *Real Presences* (Chicago: University of Chicago Press, 1989), 17.

complement, the foregoing fundamental ideas. I conclude with some overarching motifs to govern our being and acting in the world.

While the argument in this book is not directly linear, I trust that the book's unity will emerge if it is seen as an exercise in thematic recursion: from an initial statement of the problematic via H. Richard Niebuhr to an exposition of a number of aspects of that problematic in three key writers and then to an extended commendation of a particular model of cultural engagement. I intend, therefore, that the reader will close this book with a multiply reinforced sense of the global largeness of God's mission, the significance of our vocation, the hope of our destiny, and the nature of the reality we must negotiate in the meanwhile. With that sense, I hope that he or she will then be better motivated and equipped to do what God called the first man and woman to do with the world he had created: to make the best of it.

PART I

THE CLASSIC TYPOLOGY

ONE

REAPPROPRIATING H. RICHARD NIEBUHR'S *CHRIST AND CULTURE*

Theological history has been made in Constantinople, Rome, Paris, and Berlin, of course, but also in Hippo, North Africa; in Wittenberg, Saxony; in Basel, Switzerland—and in Austin, Texas. For in 1949, the Austin Presbyterian Theological Seminary hosted Yale professor of ethics H. Richard Niebuhr to deliver a series of lectures. The book that emerged out of them, *Christ and Culture,* stands as a headwater of all subsequent discussion of the huge issues he addressed, providing a set of categories that have been criticized and modified, but not abandoned, for more than half a century.

Niebuhr wove these categories out of remarkably disparate materials, as is evident in the few he mentions in his acknowledgments: not only the Bible and Augustine's *City of God,* but also sociologist Ernst Troeltsch's *The Social Teachings of the Christian Churches,* historian Etienne Gilson's *Reason and Revelation in the Middle Ages*, and psychologist Carl Jung's *Psychological Types*.[1] He drew on his considerable knowledge of church history as well to furnish examples for his generalizations. The results of this groundbreaking work—both the categories and the examples—have since been soundly criticized but, I maintain, without invalidating his project and its abiding usefulness for us today.

DEFINITIONS

Before turning to Niebuhr's categories—his formulations of the various ways in which "Christ" could relate to "culture"—we should begin with defining the crucial terms themselves.

---

1. H. Richard Niebuhr, "Acknowledgments," in *Christ and Culture,* expanded ed. with a new foreword by Martin E. Marty and a new preface by James M. Gustafson (San Francisco: Harper, 2001 [1951]), xi–xii.

Culture

One of the common understandings of "culture" associates it with refined living, sophisticated taste, and elite education. Opera, ballet, knowledge of wine and classical languages—these are marks of a cultured person. The roots of this definition lie in the early modern period, with the cosmopolitan sense of civilization that all right-thinking people were supposed to share. As counterpart to this understanding of culture—really, high culture—we have popular culture, marked in our time by supermarket tabloids, major feature films, mass consumer fads, and the like.[2]

In the nineteenth century, the definition of culture shifted, particularly as Germans, concerned to unite their various fragmented principalities into a single country, emphasized what was ethnically distinctive (and thus worthy of institutionalization in a nation-state) over against the reigning ideal of universal humanity espoused by the Enlightenment. The Germans pointed to what they characterized as their distinctive literature, philosophy, politics, music, and so on to demonstrate how different (and superior) their *Kultur* was from, say, that of the French or English. So "culture" became associated with ethnic diversity and particularly with its most elevated and characteristic expressions.[3]

Let's pull back and consider a general sense of ethnic diversity as another important way to define culture. We speak of particular "societies": that is, groups of human beings who conduct some kind of common life, whether in a state (Canadian society), a professional guild (the Society for the Scientific Study of Religion), or a service organization (the Cancer Society). We then characterize the common life of a given society as its "culture," meaning how that society has organized itself and what it then does. We thus can speak of Arab culture, or the corporate culture of Microsoft, or even the culture of the homeless.

Such a definition moves out from the value-laden sense of high or low culture into a value-free analysis of what human beings, particularly or generally, do in the world. In this vein, Martin E. Marty has defined culture as "everything humans do to, and make of, nature."[4] Culture is *what is made,* therefore, as we

---

2. See the wonderfully opinionated essay by Martha Bayles, *Hole in Our Soul: The Loss of Beauty and Meaning in American Popular Music* (Chicago: University of Chicago Press, 1994), esp. ch. 1.

3. See Kathryn Tanner, *Theories of Culture: A New Agenda for Theology* (Minneapolis: Fortress, 1997), 3–37.

4. Martin E. Marty, "Cross-Multicultures in the Crossfire," in David A. Hoekema and Bobby Fong, eds., *Christianity and Culture in the Crossfire* (Grand Rapids, MI: Eerdmans, 1997), 15. C. S. Lewis points to the ambiguities in this apparently straightforward term "nature": "Nature is a word of varying meanings, which can best be understood if we consider its various opposites. The Natural is the opposite of the Artificial, the Civil, the Human, the Spiritual,

see in the related word group of "art," "artifice," "artificial," "artisan," and so on—that is, not natural, but cultured or cultivated. Thus a scientist cultures a bacterium and a farmer practices agriculture.

Beyond this level of what we do is the level of the *meanings* a society gives to its various actions. Beyond what is made, then, we have the question "What do they make of it?" What are a society's values? Why does it do what it does, and in what symbols does it encode its preferences, fears, and loves? Ultimately, what is the worldview that is being expressed in these meanings and activities?[5] Thus, in the clever pun of Ken Myers, culture is "what we make of creation—in both senses of the word *make*."[6]

In everyday speech, we often blur the difference between "society" and "culture," using them as synonyms, and that's usually fine in this conversation also. When Richard Niebuhr himself was addressing the question of Christ and culture, he meant not high culture but society at large, the broad cultural context in which Christians are making their way:

> What we have in view when we deal with Christ and culture is that total process of human activity and that total result of such activity to which now the name *culture*, now the name *civilization*, is applied in common speech. Culture is the "artificial, secondary environment" which man superimposes on the natural. It comprises language, habits, ideas, beliefs, customs, social organization, inherited artifacts, technical processes, and values.[7]

---

and the Supernatural" (*The Abolition of Man: How Education Develops Man's Sense of Morality* [New York: Macmillan, 1947], 80–81). Thus "nature" can mean the creation, the cosmos, the whole show; it can mean wild versus cultivated; it can refer to the subhuman creation (what we sometimes call our "environment") versus humans; it can denote the original created state versus the fallen state; paradoxically, it can also be used for the fallen state versus the sanctified state; it can mean the essence of something in distinction from its nonessential or "accidental" qualities; it often means the ordinary state of something versus a perversion of it ("unnatural")—and perhaps more. Having compiled this list of definitions, it is yet my hope that the pertinent definition of "nature" in each case will be evident from the context in what follows. But we will also see, in the last part of this book, that the ambiguity of "nature" does sometimes play an important part in certain key discussions in the theology of culture—such as any instance of arguing from "what is" to "what ought to be," which might imply that nature is entirely good.

5. Lucien Legrand helpfully distinguishes what I have blurred together here: the *meanings* of the symbols, practices, and language of a society and the *values* of that society—what is variously *important* among all of these. See his *The Bible on Culture: Belonging or Dissenting?* (Maryknoll, NY: Orbis, 2000), xiv.

6. Quoted by Andy Crouch, "Interstate Nation," *Christianity Today*, 10 June 2002, 55.

7. Niebuhr, *Christ and Culture*, 32. Niebuhr's own footnote cites encyclopedia articles by James Harvey Robinson, Carl Brinkmann, and Bronislaw Malinowski, without directly citing the source for the quoted phrase in the quotation above.

This use of "culture" leads to yet another definition, namely, the dominant culture within a pluralistic society: the activities and values that characterize the majority. Thus it can make sense for a Japanese Christian to remark that Japanese culture is resistant to Christianity. She is speaking about broad and deep currents in her national culture that do not simply characterize everyone within it—they do not, obviously, characterize *her*, as a Christian herself—but that do in fact constitute the prevailing social context in which everyone in Japan must make his or her way. And it is this definition of "culture" that Niebuhr usually means in his book.

In this regard, finally, we need to remark on the fact that characteristic of modern society is the experience of *differentiation* of social sectors and groups, such that each individual negotiates a variety of societies, and thus cultures, all the time. These cultures normally share certain features, so they can be called subcultures of the dominant culture. But they can also be significantly different: the primary values of her office job (for example, producing a useful product and collecting a fair profit) are not the same as those of her athletic club (maximizing personal physical fitness), of her church (loving God, sharing life with other Christians, and serving the world), or of her work with a youth agency (providing a safe and encouraging relationship for a needy child). And as each individual in a given society brings to that society his or her experience in the other cultures in his or her life, that society also is somewhat variegated.

As Richard Madsen and his colleagues put it,

> Every interpretation of a culture takes part in a "conflict of interpretations," in Paul Ricoeur's phrase, and this conflict characterizes, indeed, constitutes culture as a multi-vocal conversation and argument. It is a conversation about how we ought to live in accord with reality as it is, and how we ought to think about how to live.[8]

We thus have further reason to beware of any monolithic sense of a culture, even one of a relatively small society. And we must be aware instead of the need for each of us—indeed, for each society—to learn to identify and interact well with the variety of cultures with which we find ourselves in contact as we make our way in the world.

Niebuhr didn't remark on it, but it remains true that there is no word in the Bible—in the languages of either Testament—for "culture." Standard Bible

---

8. Richard Madsen et al., "Introduction," in Richard Madsen, William M. Sullivan, Ann Swidler, and Steven M. Tipton, eds., *Meaning and Modernity: Religion, Polity, and Self* (Berkeley: University of California Press, 2002), xii.

study reference texts do not include an entry on it. Instead, we should look to a word that overlaps with, but must not be simply identified with "culture": "world."

World

It is worth exploring the word "world" because it resonates so negatively for many Christians. They recall snatches of Scripture—"in the world you have tribulation," "be not conformed to this world," "the world has hated me, so it will hate you" (Jn. 16:33; Rom. 12:2; Jn. 15:18)—that together constitute a spiritual collage of darkness and danger. When it comes to relating to culture, "worldliness" is the chief category of capitulation. And this is hardly a recent phenomenon in Christian sentiment: John Bunyan's pilgrim is nearly done in by the advice of Mr. Worldly-Wise and the blandishments of the world at Vanity Fair. So is the world always bad? And is it the same as culture? If so, then we can save ourselves any more theologizing and head for the hills.

The New Testament includes a range of words that are translated as "world" in English versions. The words *aiōn* (age) and *kairos* (time) have English equivalents in the sense of "the world of the dinosaurs" or "the world of Napoleon." The word *gē* emeans "soil," "land," "earth," and, by a similar derivation in English, "planet" (the way we speak of "the earth" or "Earth"). It is the root of our words "geology" and "geography." Another word, *oikoumenē,* is sometimes combined with *gē* to mean "the inhabited world," rooted as it is in *oikos* (house); thus a kind of household symbol extends to the whole household of humanity, so to say. The word *ktisis* and the expression *ta panta* are rendered "creation" or "the all," and show up also in some translations as "world." More familiar to English readers would be *kosmos,* which can mean the "whole of creation" or "the inhabited world," and also a combination of these ideas: "the world of humankind."

Clearly, then, only some of these uses of "world" are pertinent to our topic. Furthermore, while the Bible frequently speaks of the world negatively, it also refers to it neutrally or positively.

The New Testament in particular is replete with warnings about the world as an evil place, as a system of institutions, individuals, and values under evil dominion, with evil consequences. The world hates and persecutes Jesus and his disciples (Jn. 7:7; 15:18–19; 16:33; Jas. 4:4). It cannot receive the Holy Spirit (Jn. 14:17) and does not know the Father (Jn. 17:25; I Jn. 3:1). The world's entire mentality is badly confused, especially about ultimate matters (Rom. 12:2; I Cor. 1:20–21). Indeed, the current world order is under the dominion of Satan and other evil powers (Mt. 4:8–9; Jn. 12:31; Gal. 4:3; Eph. 2:2; I Jn. 5:19). As such a deranged and harmful entity, ultimately it will be condemned (I Cor. 11:32) and finally "pass away" (I Jn. 2:15–17). Thus in the few uses of the term, not surprisingly, the adjective "worldly" is bad (II Cor. 7:10; Tit. 2:12; Jude 19).

Yet again, however, the world sometimes is simply the earth or the inhabited world, a neutral thing, as in "a decree went out from Emperor Augustus that all the world should be registered" (Lk. 2:1). Moreover, the original verdict of God on his creation of the world was that it was "very good" (Gen. 1:31), and his ultimate purpose for the world is salvation (Jn. 3:16–17; II Cor. 5:19; I Jn. 4:14).[9] Therefore we cannot too quickly assume a straightforward (negative) answer to the question of how Christians are to relate to the world.

What, then, of any connection with the word "culture"? The words for world and the idea of culture clearly intersect in the sphere of human society, work, and meaning. The world is both what we're given to work with and what we then make of it. So we will refer to Biblical passages in which "world" is used if they can cast light on our questions of society and culture. For the time being, we can proceed with an openness to see the world, and culture, as not necessarily and totally bad, but hardly as necessarily good, either. The world instead is in a complex condition that is explicable both in abstract terms and in the narrative of the Bible, both of which we will turn to presently.

Church

The word "church" can mean several things, ranging from a sacred building to a local congregation, an international denomination, and even the entire community of those saved by Jesus Christ. But its central definition comes from *ekklēsia,* a gathering or assembly of those who have named Jesus as Lord and who join together to worship him, serve each other, and work with God in his mission to the world. In what follows, therefore, I will use the word in this central way: those who are committed as disciples of Jesus Christ and who band together as such. But sometimes I will mean simply the visible institution, the church as the society of those who nominally follow Jesus, however sincerely or insincerely they do so. I trust that context will make the pertinent definition clear.

---

9. I believe that this is my first use of personal pronouns for God in the present volume. I practice inclusive language for human beings, but for God I use masculine pronouns, as does the Bible and Christian tradition. As a feminist, I appreciate that this is a vexed issue, and I discuss some of the semantic and political questions here: "A Woman's Place Is in…Theology?" appendix in *Finally Feminist: A Pragmatic Christian Understanding of Gender* (Grand Rapids, MI: Baker Academic, 2005), 115–29. I ask for forbearance from readers who would prefer me to have made different choices on this question.

Kingdom of God

Jesus came preaching the Kingdom of God. Christians believe that God is always ultimately in control of the world, as God is the basis of all existence everywhere. It is not the case that Satan has somehow wrested control of this "silent planet" away from God and so must be paid off or conquered in order to free it from his grasp.[10] To be sure, Satan does enjoy a limited sphere of influence over the world, as (we should remember in this respect) do human sovereigns, and each makes a certain amount of mischief.[11] As Tom Wright puts it, "In one sense God has always been sovereign over the world and...in another sense this sovereignty, this saving rule, is something which must break afresh into the world of corruption, decay and death, and the human rebellion, idolatry and sin which are so closely linked with it."[12] There is nothing in the universe, however, that is not entirely dependent upon God's sustaining power, moment to moment—including whatever intermediate princes there may be, whether diabolical or human rulers. (The book of Daniel speaks of all three kinds of "kingdoms," and makes clear that "there is a God in heaven" [Dan. 2:28] who sees and supervises all, even as he allows subordinates a sometimes startling range of freedom.) So there is a fundamental sense in which the universe (and whatever lies beyond it) has always been, and always shall be, the realm of God, over which he exercises sovereignty.

In the Synoptic Gospels, however, we encounter a second definition of the Kingdom of God. Jesus proclaimed that "the kingdom of God is at hand" (Mt. 3:2). Jesus' life inaugurated God's direct and uncompromised rule on earth. The Kingdom of God is where, we might say, God's ways are the way, and God's rules are the rule. The Kingdom of God is where God's judgment—which both assesses good and evil and restores them to their rightful places—has taken place, and *shalom* (peace, wholeness, and goodness) characterizes all things. The Kingdom of God is thus where God's authority is joyfully embraced as legitimate and welcome.

This authority was fully evident in Jesus himself. Moreover, Jesus' life, death, resurrection, and ascension mark the irreversible beginning of the end for evil

---

10. The classic survey of such themes is Gustav Aulén, *Christus Victor: An Historical Study of the Three Main Types of the Idea of the Atonement*, trans. Jaroslav Pelikan (New York: Macmillan, 1969). In our own time, C. S. Lewis's *The Lion, the Witch, and the Wardrobe* (Harmondsworth, UK: Puffin, 1959 [1950]) doubtless has confirmed this idea in the imaginations of many readers, and the term "silent planet" comes from Lewis's novel *Out of the Silent Planet* (London: Macmillan, 1943).

11. Michael Green, *I Believe in Satan's Downfall* (London: Hodder and Stoughton, 1981).

12. N. T. Wright, *Scripture and the Authority of God* (London: Society for Promoting Christian Knowledge, 2005), 21.

everywhere and the beginning of the eternal reign of God on the earth God once made and has always cared for. This reign clearly has not begun in anything like its final fullness. The Kingdom of God is "already, but not yet," here. It is the Christian hope, however, that it will come once and for all with the triumphant return of the one who inaugurated it. And, as the Jewish Scriptures prophesied of Messiah, "his kingdom shall have no end"—neither in time nor in space.

Greater clarity on this much disputed phrase, "the Kingdom of God," can be gained by recognizing that other New Testament authors use different expressions for the same thing: John tends to use "eternal life" and Paul to use "salvation." They doubtless are reflecting the early church's mission to the Gentiles, for whom a phrase such as "Kingdom of God" might connect too closely with the particular Jewish hope for the political emancipation of the nation of Israel by a Davidic monarch, rather than with the universal offer of deliverance from the powers of this world and a blessed place in the next under the rule of God himself. Thus Jesus' terminology, appropriate for his mission to the Jews as recorded in the Synoptics, is translated—under the inspiration of the Holy Spirit—into these other, more widely relevant terms.[13]

The Kingdom of God in this sense, therefore, means the coming of God's salvation and the eternal life it brings—which is, indeed, experienced "already, but not yet," by all those who put their trust in God, follow his ways, and look forward to his eventual renewal of all things.[14]

The Church and the Kingdom

What, then, of the relationship of "church" and "Kingdom of God"? The church is not coextensive with the Kingdom of God, and in two respects.

Negatively, we observe that there are individuals and groups within the visible, institutional church who do not, in fact, follow the way of Jesus. They are "wolves in sheep's clothing" (Mt. 7:15), hypocrites, false prophets, simoniacs, and the like: those who enter the doors of the church and who take on themselves the name of Jesus without any serious intention of submitting to, much less furthering, the Kingdom of God. Moreover, we recognize that we ourselves, no matter the sincer-

---

13. See the passages in the Synoptics themselves that interchange terms: Mk. 9:43–47 par., 10: 17–30 par.; Mt. 25:31–46. And also see Jesus' discussion with Nicodemus for a similar interplay in Jn. 3.

14. A fine brief introduction to this complicated question can be found in Joel B. Green and Scot McKnight, *Dictionary of Jesus and the Gospels* (Downers Grove, IL: InterVarsity, 1992), s.v. "Kingdom of God/Heaven."

ity of our profession and the vigor of our practice, maintain pockets and episodes of infidelity in which we fail to maintain, much less extend, the Kingdom of God.

Positively, in the view of many Christians (sometimes called "inclusivists"), there are people beyond the church who have put God first in their lives and are serving him as best they can. They have not yet heard of Jesus and thus have not joined the church as self-consciously Christian disciples. By God's justifying and renewing grace, however, they have responded in faith to the Holy Spirit's testimony in their hearts and to whatever revelation God has brought to them in their particular circumstances. Thus they enjoy genuine Kingdom life and are cooperating with God to reform the world according to God's values, however seriously their outlook and experience are compromised by their lack of exposure to the gospel of Christ and their lack of contact with the church.[15]

Furthermore, the influence of God's Kingdom has been spreading, bit by bit, wherever individuals, groups, nations, and transnational realities have been influenced for the better. In our day, for example, the increased profile of universal human rights in national and international politics—with particular attention to women, children, and the poor (recognizing that women and children constitute most of the poor)—is an example of the spread of the influence of the Kingdom of God incognito, so to speak. It is obvious that the international order is far from Christian in its identity and conduct. In that crucial sense it is clearly *not* the Kingdom of God. Nonetheless, the Kingdom of God is partially and mixedly, but also really, present in the extension of these values into spheres previously not deeply shaped by them.

We see the marks of the Kingdom of God, then, wherever light penetrates darkness, wherever good makes its way against evil or inertia, wherever beauty emerges amid ugliness or vapidity, and wherever truth sounds out against error or falsity. And as we gladly recognize these marks, we also long for the complete manifestation of God's reign in the return of his Son.

We thus imply a third distinction between church and Kingdom, which is nicely set out by Richard Bauckham:

Between Old Testament Israel and the eschatological Kingdom there lie two forms of society in which the Kingdom is only partially and in dif-

---

15. For a guide to the issues here, see my "Afterword: An Agenda for an Evangelical Theology of Religions," in *No Other Gods Before Me? Evangelicals and the Challenge of World Religions*, ed. John G. Stackhouse Jr. (Grand Rapids, MI: Baker Academic, 2001), 189–201.

ferent ways anticipated: the Church and the state. The Church, because it is a voluntary, not a political, community, ought to be able to live out the religious and moral demands of God in relationship to him *more* fully than Old Testament Israel could.... [Yet] the extent to which Israel, as envisaged in the law, provides a model for the *Church* must be qualified: the specifically political element in the model finds no realization in the Church. On the other hand, the norms for human life in political society which are expressed in the Old Testament law can to some degree be realized in other political societies. But this realization will be qualified by the fact that no political society, however much influenced by biblical faith, manifests, as a political society, the kind of wholehearted commitment to the God of Israel that the law demands.[16]

As Bauckham suggests, it is crucial to distinguish the church from the Kingdom and, for that matter, to be clear that the church stands in both continuity and discontinuity with Old Testament Israel. The political dimensions of human life embodied in the Old Testament people of God are not directly manifest in the voluntary, spiritual community of the New. Indeed, the church carries on those dimensions in the quite different mode of encouraging the state under which it lives and the broader society in which it lives to realize as many of the values of the Kingdom as they will—even as the church also reminds the state and the society at large that they are *not* the Kingdom, but are only ever a deeply flawed and conflicted approximation of the city to come.

With these definitions and qualifications in hand, then, let's proceed to consider how all of these relate to each other in the encounter of Christ, his church, and his Kingdom with the world and its culture.

REAPPROPRIATING THE TYPOLOGY
OF *CHRIST AND CULTURE*

The Typology Itself

In his classic work *Christ and Culture,* H. Richard Niebuhr sets out a typology of ways in which the ideals of the Christian faith (Christ) can be related to the activities and values of a particular society (culture).

---

16. Richard Bauckham, *The Bible in Politics: How to Read the Bible Politically* (Louisville, KY: Westminster/John Knox, 1989), 29.

I. CHRIST AGAINST CULTURE

In this posture, culture is seen as hostile to the Christian faith, so Christians separate themselves from it.

Answers of the first type emphasize the opposition between Christ and culture. Whatever may be the customs of the society in which the Christian lives, and whatever the human achievements that society conserves, Christ is seen as opposed to them, so that he confronts men with the challenge of an either-or decision.[17]

Christians today might recognize forms of fundamentalist, Anabaptist, and Pentecostal Christianity in this option, with their denunciations of the world and their codes of morality formulated to guard against worldliness. Those who have left such traditions are often quick to condemn this option as extreme—which of course it is from a typological point of view, but they're speaking of real-world instances and using "extreme" as an epithet. Yet is this option so unthinkable in Nazi Germany? Stalinist Russia? Maoist China? What about in cultures such as some we know of from ancient times that were built around human sacrifice, whether the Canaanites who burned their children before their god Moloch or Mesoamerican civilizations drenched in multiple adult sacrifices? And consider contemporary North Korea, Iran, or Sudan. Are we sure that Christ is *not* standing against these cultures as interlocking institutions, values, and practices of ungodly and inhuman oppression?

We immediately encounter Niebuhr's claim that any one of his five options can be a plausible option in certain circumstances:

> It is helpful ... to recall that the repeated struggles of Christians with this problem have yielded no single Christian answer, but only a series of typical answers, which together, for faith, represent phases of the strategy of the militant church in the world.[18]

We cannot sympathetically understand these various options unless we can construe some circumstances in which they do appear plausible. I trust we can agree that, in the light of the real-world instances we have just considered, "Christ against culture" makes considerable sense.

II. CHRIST OF CULTURE

At the other end of Niebuhr's typology (though, confusingly, coming second in his exposition) is the situation of happy reinforcement of Christian values by a culture.

---

17. Niebuhr, *Christ and Culture*, 40.
18. Ibid., 2.

In them Jesus often appears as a great hero of human culture history; his life and teachings are regarded as the greatest human achievement; in him, it is believed, the aspirations of men toward their values are brought to a point of culmination; he confirms what is best in the past, and guides the process of civilization to its proper goal.... In our time answers of this kind are given by Christians who note the close relation between Christianity and Western civilization, between Jesus' teachings or the teachings about him and democratic institutions; yet there are occasional interpretations that emphasize the agreement between Christ and Eastern culture as well as some that tend to identify him with the spirit of Marxian society.[19]

Another version of "Christ of culture" can be identified also, I suggest, if we consider "second-generation" societies, in the sense of societies sufficiently transformed by Christian values as to constitute an environment in which generations can grow up without any strong sense of conflict between Christ and culture. Puritan New England was such a place for many in the late seventeenth and early eighteenth centuries. Czarist Russia might count as another. I myself have lived in three regions of North America that actually fit this type: west Texas, where people of my parents' social class worshiped at First Baptist Church and then dined with all the same folk at the country club afterward; northwestern Iowa, where Dutch-American Calvinists so dominated Sioux County that public schools were dismissed early to send children to catechism classes and the weekly church attendance averaged 90 percent of the county population; and southern Manitoba, where Mennonites sufficiently outnumbered anyone else that some small towns simply *were* Mennonite, from the mayor on down. "Christ of culture," therefore, shows up in quite a range of varieties.

III. CHRIST ABOVE CULTURE

Both extremes of "Christ against culture" and "Christ of culture" recognize no tension between the two elements of "Christ" and "culture." The extreme options relate the two elements either by separation or by conjunction. Niebuhr then posed three intermediate alternatives that do, in fact, maintain some kind of tense relationship between Christ and culture. He called people in these three categories "synthesists, dualists, and conversionists," respectively.[20]

In the first of these, a culture is viewed as being providentially supplied with good values and helpful institutions such that it is basically sound. Christ then arrives, so to speak, to both correct and especially to complement what is present in the culture:

---

19. Ibid., 41.
20. Ibid., 120.

True culture is not possible unless beyond all human achievement, all human search for values, all human society, Christ enters into life from above with gifts which human aspiration has not envisioned and which human effort cannot attain unless he relates men to a supernatural society and a new value-center.[21]

Thomas Aquinas is the great exemplar of this model, as

he combined without confusing philosophy and theology, state and church, civic and Christian virtues, natural and divine laws, Christ and culture. Out of these various elements he built a great structure of theoretical and practical wisdom, which like a cathedral was solidly planted among the streets and marketplaces, the houses, palaces, and universities that represent human culture, but which, when one had passed through its doors, presented a strange new world of quiet spaciousness, of sounds and colors, actions and figures, symbolic of a life beyond all secular concerns.[22]

Christian theology teaches society truths it has not found, and would not find, on its own—notably the gospel story itself. Christian ethics brings specific and fundamental content to the extant ethos, as the great commandments of love for God and the neighbor are enshrined in the center of life. Christian vocation teaches God's call to stewardship of the earth. And Christian preaching offers forgiveness of sin and hope of citizenship in the New Jerusalem, filling out whatever truncated version is in place (e.g., the focus on spiritual emancipation found in Indian religions, or the emphasis on social harmony in Confucianism).

Niebuhr says this:

Culture discerns the rules for culture, because culture is the work of God-given reason in God-given nature. Yet there is another law besides the law rational men discover and apply. The divine law revealed by God through His prophets and above all through His Son is partly coincident with the natural law, and partly transcends it as the law of man's supernatural life. "Thou shalt not steal" is a commandment found both by reason and in revelation; "Sell all that thou hast and give to the poor" is found in the divine law only. It applies to man as

---

21. Ibid., 42.
22. Ibid., 130.

one who has had a virtue implanted in him beyond the virtue of honesty, and who has been directed in hope toward a perfection beyond justice in this mortal existence.[23]

These last examples point to one of the zones of Christian engagement with the world in which this option has been most common: missionary work. Some missionaries have been so shocked at what they found in a particular culture that they have sought its eradication and replacement by Christianity—which, typically, they packaged with their own ethnic culture (English, French, Dutch, and so on). But many other missionaries have seen sufficient elements of truth, beauty, and goodness in a culture as to view the coming of the Christian gospel as a fulfillment of, rather than an alternative to, what was already there. The most fundamental instance of such a relationship, of course, would be the relationship of the distinctively Christian way as a fulfillment of Old Testament Israelite religion—an instance that Niebuhr himself doesn't happen to mention.

IV. CHRIST IN PARADOX WITH CULTURE

Niebuhr introduces this option with a criticism of type III and a corresponding compliment to type IV: the synthesists "do not in fact face up to the radical evil present in all human work....[T]his objection is most effectively raised by the dualists," that is, those who see "Christ and culture in paradox."[24]

Alas, type IV is arguably the least well presented option of Niebuhr's five.[25] Christians in this zone seem to be practicing a kind of Orwellian doublethink, as they serve two masters, two kingdoms, and two value systems: Christ and a not-so-Christian culture.[26] Under the general providence of God, who has ordained and who continues to supervise the structures and powers of earthly life, and particularly institutions such as family and government, Christians are to participate in, and contribute to, non-Christian or sub-Christian societies while (somehow) maintaining their ultimate allegiance to Christ:

---

23. Ibid., 135–36.

24. Ibid., 148, 149.

25. A significant attempt to correct this problem is made in Angus J. L. Menuge, ed., *Christ and Culture in Dialogue: Constructive Themes and Practical Applications* (St. Louis, MO: Concordia Academic, 1999).

26. The apostle Paul is exposited at length in this chapter of Niebuhr's *Christ and Culture* also, but it is a very Lutheran Paul (159–67). Cf. the revisionist understanding of Paul in New Testament studies introduced by N. T Wright, *What Saint Paul Really Said: Was Paul of Tarsus the Real Founder of Christianity?* (Grand Rapids, MI: Eerdmans, 1997).

To those who answer the question in this way it appears that Christians throughout life are subject to the tension that accompanies obedience to two authorities who do not agree yet must both be obeyed. They refuse to accommodate the claims of Christ to those of secular society, as, in their estimation, men in the second and third groups do. So they are like the "Christ-against-culture" believers, yet differ from them in the convictions that obedience to God requires obedience to the institutions of society and loyalty to its members as well as obedience to a Christ who sits in judgment on that society. Hence man is seen as subject to two moralities, and as a citizen of two worlds that are not only discontinuous with each other but largely opposed. In the *polarity* and *tension* of Christ and culture life must be lived precariously and sinfully in the hope of a justification which lies beyond history.[27]

A paradox is an apparent contradiction that is resolvable at some other level by some sort of qualification. The proposition "Water is a gas, a liquid, and a solid" is an apparent contradiction, but the state of water depends on the temperature—the qualification that resolves the contradiction.[28] But Niebuhr never provides the resolving qualification, the scheme within which these apparent contradictions make a single sense. Thus the Christians in this mode seem not involved in a paradox so much as in a contradiction. They seem to compartmentalize their lives into certain duties to society and then certain other duties to Christ in a kind of social implication of the law/gospel dichotomy characteristic of Lutheran thought.

Niebuhr defends Luther himself from this charge and makes some interesting suggestions about Luther's sense of Christian life in the world, which I shall take up later—both in my discussion of Dietrich Bonhoeffer, who wrestled with his Lutheran heritage on these matters, and in my own affirmations in the last part of this book. But the Luther who, Niebuhr allows, does *not* think in a compartmentalizing way nonetheless is placed by Niebuhr among a fairly world-indifferent apostle Paul, a heretically world-denying Marcion, a complacently conservative Lutheranism, an almost nonsensically paradoxical Kierkegaard, a liberally compromising Troeltsch, and a schismatic Roger Williams. This wildly varying portrait gallery results in this model remaining the least clearly presented of the five.

---

27. Niebuhr, *Christ and Culture,* 42–43.

28. Science teachers among readers of this book will be glad to know that I did learn that the state of water depends also on pressure and other factors, not just temperature.

The rest of the present book is an attempt to recover, restate, and renew a version of this option.[29] So I will not linger over Niebuhr's odd failure to make this position more intelligible, let alone plausible. (It is an especially odd failure, however, when one considers that his own brother, Reinhold—to whom the book is dedicated—fits best into this category, as Richard's brief citation of Reinhold's *Moral Man and Immoral Society* attests. We will examine Reinhold as a resource for a dialectical approach to culture before long.)[30]

V. CHRIST TRANSFORMING CULTURE

In this mode, Christians follow Christ, in the power of the Holy Spirit, to participate in God's mission of redeeming the world, bringing it back from its fallen state into blessed submission and thus into *shalom*. Sector by sector, institution by institution, and, yes, individual by individual, Christ transforms culture:

> For the conversionist, history is the story of God's mighty deeds and of man's responses to them. He lives somewhat less "between the times" and somewhat more in the divine "Now" than do his brother Christians. The eschatological future has become for him an eschatological present. Eternity means for him less the action of God before time and less the life with God after time, and more the presence of God in time. Eternal life is a quality of existence in the here and now. Hence the conversionist is less concerned with conservation of what has been given in creation, less with preparation for what will be given in a final redemption, than with the divine possibility of a present renewal.... The conversionist, with his view of history as the present encounter with God in Christ, does not live so much in expectation of a final ending of the world of

---

29. Indeed, this book might properly be seen as an attempt to recover and articulate a more plausible version of this model, just as John Howard Yoder attempted to restate and to nuance what he liked to call the "radical" version of Christianity.

30. Niebuhr, *Christ and Culture,* 183 n. 30: "Among these dualisms that eschew parallelism or the compartmentalization of the moral life may be mentioned Reinhold Niebuhr's *Moral Man and Immoral Society*, 1932"; cf. Richard Niebuhr's listing of Reinhold among "Nikolai Berdyaev, Ernest [*sic*] Troeltsch,...Gogarten (the earlier), Emil Brunner, and perhaps...Karl Barth" as exemplars of this model in the previous essay that served as the basis for these lectures: "Introduction: Types of Christian Ethics," in *Christ and Culture,* lii. This essay was written originally in 1942. The relationship of the Niebuhr brothers was fraught with misunderstanding, even in (or perhaps especially in) their public work as theologians. At one point, Richard writes to Reinhold (about a book Reinhold had dedicated to *him*), "One reason we do not understand each other, as this book makes clearer than ever to me, is that our words mean different things to us" (personal letter quoted in Richard Wightman Fox, *Reinhold Niebuhr: A Biography* [Ithaca, NY: Cornell University Press, 1996 (1985)], 153).

creation and culture as in awareness of the power of the Lord to transform all things by lifting them up to himself.[31]

Calvin transforms Geneva from the Las Vegas of its day into the Reformation's first thoroughly reformed city. The English Puritans erect a Christian commonwealth in the next century, while some of their number travel to America to do the same there for decades longer. And Dutch leader Abraham Kuyper provides a stirring call to more recent Christians of this type as he announces the claim of Christ: "There is not one inch in the entire area of our human life about which Christ, who is Sovereign of all, does not cry out, 'Mine!' "[32]

Christians in this mode have typically worked in one of three submodes: (1) converting individuals, who then will act Christianly in all things, infiltrating and influencing all sectors of society and converting others in turn, thus leading to a cumulative transformation of culture (this is the typical evangelical mode, exemplified in the preaching and career of Billy Graham, who saw the hope of America's future secured against Communism, sensuality, and other threats only by the progressive conversion of individuals); (2) constructing Christian institutions (whether schools, labor unions, news media, or political parties) as wholesome alternatives to the current options offered by other groups, in the hope that they will become sufficiently attractive and influential that successive sectors of society will be transformed by their influence (this is the Dutch neo-Calvinists' mode, which sometimes is known as "pillarization" because they provide Christian pillars of society other than those currently supporting it); and (3) conquering existing institutions with legitimate power, such as taking over businesses by buying stock, taking over legislatures by winning elections, taking over media by producing superior creative products, and so on (this is the mode of liberal Protestants, liberation theologians, the new religious right, Christian socialists, and still more otherwise disparate groups).[33]

---

31. Niebuhr, *Christ and Culture,* 195.

32. Quoted in James D. Bratt, *Abraham Kuyper: A Centennial Reader* (Grand Rapids, MI: Eerdmans, 1998), 488. I thank Hans Boersma for this citation, and for some helpful guidance regarding neo-Calvinism.

33. This list of "transformationists" shows that Oliver O'Donovan is mistaken when he says, "What matters is not to be *for* Christendom or *against* it—what earthly point could there be in either of these postures?" (*The Desire of the Nations: Rediscovering the Roots of Political Thought* [Cambridge, UK: Cambridge University Press, 1996], ix). If one is intent on using social power to effect broad cultural change, it matters quite a bit whether one is for or against Christendom as an ideal. Indeed, O'Donovan later defines this ideal in a way that any normal transformationist would approve: "it is the idea of a confessionally Christian government, at once 'secular' (in the proper sense of that word, confined to the present age) and obedient to Christ, a promise of the age of his unhindered rule" (ibid., 195).

In this last mode, it is interesting to see that this option actually connects with the apparently contradictory "Christ against culture" posture: Christians can be thoroughly against the current culture and thus either separate from it or try to take it over. The close connection between these two modes helps explain why American fundamentalism, for one important example in contemporary Christianity, has oscillated between these two approaches to American culture: they are not, in fact, so far apart.[34]

Given this sketch of Niebuhr's scheme, then, let us proceed to both understand and appropriate it for our present purposes. I want to make clear that this is what I am doing—harvesting some insights from Niebuhr, rather than defending his whole book or even expositing it thoroughly. There is much more to Niebuhr's book than his typology, and it is both rich and problematic. I am going to leave aside all but the typology itself, as it is the typology that is particularly valuable in my own constructive project and a critical discussion of other matters would only distract from that. Nonetheless, a discussion of the criticisms of the typology itself does illuminate several important themes.

Lessons from the Typology—and Its Critics

The first kind of criticism we can notice is the charge that Niebuhr's categories are wrong. What is "Christ" and what is "culture" in this scheme? Some have suggested that "Christ" really means "Christianity" or "the church," and "culture" really means "the world" or "the dominant powers and ethos of society," so Niebuhr's very terms need changing.

I'm not so sure they do, as long as we realize what Niebuhr is attempting with these categories. Niebuhr is discussing a kind of fundamental tension for

---

34. For more on H. Richard Niebuhr's categories and American fundamentalism, see George Marsden, "Christianity and Cultures: Transforming Niebuhr's Categories," *Insights* 115 (Fall 1999): 11–12. In this regard, I recall a personal conversation in which Marsden remarked that the tension between "sect" and "church" is most acute for Calvinists, whose outlook makes compromise so difficult. (Marsden's article is an unusually moderate, insightful, and constructive response to Niebuhr's work, and does not deserve the opprobrium dished out by Niebuhr's former student and apologist James Gustafson in his preface to the fiftieth edition of *Christ and Culture*, xxi–xxxv.) I recall John Howard Yoder's saying that the Swiss Brethren, the early Anabaptists in sixteenth-century Zurich, tried in fact to lead a reformation of that city—contrary to the sectarian separatism that characterized them later. Indeed, Yoder maintains, it was only upon losing the power struggle with Ulrich Zwingli's party that they then developed their "Christ against culture" posture, versus the "Christ transforming culture" mode in which they had originally sought cultural dominance. (I regret not having a formal citation for this remark, but I heard Yoder say this in a lecture at Northwestern College during a campus visit in 1989, and I discussed it with him the next day.)

the church: the tension between its fidelity to Christ (the ideal of Christian faith) and its posture toward the society from which the church is drawn and in which it must make its way.[35] How, then, does the church best construe the relationship between those two elements of its life in the world? Since that question, I believe, is Niebuhr's main concern, it would actually confuse the situation to substitute "church" or "Christianity" for "Christ," since that would be to drop out the first element of the three-element relationship: Christ—church—culture.

Yes, the church is itself a society that has its own culture, as some have pointed out—as if Niebuhr, a disciple of Ernst Troeltsch and a careful sociological inter-preter of the church, didn't recognize that fact. Indeed, his book is precisely about how the church should be relating to the other societies/cultures with which it has to interact, under the Lordship of Christ. Yes, we must also recognize that the church is always culturally embedded within and interpenetrated by other cul-tures, and so is never able to access "Christ" as an ideal without the interference of the filtering, bias, and motives of particular cultures—again, as if this would be news to one of midcentury America's more clear-eyed observers of the church in the (real) world.[36] And yes, there are subcultures within dominant cultures with which we have to interact—even multiple subcultures in a modern, pluralistic society. All of this would not be news to Niebuhr, nor does it invalidate his pro-gram. Niebuhr correctly realizes that the key question for the church is how it is to relate its basic loyalty to Christ with its life in the world, a question that goes back through church history to Augustine's extensive musings on the cities of

---

35. Niebuhr opens *Christ and Culture* by describing it as an "essay on the double wrestle of the church with its Lord and with the cultural society with which it lives in symbiosis" (xi).

36. Moreover, this embeddedness and interpenetration is not bad only—it is, in fact, generi-cally human: Christians speak German or Swahili or Urdu, not "Christian"; Christians dress and play and think and love according to particular extant cultural patterns, albeit patterns that, ideally, come under the scrutiny and refinement of the Holy Spirit. Cf. the ancient, anonymous *Letter to Diognetus:* "For Christians cannot be distinguished from the rest of the human race by country or language or customs. The do not live in cities of their own; they do not use a peculiar form of speech; they do not follow an eccentric manner of life.... Yet, although they live in Greek and barbarian cities alike, as each man's lot has been cast, and follow the customs of the country in clothing and food and other matters of daily living, at the same time they give proof of the remarkable and admittedly extraordinary constitution of their own commonwealth. They live in their own countries, but only as aliens. They have a share in everything as citizens, and endure everything as foreigners. Every foreign land is their fatherland, and yet for them every fatherland is a foreign land" (in Cyril C. Richardson, ed. and trans., *Early Christian Fathers* [New York: Macmillan, 1970], 216–17). And Richard Mouw reminds us that it is in our particularity, including our national identities, that we will enter the New Jerusalem as per Isaiah 60 (*When the Kings Come Marching In: Isaiah and the New Jerusalem* [Grand Rapids, MI: Eerdmans, 1983]).

God and of man, and the New Testament's own teachings on the matter—right back to Jesus discussing what is God's and what is Caesar's (Mt. 22:21 par.).

What does Jesus want us to do? That is really Niebuhr's question, and so his categories serve us well as a truly exhaustive list of basic possibilities. (One cannot imagine a Christian considering a "Christ below culture" option, for instance.)

The second, and quite crucial, matter to get clear is that Niebuhr intends to offer us a *typology*, not a *taxonomy*. A typology is a kind of pure intellectual construct, a setting out of the logical possibilities in a situation. Niebuhr does this in terms that relate "Christ" and "culture." Yet many readers have not understood the difference between typology and taxonomy and have thus both misunderstood and unfairly criticized Niebuhr's project. James Gustafson is right to say in Niebuhr's defense,

> It is…a mistake to interpret *Christ and Culture* as a taxonomy of Christian theological ethical literature. The typology is an ideal construct of ideas, not generalizations about literature.… The distinction between an ideal-typical and a taxonomic purpose (and they readily get mixed or confused) is this: ideal types are ideal constructs of ideas along a clearly stated axis by which particular aspects of issues of literature are illuminated. The purpose of taxonomy is to develop headings about generalizations from a variety of literature which shares similarities.[37]

A taxonomy is a classification of things as they actually are, in all their specificity: what to call, and how to relate, that red singing thing here, that white sleeping thing there, and that patterned crawling thing over yonder. Linnaeus came up with the general scheme we now use: kingdom, phylum, class, order, genus, species, and variety. So we can speak of the first creature as a cardinal, the second as a Siamese cat, and the third as a diamondback rattlesnake.

A typology offers a set of abstract possibilities in a particular zone, whether or not they describe anything in the real world as such. Such a typology might be "red birds," "blue birds," "green birds," and so on, even though no birds in reality are entirely red, blue, or green. A useful typology helps us notice things. For example, as a child discusses the locomotion of birds, she might easily equate being a bird with flying. But when her teacher sets out some abstract possibilities,

---

37. Gustafson, preface to *Christ and Culture,* xxx. John Howard Yoder spends a great deal of time barking up this tree, alas, which seriously compromises the value of much of his provocative essay, "How H. Richard Niebuhr Reasoned: A Critique of *Christ and Culture*," in *Authentic Transformation: A New Vision of Christ and Culture*, ed. Glenn H. Stassen, D. M. Yeager, and John Howard Yoder (Nashville, TN: Abingdon, 1996), 31–89.

such as "birds fly," "birds walk," "birds swim," "birds remain motionless," she then recalls birds such as penguins and ostriches that do not fly. She also notices that flying birds sometimes walk, and some of them swim. And she then observes birds motionless, especially when brooding. The typology helps her see more clearly what was already there but perhaps easily overlooked.

Furthermore, a typology can open up the imagination of creatures with self-determination, such as ourselves, to possibilities heretofore unexplored. It can help us move beyond what *is* the case to what *could be* the case by expressing the options we currently have before us in clear, abstract categories. "Human beings travel over the earth by various means—walking, swimming, riding or being towed by animals, using machines"—but what about the abstract category of space travel? Why not travel off the earth as well as on it?

Niebuhr's typology helps us in both these ways: in analyzing real-world patterns of church life and in considering possibilities for that life that might be concealed by our extant, circumscribed categories. We might well feel that the only cultural options are fight or flight, while Niebuhr provides us with three more alternatives.

Niebuhr deploys his typology to lift up aspects of the complex thought and life of various prominent individuals and movements in church history. And here we come to the third major zone of criticism, namely, the application of Niebuhr's types to real-world examples.

Most people seem (to Niebuhr) to fit nicely in just one category (e.g., Albrecht Ritschl and most of the rest of the nineteenth-century German liberal tradition in the category "Christ of culture"), while others fit in more than one and thus show up in more than one chapter (Augustine and the apostles Paul and John are the three who do so explicitly, while Niebuhr allows that Martin Luther also is "too complex to permit neat identification of an historic individual with a stylized pattern").[38] Niebuhr himself cautions us that "when one returns from the hypothetical scheme to the rich complexity of individual events, it is evident at once that no person or group ever conforms completely to a type."[39] Niebuhr's scheme thus reminds us of two more crucial ideas in this discussion.

---

38. Paul shows up in several chapters, and John chiefly in two—if one takes him to be the author of both I John (which Niebuhr exposits under type I) and the gospel bearing his name (which Niebuhr exposits under type V). Augustine, however, is confined to the "Christ transforming culture" type—even in the index—while Niebuhr does allow that "the dualistic motif is strong in Augustine" in the "Christ and culture in paradox" chapter (169), and lists the affinity of aspects of Augustine's thought with other models (207–8). Quakers appear as both representatives of "Christ against culture" and, in later periods, of "Christ of culture" (56–57). The characterization of Luther is on p. 170.

39. Niebuhr, *Christ and Culture,* 43–44.

First, it is not just that historical individuals and groups happen not to be so consistent that they fit entirely into one category. Rather, it is natural and appropriate that Christians will take one stance toward some aspects of a culture and another stance toward other aspects of a culture. John Howard Yoder puts this particularly well in this oft-cited passage:

> Some elements of culture the church categorically rejects (pornography, tyranny, cultic idolatry). Other dimensions of culture it accepts within clear limits (economic production, commerce, the graphic arts, paying taxes for peacetime civil government). To still other dimensions of culture Christian faith gives a new motivation and coherence (agriculture, family life, literacy, conflict resolution, empowerment). Still others it strips of their claims to possess autonomous truth and value, and uses them as vehicles of communication (philosophy, language, Old Testament ritual, music). Still other forms of culture are *created* by the Christian churches (hospitals, service of the poor, generalized education, egalitarianism, abolitionism, feminism).[40]

Yoder and others have understandably bristled at the way Niebuhr departs from his own deployment of his typology *as a typology* when he seems to use it as a taxonomy on Anabaptists and others in the category of "Christ against culture." Having set out their position in typological terms and adduced some historical examples to illustrate it, he then chides those historical individuals and movements for inconsistency: "the radical Christians are always making use of the culture, or parts of the culture, which ostensibly they reject"—such as the philosophy and science of the day, and language itself.[41] Nor, Niebuhr continues, can they do otherwise: "They cannot separate themselves completely, therefore, from the world of culture around them, nor from those needs in themselves which make this culture necessary."[42]

---

40. Yoder, "How H. Richard Niebuhr Reasoned," 69. Martin E. Marty offers a similar observation from his Lutheran vantage point: "Calvin and his cohorts embody 'Christ Transforming Culture' impulses in respect to politics. Luther meanwhile needs to post a dualism, 'two kingdoms.' One of them always displays the way 'the demonic pervades the structures of existence.' However, when it comes to affirming images in church building, the arts, and music, it is Luther who is the culture-affirmer....He minimizes the dualism there and sees possibility in converting at least some aspects of the culture" (foreword to Niebuhr, *Christ and Culture*, xviii).

41. Niebuhr, *Christ and Culture*, 69. Yoder returns to this criticism several times in his "How H. Richard Niebuhr Reasoned."

42. Niebuhr, *Christ and Culture*, 73.

Yoder and company, however, would simply agree with these observations as truistic. But they would go on to reply that this charge of inconsistency is the result of applying a pure type to an utterly, which is to say ludicrously, consistent extreme. Are the Amish supposed to avoid the very roads built by the "English"? Are these separatists supposed to invent their whole language, dress, familial relations, and so on out of whole cloth—cloth without any element, let alone pattern, of the world? This sort of criticism is itself inconsistent in two respects: Niebuhr seems ruthlessly critical of this type in a way he doesn't criticize any other, and he does so by confusing taxonomy with typology.

Perhaps one thing more should be said on this matter, however. Perhaps Niebuhr's critique is more searching than has been acknowledged by his Anabaptist critics. For one might well ask just how "unspotted by the world" is *anything* taken from it. Buttons versus zippers seems like a silly Amish controversy to most outsiders, but buttons can be made entirely by the community, while zippers implicate the community in external—indeed, international, and perhaps exploitative—trade. Language itself is of course an encoding of values, and many of those values will not be Christian, even if Christians do, as Yoder suggests, try conscientiously to strip language of "claims to possess autonomous truth and value." Can one use a racist or sexist epithet, for example, in anything other than a value-laden way? Can one use "he" and "man" nowadays as generic references to human beings without implying a stance on certain matters of gender?

Perhaps, for all its faults, Niebuhr's point is worth making. Yes, the Anabaptist criticisms remain. But Niebuhr's typology, and even his own inconsistent application of it in this instance, at least can remind us of just how subtle and complex is the question of distinguishing "Christ" from "culture" for every Christian person and group. The typology also can help us analyze varieties of cultural stances within an apparently homogeneous group, such as the spectrum of Anabaptist models of cultural engagement and disentanglement ranging from urban Mennonites to Amish colonies.

Having considered, then, the first idea that groups do not, and should not, fit nicely and always into one or another scheme, we turn to a second, complementary idea, which is pointed out by George Marsden. It is that individuals and groups demonstrate that one or another of Niebuhr's categories does describe their *dominant* mode of engagement:

> By usually speaking as though his ideal types characterize real historical figures, [Niebuhr] leaves the impression that each Christian or group can be adequately typed by one or the other of the cultural attitudes. To correct this misleading

impression, what we need to emphasize is that the categories are simply, as Niebuhr himself acknowledges, leading motifs. A motif should be seen as a dominant theme with respect to some specific cultural activities. It suggests a musical analogy. A dominant motif may be subordinated in one part of a symphony while another takes over. Identifying a dominant motif in a particular Christian group toward some specific cultural activity should not lead to the expectation that this group will not adopt other motifs toward other cultural activities.[43]

Most birds really do fly most of the time (albatrosses), while others swim most of the time (ducks), and some walk most of the time (emus). A typology thus can keep us from oversimplification of two sorts, whether mistaken generalizations ("All birds fly") or excessive complication ("Birds move in lots of different ways and some differently than others"). Niebuhr's scheme both helps us see more complexity in our subjects than we might otherwise see and helps us discern the fundamental postures of individuals and groups.

One final qualification here is made by Niebuhr himself:

Many a Protestant who has abandoned the Ritschlian answer is attracted to Thomism without being tempted to transfer his allegiance to the Roman church, while in Anglican thought and practice his system is normative for many; on the Christ-culture issue the lines drawn among Christians cannot be made to coincide with the historic distinctions among the great churches.[44]

What Niebuhr says about Thomism is true about other models in other contexts: some Reformed Christians live more in type IV than in type V (Marsden himself, a conservative Presbyterian, advocates type IV at the end of his essay on Christ and culture); some Pentecostals, whom one might assume are in type I, are busy in type V; and we have seen how various groups that historically would be identified with type I (Baptists, Mennonites) or type V (Calvinists) in certain places in America are comfortably practicing type II. Niebuhr's typology thus helps us again, as it provides us categories to discern this kind of complexity in the real world, where labels ("Mennonite," "Calvinist") can easily mislead us into assumptions (Mennonite = type I, Calvinist = type V) that do not match the facts.

---

43. Marsden, "Christianity and Cultures," 10.
44. Niebuhr, *Christ and Culture*, 129.

The fourth major zone of criticism centers on Niebuhr's obvious preference for the last of his five types, the "transformation" option.[45] Many readers have remarked on how this is the one of the five that comes in for the least criticism—indeed, it is hard to discern any criticism at all, and there is no section of critique at the end to parallel those in the other chapters. Other readers have noticed that the placing of this scheme at the end of his book "loads" the discussion toward it as a kind of natural and satisfying end point, its virtues played off the deficiencies of the others, even though it is, in fact, somewhere in the middle of Niebuhr's scheme, with types I and II being the limits between which the others are located. One might remark, finally, that Niebuhr's choice of examples for each category tends to tilt the discussion toward the last two options. His midcentury Protestant audience was not likely to be inspired by the likes of Tertullian and Tolstoy (type I), Peter Abelard and Albrecht Ritschl (type II), or Clement of Alexandria and Thomas Aquinas (type III).[46] They would certainly be impressed by Paul and by Luther, portrayed in type IV. But then Niebuhr enlists Augustine, Calvin, John Wesley, and Jonathan Edwards for type V, which ought to have impressed particularly his original audience of Presbyterian seminarians. Indeed, the one risk Niebuhr takes in this regard is concluding with a commendation of F. D. Maurice, the nineteenth-century British Christian socialist whose views might not have squared immediately with Texan Christian political instincts of a century later.

---

45. An irresponsible reading of Niebuhr—irresponsible theologically, hermeneutically, and ethically—occurs in what has been, alas, a popular book: Stanley Hauerwas and William H. Willimon, *Resident Aliens: Life in the Christian Colony* (Nashville, TN: Abingdon, 1989), 40–43. No one who has read this far in the present volume can interpret my remarks as an uncritical apologetic for Niebuhr. Criticism is entirely in order. But Hauerwas and Willimon caricature Niebuhr. Indeed, they do so in so many ways that I cannot linger over them all. A few might suffice to illustrate the point: "Niebuhr set up the argument as if a world-affirming 'church' or world-denying 'sect' were our only options' [we have seen that Niebuhr does not do that, but rather affirms several options as plausible], as if these categories were a faithful depiction of some historical or sociological reality in the first place [which, we have also seen, is what Niebuhr does *not* do in setting out a typology]." Hauerwas and Willimon go on to cast Niebuhr as an unwitting apologist for midcentury America in toto, including its bombing of Hiroshima. Hauerwas and Willimon are demonstrably intelligent and well-meaning men who might simply have been carried away by zeal. But readers ought to be on their guard against the tissue of misrepresentations of Niebuhr and his project in these few pages (40–43).

46. Niebuhr's exposition of the types is biased even more strongly toward type V in that he uses heretics as examples of three of the other types, beyond those listed above, the orthodoxy of some of whom would of course be contested: Montanism for type I, Gnosticism for type II, and Marcion for type IV. It has been widely observed, by the way, that Niebuhr's characterization of Gnosticism is itself largely off the mark: see, for example, Yoder, "How H. Richard Niebuhr Reasoned," 36–37.

Yet let us also take Niebuhr at his word when he remarks affirmatively that different cultures can require different stances.[47] It is because this is, in fact, a good point to make that I provided what I hope are more plausible examples of each type in the discussion above. However much one might champion one of the intermediate types as perhaps the most common or most typical or most realistic stance for Christians to assume most of the time, I affirm that Christians have faced certain extreme situations in which "Christ against culture" or even "Christ of culture" makes sense, despite Niebuhr's obvious antipathy toward them.

As we have remarked, furthermore, not only can it be appropriate for Christians to take different stances on different aspects of the same culture, but it typically *is* appropriate. Again, the evangelical tradition is an interesting case in point, exploiting as it has for more than two centuries the latest in communications and organizational technologies to preach a traditional message—whether George Whitefield deploying the dramatic arts of the theater of his time and John Wesley developing a sophisticated network of Methodist fellowship groups, or nineteenth-century evangelists formulating "New Measures" of church architecture (the "anxious bench" on which those who were spiritually questing could sit, and the tents that let the evangelists set up wherever they liked, with or without local clerical support), or Jerry Falwell using a state-of-the-art television studio to broadcast, of all things, *The Old-Time Gospel Hour*.[48] What is true of evangelicals has also been true of Roman Catholics, whether Matteo Ricci exploiting Confucianist traditions in which to present his Christian teaching in sixteenth-century China or John Paul II appearing on stadium JumboTrons around the world as a Catholic Billy Graham in the late twentieth century. In fact, since cultures are not monolithic, to adopt just one stance toward everything is to refuse the responsibility to think carefully about which stance is the best in this or that instance.

The last point I want to make, however, is one that Niebuhr implies, if he doesn't say it outright. I think it is well worth considering as a way of making

---

47. Niebuhr addresses questions of cultural relativity in his opening and closing sections of *Christ and Culture:* see 2, 39–40, 232, 234–41, 249–53. Indeed, almost his last sentence is as follows: "To make our decisions in faith is to make them in view of the fact that no single man or group or historical time is the church; but that there is a church of faith in which we do our partial, relative work and on which we count" (256).

48. Martin E. Marty and Scott Appleby were among the first to remark on fundamentalists being only *selectively* conservative and *selectively* anti-modern: Martin E. Marty and R. Scott Appleby, eds., *Fundamentalisms Observed* (Chicago: University of Chicago Press, 1991); and Martin E. Marty and R. Scott Appleby, *The Glory and the Power: The Fundamentalist Challenge of the Modern World* (Boston: Beacon, 1992).

some sense of what we see in Christian history, namely, Christian individuals and groups ranged on more than one side of a controversial issue. To be sure, sometimes Christians disagree because one side is just wrong—motivated by greed, pride, stupidity, and so on. And sometimes both sides are wrong. But I want to suggest that sometimes both sides might be right.

In some orthodox circles there is an invocation of the law of non-contradiction as a kind of logical razor meant to carve away all options but one in a dispute. Yet our world is not always that neatly divisible into right and wrong.

Let us take the vexed question of war, for example. I want to suggest that there have been times in which Christians have properly gone to war. Recent examples would include the fight against Nazi Germany, the fight to stop ethnic cleansing in the former Yugoslavia, and the fight to keep the Taliban from power in Afghanistan. War is something God ordered his people to undertake in the Old Testament. War is something God himself will undertake in the Second Coming of Christ. Most Christians through most of the centuries have understood war to be the "awful option" to deal with evil when all other means have failed.

Yet war is clearly not Christ's ideal. He is the Prince of Peace who himself suffered and died unjustly in order to redeem the world from its various wars— within the human soul as well as without. And the Biblical vision of our destiny is that of the "peaceable kingdom," without any more conflict (Isa. 2:2–4; 11:6–9). Furthermore, even a "just war" is fraught with danger—not only the obvious physical dangers of injury, death, loss of loved ones, and waste of resources, but also the dangers of pride, jingoism, bloodlust, atrocity, and vengeance.

How, then, to keep warriors humble, to keep violence to a minimum, to affirm that war is a regrettable, temporary measure, fit only for our badly topsy-turvy world until Jesus returns to set things straight? Even more difficult, how to both prosecute a war and simultaneously testify to God's ultimate desire for peace? If the former task is difficult, the latter seems impossible—simply contradictory. How can a group of people both fight a war and bear witness against war?

The law of non-contradiction won't help us here. If undertaking war is right, then opposing options are wrong, and conscientious objectors are resisting the will of God. If radical peacemaking is right, then no wars must be fought, ever, and most Christians through most of history have been terribly, bloodily disobedient.

But what about another possibility? If the "whole counsel of God" on this matter is, in fact, impossible for one group to live out, why not instead consider that God has called most Christians in a society to wage war—most, in order to maximize resources for the struggle—and yet also called some other Christians to maintain a witness of radical peacemaking and a prophetic voice against the evils of war?[49]

Niebuhr himself makes this point:

> The radically Christian answer to the problem of culture [he means type I] needed to be given in the past, and doubtless needs to be given now. It must be given for its own sake, and because without it other Christian groups lose their balance.... If Romans 13 is not balanced by I John, the church becomes an instrument of state, unable to point men to their transpolitical destiny and their suprapolitical loyalty; unable also to engage in political tasks, save as one more group of power-hungry or security-seeking men.[50]

Niebuhr goes on to criticize this option as "inadequate" to accomplish the work of God in the world, and I will do the same in Part Three. But while I agree with Niebuhr that this stance does not position Christians to say and do all that must be said and done in the world, I am suggesting, perhaps more forcibly than he did, that Christians in this mode and in these circumstances might be *entirely in the will of God—for them, at that time*. I say this because my main point is that in some cases no single stance says and does all that must be said and done, and therefore more than one posture might be necessary to cumulatively bear witness to the broad scope of God's word and will in a complex matter. Niebuhr affirms this sort of pluralism in similar language as he testifies to his "conviction that Christ as living Lord is answering the question [of cultural engagement] in the totality of history and life in a fashion which transcends the wisdom of all his interpreters yet employs their partial insights and their necessary conflicts."[51]

---

49. David Martin makes this point as well: "In my view, the radical peace witness acts to inject a powerful idea into the public mind but has mainly to be carried by small separatist groups because it is incapable of generalization to the state as such" (*Reflections on Sociology and Theology* [Oxford: Clarendon, 1997], 135).

50. Niebuhr, *Christ and Culture*, 68. He also refers to F. D. Maurice's involvement with Christians of various types in the Christian Socialist movement and suggests that Maurice would have remarked that "no Christian thought can encompass the thought of the Master, and that as the body is one but has many members so also the church" (229). I am extending these suggestive thoughts of Niebuhr in a direction I trust he himself would judge plausible.

51. Ibid., 2. He says something similar at the beginning of his "Concluding Unscientific Postscript," in *Christ and Culture*, 231–32. And he published a related version of these sentiments more than a decade earlier: "The invisibility of the catholic church is due not only to the fact that no one society or nation of Christians can represent the universal but also to the fact that no one time, but only all times together, can set forth the full meaning of the movement towards the eternal and its created image" (*The Kingdom of God in America* [New York: Harper, 1959 (1937)], xv).

I highlight this point because most readers seem to conclude that the thrust of his book is so strongly toward type V as to make it not just the best option but simply normative.

Certainly this conjecture that more than one option can be affirmed in a given instance is a possibility around which lurk the perils of relativism and of a lazy refusal to confront conflict among Christians. Certainly this idea could be used to avoid hard decisions among difficult options.[52] At this point, all I am asserting is that it is a plausible possibility in at least some cases. Put a little more strongly, I think it makes sense of a fundamental historical reality: Christians of obvious good sense and good faith have disagreed about lots of things, and it's not clear to me, at least, that one side or another was always just wrong. I recognize that I have placed a kind of bracket around these views, thus undercutting their claim to represent God's truth entirely and clearly. Indeed, I recognize that I am implicitly resolving the paradox in this example in favor of a just-war position that is held in a vital kind of check by a vigorous peace witness. But I have done so with sincere appreciation of both sides' moral seriousness and theological integrity. Such an outlook cannot possibly please everyone, of course, and especially not purists of any one option. But I hope it is at least a viewpoint worth considering, and we shall revisit this viewpoint in Part Three.

If Niebuhr's typology, therefore, can help us see that different cultures can prompt different stances by Christians and that different aspects of the same culture can prompt different stances by Christians, then perhaps it can help us see that different aspects of the same culture can prompt different stances by different Christians. This conclusion is indeed paradoxical. It is only the first of several that will take me the rest of this book to set out.

Thus I conclude my project of defending Niebuhr's basic typology as a still-useful guide to many issues.[53] I shall use it occasionally in the remainder of this volume. And I shall spend the last part of this book suggesting that Niebuhr's odd type IV—"Christ in paradox with culture"—is worth another, better look. I shall be recommending a kind of hybrid of types IV and V. Let us consider the phrase now common in consideration of the Kingdom of God: "already, but not yet." It seems to me that we can see two of Niebuhr's types as various versions of an "already" motif: "Christ of culture" and "Christ above culture." We can also see "not yet" as characteristic of "Christ against culture." Niebuhr's fifth type,

52. Yoder accuses Niebuhr of exactly these sins: "How H. Richard Niebuhr Reasoned," 79–83.
53. For an example of the abiding relevance of Niebuhr's typology, see Michael W. McConnell, Robert F. Cochran Jr., and Angela C. Carmella, eds., *Christian Perspectives on Legal Thought* (New Haven, CT: Yale University Press, 2001).

"Christ transforming culture," does maintain, at least temporarily, the tension of "already, but not yet." But only Niebuhr's fourth type, "Christ in paradox with culture," maintains the full and abiding tension of "already, but not yet"—itself literally a paradox.

Thus I will offer in what follows a new version of the Christian Realism usually associated with Niebuhr's brother, Reinhold. But I see it qualified through the life and work of both C. S. Lewis and Dietrich Bonhoeffer, who are, along with Reinhold, the subjects of Part Two.

PART II

SOME RESOURCES FOR THE
RECOVERY OF CHRISTIAN
REALISM

Perhaps there are theologians who can survey all of the relevant literature—
Biblical, historical, and contemporary—to arrive at a comprehensively informed
theology of culture. Given the tremendous scope of all of that literature, however, I doubt that there are such people. I certainly am not one who could claim
such expertise. Instead, I offer what I have learned in order to help readers along
their own journeys with Christ, equipping not only individuals but also Christian
churches and other groups to understand and fulfill their vocations better: more
clearly, more comprehensively, more coherently, more effectively, more hopefully, and more joyfully.

Let's proceed, then, to an examination of three key resources: the work of
three individuals from the middle of the twentieth century, C. S. Lewis, Reinhold
Niebuhr, and Dietrich Bonhoeffer.

The choice of these three subjects for chapter-length study is not completely
idiosyncratic. Readers will be comforted to know that these three are not the
only authors I have ever read on the subject, and other people quote them frequently on these matters. They are not even the three authors with whom I agree
the most. But they do have important things to say. Furthermore, along with the
benefit of the substance of their writings, I set them out here also as examples of
different modes of Christian engagement with culture that are instructive both
positively and negatively.

I do not pretend to offer incisive original investigations of these widely studied
men, nor will I offer extensive criticisms. Indeed, I daresay that specialists in

Lewis, Niebuhr, or Bonhoeffer—they are legion, and I am not in their number—cannot expect to learn much that is new from these chapters. What I hope will be beneficial to most readers, and perhaps even to such specialists also, will be the harvesting of ideas and examples from these Christian brothers in the aid of the main project of this book, namely, the articulation and defense of a realistic Christian mode of engagement with most modern cultures today.

TWO

C. S. LEWIS

The Christian Individual

There is a comical sense in which it is appropriate that I, a North American evangelical scholar, would involve C. S. Lewis in my discussion of theology of culture. It is appropriate because, as has been widely observed, evangelical scholars tend to invoke the eminent Oxford and (later) Cambridge professor of literature on *every* topic they discuss. Lewis is an evangelical hero in North America, occupying a status surpassing, I am led to understand, his eminence among his British compatriots. Many an evangelical argument has been settled by the solemn invocation of his authority: "Well, C. S. Lewis says..."

Lewis is a hero not only among evangelicals, however. Anglo-Catholics have claimed him as one of the brightest of their own, liberal Protestants see him as an exemplar, and Kallistos Ware even tried to locate Lewis as a crypto-Orthodox (although perhaps with tongue in cheek).[1] So if we can find that Lewis has interesting things to say about our subject (he has) and that he himself models an interesting way of engaging culture (he does), then he will speak yet to a wide range of Christians. Furthermore, if we find that Lewis's views and practices are in some important way limited, even deficient, then we will do well to recognize those shortcomings and seek to move beyond them.

In this chapter and in the two that follow, I will proceed by culling insights from a wide range of our subject's writings (what we will call his "preaching"), all the while also noticing aspects of his life choices that might instruct us as well (what we will call his "practice"). In this particular chapter, moreover, we will conclude by reflecting on Lewis's encoding of so many of his values in his imaginative fiction, thus briefly exploring his "parables" to confirm the main lessons we have garnered from these other sources.

---

1. Kallistos Ware, "God of the Fathers: C. S. Lewis and Eastern Christianity," in *The Pilgrim's Guide: C. S. Lewis and the Art of Witness,* ed. David Mills (Grand Rapids, MI: Eerdmans, 1998), 234.

Let us begin, then, with a paradox. Chad Walsh, who was among the earliest to promote Lewis to North American audiences, in his enthusiasm for Lewis nonetheless observed, "For a Christian social philosophy one turns to Maritain, Niebuhr, Berdyaev, George MacLeod and many others—not to C. S. Lewis."[2] Yet let us turn to Lewis nonetheless, for he has much to offer our social philosophy, despite his apparent lack of one.

THE CHRISTIAN STORY

The Christian Scriptures include a wide range of genres: poetry, prophecy, parable, apocalyptic, proverb, psalm, epistle, and more. But unlike the sacred scriptures of any other major religion in the world—including even the Jewish Scriptures, which Christians take up into their canon—the Christian Bible has a distinctly narrative shape. It has a beginning (creation and Fall), a middle (redemption), and an end (consummation), with lots of connective narrative throughout.

Lewis, himself both a scholar of stories and a composer of them, naturally related to the Christian revelation as narrative—long before narrative was emphasized in academic theology, as it has been over the last few decades. Lewis thus can help us set out this fundamental schema of the Christian religion, with all of the implications that come from knowing where we have been, where we are, and where we are going. Such a narrative emphasis is, indeed, teleological—all about "the end," not merely in terms of how things finish but why things are, in terms of their purpose in the plot of history. Such an understanding tells us what the world is, who we are, and what we therefore are to be and to do.

We will return to the Christian Story in Part Three to take it up generically, but for now let us see how it figured in Lewis's thought—and what, for him, are some of the many implications that follow from this Story.

THE ELEMENTS AND SHAPE
OF THE STORY
Creation

Lewis follows the Genesis account in understanding the world to have been created good, but also as immature. The world thus leans forward, so to speak, to its future, to its cultivation and maturation and fulfillment:

---

2. Chad Lewis, *C. S. Lewis: Apostle to the Skeptics* (New York: Macmillan, 1949), 160; cited in Gilbert Meilaender, *The Taste for the Other: The Social and Ethical Thought of C. S. Lewis* (Grand Rapids, MI: Eerdmans, 1978), 1.

We ask how the Nature created by a good God comes to be in this condition? By which question we may mean either how she comes to be imperfect—to leave "room for improvement" as the schoolmasters say in their reports—or else, how she comes to be positively departed. If we ask the question in the first sense, the Christian answer (I think) is that God, from the first, created her such as to reach her perfection by a process in time. He made an Earth at first "without form and void" and brought it by degrees to its perfection.... In that sense a certain degree of "evolutionism" or "developmentalism" is inherent in Christianity.[3]

Adam and Eve themselves were morally innocent but not morally mature.[4] Unformed and unconfirmed in habits of righteousness, they were free to sin in a way that a morally mature individual—angel or human—is not, because of that individual's deeply formed character that inclines away from sin and toward goodness.

Moral reality, for Lewis, is as real a part of the world as its physicality. He argued for this view at length in *The Abolition of Man*, particularly in terms of a great "Way" of the world, morally speaking, which he discerned in the widespread moral consensus of civilizations.[5] To label this consensus, he borrowed the Chinese word *tao* (way) and provided an appendix of similar moral maxims culled from the scriptures of the world's great religions. Morality thus is a matter neither merely of social convention nor simply of biological impetus; rather, it is part of the very structure of things, the *Tao*—to defy which is as foolish and harmful as to defy physical realities such as the force of gravity or the power of electricity. Thus the moral imperative simply stems from the moral indicative: "You ought (not) do this because that is the way things are."

This thing which I have called for convenience the *Tao*, and which others may call Natural Law or Traditional Morality or the First Principles of Practical Reason or the First Platitudes, is not one among a series of possible systems of value. It is the sole source of all value judgments.... There never has been, and never will be, a radically new judgement of value in the history of the

---

3. C. S. Lewis, *Miracles* (San Francisco: Harper, 2001 [1947; rev. ed. 1960]), 195. It should be acknowledged that Lewis is a little ambiguous here. He begins by implying that Nature is currently imperfect and marred by evil, but then he sounds as though God eventually brought Nature to perfection at some time in the past. I think the more consistent reading is the former, and the latter is a slip: Lewis did *not* think Nature was perfect in the strong sense of "mature and complete" at the time of original creation.

4. Lewis explores this topic in *The Problem of Pain* (New York: Collier, 1962), 77–88.

5. See the appendix to C. S. Lewis, *The Abolition of Man: How Education Develops Man's Sense of Morality* (New York: Macmillan, 1947).

world.... The rebellion of new ideologies against the *Tao* is a rebellion of the branches against the tree: if the rebels could succeed they would find that they had destroyed themselves. The human mind has no more power of inventing a new value than of imagining a new primary color, or, indeed, of creating a new sun and a new sky for it to move in.[6]

Lewis drew an important lesson from this understanding of what we might call his "moral realism," that is, his belief that the moral nature of things is *really* there *in them,* rather than creatively imposed upon them by our imaginations. He asserted that moral education is highly useful, while moral exhortation isn't. Either people see reality and act accordingly (including moral reality), or they don't. Either someone understands enough about electricity not to cross the red and white wires, or he doesn't understand and proceeds in confidence that what he is doing is right. Pleading with him might work for the moment, if he is moved by your anguish and doesn't want it to continue. But if you want him *never* to cross those wires, pleading isn't the solution. Teaching him about electricity is.

To be sure, Lewis understood the perversity of the human heart better than most. *The Screwtape Letters* makes that clear by itself. And Lewis recognized that some people will defy good teaching and proceed to destruction in their foolish conceit. As a lifelong educator, he had no illusions that education was the panacea for human ills.[7] He simply indicated something fundamental about moral formation: showing people the way things are and then showing them how to negotiate that reality successfully is a better way to encourage goodness than mere exhortation from whatever position of authority or sympathy one happens to enjoy.[8]

Just as understanding and then contending well with physical reality are not always simple matters, however, so it is that moral training is required as well. One can sit in a classroom and be correctly informed about the nature of gravity, friction, snow, and so on, but the skill of negotiating the physical reality of a mountainside on skis must be learned only with exertion and perseverance. So, too, moral training means inculcating, fostering, and confirming moral habits over time, with similar exertion and perseverance. Thus Lewis affirms moral education as both rigorous and sustained (again, especially in *The Abolition of Man*).

---

6. See the appendix to C. S. Lewis, *The Abolition of Man: How Education Develops Man's Sense of Morality* (New York: Macmillan, 1947). 56–57.

7. Nor was being "cultured," as C. S. Lewis argues in "Lilies That Fester," in *The World's Last Night and Other Essays* (New York: Harcourt Brace Jovanovich, 1952), 31–49.

8. Lewis practices this principle in the well-known apologetic of Book One of *Mere Christianity* (Glasgow: Collins/Fount, 1977 [1952]).

The summum bonum of human existence for Lewis is shown us in Eden and its portrait of nascent *shalom:* a condition in which each individual thing is fully and healthily itself and in which it enjoys peaceful, wholesome, and delightful relations with God, with itself, and with all of the rest of creation. The world enjoys a kind of *perichorēsis* of love, to borrow a term from the Cappadocian Fathers, a kind of intertwining dance of mutuality, cooperation, hierarchies, roles, service, and delight. In fact, the dance is a chief image of Lewis both for God's own life and for the life of humanity.[9]

Fall

Few writers have exposed the nature of human—and, indeed, diabolical—evil better than C. S. Lewis. Dostoyevsky, Balzac, Dickens, O'Connor, Nabokov, and other great writers have painted their classics of debauchery, decadence, and destruction. Lewis, too, was a master of this subject, and particularly in bringing to light what we might call "everyday evil," the ordinary ways in which people torment and exploit each other, harm themselves, and cooperate with nefarious spiritual powers. Lewis's depictions of evil—most notably in *Screwtape,* of course, but in many of his other works as well, including his theology and literary criticism—indicate his belief in a phrase I'm not confident he ever used, much less affirmed: "total depravity." This doctrine is often misunderstood as suggesting that because of the Fall, human beings are as bad as they can possibly be. Lewis clearly didn't believe that—nor have any of the historical churches or their leading theologians, for that matter. That's not what total depravity means. Instead, "total depravity" is a phrase that indicates the *extent* of evil in our lives, and Lewis appreciated that evil has touched, and harmed, every part of us: our moral natures, yes, but also our rationality, our aesthetic sensibility, our sexuality—our very view of the world and our most fundamental motives.

In the light of this clear-eyed view of sin, Lewis writes, "Our leisure, even our play, is a matter of serious concern. There is no neutral ground in the universe: every square inch, every split second, is claimed by God and counterclaimed by Satan."[10] Lewis thus made clear that education, no matter how rigorous or

---

9. Ibid., 149–50. See also C. S. Lewis, *Letters to Malcolm: Chiefly on Prayer* (New York: Harcourt, 1992 [1963]), 92–93. Lewis's view of hierarchy indicates both that he affirmed this ordering of things and also that such orders were not always fixed but could shift in changing circumstances: see Meilaender, *Taste for the Other,* 70 ff.; Lewis, *Miracles,* 189; Lewis, "Membership," in *The Weight of Glory and Other Addresses* (Grand Rapids, MI: Eerdmans, 1949), 30–42.

10. C. S. Lewis, "Christianity and Culture," in *Christian Reflections,* ed. Walter Hooper (Grand Rapids, MI: Eerdmans, 1997 [1967]), 33.

sustained, will not suffice to solve our deep and broad moral afflictions. Our current sinful condition makes it not just difficult but finally impossible to improve enough. Virtue can become a passion for us only as we are "born again."[11] Thus, he notes often, the Bible and Christian tradition are replete with imagery of death and resurrection or new birth.

Redemption

Lewis never tires of this theme—that new life, which we all need, requires death of a sort. The gospel paradox of "losing one's life to save it" (Mt. 10:39) is perhaps the most quoted Scriptural phrase in Lewis's corpus:

> Christ says, "Give me All. I don't want so much of your time and so much of your money and so much of your work: I want You. I have not come to torment your natural self, but to kill it. No half-measures are any good. I don't want to cut off a branch here and a branch there. I want to have the whole tree down. I don't want to drill the tooth, or crown it, or stop it, but to have it out. Hand over the whole natural self, all the desires which you think innocent as well as the ones you think wicked—the whole outfit."[12]

As Gilbert Meilaender puts it, "Talk of elevation or even transformation cannot now stand alone. It is necessary to talk also of killing the natural self and replacing it with a new one."[13] "Ye must be born again" (Jn. 3:7 KJV).

Yet the paradox deepens. "Grace perfects nature," Lewis declares.[14] Elsewhere he says, "All that you are, sins apart, is destined, if you will let God have His good way, to utter satisfaction."[15] What we are reborn *to*, then, is not a negation of everything we felt and enjoyed and wanted before. This new life is but a purification and elevation of all of that to its shining best. Lewis puts it this way in his book *Miracles:*

> The first innocent and spontaneous desires have to submit to the deathlike process of control or total denial: but from that there is a reascent to fully formed character in which the strength of the original material all operates but in a new

11. Meilaender, *Taste for the Other,* 210–11.

12. Lewis, *Mere Christianity,* 165.

13. Meilaender, *Taste for the Other,* 172.

14. Lewis, *Letters to Malcolm,* 10.

15. Lewis, *The Problem of Pain,* 147.

way. Death and Rebirth—go down to go up—it is a key principle. Through this bottleneck, this belittlement, the highroad nearly always lies.[16]

So *eros* is completed, not negated, by *agapē*.[17] So also *bios,* our natural life, is taken up into what Lewis calls our "spiritual" life of *zoē*.[18] Thus we encounter a theme that shows up throughout this conversation, what we might call the continuity/discontinuity question. How much of our new life in Christ is to be undertaken properly in continuity with what was before, and how much in discontinuity? How new is "new"?

Meilaender puts Lewis's view of our experience of the tension, even conflict, between the old and the new this way: "Existentially,... we experience not a harmony but a rivalry between our love for God and our natural loves." In fact, he goes on, "the pictures of the natural loves harmoniously perfected by divine love must never blind our eyes to what this may mean in any person's experience. It may mean conflict, rivalry, renunciation, and grief." "For a fallen creature to [turn to God] will seem like a death of the self. It cannot be experienced simply as a turning from one good to a higher good but instead must often be experienced as a negation not only of the thing but of the self."[19]

Lewis thus speaks of "Nature wounded by Grace," but as a dentist or surgeon hurts in order to heal.[20] Indeed, it is this view of redemption that prompted Lewis occasionally to defend the prospect of purgatory, an intermediate state in which believers are purged of their remaining impurities and confusions and made ready to enjoy the life to come.[21]

Clearly, then, Lewis affirms a certain "Christ against culture" theme in his assertion of the necessity of death and rebirth. But he also sounds like "Christ above culture" and "Christ transforming culture" in this discussion. Lewis wants to affirm what is good in not yet fully redeemed cultures around the world, and to see Christianity as the fulfillment, the final reality, of what were shadows and

---

16. Lewis, *Miracles,* 180.

17. This point is central to the argument of C. S. Lewis, *The Four Loves* (London: Fontana, 1960).

18. This transformation is a theme of Book Four of *Mere Christianity*.

19. Meilaender, *Taste for the Other,* 169, 175, 27.

20. C. S. Lewis, "Williams and the Arthuriad," in Charles Williams and C. S. Lewis, *Arthurian Torso* (Oxford: Oxford University Press, 1948), 175; quoted in Meilaender, *Taste for the Other,* 135.

21. For a literary discussion of purgatory, see C. S. Lewis, *The Great Divorce: A Dream* (San Francisco: Fount, 1997 [1946]). For an explicit defense, see *Letters to Malcolm,* 106–9. Lewis only hints at it in his much better-known *Mere Christianity*: "The job [of producing holiness in us] will not be completed in this life: but He means to get us as far as possible before death" (171).

hopes and preliminaries and preparations in other cultures. Thus he spoke of "good dreams" in other cultures that became "true myths" in the Christian Story.[22] One hears bits of the great theme in the opening movements of the symphony, and then they fuse together in glorious harmony in the finale.[23]

The dominant mode of response to God's initiative in salvation, for Lewis, is in the Christian tradition of the *imitatio Christi* (imitation of Christ). To be sure, faith, as both assent to the truth of Christian teaching and trust in the person of Christ as Savior, is central to Lewis's religion. But it seems fair to say that sanctification was more dominant in Lewis than justification. Faith typically is portrayed by him as lived commitment. This committed life, furthermore, has a trajectory. It is headed for a particular destination, and it makes progress toward that goal step by step. Meilaender comments, "There is no jumping ahead to [the end]. The way must be traversed. Just as important [as hope in our ultimate salvation] in Lewis' vision of life, therefore, is his attention to our pilgrimage toward that end and his constant suggestion that this journey is likely to be a painful one."[24]

Paradoxes continue, however. Yes, the discipline of the Christian walk is hard—indeed, it requires a kind of death *and* a daily willingness to march toward death as one shoulders one's cross in the train of the Crucified One. Preparation for the eventual Great Dance requires discipline: "Discipline, while the world is yet unfallen, exists for the sake of what seems its very opposite—for freedom, almost for extravagance....The heavenly frolic arises from an orchestra which is in tune; the rules of courtesy make perfect ease and freedom possible between those who obey them."[25] As Meilaender goes on to comment, "Lewis does not for a moment think that freedom and discipline can be harmoniously combined in our present life."[26]

---

22. Lewis, *Mere Christianity*, 51. See also "Religion Without Dogma?" (which uses the more traditional theological term *preparatio evangelica*) in C. S. Lewis, *God in the Dock: Essays on Theology and Ethics*, ed. Walter Hooper (Grand Rapids, MI: Eerdmans, 1970), 129–46.

23. Wesley Kort, true to his theological liberalism, articulates Lewis in a liberal mode thus: "What one receives in reading the Bible is this: what one longs to be true in reading other stories is clarified as true in the reading of this story" (Wesley A. Kort, *C. S. Lewis Then and Now* [Oxford: Oxford University Press, 2001], 96). But Lewis's point is far stronger, and orthodox: what one longs to be true in reading other stories is not just *clarified* in the Bible—as if the Christian revelation is merely the clearest rendition (yet?) of the timeless truths of religion—but *realized* in the Christian story, and especially in the career of Jesus Christ; it is the "true myth" at the heart of everything else. Lewis's most important and sustained theological work, *Miracles*, deals frequently with other religions, myths, and so on: see, for example, 218–31.

24. Meilaender, *Taste for the Other*, vii.

25. C. S. Lewis, *A Preface to Paradise Lost* (Oxford: Oxford University Press, 1942), 81.

26. Meilaender, *Taste for the Other*, 51.

Yet this severe renunciation is accompanied by deep enjoyment. God strews our way with pleasures, which affirm to us the goodness of God, the goodness of the world, the goodness of each other, and the goodness of ourselves. Pleasures draw us out from ourselves to this larger cosmos and finally to God himself. Indeed, Lewis sometimes harks back to the mystical tradition of erotic delight in God: we want God and he wants us, and we take pleasure in each other.[27]

Lewis makes this point powerfully in the mouth of the authoritative demon Screwtape:

> He [God] is a hedonist at heart. All those fasts and vigils and stakes and crosses are only a façade. Or only like foam on the sea shore. Out at sea, out in His sea, there is pleasure and more pleasure. He makes no secret of it; at His right hand are "pleasures for evermore." Ugh! I don't think he has the least inkling of that high and austere mystery to which we rise in the Miserific Vision. He's vulgar, Wormwood. He has a bourgeois mind. He has filled His world full of pleasures. There are things for humans to do all day long without His minding in the least—sleeping, washing, eating, drinking, making love, playing, praying, working.[28]

Yet the switchbacks, the dialectics in Lewis's thought, continue. There is fundamentally a choice: to seek pleasure, thus drawing the world in to oneself, devouring it and shrinking at the same time—as Satan is depicted in *Screwtape* as the supreme and shrinking narcissist—or to seek God, thus being drawn out into the world to enjoy it, God, and oneself fully and forever. As Meilaender puts it, Lewis commends to us the attitude of faithful receptivity, a freedom both to receive anything gratefully from God and to just as freely relinquish anything back to God.[29] And Lewis brings several of these themes—renunciation, pleasure, pilgrimage, hope, faith, and sanctification—brilliantly to a point: "What is unforgivable if judged as an hotel may be very tolerable as a reformatory."[30]

---

27. See Meilaender, *Taste for the Other,* on this theme, plus the entire chapter on "Pleasure" in Kort, *C. S. Lewis Then and Now.*

28. C. S. Lewis, *The Screwtape Letters* (Old Tappan, NJ: Revell, 1976), 106. We will see Dietrich Bonhoeffer making a similar point (without diabolical irony, of course) in his theme of "the natural, " discussed below in Chapter 4.

29. Meilaender, *Taste for the Other,* 21.

30. C. S. Lewis, "Preface," in *Essays Presented to Charles Williams,* ed. C. S. Lewis (Grand Rapids, MI: Eerdmans, 1966), xiii; quoted in Meilaender, *Taste for the Other,* 125. Lewis extends the metaphor in "Answers to Questions on Christianity," in *God in the Dock,* 52.

What, then, of culture and our everyday life in the world? Lewis addresses Christianity and culture directly in just one essay—it was not a theme to which he turned often. And he seems to have had in mind here mostly the definition of "culture" as high culture, particularly intellectual and aesthetic activity, although he does relate this plane to the other levels of human life.[31]

Lewis begins by referring to his own study of the Bible on this question, and particularly the attitude of the New Testament: "Here I found...a demand that whatever is most highly valued on the natural level is to be held, as it were, merely on sufferance, and to be abandoned without mercy the moment it conflicts with the service of God." He continues: "On the whole, the New Testament seemed, if not hostile, yet unmistakably cold to culture. I think we can still believe culture to be innocent after we have read the New Testament; I cannot see that we are encouraged to think it important."[32]

By "innocent," Lewis seems to mean that it can still be seen as a good thing to be undertaken, rather than intrinsically something evil to be avoided. But, particularly for a man whose profession it was to teach literature to privileged students in a great university, Lewis sets out an intriguing list of reasons why culture (of this sort) can be a proper undertaking:

1. The need to earn a living.
2. Culture can be harmful, so "it is therefore probably better that the ranks of the 'culture-sellers' should include some Christians—as an antidote."[33]
3. Pleasure.
4. To awaken the unconverted to "something more" that points toward the gospel.

While there is nothing objectionable on this list, it is also curiously bereft of any large vision of "Christ transforming culture"—indeed, bereft of any missional purpose at all beyond evangelism. There are no references here to the so-called cultural mandate of Genesis 1 to "fill the earth and subdue it," to cultivate the world as the primary calling of all humanity, which we shall discuss much more in Part Three.

Lewis does add one more element to the mix. As converted people, he says, we ought to do our work "unto the Lord" to glorify him thereby. "The work of

---

31. Lewis, "Christianity and Culture," 12.

32. Ibid., 14, 15.

33. Ibid., 15. Cf. C. S. Lewis, "Learning in War-Time": "Good philosophy must exist, if for no other reason, because bad philosophy needs to be answered" (in *The Weight of Glory and Other Addresses*, 50).

a charwoman and the work of a poet become spiritual in the same way and on the same condition.... Let us stop giving ourselves airs."[34] Lewis echoes this sentiment in another essay in which he writes, "The work of a Beethoven, and the work of a charwoman, become spiritual on precisely the same condition, that of being offered to God, of being done humbly 'as to the Lord.' "[35]

In sum, then, for Lewis, "culture, though not in itself meritorious, was innocent and pleasant, might be a vocation for some, was helpful in bringing certain souls to Christ, and could be pursued to the glory of God."[36] Again, quite what Lewis means by bringing glory to God in our work is not spelled out—a curious lapse for an author normally so explicit.

This is not the only remarkable lacuna in Lewis's posture toward society, however. Lewis's focus almost always rests on the sphere of the individual life, Christian or otherwise. It helps give his writing its remarkably intimate appeal. But when one steps out of that almost cozy chat one is having with Lewis as one reads, one realizes that Lewis has relatively little to say about church life or about society as a whole.

His Cambridge acquaintance Richard Ladborough comments that "neither in conversation nor in his works did he show much interest in organized religion. He was orthodox in belief but seemed to have little sense of the Church."[37] His learned clerical friend Alan Bede Griffiths remarks also on Lewis's "almost total lack of concern about the Church as an institution."[38] Lewis himself testified in his autobiography thus: "To me, religion ought to have been a matter of good men praying alone, and meeting by twos and threes to talk of spiritual matters."[39] To be sure, this is Lewis writing of his views as a mere theist and *before* he became a Christian, but it is not clear that he changed them very much on this score afterward. The individual remained his primary focus. Thus Lewis has Screwtape declare,

> I would not—Hell forbid!—encourage in your own minds that delusion which you must carefully foster in the minds of your human victims. I mean the delu-

---

34. Lewis, "Christianity and Culture," 24.

35. Lewis, "Learning in War-Time," 48–49.

36. Lewis, "Christianity and Culture," 28.

37. Richard W. Ladborough, "In Cambridge," in *C. S. Lewis at the Breakfast Table and Other Reminiscences* (rev. ed.), ed. James T. Como (New York: Harcourt Brace Jovanovich, 1992 [1979]), 103.

38. Alan Bede Griffiths, "The Adventure of Faith," in *C. S. Lewis at the Breakfast Table,* ed. Como, 19.

39. C. S. Lewis, *Surprised by Joy: The Shape of My Early Life* (New York: Harcourt Brace Jovanovich, 1955), 234.

sion that the fate of nations is *in itself* more important than that of individual souls. The overthrow of free peoples and the multiplication of slave-states are for us a means (besides, of course, being fun); but the real end is the destruction of individuals. For only individuals can be saved or damned, can become sons of the Enemy or food for us.[40]

It is interesting in this regard to ask what Lewis thought about cities, those symbols of human social life. Wesley Kort avers, "While Lewis affirms the importance of social spaces that accommodate and stimulate the potentials of persons and grant to persons a sense of being a home, he offers no realistic models of social space equivalent to those he gives for personal spaces and open landscapes."[41] Compare also the testimonial of Helen Gardner, as Meilaender introduces it: "Despite the fact that much of his [academic] work concerned the debt of English literature to the literature of the Renaissance, no vision of 'cities, large and small, with splendid public monuments' ever played a large role in his imagination. For Lewis, she suggests, the simple loyalties of the *comitatus* were never replaced by the more complex loyalties of the 'city.' "[42]

Even more generally, work, the workplace, and the economy at large were seen by Lewis as cursed by stupidity, uselessness, alienation, unfair wages, and more. Meilaender notes, "What is important, he believes, is not to assign blame but to learn to live within such a society. Here again he returns to personal entry into the dialectic. To seek really good work—work which offers possibility for delight—may require 'considerable mortification of our avarice.' "[43] Sounding every bit the embattled but faithful individual pilgrim in a hostile and misguided society, Lewis advises, "The main practical task for most of us is not to give the Big Men advice about how to end our fatal economy—we have none to give and they wouldn't listen—but to consider how we can live within it as little hurt and degraded as possible."[44]

C. S. Lewis thus sounds the "Christ against culture" theme again. Yet this individualism is not self-absorption. Quite the contrary. The individual is ful-

---

40. C. S. Lewis, "Screwtape Proposes a Toast," in *The World's Last Night,* 68.

41. Kort, *C. S. Lewis Then and Now,* 69.

42. Helen Gardner, "Clive Staples Lewis, 1898–1963," *Proceedings of the British Academy* 51 (1965): 420; quoted in Meilaender, *Taste for the Other,* 42.

43. Meilaender, *Taste for the Other,* 44; the quotation from Lewis is from "Good Work and Good Works," *The World's Last Night,* 78. Earlier in this same essay Lewis avers that "work with doing apart from its pay, enjoyable work, and good work [have] become the privilege of a fortunate minority" (76).

44. "Good Work and Good Works," 77.

filled precisely by communion with church and society—and nature. Kort explains,

> For him it is essential that the Christian not think of belief as a way of bringing something in to his or her life but, rather, as a way of being brought out into a larger world or sense of the world....Lewis militates constantly against self-preoccupation and especially against narcissism. An interest in Christianity that would amount to accepting something into one's life would be only another form of self-expansion. The direction of conversion for Lewis is very much the opposite, of moving outward into something larger and more important than the self.[45]

Furthermore, Lewis affirms a principle of difference—or even what sociologists of modernity call "differentiation"—in one's vocation that contributes toward the common good.[46] He demonstrates this understanding by characterizing himself as a literary scholar, cultural critic, and apologist—not as political theorist or clergyman. In particular, he once wrote, "Of forms of government, of civil authority and civil obedience, I have nothing to say."[47] Each of us plays his or her role in the complex interactions of modern society, and all benefit:

> The application of Christian principles, say, to trade unionism or education, must come from Christian trade unionists and Christian schoolmasters: just as Christian literature comes from Christian novelists and dramatists—not from the bench of bishops getting together and trying to write plays and novels in their spare time.[48]

This benefit, to be sure, is largely for the meanwhile. And Christians look forward to the New Society that is to come upon Christ's return.

Consummation

Lewis has sometimes been called a Platonist, and presently we shall examine at least one way in which that characterization makes sense. But his fundamental

---

45. Kort, *C. S. Lewis Then and Now,* 22. A characteristically graphic and powerful discussion of the ethics of masturbation nicely illustrates this theme: see Lewis's letter (too long to quote here) to a Mr. Masson, quoted in Richard Purtill, *C. S. Lewis's Case for the Christian Faith* (San Francisco: Harper & Row, 1985), 97–98.

46. Lewis, *Problem of Pain,* 150.

47. Ibid., 115.

48. Lewis, *Mere Christianity,* 75.

view of the world to come is not Platonic, even in a Christian mode. Indeed, it differs from most of his beloved medieval and Renaissance authors in that the goal of human life is not the Beatific Vision, the endless mystical contemplation of the Beloved as is pictured at the end of Dante's *Paradiso:*

> The promises of Scripture may very roughly be reduced to five heads. It is promised, firstly, that we shall be with Christ; secondly, that we shall be like Him; thirdly, with an enormous wealth of imagery, that we shall have "glory"; fourthly, that we shall, in some sense, be fed or feasted or entertained; and finally, that we shall have some sort of official position in the universe—ruling cities, judging angels, being pillars of God's temple.[49]

Lewis loved to consider how this world prefigures and leads on to the next:

> When human souls have become as perfect in voluntary obedience as the inanimate creation is in its lifeless obedience, then they will put on its glory, or rather that greater glory of which Nature is only the first sketch....Nature is mortal; we shall outlive her....Nature is only the image, the symbol; but it is the symbol Scripture invites me to use. We are summoned to pass in through Nature, beyond her, into that splendour which she fitfully reflects.[50]

In that passage, Lewis *does* sound a bit Platonic, as if nature is merely a symbol of a spiritual reality to come, to be enjoyed by "human souls." And this motif of radical disruption shows up elsewhere in his writing:

> The doctrine of the Second Coming is deeply uncongenial to the whole evolutionary or developmental character of modern thought. We have been taught to think of the world as something that grows slowly towards perfection, something that "progresses" or "evolves." Christian Apocalyptic offers us no such hope....It foretells a sudden, violent end imposed from without: an extinguisher popped onto the candle, a brick flung at the gramophone, a curtain rung down on the play—"Halt!"[51]

Yet while this disruption is itself radical, it is not as comprehensively destructive quite as Lewis's metaphors suggest. The New Testament account of Christ's resurrection and ascension

---

49. Lewis, "The Weight of Glory," 7.
50. Ibid., 13.
51. Lewis, "The World's Last Night," 100–1.

is not the picture of an escape from any and every kind of Nature into some unconditioned and utterly transcendent life. It is the picture of a new human nature, and a new Nature in general, being brought into existence. We must, indeed, believe the risen body to be extremely different from the mortal body: but the existence, in that new state, of anything that could in any sense be described as "body" at all, involves some sort of spatial relations and in the long run a whole new universe. That is the picture—not of unmaking but of remaking. The old field of space, time, matter, and the senses is to be weeded, dug, and sown for a new crop. We may be tired of that old field: God is not.[52]

Lewis uses the image of a house to nicely show the ambiguity of this theme of continuity and discontinuity: "A new Nature is being not merely made but made out of an old one. We live amid all the anomalies, inconveniences, hopes, and excitements of a house that is being rebuilt. Something is being pulled down and something going up in its place."[53] One might well ask of Lewis whether something is being remade or replaced. I expect he would reply that the answer is both: out of the one comes the other, with resemblance but also transcendence—just like Jesus' resurrection body, which is our one glimpse of the new creation physically, so to speak, beyond John's visions in the Apocalypse.

With such a view of what is to come, Lewis celebrates *Sehnsucht,* his longing for joy. This longing, he says, is vital to our well-being, as it keeps us from settling for what cannot satisfy, and draws us upward and forward to the new world in which all is finally well. His most popular sermon furnishes us with this oft-quoted observation:

If we consider the unblushing promises of reward and the staggering nature of the rewards promised in the Gospels, it would seem that Our Lord finds our desires, not too strong, but too weak. We are half-hearted creatures, fooling about with drink and sex and ambition when infinite joy is offered us, like an ignorant child who wants to go on making mud pies in a slum because he cannot imagine what is meant by the offer of a holiday at the sea. We are far too easily pleased.[54]

---

52. Lewis, *Miracles,* 244.

53. Ibid., 253; cf. the same use of George MacDonald's image in Lewis, *Mere Christianity,* 172.

54. Lewis, "Weight of Glory," 1–2.

THEMES IN A THEOLOGY
OF CULTURE

Before we move on from Lewis's preaching to his practice, we can pause to elaborate briefly upon a few themes from the foregoing.

"Sanctification" of Self—and Society?

We have seen that Lewis focuses particularly on the sphere of the individual Christian faithfully making his way along the path of sanctification, looking for the world to come, taking pleasure as he finds it, and contributing to the common good as he can.

Inasmuch as the cumulative influence of Christians in a society affects public institutions, however, Lewis's concern was not to *subvert* public institutions nor to *convert* them to their final messianic state, but to *revert* them back to their traditional sources and purposes in God's providence. In this view Lewis was truly a cultural conservative (and not merely reactionary or contrarian), not because he entertained any romantic view of the inherent goodness of society at some point in the past, but in the deep sense of one who continued to see the goodness and order of God over and in all earthly affairs. Lewis had not given up on the structures God has placed in the world, and he believed that the Christian is to contribute as he can to any attempt to recover these healthful, helpful gifts.

That was the positive side of his conservatism. There was a negative side as well:

Being a democrat, I am opposed to all very drastic and sudden changes of society (in whatever direction) because they never in fact take place except by a particular technique. That technique involves the seizure of power by a small, highly disciplined group of people; the terror and the secret police follow, it would seem, automatically. I do not think any group good enough to have such power. They are men of like passions with ourselves.[55]

Realism as well as hope, therefore, constantly shaped Lewis's outlook. He himself found it natural to think in terms of hierarchy, believing that it was ultimately the correct order of things.[56] This disposition accounts at least partly for

---

55. C. S. Lewis, "A Reply to Professor Haldane," in *Of Other Worlds: Essays and Stories* (New York: Harcourt, 1994 [1966]), 82.

56. Lewis argues backward, so to speak, by having Screwtape promote "democracy"—really, a form of envious leveling—in "Screwtape Proposes a Toast," 51–70. He argues positively in a number of places, including in "Christianity and Literature," in Lewis, *Christian Reflections,* 4–11.

why he was so "at home" in the Middle Ages, and particularly in its imaginative literature. But when it came to the actual political life of human beings in his own time, Lewis recommends democracy, not hierarchy, because of the Fall. The "real reason for democracy," he says, is that we are "so fallen that no man can be trusted with unchecked power over his fellows."[57] As Meilaender comments, "Lewis states explicitly that we should not even try to reinstitute the hierarchical ideal.... We are settling for something which, though necessary, is second-best."[58]

Lewis knew enough of world history to see a kind of tension in God's call to each society. Each culture is peculiar and deals with its particular historical moment. It does so, however, in the light of the universal *Tao,* and any Christian culture does so particularly in the light of God's revelation in the Bible. Ultimately, of course, particular societies will give way to the New Jerusalem under the reign of Messiah. In the meanwhile, however, they each make their way and play their part. Lewis thus was much more appreciative of what he knew of foreign cultures than many of his readers would be aware of simply from, say, his rather stereotypical depiction of Calormen in the Narnia stories.

Finally, Lewis sees redemption for Nature herself: "She, like ourselves, is to be redeemed.... She will be cured in character: not tamed (Heaven forbid) nor sterilised."[59] So, again, while Lewis focuses most of his attention on human beings, and on individuals at that, his vision does extend well beyond ourselves to the whole world under God's care.

Conversion—Both Evangelism and Edification—as Chief Mission and Yet Scholarship as Worthy Occupation

Lewis, as we have seen, naturally thought in terms of hierarchy and unity. Christians, he maintained,

> live in a graded or hierarchical universe where there is a place for everything and everything should be kept in its right place. The Supernatural is higher than the Natural, but each has its place; just as a man is higher

---

57. C. S. Lewis, "Equality," *The Spectator* 171 (27 August 1943), 192; reprinted in *Present Concerns: Essays by C. S. Lewis,* ed. Walter Hooper (New York: Harcourt Brace, 1986), 17. Lewis repeats this sentiment almost verbatim in "A Reply to Professor Haldane," 81. He goes on to comment, "A political program can never in reality be more than probably right. We never know all the facts about the present and we can only guess the future. To attach to a party programme—whose highest real claim is to reasonable prudence—the sort of assent which we should reserve for demonstrable theorems, is a kind of intoxication" (81–82).

58. Meilaender, *Taste for the Other,* 83.

59. Lewis, *Miracles,* 105.

than a dog, but a dog has its place. It is, therefore, to us not at all surprising that healing for the sick and provision for the poor should be less important than (when they are, as sometimes happens, alternative to) the salvation of souls; and yet very important. Because God created the Natural—invented it out of His love and artistry—it demands our reverence; because it is only a creature and not He, it is, from another point of view, of little account. And still more, because Nature, and especially human nature, is fallen it must be corrected and the evil within it must be mortified. But its essence is good; correction is something quite different from Manichaean repudiation or Stoic superiority.[60]

In one of the most quoted passages in all of Lewis's highly quotable corpus, he points particularly to the value of human beings:

It may be possible for each to think too much of his own potential glory hereafter; it is hardly possible for him to think too often or too deeply about that of his neighbour. The load, or weight, or burden of my neighbour's glory should be laid daily on my back, a load so heavy that only humility can carry it, and the backs of the proud will be broken. It is a serious thing to live in a society of possible gods and goddesses, to remember that the dullest and most uninteresting person you talk to may one day be a creature which, if you saw it now, you would be strongly tempted to worship, or else a horror and a corruption such as you now meet, if at all, only in a nightmare. All day long we are, in some degree, helping each other to one or other of these destinations. It is in the light of these overwhelming possibilities, it is with the awe and circumspection proper to them that we should conduct all our dealings with one another, all friendships, all loves, all play, all politics. There are no *ordinary* people. You have never talked to a mere mortal. Nations, cultures, arts, civilizations—these are mortal, and their life is to ours as the life of a gnat. But it is immortals whom we joke with, work with, marry, snub, and exploit—immortal horrors or everlasting splendours.[61]

Lewis thus had a strong concern that we help our neighbors come to faith and then grow up into faithful maturity. Yet he recognized that most Christians are called to spend most of their time in activity that isn't obviously and directly evangelistic or otherwise obviously spiritually edifying:

---

60. C. S. Lewis, "Some Thoughts," in *God in the Dock*, 148–49.
61. Lewis, "Weight of Glory," 14–15.

Before I became a Christian, I do not think I fully realized that one's life, after conversion, would inevitably consist in doing most of the same things one had been doing before: one hopes, in a new spirit, but still the same things.... Christianity does not exclude any of the ordinary human activities. St. Paul tells people to get on with their jobs. He even assumes that Christians may go to dinner parties, and, what is more, dinner parties given by pagans. Our Lord attends a wedding and provides miraculous wine. Under the aegis of His Church, and in the most Christian ages, learning and the arts flourish. The solution of this paradox is, of course, well known to you. "Whether ye eat or drink or whatsoever ye do, do all to the glory of God."

All our merely natural activities will be accepted, if they are offered to God, even the humblest: and all of them, even the noblest, will be sinful if they are not. Christianity does not simply replace our natural life and substitute a new one: it is rather a new organization which exploits, to its own supernatural ends, these natural materials.... There is no essential quarrel between the spiritual life and human activities as such.[62]

Thus we encounter Lewis making the paradoxical point about learning being done for its own sake, which is to the glory of God, *without* thereby bending the research to come to edifying conclusions or to show its relevance somehow to Christian life:

By leading that [learned] life to the glory of God I do not, of course, mean any attempt to make our intellectual inquiries work out to edifying conclusions.... I mean the pursuit of knowledge and beauty, in a sense, for their own sake, but in a sense which does not exclude their being for God's sake. [Now Lewis sounds a "Christ above culture" motif.] An appetite for these things exists in the human mind, and God makes no appetite in vain. We can therefore pursue knowledge as such, and beauty, as such, in the sure confidence that by so doing we are either advancing to the vision of God ourselves or indirectly helping others to do so. [It is interesting that in this passage he speaks not of *shalom* more broadly as the goal but of the Beatific Vision.] Humility, no less than the appetite, encourages us to concentrate simply on the knowledge or the beauty, not too much concerning ourselves with their ultimate relevance to the vision of God. That relevance may not be intended for us but for our betters—for men who come after and find the spiritual significance of what we dug out in blind and humble obedience to our vocation.[63]

62. Lewis, "Learning in War-Time," 46, 47–48.
63. Ibid., 49.

Lewis wants his readers to be clear that his is no vision of liberal optimism, as we have seen:

> If we thought we were building up a heaven on earth, if we looked for something that would turn the present world from a place of pilgrimage into a permanent city satisfying the soul of man, we are disillusioned, and not a moment too soon. But if we thought that for some souls, and at some times, the life of learning, humbly offered to God, was, in its own small way, one of the appointed approaches to the Divine reality and the Divine beauty which we hope to enjoy hereafter, we can think so still.[64]

Indeed, Lewis sharpens the point of the value of our work as intrinsic rather than instrumental: "I do not mean that a Christian should take money for supplying one thing (culture) and use the opportunity thus gained to supply a quite different thing (homiletics and apologetics). That is stealing."[65]

The point for everyone, then, is that if even the relatively rarefied activity of advanced scholarship is justified on Christian terms, all the more are more practical activities thereby justified: child rearing, business, health care, and so on. And Lewis knew about these things, too, as we shall now see.

Work and Domesticity

I grew up in a home in which C. S. Lewis was revered. My parents bought a book that depicted Lewis's life through photographs and text, and I remember musing over it as a thirteen-year-old already entranced by the idea of the university. I had moved through school quickly and was in the tenth grade. High school had only a few intellectual charms for me. But *university*: that was where cultivated people sipped tea—or even wine (I was raised in an abstinent tradition, so wine seemed almost unimaginably sophisticated)—and conversed wisely and wittily about great things. The volume about Lewis nicely filled in my mental pictures of such life with photographs of Lewis's college rooms, exteriors of Magdalen College and the "dreaming spires" of Oxford, and the High Street, on which walked the demigods of one of the world's great universities.[66]

---

64. Ibid., 53–54.

65. Lewis, "Christianity and Culture," 21.

66. Douglas Gilbert and Clyde S. Kilby, *C. S. Lewis: Images of His World* (Grand Rapids, MI: Eerdmans, 1973).

A particular photograph, however, stood out in my mind. It was a shot of Addison's Walk, the path near the River Cherwell upon which Lewis would stroll with his friends.[67] Along with the building photographs, it nicely impressed upon me the picture of Lewis enjoying the life of the scholar bachelor: his rooms tidied by "scouts," his meals prepared by the college kitchen, his days filled with reading, writing, walking, conversation, and the pleasure of delivering another brilliant lecture to an adoring audience. And as I went on to read Lewis over the ensuing years, in the back of my mind was a sort of qualification of my admiration for him: he could produce so much, at such a high level, I was sure, because he enjoyed this life of leisurely intellection, forever strolling on Addison's Walk with Barfield or Tolkien, between reading in the Bodleian and writing in his Magdalen rooms.

It was A. N. Wilson's biography of Lewis—easily the least favorite biography among Lewis fans, and understandably reviled by their number for its sarcasm and occasional cheap Freudian speculation—that shattered this myth and so helpfully knocked Lewis off his pedestal.[68] Wilson depicts Lewis running from his endless tutorial sessions with more-or-less motivated Oxford undergraduates to pick up groceries on his way out to a house in Headington and the demanding (we would say "dysfunctional") quasi-family he maintained with the odd Mrs. Moore, her apparently normal daughter, and his alcoholic brother; *this* domestic Lewis, *this* sometimes harried and always busy man with his shirtsleeves rolled up over the day's dishes in the sink, was the C. S. Lewis who had produced all of *that*? Lewis's star shone all the brighter in my mind as I closed Wilson's biography and thought, *He did all that in the real world, not in some misty Oxonian Neverland.* C. S. Lewis was, indeed, a common man who somehow managed to be an uncommon scholar.

The college servants who looked after him at Cambridge in his later career were said to have "respected and admired him" as "a *real* gentleman" who

---

67. Ibid., 32. My wife and I happened upon Addison's Walk on our first visit to Oxford by sneaking into Magdalen College's grounds. It was a genuine thrill to walk it, fifteen years after I had seen the photograph for the first time.

68. A. N. Wilson, *C. S. Lewis: A Biography* (New York: Norton, 1991). Lewis seems eerily prophetic of Wilson's biography as he writes about "another type of critic who speculates about the genesis of your book [as an] amateur psychologist. He has a Freudian theory of literature and claims to know all about your inhibitions. He knows what unacknowledged wishes you were gratifying.... And now, come to think of it, I have seldom seen [this kind of criticism] practiced on a dead author except by a scholar who intended, in some measure, to debunk him. That in itself is perhaps significant. And it would not be unreasonable to point out that the evidence on which such amateur psychologists base their diagnosis would not be thought sufficient by a professional. They have not had their author on the sofa, nor heard his dreams, and had the whole case-history" ("On Criticism," in *Of Other Worlds,* 50–51).

showed genuine interest in their well-being—in a place in which such interest was remarkable.[69] More remarkable was his much earlier decision to keep a war-time commitment to his fellow soldier Paddy Moore, with whom he had formed a pact to care for the other's family in the event one was killed. So Lewis cared for Mrs. Moore and her daughter for years. And then he spent his last years with a second family, caring for Joy Davidman and her two sons. Of course domestic life had its rewards for Lewis himself. But those two families featured terrible and extended demands, with Mrs. Moore slowly declining into a bitter, selfish senility while later Joy Davidman slowly succumbed to cancer.

One of Lewis's former Oxford students remarks:

> Most of the time that I was an undergraduate, he went home to his house in Headington in the evenings, though I think he spent all his days in college. He once said how irritating it was that one seemed to get one's best ideas with both hands in hot water doing the washing up, unable to make notes. One of my friends after the war expressed his regret at his own lack of domesticity. "Ah," said Lewis. "You have too little of it and I have too much."[70]

Yet Lewis connected not only his scholarship with his domesticity—if only ironically in this instance—but also his piety. During your prayers, he once counseled, as you pray to be conformed more and more to the likeness of Christ, "you may realize that, instead of saying your prayers, you ought to be downstairs writing a letter, or helping your wife to wash-up. Well, go and do it."[71]

Lewis did not, however, simply fly back and forth between university and family. He enjoyed extended walking tours with male friends—and occasionally female companions joined the company as well. These trips featured friendship, beer and food, conversation, and encounter with nature—all of which Lewis esteemed highly:

---

69. Ladborough, "In Cambridge," 102–3.

70. Derek Brewer, "The Tutor: A Portrait," in *C. S. Lewis at the Breakfast Table,* ed. Como, 56. Lewis writes powerfully that "if Christian teachers wish to recall Christian people to domesticity—and I, for one, believe that people must be recalled to it—the first necessity is to stop telling lies about home life and to substitute realistic teaching.... Since the Fall no organization or way of life whatever has a natural tendency to go right.... [D]omesticity is no passport to heaven on earth but an arduous vocation—a sea full of hidden rocks and perilous ice shores only to be navigated by one who uses a celestial chart.... The family, like the nation, can be offered to God, can be converted and redeemed, and will then become the channel of particular blessings and graces. But, like everything else that is human, it needs redemption" ("The Sermon and the Lunch," in *God in the Dock*, 284–85). This essay is a brilliant dose of realism that ought to be required reading for premarital counseling.

71. Lewis, *Mere Christianity,* 159.

My happiest hours are spent with three or four old friends in old clothes tramp-
ing together and putting up in small pubs—or else sitting up until the small
hours in someone's college rooms talking nonsense, poetry, theology, metaphysics over beer, tea, and pipes.[72]

I remark on these trips because Lewis undertook them gladly and was sorry
whenever one would have to be canceled because of a crisis. He never saw these
extended outings as "taking away from" either his family duties or his scholarly
vocation.

Still, his scholarly vocation occupied most of his waking hours. And we can learn
much from him on this score as well, no matter our own occupations. The primary thing perhaps to notice is that upon his conversion, Lewis didn't leave Oxford
and the teaching of literature for a divinity college career or a preaching ministry.
Despite his status as the twentieth century's most influential apologist, such work
was a sideline for him, and he seems never to have seriously considered either a
church career or a job in academic theological education. Nor do any of Lewis's
biographers that I have read indicate that someone ever suggested he do so. In
Lewis's world, devotion to literature hundreds of years old was a perfectly worthy
thing for a Christian. Indeed, despite Lewis's own writing that implies a hierarchy
of activities for the Christian with evangelism at its putative peak, for all his evangelistic talents he seems never to have considered an evangelistic career. His practice
was to carry on the work God had already called him to do and to which he was
obviously well-suited. As Wesley Kort nicely puts it, "Lewis does not respond to the
cultural despisers of religion by becoming a religious despiser of human culture."[73]

Yet it is not as if there was no evangelistic element in Lewis's main, scholarly
work. Kort observes,

For Lewis the crucial failure of modern culture is that it renders people unprepared to give an account of the world in which they find themselves and of
their behavior in it. They are unprepared because the narcissist and materialist
assumptions under which they operate are unable to provide an account that is
adequate and coherent. . . . [And c]ynicism and skepticism are [merely] defenses
against giving an account.[74]

---

72. Letter to Macmillan, his American publisher, quoted in Alan Jacobs, *The Narnian: The Life
and Imagination of C. S. Lewis* (San Francisco: Harper, 2005), xix.

73. Kort, *C. S. Lewis Then and Now*, 177.

74. Ibid., 25.

Lewis was especially good at giving an account of the Christian life, which he did in his literary history and criticism as in everything else. And to do that was both evangelistic and edifying.[75] Meilaender allows,

> He strives to present his theology consistently. But it is, he thinks, a consistent picture of an untidy world. The world as Lewis experiences it resists complete systematization—which is what we should expect from one who knows himself to be a pilgrim. Not all questions can be answered this side of "the land of the Trinity."[76]

Many readers, of course, have been spiritually assisted both by Lewis's theological prose and by his imaginative tales that depict good and evil so memorably. But many others have been touched by Lewis's Christian view of things in his literary scholarship, whether they recognize it as Christian or not.

Furthermore, the very Christian worldview he was articulating is a worldview that prizes literature and encourages its study by those gifted in such scholarship. The Kingdom of God, that is, includes the enjoyment of literature. So Lewis literally lived out good news about that Kingdom by continuing his scholarship, as well as in his various more explicitly religious writings.

The many, many fans of Lewis's fiction—from *Screwtape* to *The Great Divorce* to the space trilogy to Narnia—need to consider that this eminent scholar and equally eminent apologist was taking considerable time away from those two respectable jobs to *write stories*—not always a highly respected vocation among the pious. Lewis's easy transition from one type of writing to another demonstrates his wide vision of what "counts" as worthwhile work in the world.

Kort again comments, "Lewis the convert locates himself not first of all in an institution or community but, rather, in a world differently constituted and differently understood. Conversion did not call him out of the culture and into the church but to work at the complex relation of Christian beliefs, values, and norms to the culture."[77] Lewis did work at this "complex relation" in a startlingly broad range of genres. But the quality and reception of the work indicate that he wasn't

---

75. Anthropologist Clifford Geertz comments: "It is this placing of proximate acts in ultimate contexts that makes religion, frequently at least, socially so powerful. It alters, often radically, the whole landscape presented to common sense, alters it in such a way that the moods and motivations induced by religious practice seem themselves supremely practical, the only sensible ones to adopt given the way things 'really' are" (*The Interpretation of Cultures* [New York: Basic Books, 1973], 122).

76. Meilaender, *Taste for the Other*, 5.

77. Kort, *C. S. Lewis Then and Now*, 23.

straining outside his calling. Poetry, which he had hoped would be his main call-ing, was the one genre he undertook in which he is generally acknowledged to have failed. It thus is perhaps an impressive (negative) confirmation of what he *did* do so well in so many other ways.[78]

Hope and Vocation

Lewis was a scholar of medieval and Renaissance literature but, again, he was no romantic, longing for some previous idyll of fair maidens, noble knights, and a culture of courtesy. Indeed, his historical scholarship equipped him well to cast a gimlet eye on all civilizations. Thus he characterized contemporary culture as nei-ther the apex of civilization's advance (so the self-flattery of modernity) nor as the nadir of pseudo-sophisticated barbarism (so both the premodern and postmodern critics). Lewis saw modern society as he saw all societies: as a mixed field, showing the fruit of worthy human efforts under Providence and also showing the fruit of evil human efforts aided by the Evil One.

For Lewis, culture always demonstrates three elements in tension:

1. Culture is always plastic: we are always shaping it (as, to be sure, it shapes us), and it is not inexorable, permanent, or linear.
2. Culture always is also marked by the intransigence of evil and the active resistance of evil agents, human and diabolical.
3. Culture is yet under the providence of God, who has promised to redeem the whole world. Thus Lewis felt neither optimism nor pessimism was appropriate; rather, he advocated a realistic hope for both now and the future.

We should therefore live in the present—with our hope for the future secure in the coming Kingdom, but not always living for the future and therefore unhappy until it comes in all its fullness. So Screwtape advises Wormwood,

---

78. Lewis once testified: "The imaginative man in me is older, more continuously operative, and in that sense more basic than either the religious writer or the critic. It was he who made my first attempt (with little success) to be a poet. It was he who, in response to the poetry of oth-ers, made me a critic, and in defense of that response, sometimes a critical controversialist. It was he who, after my conversion led me to embody my religious belief in symbolic or mytho-poeic forms, ranging from *Screwtape* to a kind of theologised science-fiction. And it was, of course, he who has brought me, in the last few years to write the series of Narnian stories for children" (*Letters of C. S. Lewis,* ed. W. H. Lewis and Walter Hooper, rev. ed. [New York: Harcourt Brace Jovanovich, 1993], 444; quoted in Jacobs, *The Narnian,* xxiv–xxv).

To be sure, the Enemy wants men to think of the Future too—just so much as is necessary for *now* planning the acts of justice or charity which will probably be their duty tomorrow. The duty of planning the morrow's work is *today's* duty; though its material is borrowed from the Future, the duty, like all duties, is in the Present. This is not straw splitting. He does not want men to give the Future their hearts, to place their treasure in it. We do! His ideal is a man who, having worked all day for the good of posterity (if that is his vocation), washes his mind of the whole subject, commits the issue to Heaven, and returns at once to the patience or gratitude demanded by the moment that is passing over him. But we want a man hag-ridden by the Future—haunted by visions of an imminent heaven or hell upon earth—ready to break the Enemy's commands in the Present if by so doing we make him think he can attain the one or avert the other—dependent for his faith on the success or failure of schemes whose end he will not live to see. We want a whole race perpetually in pursuit of the rainbow's end, never honest, nor kind, nor happy *now,* but always using as mere fuel wherewith to heap the altar of the Future every real gift which is offered them in the Present.[79]

Thus Lewis counsels us to do what we know we are to do: "We are on the stage. To play well the scenes in which we are 'on' concerns us much more than to guess about the scenes that follow it."[80] To be sure, one plays a character better if one knows the whole play, or even just the outline of it. And Lewis himself agrees, for he knows we Christians do have some sense of the final act of the drama. In the same essay in which he offers this advice, he remarks, "What is important is not that we should always fear (or hope) about the End but that we should always remember, always take it into account."[81]

Lewis's main point is that we have only an outline, and furthermore an outline only of the Grand Narrative. We do not have such a sketch of our own lives, or the lives of others, or of our churches or families or nations or civilizations. In that sense, Lewis's advice is bracing:

We do not know the play. We do not even know whether we are in Act I or Act V. We do not know who are the major and who the minor characters. The Author knows. The audience, if there is an audience (if angels and archangels and all the company of heaven fill the pit and the stalls) may have an inkling.

---

79. Lewis, *Screwtape Letters,* 78–79.
80. Lewis, "World's Last Night," 104.
81. Ibid., 110.

But we, never seeing the play from outside, never meeting any characters except the tiny minority who are "on" in the same scenes as ourselves, wholly ignorant of the future and very imperfectly informed about the past, cannot tell at what moment the end ought to come.... We are led to expect that the Author will have something to say to each of us on the part that each of us has played. The playing it well is what matters infinitely.[82]

So Lewis concludes,

For what comes is Judgment: happy are those whom it finds labouring in their vocations, whether they were merely going out to feed the pigs or laying good plans to deliver humanity a hundred years hence from some great evil. The curtain has indeed now fallen. Those pigs will never in fact be fed, the great campaign against White Slavery or Governmental Tyranny will never in fact proceed to victory. No matter; you were at your post when the Inspection came.[83]

History and Imagination: Diagnosis and Ways Forward

C. S. Lewis combined abilities to look backward and forward in unusual measure. Most of his readers know he was a literary critic, but he spent little time reviewing authors among his contemporaries. He was, instead, a literary historian, an explorer particularly of medieval and Renaissance literature. He thus was committed to the importance of history to provide us not only with more or less interesting accounts of the past to satisfy our curiosity but also with an accurate understanding of how we got here—and what "here" actually is. Lewis is, as usual, eloquent on his theme:

We need intimate knowledge of the past. Not that the past has any magic about it, but because we cannot study the future, and yet need something to set against the present, to remind us that the basic assumptions have been quite different in different periods and that much which seems certain to the uneducated is merely temporary fashion. A man who has lived in many places is not likely to be deceived by the local errors of his native village: the scholar has lived in many times and is therefore in some degree immune from the

82. Ibid., 105–6.
83. Ibid., 111–12.

great cataract of nonsense that pours from the press and the microphone of his own age.[84]

Lewis thus counsels us to seek out and read old books along with new ones. If we read only our contemporaries, Lewis warns,

> where they are true they will give us truths which we half knew already. Where they are false they will aggravate the error with which we are already danger-ously ill. The only palliative is to keep the clean sea breeze of the centuries blow-ing through our minds, and this can be done only by reading old books. Not, of course, that there is any magic about the past. People were no cleverer then than they are now; they made as many mistakes as we. But not the *same* mistakes. They will not flatter us in the errors we are already committing; and their own errors, being now open and palpable, will not endanger us. Two heads are better than one, not because either is infallible, but because they are unlikely to go wrong in the same direction. To be sure, the books of the future would be just as good a corrective as the books of the past, but unfortunately we cannot get at them.[85]

Lewis, of course, was gifted also with an extraordinary imagination. He felt keenly, however, that this gift was to be used not to avoid reality but to envision how things could be better and how to make them better—to construct not escap-ist fantasies but useful, invigorating visions. Wesley Kort perhaps downplays the importance of critique, but his emphasis is correct: "The urgent need is to mobi-lize the energy that is now given to protesting and taking exception and to direct it toward formulating alternative accounts of how things should be."[86]

Lewis did not himself, however, do much imagining in any realistic, literal sense of what a renewed, or even improved, society would look like or how it could be achieved.[87] His imaginary worlds—whether of Narnia, our solar system, classical mythology, or the world to come—depict enduring virtues and implicitly (and occasionally explicitly) point to contemporary issues and their resolution.[88]

---

84. Lewis, "Learning in War-Time," 50–51.

85. C. S. Lewis, "On the Reading of Old Books," in *God in the Dock*, 202.

86. Kort, *C. S. Lewis Then and Now*, 170.

87. The one professional field on which Lewis did frequently opine was his own, education. *The Abolition of Man* is his longest contribution, but most of his essay collections contain at least one article on education, and other works contain at least passing, and passionate, mention of it.

88. *The Silver Chair* (Harmondsworth, UK: Puffin, 1965 [1953]), for instance, strikes a few blows against unhappy trends in elementary education in the form of "Experiment House"; and *That Hideous Strength* (London: Pan, 1976 [1955]) scores numerous points against various

Generally, however, he left to others who were more politically knowledgeable the task of portraying social and cultural alternatives. He remained the individual who enjoyed small societies and who, from that basis, offered what he could by way of critique and suggestion to the larger societies of which he was a member—church, university, nation, and Western civilization at large.[89]

Enjoying the World—and Its Maker

We began by noticing how American evangelicals have taken Lewis to heart. Many observers of this phenomenon, however, have noted with delicious glee that Lewis is hardly an exemplar of contemporary American evangelicalism, particularly in his convivial love of beer, his frank celebration of sex and of love in all its legitimate forms, his devotion to poetry, and his appreciation that each of us is both gifted and limited, thus telling theologians and ecclesiastics to leave politics largely to politicians.[90]

Lewis's brother, Warnie, speaks of him encountering a tramp while on a country walk. Finding the fellow had some appreciation of poetry, Lewis asked the man to wait. He hurried home and returned with a twofold gift: a book of collected verse and several bottles of beer. As Richard Purtill sums up: "The combined gift from Lewis's own library and larder seems to strike just the right note of human

---

contemporary philosophical and political attitudes. *The Pilgrim's Regress: An Allegorical Apology for Christianity, Reason, and Romanticism* (San Francisco: Fount, 1998 [1953]), of course, is all about contemporary alternatives to Christianity through which Lewis himself had traveled.

89. Indeed, even when Lewis does offer political advice—for instance, on the question of forming a Christian Party in Britain—he offers some shrewd counsel, but concludes on a note so individualistic and evangelistic it could have come from Billy Graham: "There is a third way [to influence politics as Christians]—by becoming a majority. He who converts his neighbour has performed the most practical Christian-political act of all" ("Meditation on the Third Commandment," in *God in the Dock*, 199.) Lewis complexifies the situation even further in *Mere Christianity*, where he prescribes two courses of action, neither of which is evangelistic: "I have said that we should never get a Christian society unless most of us became Christian individuals. That does not mean, of course, that we can put off doing anything about society until some imaginary date in the far future. It means that we must begin both jobs at once—(1) the job of seeing how 'Do as you would be done by' can be applied in detail to modern society, and (2) the job of becoming the sort of people who really would apply it if we saw how" (79). My sense is that Lewis is not contradicting himself, but rather is nowhere articulating anything approaching a comprehensive philosophy of Christian political engagement. It is coherent, of course, for him to affirm all three elements: Christian rectitude, evangelism of others, and cultural work that brings as much *shalom* as possible. We can note that individualism is the governing category of all three.

90. Walter Hooper, Lewis's literary executor, comments that Lewis "came to detest [politics] later in this life," particularly since, as his brother testifies, "politics...was a topic he almost always heard his elders discussing" (preface to Lewis, *Of Other Worlds*, vii).

comradeship."[91] (To be sure, this scene might strike us as being as removed from our experience as Lewis's beloved Middle Ages themselves: who among us has a book of poetry on hand to give away, quite apart from the beer?)[92]

In his enjoyment of the world, Lewis sometimes practices better than he preaches. Some have seen his writing as if in the grip of an Augustinian binary view of things, namely, that everything is to be enjoyed only as it points to the glory of God. Lewis writes as if we are to look not *at* things but *through* them or *along* them to God:

> The books or the music in which we thought the beauty was located will betray us if we trust to them; it was not *in* them, it only came *through* them, and what came through them was longing. These things—the beauty, the memory of our own past—are good images of what we really desire; but if they are mistaken for the thing itself they turn into dumb idols, breaking the hearts of their worshippers. For they are not the thing itself; they are only the scent of a flower we have not found, the echo of a tune we have not heard, news from a country we have never yet visited.[93]

Readers of Lewis's various books will recognize this as a recurring idea. Thus he puts it in another work, "All joy reminds. It is never a possession, always a desire for something longer ago or further away or still 'about to be.'"[94] And Meilaender sums up: "To turn from the image in the thing to the glory itself, from created thing to the Creator, is to find one's life and the end to which one was created."[95]

It may be that Lewis is pushing so hard in this direction—perhaps too hard—because he is pushing against a particular evil, the evil of secularism, or naturalism, construing this world as all there is: "You and I have need of the strongest spell that can be found to wake us from the evil enchantment of worldliness [by which I think Lewis means "secularism"] which has been laid upon us for nearly a hundred years."[96] But this quasi-Platonic answer of Lewis's

---

91. The story is told in *Letters of C. S. Lewis,* ed. W. H. Lewis (New York: Harcourt Brace Jovanovich, 1966), 21; told in Purtill, *C. S. Lewis's Case for the Christian Faith,* 104.

92. See John McWhorter, *Doing Our Own Thing: The Degradation of Language and Music and Why We Should, Like, Care* (New York: Gotham, 2003), esp. ch. 3.

93. Lewis, "Weight of Glory," 4–5.

94. Lewis, *Surprised by Joy,* 78.

95. Meilaender, *Taste for the Other,* 27.

96. Lewis, "Weight of Glory," 5.

not only seems to push too far in the other direction but is against Lewis's own practice (and "preaching") on other occasions. Because this idea is so crucial to life in the world, and because Lewis has been so influential, let's explore it a little further.

Despite what he says in the passages above, it is obvious that for C. S. Lewis, beer, sex, and poetry, among many other things, are *intrinsically* good. God pronounced the creation "good" in Genesis 1 with no hint that it was good only because it somehow pointed to him. And I think the Lewis biographies, as well as his own writings, indicate that he was not, in fact, forever thinking, *I enjoyed this friend's company because he reminds me of God,* or *I enjoyed this pint of bitter because it reminds me of God,* and so on.[97]

Indeed, I suggest that this idea is both unnecessary and unhelpful. It renders things translucent, even shadowy, as if we are always to see through them to God. (This is particularly ironic from the author of *The Great Divorce*, in which heaven is precisely the place in which things become *more* firm, thick, and vivid.) Lewis himself indicates that he loathes the idea of nature being something other than itself, being a kind of "arrangement" meant to "do something" rather than just "be."[98] And as he writes elsewhere: "Those who read poetry to improve their minds [or to discover and glorify God?] will never improve their minds by reading poetry. For the true enjoyments must be spontaneous and compulsive and look to no remoter end. The Muses will submit to no marriage of convenience."[99]

I think he is right about that, and I think such an outlook is true to what we know of his life. Our enjoyment of nature, however, certainly can be enhanced by seeing it, as Lewis wants us to do, as being a creature, and therefore seeing it within a broader frame that includes God himself as Creator: "Only Supernaturalists really see Nature.... Come out, look back, and then you will see...this astonishing cataract of bears, babies, and bananas: this immoderate deluge of atoms, orchids, oranges, cancers, canaries, fleas, gases, tornadoes and toads.... She is herself. Offer her neither worship nor contempt."[100]

It would be more consistent for Lewis to say that we will receive and enjoy them more fully not by making them into idols, which strains them past their actuality (and thus can stretch them out to a grotesque thinness, so to speak), but

---

97. See Lewis's "ideal day" in *Surprised by Joy*, 141–43.

98. Lewis, *Miracles*, 101.

99. Lewis, "Lilies That Fester," 35.

100. Lewis, *Miracles*, 104–5.

as works of the great Artist. We enjoy *both* the artifact *and* the artist, and each shows us something about the other to the greater enjoyment of both.[101]

Lewis also sometimes overstates things in his love of the powerful image. In this same vein, he can diminish what is good while he is trying to praise what is better: recall the famous passage in "The Weight of Glory" in which he contrasts human life without salvation as the child's mud pies versus a holiday at the sea,[102] or the well-known depiction of the Incarnation in *Mere Christianity* as a human being becoming a slug or a crab.[103] Each of these analogies overdoes things because the mud pies are *not* intrinsically good, and the slug or crab does not in any obvious way bear the image of the maker. So we, too, must beware of images that underplay the God-given goodness of things—even as we recall, in Lewis's defense, that in this regard he has good company in even Biblical writers: the nations are as grass, as chaff, as dust, as drops in the bucket, and so on.

The key seems to be to delight in things without inordinate love, and enjoying all of life to the glory of God.[104] Meilaender paraphrases Lewis thus:

> True Christian asceticism never involves a rejection of the created thing. One must say: "Marriage is good, though not for me; wine is good, though I must not drink it; feasts are good, though today we fast." What is sought is an attitude which leaves a person free both to enjoy his breakfast *and* to mortify his inordinate appetites.[105]

Lewis, then, never seems quite to connect all the dots in one place: the intrinsic value of all worthy work and the pleasures to be enjoyed along life's pilgrimage; the goodness built into the institutions of the world, however currently corrupt; the relationships among the individual, the church, social institutions,

---

101. And Lewis does sometimes say this, as he concludes one essay on this theme with the following: "One must look both *along* [to God] and *at* everything" ("Meditation in a Toolshed," in *God in the Dock*, 215).

102. Lewis, "Weight of Glory," 2.

103. Lewis, *Mere Christianity*, 152.

104. Lewis, *Abolition*, 26. Lewis puts it hierarchically here: "Our deepest concern should be for first things, and our next deepest for second things, and so on down to zero—to total absence of concern for things that are not really good, nor means to good at all" (*Letters to Malcolm*, 22).

105. This is Meilaender's paraphrase and quotation of "Some Thoughts," in *God in the Dock*, 149; quoted in Meilaender, *Taste for the Other*, 32. In this sentiment, as in many others, Lewis demonstrates his agreement with Augustine—an author whom he rarely quotes, however; see Augustine's *City of God*, XI, 25.

society at large, and nations; the world to come as a garden city, and not merely as a viewing stand from which we all look at God (again, as in Dante's *Paradiso*); the continuity and discontinuity between this world, this life, and the next. He sometimes sounds Platonic or even Gnostic in his focus on the spiritual; other times he sounds strongly affirmative of the world at every level. He sometimes acutely sees huge cultural changes swirling around him and sounds as if he is on the verge of a call to wide social action, but he usually settles for some homey, prudent advice for the individual reader. For a vision of Christian engagement beyond that individual level, we need to look elsewhere—as Chad Walsh advised us. But there is much to be learned from C. S. Lewis on that crucial level of the Christian individual—and his or her family and friends.

C. S. LEWIS'S "PARABLES"

"This is my Father's world," the hymn proclaims, and Lewis believed it. But this world is currently under the sway of evil, both demonic and human. It is out of touch with the rest of creation, a "silent planet" that needs to be connected up once again with God's cosmic *shalom*—and it *will* be reconnected someday.

That *shalom* is figured in the community of St. Anne's at the conclusion of *That Hideous Strength,* in the innocence of Malacandra, and throughout Narnia once it is relieved of oppressive overlords. In each of these places there is a community of transformed—but still what we might call "identical or at least identifiable"—humans, beasts, other sentient creatures, angels, and God in a beautiful, nourishing environment. Thus *Perelandra*'s redemption story ends with a Great Dance, and dances of all (good) creatures recur in other tales as well, particularly throughout the Narnia stories.

Yet beyond these pictures of social harmony, Lewis seems never to have reconciled himself to *cities*. London itself appears in the Narnia chronicles, but always as negative (particularly in *The Magician's Nephew,* but it is also war-torn London from which the children must be sent away in *The Lion, the Witch, and the Wardrobe* as well).[106] All of the other cities in the Narnia chronicles are evil—from Charn to Calormen. Hell itself is a city in *The Great Divorce,* but Heaven is a countryside. I shall leave as homework for Lewis aficionados this question: does anything good happen in a city in any of Lewis's writings? One wonders if

---

106. Lewis comments on his distance from London in "Hedonics," in *Present Concerns,* 50–51.

C. S. Lewis himself stood in need of some imaginative conversion by the Bible's own images of the New Jerusalem.

It is in the Narnia tales that Lewis perhaps figures best his fundamental understanding—both Christian and, indeed, more than a little Platonic—of how this world relates to the next. In the spirit of both Christian and ancient Greek teleology, therefore, let us look at the "last things"—the final volume of those tales, *The Last Battle*. (In what follows, I shall presume the reader's familiarity with the basic plot and characters of these famous stories.)

Lewis depicts both the best of Narnia *and* the best of England as residing within Aslan's country. From either place, we are invited not to despise it but to mount up from it: "farther up and farther in!"

Narnia itself is destroyed finally by water and then frozen; its sun is extinguished and then dismissed, its cosmic role accomplished. Yet those who have fought on Aslan's side in the final conflict now continue in a land very much like Narnia, only better: green, vital, and good. They arrive at a splendid walled garden, and Lucy begins to see the way things really are. The old Narnia was a shadow or copy of the real one:[107]

> Lucy looked hard at the garden and saw that it was not really a garden at all but a whole world, with its own rivers and woods and sea and mountains. But they were not strange: she knew them all.
>
> "I see," she said. "This is still Narnia, and, more real and more beautiful than the Narnia down below, just as *it* was more real and more beautiful than the Narnia outside the Stable door. I see...world within world, Narnia within Narnia..."
>
> "Yes," said Mr Tumnus, "like an onion: except that as you go in and in, each circle is larger than the last."

Lucy spots what she recognizes as England. And her friend Tumnus explains: "But you are now looking at the England within England, the real England just as this is the real Narnia. And in that inner England no good thing is destroyed."[108]

Then the children see their dead parents walking toward them smiling and waving, very much alive. The faun again explains: "That country [of the dead] and this country—all the *real* countries—are only spurs jutting out from the great

---

107. Lewis, *The Last Battle* (Harmondsworth, UK: Puffin, 1964 [1956]), 153; Plato is explicitly invoked on 154.
108. Ibid., 163–64.

mountains of Aslan. We have only to walk along the ridge, upward and inward, till it joins on."[109]

Thus Aslan pronounces: "The term is over: the holidays have begun. The dream is ended: this is the morning."[110]

Lewis's narrator concludes: "But for them it was only the beginning of the real story. All their life in this world and all their adventures in Narnia had only been the cover and the title page: now at last they were beginning Chapter One of the Great Story which no one on earth has read: which goes on for ever: in which every chapter is better than the one before."[111]

As we take our leave of C. S. Lewis, then, we move into a very different situation: from Narnia to New York City, from the United Kingdom to the United States, and from medieval romance to modern politics. This is the world of Reinhold Niebuhr, from whom we have much to learn as well.

---

109. Ibid., 164.
110. Ibid., 165.
111. Ibid.

THREE

REINHOLD NIEBUHR

Prophet of Christian Realism

Time, Life, and *Saturday Review* magazines all acclaimed Reinhold Niebuhr as America's premier theologian in the mid-twentieth century.[1] An indefatigable speaker in colleges, universities, churches, conferences, political rallies, and other venues—until a stroke halted him in 1952, in his sixtieth year—the most famous professor at Manhattan's Union Theological Seminary also authored 21 books, contributed to 126 more, and wrote at least 2,600 articles.[2] In September 1964, President Lyndon Johnson awarded him the Medal of Freedom, the nation's highest civilian honor. And, as Larry Rasmussen recalls,

> when Harvard University sought a keynote speaker for its 350th anniversary celebration in 1986, an occasion which called for a public intellectual with a commanding presence who could speak across the disciplines, American literature professor Alan Heimert told President Derek Bok that only two people in the last twenty years could have made that speech—Walter Lippmann and Reinhold Niebuhr—and they were both gone.[3]

Observers as different as Stanley Hauerwas and Langdon Gilkey have argued, however, that the world such men spoke *for* is gone as well.[4] Hauerwas

---

1. Larry Rasmussen, "Introduction," in Reinhold Niebuhr, *Reinhold Niebuhr: Theologian of Public Life,* ed. Larry Rasmussen (Minneapolis: Fortress, 1991), 2. Martin Halliwell notes that *Time* named Niebuhr as one of America's three most influential intellectuals, numbering him with Lionel Trilling and Edmund Wilson (*The Constant Dialogue: Reinhold Niebuhr and American Intellectual Culture* [Lanham, MD: Rowman and Littlefield, 2005], 3).

2. Rasmussen, "Editor's Note," in Niebuhr, *Reinhold Niebuhr,* ix; citing statistics from David Gushee without further reference.

3. Rasmussen, "Introduction," 1.

4. Stanley Hauerwas, *With the Grain of the Universe: The Church's Witness and Natural Theology* (Grand Rapids, MI: Brazos, 2001), ch. 4.; Langdon Gilkey, *On Niebuhr: A Theological Study* (Chicago: University of Chicago Press, 2001): "It has been the rather swift breakup of this massive

and others have in fact assailed Niebuhr as a "chaplain to power" who helped legitimize American imperialism and self-righteousness during the Cold War.[5] Furthermore, Niebuhr's general theologico-ethical outlook, known as "Christian Realism," has been accused of promoting an un-Christian defeatism, a willingness to compromise with evil, and a repudiation of the transforming power of God.[6] Finally, while once he had the attention not only of Christian America but of America itself, Reinhold Niebuhr now is largely ignored by younger theologians, Christian activists, historians of American religion, and society at large.[7]

So what is Christian Realism, and why should we care, decades after Niebuhr's death in 1971?

IS CHRISTIANITY REALISTIC?

The first thing to acknowledge in any discussion of Christian Realism is that there is a very long, and now academically dominant, tradition in Western civilization that would say that Christian Realism must be a contradiction in terms. According to this outlook, religion in general is not realistic but instead delusional, both misguided and misguiding.

Biblical and theological consensus that has accounted for the sharp reduction in the authority and prominence of Niebuhr's thought from the 1960s on" (224).

5. Stanley Hauerwas is only one of several who have made this charge: see Stanley Hauerwas and Mike Broadway, "The Irony of American Christianity: Reinhold Niebuhr on Church and State," *Insights* 108 (Fall 1992): 33–46. This article quotes an even more antagonistic Noam Chomsky.

Niebuhr was not blind to the lure of proximity to power. He chided Billy Graham, among other clergy, for cooperating with Richard Nixon's institution of religious services in the White House in 1969: "It is wonderful what a simple White House invitation will do to dull the critical faculties, thereby confirming the fears of the Founding Fathers. The warnings of Amos are forgotten" (*Christianity and Crisis,* 4 August 1969, 211; anthologized in Niebuhr, *Reinhold Niebuhr,* 271). As Richard Wightman Fox's biography makes clear, Niebuhr was no stranger to such corridors of power himself, and struggled in his later decades with his enjoyment of prominence and his fear of being co-opted (*Reinhold Niebuhr: A Biography* [Ithaca, NY: Cornell University Press, 1996 [1985]). Still, he testified late in life to his conviction that "a realist conception of human nature should be made the servant of an ethic of progressive justice and should not be made into a bastion of conservatism, particularly a conservatism which defends unjust privileges" (*Man's Nature and His Communities* [New York: Charles Scribner's Sons, 1965], 24–25; cited in Robert McAfee Brown, "Introduction," in Reinhold Niebuhr, *The Essential Reinhold Niebuhr: Selected Essays and Addresses,* ed. Robert McAfee Brown [New Haven, CT: Yale University Press, 1986], xxii).

6. Robin Lovin is especially helpful in discerning in what ways "Christian realism" is, and is not, a good description of Niebuhr's thought: see his "Introduction to Christian Realism" in *Reinhold Niebuhr and Christian Realism* (Cambridge, UK: Cambridge University Press, 1995), 1–32.

7. The impressively erudite study of Niebuhr by Martin Halliwell notes the paradox (!) that Niebuhr both has generated a steady stream of dissertations, articles, and books and is being rediscovered in more popular media, while historians of American religious history have almost entirely left him out of recent accounts. The former phenomena, I daresay, bear tribute to

Sociologist Rodney Stark provides a brief catalogue of philosophical and social scientific luminaries who share this low opinion of religion, and of Christianity in particular:

> Thomas Hobbes, one of the celebrated "founders" of social science, dismissed all religion as "credulity," "ignorance," and "lies" and Gods as "creatures of...fancy." A century later, David Hume echoed Hobbes, dismissing all "[belief in] miracles as limited to ignorant and barbarous nations." During the nineteenth century antireligious social science was rampant. Auguste Comte coined the word "sociology" to identify a new field that would replace religious "hallucinations" as the guide to morals. Then, Ludwig von Feuerbach "discovered" that humans create Gods in their own image, while Karl Marx and Friedrich Engels found God in the economy, busy sanctifying "wage slavery." At the start of the twentieth century, the famous French sociologist Emile Durkheim taught that the fundamental reality is that society itself is always the true object of religious worship: "god...can be nothing else than [society] itself, personified and represented to the imagination." Next came Sigmund Freud, who explained on [just] *one page* of his celebrated psychoanalytic exposé of faith, *The Future of an Illusion,* that religion is an "illusion," a "sweet—or bittersweet—poison," a "neurosis," an "intoxicant," and "childishness to be overcome." Even more recently, no reviewer as much as flinched when, on the first page of his book *Mystical Experience,* Ben-Ami Scharfstein revealed that "mysticism is...a name for the paranoid darkness in which unbalanced people stumble so confidently," and went on to identify the supernatural as a "fairy tale." In similar fashion, Oxford's distinguished Bryan Wilson identified "supernaturalist thinking" as an "indulgence."[8]

I take the time to quote this catalogue because Reinhold Niebuhr was well aware of this settled prejudice against religion, and particularly the prejudice against the dominant religion of the West, Christianity. In the teeth of it, he embraced philoso-

---

the enduring value of Niebuhr's thought, while the latter is entirely due to the recent fad in American religious history to "decenter" the narrative and, above all, to avoid privileging the story of American mainline Protestantism—of which Niebuhr has got to be everyone's choice as leading representative in the middle half of the twentieth century. One hopes this latter reaction, understandable as it is—my own career in North American religious history coincides precisely with the reaction against Sydney Ahlstrom's magisterial (and Puritan-favoring) history of American religion—will soon swing toward an appropriately balanced view that no longer commits the historical sin of purposely ignoring vast reaches of American history because other parts were previously neglected. See Halliwell, *Constant Dialogue,* 19–21.

8. Rodney Stark, *One True God: The Historical Consequences of Monotheism* (Princeton, NJ: Princeton University Press, 2001), 4–5.

phy and social science, integrating them fully into his way of looking at the world. But he also judged them to be deficient precisely in the light of the religion so many philosophers and social scientists had been so willing to despise.

Indeed, Niebuhr's fundamental public claim for Christianity is that it does a better job—a more rationally satisfying, as well as a more existentially satisfying, job—of explaining the world than does any other worldview, including the worldviews of Hobbes, Hume, Comte, Marx, Freud, or anyone else. Far from being an escape from reality into narcotically soothing aspirations or comforting wish fulfillment, Christianity is the most realistic view of things on offer.

I would like to exposit Niebuhr's version of Christian Realism, then, under three large themes: epistemology, human nature, and history. Then we will trace out some implications of Niebuhr's thought for our project of reconsidering the Christian attitude toward culture.[9]

WHAT IS CHRISTIAN REALISM?

Epistemology

We properly draw on experience to tell us what we can know of the world.
Reinhold Niebuhr relied heavily upon experience, by which he meant both formal, scientific study of the world and also introspective analysis of ourselves. Larry Rasmussen notes,

> Much of Niebuhr's writing was given to a lively factual and historical description of events and developments, and could go on for pages without using the language of Christian traditions. This reflected his insistence that empirical analysis was essential to criticism and a well-made case.[10]

Langdon Gilkey elaborates, "This continuing and dominant interest in social and historical matters means that social science and social philosophy, social psychology, anthropology, social ethics, and, above all, philosophies of human nature and of history represent the materials with which Niebuhr largely worked."[11]

---

9. This expositional structure is hardly original with me, following as it does Niebuhr's own writing, especially in *The Nature and Destiny of Man: A Christian Interpretation*, 2 vols. (New York: Charles Scribner's Sons, 1964 [1941, 1943]). A recent exposition along these lines is offered in Gilkey, *On Niebuhr,* Part 2.

10. Rasmussen, "Introduction," 3.

11. Gilkey, *On Niebuhr,* 21.

In fact, Niebuhr believed that if this or that form of analysis proves to be unfruitful, or even results in evil (e.g., Marxism), then it simply must be replaced. In this respect he was unusual among left-leaning American intellectuals of his day in that his youthful use of Marxian categories was followed by his relatively early recognition of the evils of Stalinism and his later general rejection of Marxism. On another front, Niebuhr eventually allowed his ongoing analysis of Britain to correct his earlier mythologizing of that nation as a foil for criticizing America. The facts didn't fit the generalizations, so the generalizations had to change.

A generation later, historian Mark Noll chided his fellow evangelicals for what might be called their biblicistic non-empiricism. Noll scored the typical evangelical mind-set that considered events in the world by looking at what (they thought) the Bible said about the events (for example, conflict in the Middle East) and then interpreting the news of the day through this grid. Evangelicals did the same thing in the vexed arena of natural science, most notoriously in the debates around "creation science," in which evangelicals showed that they were so satisfied that they knew what the Bible was saying in Genesis that they knew what science *had* to say about the origins of the planet and its inhabitants. To be sure, Noll affirmed, a Biblically informed worldview is essential to good Christian thinking about any subject. But with that worldview in place, one should look directly at the subject, examining it with the God-given resources of the appropriate intellectual discipline (geology or psychology or aesthetics) in order to see it as clearly as possible. Noll puts it with characteristic concision: "To understand something, one must look at that something."[12]

This syndrome of ideological blinkers affects more than evangelicals, of course. It is common among ideologues on the left, on the right, and in between. Data are fitted into the theory, and new data are not even industriously sought, since we already "know" the theory is right.

Niebuhr's determination to investigate reality and keep seeking more truth is a stance reflecting both epistemic and metaphysical humility. We ought to submit to reality, he says, at least as we perceive it, and thus recognize our small, limited place in the scheme of things. In such a posture we serve God and our fellow creatures aright, rather than narcissistically distorting our construal of reality in order to suit our preferences—a motive that is, as psychiatrist Scott Peck reminds us, a fundamental trait of evil.[13]

---

12. Mark A. Noll, *The Scandal of the Evangelical Mind* (Grand Rapids, MI: Eerdmans, 1994), 199.
13. M. Scott Peck, *People of the Lie: The Hope for Healing Human Evil* (New York: Simon and Schuster, 1983).

What we can find out that way, however, prompts us to realize that we cannot know it all, and mystery is an irreducible element in any adequate description of the world.

Long before "postmodernism" arose as a term, let alone a watchword, of cultural sophistication, Niebuhr recognized that human reason has the paradoxical quality of being able both to transcend itself—to keep learning, to critique its own previous opinions, and to creatively form new ways of thinking—and yet also to recognize its finitude, that its sense of reality and its reflections upon reality were always beams of light in an indefinably larger darkness. Thus Niebuhr was impressed with the relativity of all human knowledge, but also with its finitude and with its recognition of its own finitude. We ourselves, he affirms, know that we cannot know it all—even about ourselves, let alone about the origin and destiny of our race, and a fortiori of the universe itself.

Therefore, he avers, the best worldview is the one that properly identifies both human ability and human limitation. To put it more pointedly, any worldview, philosophy, or religion that provides a completely comprehensive and coherent account of reality is necessarily false: it simply must be leaving out too much and is substituting the part for the whole. "Mystery does not annul meaning," Niebuhr says, "but enriches it. It prevents the realm of meaning from being reduced too simply to rational intelligibility and thereby being given a false center of meaning in a relative or contingent historical force or end."[14] Paradoxically (an adverb that shows up frequently in discussions of Niebuhr), without a coherent inclusion of the category of mystery, any explanation of the world is necessarily reductionistic.[15]

We might note that, as in most things theological for Niebuhr, this idea has political ramifications. In particular, epistemic humility is the key to religious tolerance in a pluralistic democracy (as it was, one might note, for thinkers at least as far back as John Locke, and then John Milton in his *Areopagitica*):

> Religious humility is in perfect accord with the presuppositions of a democratic society. Profound religions must recognize the difference between divine majesty and human creatureliness; between the unconditioned character of the divine and the conditioned character of all human enterprise.... Religious faith ought therefore to be a constant fount of humility; for it ought to encourage

---

14. Reinhold Niebuhr, *Faith and History: A Comparison of Christian and Modern Views of History* (New York: Charles Scribner's Sons, 1951), 103.

15. Niebuhr discusses this question in terms of "the perils of making coherence the basic test of truth," in "Coherence, Incoherence, and Christian Faith," and see also his "Mystery and Meaning," both anthologized in *Essential Reinhold Niebuhr,* 218–36 and 237–49.

men to moderate their natural pride and to achieve some decent consciousness of the relativity of their own statement of even the most ultimate truth...

Religious toleration through religiously inspired humility and charity is always a difficult achievement. It requires that religious convictions be sincerely and devoutly held while yet the sinful and finite corruptions of these convictions be humbly acknowledged; and the actual fruits of other faiths be generously estimated.[16]

Christian theology provides the best conceptuality by which to articulate this reality: God created and sustains the world, and made us able to understand it. He then enables us to coordinate that understanding with the understanding he grants us of theology as well.

Niebuhr believed that the best comprehension of reality will be gained by analysis of the world and analysis of theological resources, with both analyses then being brought into conversation. A generation before liberation and feminist theologies emphasized the praxis/theoria dynamic, Niebuhr affirmed that there must be a dialectic among these modes of accessing reality, and he practiced such a dialectic. Rasmussen offers a nice summary of Niebuhr's method:

> Niebuhr wrestled with the moral and political bulk of some issue into which he had thrown his considerable energy and talent. And then, in the midst of that engagement, he would grab insight from the reservoir of theological ideas which were part of a faith he had held from his youth onward....With an acute historical consciousness, and a feeling for the imprint of events, he would simply raid theology to help discern "the signs of the times" and move everyone he could into a committed response to those events. Niebuhr consistently traveled a methodological circle, employing Christian symbols to illumine the human drama that fascinated him, and then revising the articulation of those symbols in light of the drama as it unfolded. He let faith discern the truth of

---

16. Reinhold Niebuhr, *The Children of Light and the Children of Darkness: A Vindication of Democracy and a Critique of Its Traditional Defense* (New York: Charles Scribner's Sons, 1944), 135, 137. This epistemic humility grounding pluralistic tolerance upsets critics of both Reinhold and Richard Niebuhr. These critics assail the Niebuhrs for compromising the stark truth of the Gospel in order to covertly defend liberal democracy and its cultural and consumerist relativism. See John Howard Yoder, "How H. Richard Niebuhr Reasoned: A Critique of *Christ and Culture,*" in *Authentic Transformation: A New Vision of Christ and Culture,* ed. Glenn H. Stassen, D. M. Yeager, and John Howard Yoder (Nashville, TN: Abingdon, 1996), 31–89; Stanley Hauerwas, "The Democratic Policing of Christianity," *Pro Ecclesia* 3 (Spring 1994): 227–29; and Hauerwas, "Reinhold Niebuhr's Natural Theology," in *With the Grain of the Universe,* esp. 135–40. I shall offer my own thoughts about epistemic humility and its cultural implications for Christians in due course.

his experience and at the same time let the reality of human experience be his standard guide into theology.[17]

Langdon Gilkey comments on Niebuhr's convictions that emerged in this dialectic:

> The Christian scheme of meaning, [Niebuhr] argued, makes more sense than the others on three important grounds: (1) it makes intelligible the contradictions and confusions of ordinary, and especially historical, experience; (2) it deals most creatively with the deep anxieties of being human; and (3) it guards against the twin perils of idolatry and despair. To him each of the secular alternatives to Biblical faith takes some finite and partial aspect of human life as both ultimate and saving. This inevitably leads on the one hand to reflective misunderstanding, and on the other it creates the condition for idolatry.[18]

Niebuhr himself testifies thus of his experiences as a politically activistic pastor and professor:

> Since I am not so much scholar as preacher, I must confess that the gradual unfolding of my theological ideas has come not so much through study as through the pressure of world events. Whatever measure of Christian faith I hold today is due to the gradual exclusion of alternative beliefs through world history. As did Peter, I would preface my confession, "Thou hast words of eternal life," with the question, "Lord, to whom shall we go?" Even while imagining myself to be preaching the Gospel, I had really experimented with many alternatives to Christian faith, until one by one they proved unavailing.[19]

God has provided information and insight that we never could have discovered on our own—thus we need God's revelation.

Niebuhr says this: "Faith in God ... depends upon faith in His power to reveal Himself. The Christian faith in God's self-disclosure, culminating in the revelation of Christ, is thus the basis of the Christian concept of personality and individuality."[20] Niebuhr tirelessly repeats our need for God to reveal himself and his truths not only in general revelation (such as in nature and in our consciences)

---

17. Rasmussen, "Introduction," 2.
18. Gilkey, *On Niebuhr,* 55.
19. Quoted in Rasmussen, "Introduction," 4 n. 6.
20. Niebuhr, *Nature and Destiny,* I:15.

but also in the special revelation of the Bible and particularly the career of Jesus Christ:

> The God whom we meet as "The Other" at the final limit of our own conscious-ness, is not fully known to us except as specific revelations of His character aug-ment this general experience of being confronted from beyond ourselves.
>
> In Biblical faith these specific revelations are apprehended in the context of a particular history of salvation in which specific historical events become special revelations of the character of God and of His purposes....
>
> ...Man does not know himself truly except as he knows himself confronted by God....It is for this reason that Biblical faith is of such importance for the proper understanding of man.[21]

For example, we recognize that we do both good and evil, and that everyone does so. We further recognize that no one lives up to his or her own moral code, let alone any pure and universal standard that may be held up by a God or gods. We also recognize that we regret much or all of our misbehavior, and yet we con-tinue to perform similar acts. Niebuhr suggests that these phenomena all deserve attention—none should be ignored in the interest of formulating a tidy moral anthropology—and that the Christian theological category of "sin," as revealed in the Bible and exposited in the Christian tradition, offers a category that is both intellectually and existentially satisfying.[22]

In this way, and in many others, Biblical revelation not only answers human questions but reframes some of them so that they are oriented more accurately. In fact, Niebuhr affirms that Biblical revelation properly redirects our attention even from general experiences of God to the particular figure of Jesus Christ:

> Christian faith sees in the Cross of Christ the assurance that judgment is not the final word of God to man; but it does not regard the mercy of God as a forgiveness which wipes out the distinctions of good and evil in history and makes judgment meaningless. All the difficult Christian theological dogmas

---

21. Ibid., I:130–31.

22. This particular argument, of course, was articulated to an even broader audience by C. S. Lewis in *Mere Christianity*, but its heritage goes back at least to Kant, if not to Paul's Epistle to the Romans itself. Niebuhr, however, is not a moral realist quite in the way Lewis is. As Robin Lovin explains, moral realists "are not committed [as I think Lewis was] to the metaphysical claim that 'good' and 'evil,' or 'right' and 'wrong,' are metaphysical properties that exist apart from the natural, empirical properties of things" (*Reinhold Niebuhr and Christian Realism,* 14). Niebuhr is an Aristotle to Lewis's Plato, so to say.

of Atonement and justification are efforts to explicate the ultimate mystery of divine wrath and mercy in its relation to man....

Christian faith regards the revelation in Christ as final because this ultimate problem is solved by the assurance that God takes man's sin upon Himself and into Himself and that without this divine initiative and this divine sacrifice there could be no reconciliation and no easing of man's uneasy conscience.[23]

To reveal truth in a way that properly balances various elements and communicates well across a variety of cultures, God has resorted to the genre of story, of myth—understood as a narrative and symbol set that articulate abiding truth ("this is the way things are and have been") but not, as Christian tradition has believed, historical truth ("this is the way things once happened").

Niebuhr frequently resorts to paradoxes, and claims that he is merely trying to explicate what is inherent in both our experience and in divine revelation. Theology cannot fully explain the human condition, therefore, but the Bible's stories—from Eden to the New Jerusalem—depict it powerfully and coherently. Theology cannot articulate clearly the Incarnation of God in Jesus Christ, but the Gospels show it. Orthodox Christological affirmations do the best justice that doctrinal formulation can do to this portrait, but it is this portrait itself that makes the most sense of God's wrath and mercy.

Again, the doctrine of sin furnishes a rich example. Niebuhr is orthodox in that he believes we all are, indeed, affected by sin in the core of our beings. We are not basically good people who, strangely and occasionally, commit evil, but deeply

---

23. Niebuhr, *Nature and Destiny*, I:142–43. It is not clear to me how Hauerwas and others who criticize Niebuhr as anthropocentric—even as functionally atheistic (which I think is the implication of *With the Grain of the Universe*, in order to depict Hauerwas's heroes, especially Karl Barth, all the more brightly as true Christians)—would deal with a passage such as this. To be sure, Niebuhr's extended Christological musings in volume II of *The Nature and Destiny of Man* do not always read as precise affirmations of orthodoxy. But perhaps Langdon Gilkey makes the main point about Niebuhr: "The religious relation to God is hence no longer an expression of the human quest for the good and so of the goodness and idealism of human being, as it was in much of liberalism. On the contrary, the quest for God can only be infinitely frustrated until the actual religious relation to God is rectified—and that becomes possible only through God's initiative, through revelation and through grace" (*On Niebuhr*, 25). And Gilkey later concludes, "Despite its major concentration on an empirical look at human social behavior, on the real characteristics of political existence, and on the actual shape of the contours of history, Niebuhr's theology is...a 'God-centered' theology and not a humanistic or naturalistic one. As a consequence it cannot possibly be understood—as many have sought to do—as primarily brilliant social commentary with the pious icing, so to speak, of theological or Biblical rhetoric. Without God—and God's judgment and mercy—there are only the possibilities of idolatry and destruction or despair and enervation; without God, therefore, there is hope of neither meaning nor renewal in life or in history" (ibid., 188).

conflicted people who recognize within our souls both the desire to do good (the "image of God") and the desire to do evil ("original sin"). The Biblical narrative of sin, Niebuhr maintains, best depicts our lived reality. The doctrine of original sin, Niebuhr famously quipped, is the one empirically verifiable doctrine of Christian faith.[24] As Gilkey puts it, "Niebuhr really means it when he says...'There is none righteous, no, not one' (Rom. 3:10)."[25] This is a reality that analytical, ontological speech can clarify to some extent, but does so at the risk of (to borrow a Wordsworthian phrase) "murdering to dissect." The story, by contrast, keeps all of the elements together and in proper relation in a way that ontology cannot.

There has been a lot of unhappy history since Niebuhr's day. His own country has endured a long list of crises, only some of which are recalled by such references as Vietnam, Watergate, Iran-contra, savings and loan, Drexel, 9/11, and Iraq. Internationally, we have glimpsed repression in North Korea, China, Burma (Myanmar), and beyond; corruption throughout Africa and Latin America; and atrocities in Cambodia, Rwanda, Yugoslavia, Sudan, and elsewhere. Niebuhr would not have been surprised. In 1940 he wrote:

> History does not move forward without catastrophe, happiness is not guaranteed by the multiplication of physical comforts, social harmony is not easily created by more intelligence, and human nature is not as good or as harmless as had been supposed. We are thus living in a period in which either the optimism of yesterday has given way to despair, or in which some of the less sophisticated moderns try desperately to avoid the abyss of despair by holding to credos which all of the facts have disproved.[26]

Niebuhr would ask his fellow liberals, but he would also ask us all, whether we recognize and take seriously the presence and power of sin everywhere and in everyone: Do we get it? *Do* we? Or are we still shocked by it, as if it is a terrible surprise rather than a dark, abiding reality with which we should wisely contend?[27]

---

24. Brown, "Introduction," xii; Brown refers to Niebuhr's *Man's Nature and His Communities* but provides no further information.

25. Gilkey, *On Niebuhr,* 109.

26. Niebuhr, "Optimism, Pessimism, and Religious Faith," anthologized in *Essential Reinhold Niebuhr,* 9.

27. Oddly, Niebuhr consistently assails the term "total depravity" as if it means that human beings are completely corrupt and lack all remnants of the image of God (e.g., *Nature and Destiny,* 1:266–67). It is particularly strange when one considers that Niebuhr's theological training was primarily in the magisterial Protestant traditions (Lutheran and Reformed) that define this idea instead as dealing with the *extent* of sin—namely, that every part of our

Still, this traditional warning about sin from Niebuhr comes in a neo-orthodox mode in that he does not believe in a literal Adam and Eve.[28] He simply takes for granted the evolutionary theory of his day, and presumes that this Bible story is a "myth." Unlike Lewis, who believes that a myth can also be historically factual (with the career of Jesus being the True Myth at the heart of all mythology), Niebuhr believes that the Bible presents us with myths in the sense of narratives that do not describe an event in the past but refer pictorially to our perennial human predicament.[29] He writes,

> The myth alone is capable of picturing the world as a realm of coherence and meaning without defying the facts of incoherence. Its world is coherent because all facts in it are related to some central source of meaning; but is not rationally coherent because the myth is not under the abortive necessity of relating all things to each other in terms of immediate rational unity.[30]

Things happen in a story in a way that makes sense *within the world of the story,* even if they are not plausible to us in strictly scientific, philosophical, or historical senses. Biblical myths function this way, connecting ideas and events the coherence of which rational analysis cannot (yet) apprehend. Gilkey concludes:

> Once affirmed, these paradoxes are validated over and over by the "facts" or the "stuff of experience," both because other more rational alternatives

---

humanity is affected by it (over against Roman Catholic distinctions between nature and "supernature," as per Aquinas). It would have been more consistent for Niebuhr to embrace this terminology, not to (mis)use it as a foil. See his discussion of "The Locus of Original Righteousness" for a place in which Niebuhr is, in fact, defending "total depravity" without using the name: *Nature and Destiny,* I:276–80. Cf. also this passage: "There is no level of human moral or social achievement in which there is not some corruption of inordinate self-love" (*Children of Light,* 17). Langdon Gilkey testifies movingly to a liberal's shock at evil among some very nice people, despite his already having "read and re-read Niebuhr" (*On Niebuhr,* 116–23; based on Gilkey's book *Shangtung Compound* [New York: Harper & Row, 1966]).

28. A classic passage of Niebuhr's *Nature and Destiny* deals with the Fall as mythical and not historical (I:267–69). Gilkey puts this belief nicely in context: "Niebuhr clearly accepts this evolutionary view of nature's and of humanity's past; he knows from biological and from anthropological science that there was no beginning of all things and no first human pair some six thousand years ago. But like most neo-orthodox theologians he hardly ever refers to the scientific sources of much of his own thinking. What he does refer to are the very good theological reasons for this de-literalization which his view of human being entails" (Gilkey, *On Niebuhr,* 93; see also his discussion on 233–36).

29. Lewis directly contrasts his view of myth with Niebuhr's in *The Problem of Pain* (New York: Collier Books, 1962), 77 n. 1.

30. Reinhold Niebuhr, *An Interpretation of Christian Ethics* (London: Student Christian Movement, 1936), 36.

falsify experience…and because to our surprise these same paradoxes make the strange and even irrational contours of experience intelligible.… And it is this "empirical" justification of what seems at first glance to be absurd that Niebuhr's theology seeks continuously to present to us.[31]

To be sure, Niebuhr does not believe that the whole Bible is mythological in this way—he seems to be more historically confident about much of the career of Jesus—but he does hold to this view of myth as the most helpful way for us moderns to appropriate the ongoing relevance of the truth revealed in Scripture. In this, then, he reflects his liberal identity, as do most so-called neo-orthodox in this respect, as they stand in the tradition going back to David Friedrich Strauss's *Life of Jesus* as seeing the Bible as speaking in importantly mythological terms.[32]

Christian Realism, therefore, is epistemologically realistic in terms of both metaphysics and morality.

In terms of metaphysics, Christianity helps us to see the world the way it really is: to see ourselves, each other, the planet, and God. In terms of morality, Christianity also helps us to see the world the way it really is: morality is not merely a construct of individual preference or social convention. Niebuhr affirms that "there are essentially universal 'principles' of justice"—what he also called "transcendent principles of justice" and, later, "regulative principles"—that clearly help or harm human life, and are therefore objectively right or wrong.[33]

This realism, however, must be qualified by the previous acknowledgments of both mystery and myth. We do not see everything, nor do we see anything so clearly

---

31. Gilkey, *On Niebuhr,* 66.

32. Niebuhr seems resistant to other traditional ideas as well, such as the idea that corruption in the rest of creation stems from human sin, and that God responds to prayer by actively intervening in natural and human processes: see, for example, "Optimism, Pessimism, and Christian Faith" and "The Providence of God," anthologized in *Essential Reinhold Niebuhr,* 14–16 and 33–40. To be sure, however, not all traditional Christians are committed to the literalism of so-called creation science and its belief in a "young earth" created in six 24-hour days. Many conservative Christian believers since Darwin have had little trouble in holding to some form of evolutionary theory and one of a wide range of views of the historical and theological nature of the Genesis account. See David N. Livingstone, *Darwin's Forgotten Defenders: The Encounter Between Evangelical Theology and Evolutionary Thought* (Grand Rapids, MI: Eerdmans, 1984); and James R. Moore, *The Post-Darwinian Controversies: A Study of the Protestant Struggle to Come to Terms with Darwin in Great Britain and America, 1870–1900,* new ed. (Cambridge: Cambridge University Press, 2003). On myth and history in the Old Testament, see the unusually lucid discussion in Part One of Iain W. Provan, V. Philips Long, and Tremper Longman III, *A Biblical History of Israel* (Philadelphia: Westminster John Knox, 2003).

33. Niebuhr, *Nature and Destiny,* II:254; see Lovin, *Reinhold Niebuhr and Christian Realism,* 213–34, for a discussion of "regulative principles."

and comprehensively that we can claim certainty for our perceptions and inferences. Much of what we do see, moreover, is expressed best in story, in myth, and not in the discursive speech preferred by most scientists and philosophers. Indeed, these acknowledgments are themselves "realistic." They conform to the way things really are: the way we are, the way the world is, the way God is, and so on.

Furthermore, Niebuhr's epistemological realism is qualified not only by our limitations but also by our faults—namely, our sin. This theme, that of human nature, we will explore next.

One interesting implication for preachers and teachers alike arises out of Niebuhr's epistemological realism, which embraced moral realism as well. This implication almost exactly parallels C. S. Lewis's feelings on the question of the relative efficacy of moral exhortation versus moral education. Niebuhr says, "I am a preacher and I like to preach, but I don't think many people are influenced by admonition. Admonitions to be more loving are on the whole irrelevant. What is relevant are analyses of the human situation that discuss the levels of human possibilities and of sin."[34] With Lewis, then, Niebuhr understands that people may resist moral teaching, but we must try to help them see that they are resisting not us, our opinions, or our wishes but *reality,* the way things simply are.

Human Nature

Human beings have a twofold nature: we are creatures, and thus human (of the humus, the earth)—finite in awareness, in ability, in mortality. But we are also created in the image of God, and thus enjoy transcendence—to get beyond ourselves to see ourselves, to get beyond the present circumstances to imagine and create a new situation, and to aspire to get beyond ourselves and this world to arrive at a more glorious destiny.

Niebuhr begins his magisterial discussion in *The Nature and Destiny of Man* with this observation: "The obvious fact is that man is a child of nature, subject to its vicissitudes, compelled by its necessities, driven by its impulses, and confined within the brevity of the years which nature permits its varied organic form[s].... The other less obvious fact is that man is a spirit who stands outside of nature, life, himself, his reason and the world."[35]

---

34. Quoted in Rasmussen, "Introduction," 5 n. 8. Most commentators on Niebuhr discuss the question of the aptness of "neo-orthodox" as a description of his thought. Langdon Gilkey offers some particularly helpful insights, including this: "Niebuhr can as easily be termed a 'neo-liberal' as he can be called neo-orthodox" (*On Niebuhr,* 26–28; the quoted passage is on 27).

35. Niebuhr, *Nature and Destiny,* I:3.

He goes on: "In its purest form the Christian view of man regards man as a unity of God-likeness and creatureliness in which he remains a creature even in the highest spiritual dimensions of his existence and may reveal elements of the image of God even in the lowest aspects of his natural life."[36]

In these affirmations, Niebuhr echoes the Psalmist:

When I look at your heavens, the work of your fingers, the moon and the stars that you have established; what are human beings that you are mindful of them, mortals that you care for them? Yet you have made them a little lower than God, and crowned them with glory and honor. You have given them dominion over the works of your hands; you have put all things under their feet. (Ps. 8:3–6)

Niebuhr's entire ethical project revolves around this dual nature of humanity and our need for God to help us achieve our aspirations, aspirations that he has given us and that yet lie beyond our own power to achieve.

Human beings have the ability to choose to a considerable extent what to believe, feel, and do. And yet we are also bound in our beliefs, feelings, and actions, not only by our intrinsic creaturely limitations but also by our sin.
Niebuhr avers that "the Christian view of human nature is involved in the paradox of claiming a higher stature for man and of taking a more serious view of his evil than other anthropology."[37] He continues,

The high estimate of the human stature implied in the concept of "image of God" stands in paradoxical juxtaposition to the low estimate of human virtue in Christian thought. Man is a sinner. His sin is defined as rebellion against God. The Christian estimate of human evil is so serious precisely because it places evil at the very center of human personality: in the will. This evil cannot be regarded complacently [Take that, fellow liberals!] as the inevitable consequence of his finiteness or the fruit of his involvement in the contingencies and necessities of nature. Sin is occasioned precisely by the fact that man refuses to admit his "creatureliness" and to acknowledge himself as merely a member of a total unity of life. He pretends to be more than he is. Nor can he...dismiss his sins as residing in that part of himself which is not his true self, that is, that part of himself which is involved in physical necessity....Man is not divided against himself so that the essential man can be extricated from the nonessential. Man

---

36. Ibid., I:150.
37. Ibid., I:18.

contradicts himself within the terms of his true essence. His essence is free self-determination. His sin is the wrong use of his freedom and its consequent destruction.[38]

Thus Niebuhr champions a Biblical anthropology over the extant alternatives. Whether Marxian, psychoanalytical, liberal Christian, or otherwise, all of these alternatives are reductionistic in just this way: they fail to take into account—into proper, balanced, and paradoxical account—both human freedom and responsibility, and also human bondage and our need for salvation from a source outside ourselves.

This kind of balancing is done frequently with paradoxes. And it is here that we can see several threads of Niebuhr's thought come together: the transcendence and immanence of God, the freedom and bondage of humanity, the divinity and humanity of Christ, the scope and limitation of human knowledge, the greatness and depravity of the human heart—all of these themes and more are expressed by Niebuhr in discursive prose, yes, but they are based, for Niebuhr, in narrative. Again, only this portrait makes sense of God's wrath and mercy, and only orthodox Christological affirmations, precisely in their paradoxes derived from these stories, can do justice to this portrait.

History

Human beings can look forward to a great destiny, by the grace of God. This world is not all there is, and there is a better world ahead.
Niebuhr warns his audiences that "the Biblical symbols cannot be taken literally because it is not possible for finite minds to comprehend that which transcends and fulfills history."[39] More memorably, he quips: "It is unwise for Christians to claim any knowledge of either the furniture of heaven or the temperature of hell; or to be too certain about any details of the Kingdom of God in which history is consummated."[40]

This counsel seems prudent enough. But in his extended discussion at the conclusion of *The Nature and Destiny of Man*, Niebuhr, perhaps surprisingly, goes on to proclaim traditional doctrines: the second coming of Christ as a vindication of

---

38. Niebuhr, *Nature and Destiny*, I:16. This passage should be paired with ch. 7 of vol. II of Niebuhr's *Nature and Destiny* to question Langdon Gilkey's repeated claim that for Niebuhr, sin was fundamentally injustice toward others in contradistinction to what Gilkey calls the traditional view of sin as estrangement from God and self-destruction (*On Niebuhr*, 204, 228).

39. Niebuhr, *Nature and Destiny*, II:289.

40. Ibid., II:294.

Christ and of God's redeeming love; the last judgment, which both affirms the hope that evil will not continue and confirms the truth that history will not redeem itself; and the resurrection as the vindication of the meaningfulness of our historical existence (versus the doctrine of the immortality of the soul, which in Greek and Indian thought tends to negate the value of our historical, bodily life).[41]

What Niebuhr anticipates is not entirely clear, even to himself. Gilkey characterizes Niebuhr's eschatological conclusions as "frustratingly brief and astoundingly short in descriptive adequacy."[42] Niebuhr writes that "the idea of the resurrection of the body can of course not be literally true." (The "of course" is an interesting remark, given that the vast majority of Christians through history have affirmed that the resurrection of the body is "of course" literally true.)[43] Niebuhr immediately goes on: "But neither is any other idea of fulfillment literally true. All of them use symbols of our present existence to express conceptions of a completion of life which transcends our present existence." And Niebuhr affirms the doctrine of the resurrection of the body, particularly because "it expresses at once a more individual and a more social idea of human existence."[44] Niebuhr thus is consistent: the exact nature of the world to come is figured only in Biblical myths, the literal details of which should not be believed in as such. But those myths convey encouraging truths to us that provide us with the hope we need to move forward in faith.

---

41. Ibid., II:290–98.

42. Gilkey, *On Niebuhr,* 221.

43. Niebuhr was scored for this and other departures from basic orthodoxy by many critics, including some associated with Union Seminary itself: see Fox, *Reinhold Niebuhr,* for a summary of searching reviews of Niebuhr's *Beyond Tragedy: Essays on the Christian Interpretation of History* (New York: Charles Scribner's Sons, 1937), including those of his friends John Bennett, Cyril Richardson, and Joseph Haroutunian (182–83). And see Fox also for snippets of Niebuhr's views on resurrection, life after death, and such—on which set of subjects Niebuhr was, at best, agnostic (215).

44. Quotations are from Niebuhr, *Beyond Tragedy* (1937), anthologized in Niebuhr, *Reinhold Niebuhr,* 109, 113. Niebuhr says elsewhere that "we do not believe in the virgin birth, and we have difficulty with the physical resurrection of Christ" because, as I have noted, he had given up belief in God's miraculous intervention ("Coherence, Incoherence, and Christian Faith," 232). Niebuhr never argues at length for this conviction of a "closed universe," but rather seems to assume it as just what all right-thinking people now assume. Niebuhr clearly recognizes the danger here: that the historical particularities of the Christian *kerygma* are imperiled by this kind of attitude, thus threatening to dissolve liberal Christianity into "yet another [perennial] philosophy." He seems to worry aloud: "We say we take historical facts seriously but not literally; but that may be on the way of not taking them as historical facts at all." He concludes, "There is no simple solution for this problem" (233). One thinks of C. S. Lewis's *Miracles* as a book Niebuhr would have read with profit, since Niebuhr seems to be giving up a belief that Lewis shows he doesn't need to relinquish in order to remain a respectable Christian intellectual.

Meanwhile, however, our duty is to approximate the goodness of that better world, in full and prudent realization of the limitations of this one.

This is the ethical stance for which Niebuhr is perhaps best known: the stance of working for the best, under a Providence that guides history to its own beneficent purposes while expecting resistance, confusion, compromise, trade-offs, and sometimes even failure along the way. Gilkey asserts,

> In this emphasis on history, Niebuhr is clearly a modern and Western thinker. Evidently he is also on this issue an example of "liberal" theology in the sense that here the central focus of religious faith and piety has moved from the question of salvation in the next life to that of the meaning of this life.[45]

Niebuhr concludes his great work, *The Nature and Destiny of Man,* with these words:

> By its confidence in an eternal ground of existence which is, nevertheless, involved in man's historical striving to the very point of suffering with and for him, this faith can prompt men to accept their historical responsibilities gladly....
>
> Thus wisdom about our destiny is dependent upon a humble recognition of the limits of our knowledge and our power. Our most reliable understanding is the fruit of "grace" in which faith completes our ignorance without pretending to possess its certainties as knowledge; and in which contrition mitigates our pride without destroying our hope.[46]

Niebuhr thus strikes a balance between those who would abandon the world and those who still think we can solve whatever is wrong—or, at least, the Important People can, if they would just get busy. (As a columnist in the satirical newspaper *The Onion* once asked plaintively, "Why doesn't someone just fix all the problems?") Niebuhr strives to maintain a realism between cynicism and idealism. By our own efforts, even aided by divine grace, he believes, there will be no "arrival" at the "end of history" or the "ultimate society," since wherever we go,

---

It will be clear by now that a precise fix on Niebuhr's theology on the classic loci of systematic theology is sometimes elusive. As a liberal, he was free to articulate Christian doctrine as he saw fit, and to change his views as well. He also was simply not all that interested in doctrine per se. Happily, however, pinning down Niebuhr's doctrine is not essential to the present project.

45. Gilkey, *On Niebuhr,* 54.

46. Niebuhr, *Nature and Destiny,* II:321.

there we are—*simul justus et peccator*.[47] But this does not mean we should therefore abandon our cultural responsibilities, as various sorts of Christians suggest:

> A simple Christian moralism is senseless and confusing. It is senseless when, as in the [First] World War, it seeks uncritically to identify the cause of Christ with the cause of democracy without a religious reservation. It is just as senseless when it seeks to purge itself of this error by an uncritical refusal to make any distinctions between relative values in history. The fact is that we might as well dispense with the Christian faith entirely if it is our conviction that we can act in history only if we are guiltless. This means that we must either prove our guiltlessness in order to be able to act; or refuse to act because we cannot achieve guiltlessness. Self-righteousness or inaction are the alternatives.[48]

In facing hard realities, Niebuhr can shock his liberal friends, as well as others:

> The responsible leader of a political community is forced to use coercion to gain his ends. He may, as Mr. Gandhi, make every effort to keep his instrument under the dominion of his spiritual ideal; but he must use it, and it may be necessary at times to sacrifice a degree of moral purity for political effectiveness.[49]

The world, affected by the Fall, is a place in which extraordinary measures are necessary even to approximate God's ideal in this situation—which is all we can accomplish. Thus we must sometimes undertake action that is necessarily under God's condemnation—in the sense that it "falls short of the glory of God" (Rom. 3:23)—but also is the best we can do in the situation in which we find ourselves. It is "best" in the sense that it achieves the most justice and, all going well, also manifests the most love.[50]

---

47. The Latin is a phrase of Luther's: "at once both justified and a sinner." Niebuhr cites it in his reflections on "Augustine's Political Realism," anthologized in *Essential Reinhold Niebuhr*, 135. Niebuhr thus concludes: "There is no escape from the paradoxical relation of history to the Kingdom of God. History moves towards the realization of the Kingdom but yet the judgment of God is upon every new realization" (*Nature and Destiny*, II:286).

48. "Why the Christian Church Is Not Pacifist," anthologized in *Essential Reinhold Niebuhr*, 118.

49. Reinhold Niebuhr, *Moral Man and Immoral Society* (New York: Charles Scribner's Sons, 1960 [1932]), 244.

50. The relationship between justice and love, particularly in politics, evolves from a pretty stark disjunction in Niebuhr's earlier writings to a more positive relation in his later ones. Beyond the contrast between *Moral Man* and *Nature and Destiny*, see also Reinhold Niebuhr, "Beyond Law and Relativity," in *Faith and History: A Comparison of Christian and Modern Views of History* (New York: Charles Scribner's Sons, 1951), 171–95. We will come back to the question of justice and love in chapter 9.

Thus Niebuhr negotiates the ideal and the real. The Biblical ideals (in the sense of Niebuhr's "regulative principles," which set out general considerations that conduce to *shalom*, not timeless descriptions of what *shalom* looks like in every particular) perform several valuable functions. They inspire us to greater effort and imagination than we might otherwise put forth; they set limits on what we can and cannot do; and they judge whatever we do as, finally, flawed and "not yet" the Kingdom of God.[51] "According to Christian faith," he says, "life is and always will be fragmentary, frustrating, and incomplete. It has intimations of a perfection and completeness which are not attainable by human power."[52]

Still, some societies are better than others, and can be recognized as such. (Niebuhr worries that both Barth's theology and classical pacifism in their own ways refuse to make moral distinctions among various governments and societies in the name of God's absolute righteousness, by the perfection of which all are

---

51. Niebuhr puts this sharply in the title of a chapter in his *Interpretation of Christian Ethics*, "The Relevance of an Impossible Ethical Ideal," in which occurs his famous characterization of biblical ideals, and particularly of universal love, as the "impossible possibility" (124). Indeed, Niebuhr is well known, and often criticized, for his contention that the ethics of Jesus present a kind of eschatological ideal that judges all of our work in the interim between his advents but does not provide an ethics for that interim. John Howard Yoder's *The Politics of Jesus* is, in some ways, a direct response to that contention.

One might detect Niebuhr implicitly mapping the "ideal/real" distinction onto the "individual/community" distinction in *Moral Man*. See passages such as the following: "Whenever religious idealism brings forth its purest fruits and places the strongest check upon selfish desire it results in policies which, from the political perspective, are quite impossible.... It would therefore seem better to accept a frank dualism in morals than to attempt a harmony between the two methods which threatens the effectiveness of both. Such a dualism would have two aspects. It would make a distinction between the moral judgments applied to the self and to others; and it would distinguish between what we expect of individuals and of groups" (*Moral Man*, 270–71). (It is interesting that Richard Niebuhr did not note that his brother's "dualism" has this shape, at least in this book—an observation which would have helped make more intelligible his sketch of "Christ and Culture in Paradox.") Reinhold Niebuhr moved away from such associations and later softened the "sharp distinction" between the individual and the corporate (p. xi). Indeed, he revised the moral possibilities of communities upward and those of individuals downward in his mature work, notably in *Nature and Destiny*.

52. *Christianity and Society*, Autumn 1949, 3; anthologized in Niebuhr, *Reinhold Niebuhr*, 131. Niebuhr strikes these themes in many other places, including this one: "There is the promise of a new life for men and nations in the gospel, but there is no guarantee of historic success. There is no way of transmuting the Christian gospel into a system of historical optimism. The final victory over man's disorder is God's and not ours; but we do have responsibility for proximate victories. Christian life without a high sense of responsibility for the health of our communities, our nations, and our cultures degenerates into an intolerable other-worldliness. We can neither renounce this earthly home of ours nor yet claim that its victories and defeats give the final meaning to our existence" ("The Christian Witness in the Social and National Order," anthologized in *Essential Reinhold Niebuhr*, 100).

condemned. Such views, he maintains, paralyze any effort to champion the better option, however flawed, over the worse.)[53] Thus we can and must work for the most justice, and the most human flourishing, that we can:

If the Christian conception of grace be true then all history remains an "interim" between the disclosure [in Christ] and the fulfillment of its meaning [at the end of the world]. This interim is characterized by positive corruptions, as well as by partial realizations and approximations of the meaning of life. Redemption does not guarantee elimination of the sinful corruptions, which are in fact increased whenever the redeemed claim to be completely emancipated from them. But the taint of sin upon all historical achievements does not destroy the possibility of such achievements nor the obligation to realize truth and goodness in history. The fulfillments of meaning in history will be the more untainted in fact, if purity is not prematurely claimed for them. All historical activities stand under this paradox of grace.[54]

One fundamental and significant implication for Niebuhr was the act of participating in elections. He left behind his earlier idealism (now in the colloquial sense of idealism as "wishful thinking") and opted instead for the "best of the real choices" in elections, with "best" being defined as the one who would most likely achieve the most according to the values of the Kingdom of God. The unpalatable and irresponsible alternatives, he believed, were either refusing to vote, which does nothing to resist the most evil of the choices, or voting for the purest candidate, who would certainly lose. Making such choices meant that one could congratulate oneself on one's putative integrity while doing precisely nothing to improve the actual situation.

Let us now proceed to consider further implications of this outlook.

---

53. See, respectively, "Coherence, Incoherence, and Christian Faith" and "Why the Christian Church Is Not Pacifist," anthologized in *Essential Reinhold Niebuhr*, 218–36 and 102–19.

54. Niebuhr, *Nature and Destiny*, II:213. The tension between the ideal and the real is not unique to American culture, of course, but it is particularly obvious therein—as observers at least as far back as Tocqueville have observed. The Puritan sense of having an "errand into the wilderness" (as Perry Miller put it) in order to set up a "city on a hill" (John Winthrop) has impelled both American expansionism and charity, even as self-interest and limited resources have compelled American isolationism and expediency. Niebuhr thus shows himself a true American, even though I don't know of a place in his writing in which he himself makes this connection. It is interesting in this regard to note a recent issue of *The Atlantic* that features precisely this tension in a retrospective collection of previously published essays, with national correspondent James Fallows selecting one essay in particular as "eerily timely," the one by Reinhold Niebuhr. See "Idealism and Practicality," *The Atlantic*, July 2006, 57–60.

IMPLICATIONS OF CHRISTIAN REALISM

The Evil of Pride—and Sensuality

Niebuhr is well known for admonishing us for the sin of pride, whether in thinking we can replace the current order with one that will work nicely for everyone or in congratulating ourselves that we already have achieved a perfectly just order in this or that institution:

> Western culture has paid for [the] boon of historical dynamic with two evils inhering in the historical emphasis. One is the evil of fanaticism, the consequence of giving ultimate significance to historically contingent goals and values. The other is the creative, but also confusing, Messianism, the hope for a heaven on earth, for a kingdom of universal peace and righteousness.[55]

Communism is one of Niebuhr's main examples of the latter delusion, but he relentlessly chides his fellow liberals for their unwarranted and dangerous optimism about democracy and capitalism as well.[56]

Niebuhr also, however, cautions us against the complementary sin, a sin that is perhaps in more need of exposure today in a time of greater doubt, even despair, over the possibility of real, lasting, and beneficial transformation of ourselves or of the institutions in which we work. Niebuhr warns us against "sensuality," though he defines the term as the abandonment of our freedom in order to take refuge in the status quo—what Karl Barth perhaps more helpfully called "sloth." Writes Niebuhr: "Sensuality represents an effort to escape from the freedom and the infinite possibilities of spirit by becoming lost in the detailed processes, activities

---

55. Niebuhr, *Nature and Destiny,* II:viii.

56. Criticism of both Marxism and liberalism shows up often in Niebuhr's writings, as in "Ideology and the Scientific Method," anthologized in *Essential Reinhold Niebuhr,* 205–10. Niebuhr began assailing capitalism in his first career as a pastor in Detroit, particularly in the person of Henry Ford and his autocratic exploitation of auto workers. See his *Leaves from the Notebook of a Tamed Cynic* (New York: Willett, Clark, 1929) and the relevant sections of Fox's biography. Warnings about democracy, including a straightforward characterization of it as a "false religion," can be found in Reinhold Niebuhr, *Reinhold Niebuhr on Politics: His Political Philosophy and Its Application to Our Age as Expressed in His Writings,* ed. H. R. Davis and R. C. Good (New York: Charles Scribner's Sons, 1960). These warnings can be taken together with Niebuhr's extended consideration and commendation of democracy in *Children of Light.* Indeed, one of Niebuhr's most quoted lines comes from this book, and it sounds much like C. S. Lewis on the latter theme: "Man's capacity of justice makes democracy possible; but man's inclination to injustice makes democracy necessary" (xiii). As for liberal optimism, Niebuhr offers an extended critique of all straightforward ideas of (American or global) progress in *The Irony of American History* (New York: Charles Scribner's Sons, 1952).

and interests of existence, an effort which results inevitably in unlimited devotion to limited values."[57]

Robin Lovin offers a brilliant and sensitive exposition of this theme:

> What marks sensuality is that it holds anxiety at bay by total absorption in an activity that raises no questions beyond itself.... Sin is present not merely in the ambition that remakes the world to suit its own plans, but in the sensuality that loses itself in immediate possibilities, in the sloth that absorbs itself in petty concerns and excuses its mediocre performance, and even in the disciplined pursuit of excellences that have been carefully defined by someone else.... Unless persons and nations are straining toward a good that stands in judgment on every concrete form of excellence they know and have achieved, they have yielded to the temptations of sensuality and of sloth. In their anxiety, they have sought to achieve freedom by denying that they are free, and this is true even for those heirs of Puritanism who compound the contradiction by working very hard at being slothful.[58]

Lovin points to those heirs busily working away in business, the arts—and scholarship. What is going on? Lovin continues:

> Those who find their work meaningless and who lack significant personal relationships will find much encouragement in a consumer-oriented society to devote themselves to new forms of gadgetry and to establish a firm decorative control over their limited personal environment. These evasions of freedom, along with the forms of indulgence more usually associated with "sensuality," must be seen as genuine forms of sin.
>
> ...We must also identify a form of institutional sin that elicits sensuality or sloth from persons by demanding commitments that preclude responsible attention to the range of choices and responsibilities that they ought to be attending to for themselves. The "up or out," "publish or perish" career trajectories imposed by businesses, law firms, and academic institutions provide familiar examples of this sort of pressure.... Those who yield to these pressures are often pictured as ambitious, "fast-track" achievers whose chief temptation would seem to be to emulate the pride of their seniors and superiors. In fact,

---

57. Niebuhr, *Nature and Destiny,* I:185.

58. Lovin, *Reinhold Niebuhr and Christian Realism,* 145–48. For some contemporary reflections on both pride and sloth, see Jean Bethke Elshtain, *Who Are We? Critical Reflections and Hopeful Possibilities* (Grand Rapids, MI: Eerdmans, 2000), chs. 2 and 3.

however, their achievements are often expressions of sensuality and sloth. The rising executive or scholar abandons the difficult balancing of obligations that marks a life of freedom constrained by human finitude, and substitutes a single set of goals defined by outside authorities. . . . The over-achiever stills anxiety in precisely the way that Niebuhr describes the sensual evasion, "by finding a god in a person or process outside the self."[59]

This idolatry also serves the self, of course, and Niebuhr rightly recognizes in sensuality both an inordinate self-love and an inordinate love for something else, the idol.

David Martin, a latter-day Niebuhrian, warns of these twin perils of pride and sensuality/sloth in his distinctive way:

One [peril] is the danger of locating the kingdom as *here* and *there:* the falsehood of premature identification. This danger is greatest when any nation or party identifies itself as the embodiment of promise. A political party or nation seeing itself as a secular realization of God's kingdom on earth proclaims an omnipotence and omniscience it cannot possibly have, and is a harbinger of repression and violence. . . .

The other danger is forgetfulness of promise, and immersion in the everyday. When that happens everything that *is* appears indefinitely prolonged. Material wants and satisfactions set the limit on desire and cut off the horizon of hope. People cease to hear any more this prophetic warning that God remains God and that the demands of righteousness and justice are not set aside.[60]

We might say, then, that Niebuhr's realism—the belief that there is a transcendent standard and, indeed, a transcendent God, which both judge us and lure us on to excellence—chastens the modern idea of progress for its pride, but also

---

59. Lovin, *Reinhold Niebuhr and Christian Realism,* 150. Niebuhr dwells particularly on sex in his exposition of sensuality (*Nature and Destiny,* I:228–40). But his conclusions are applicable much more widely, as he suggests: "What sex reveals in regard to sensuality is not unique but typical in regard to the problem of sensuality in general. Whether in drunkenness, gluttony, sexual license, love of luxury, or any inordinate devotion to a mutable good [and Lovin's examples in *Reinhold Niebuhr and Christian Realism* helpfully clarify and broaden this generalization from Niebuhr's more typical examples], sensuality is always: (1) an extension of self-love to the point where it defeats its own ends; (2) an effort to escape the prison house of self by finding a god in a process or person outside the self; and (3) finally an effort to escape from the confusion which sin has created into some form of subconscious existence" (*Nature and Destiny* I:239–40).

60. David Martin, *Christian Language in the Secular City* (Aldershot, UK: Ashgate, 2002), 120.

chastens the postmodern idea of radical relativism for its despair.[61] We must not assume that we can completely remake anything in our world, but we also must not assume that things must remain as they are. Instead, we must make the best of them, neither in proud confidence nor in slothful acquiescence, but in hopeful faithfulness to, and in, the command and power of God.

The Requirement of (Political) Action

Niebuhr's wife, Ursula, and his daughter, Elisabeth, have testified to the continual family conversation about politics.[62] Despite his clerical training and his lifelong work in either the church or the academy, Niebuhr was fascinated by politics. He engaged in considerable political action himself: countless speeches, membership and committee work in several successive parties, leadership in what we now call political action committees, public endorsements of candidates, and even ill-starred candidacies of his own.

Pragmatism was his watchword, not in any deep philosophical sense, but in the colloquial sense of valuing *results*.[63] In fact, political results were so important to him that even when given the honor of presenting the Gifford Lectures in Scotland (which became *The Nature and Destiny of Man*), Niebuhr struggled to make time to write them with appropriate academic focus and thoroughness, occupied as he was by the campaigns of that time. Paradoxically, however, it is astonishing to consider the sheer volume of his literary output, regardless of one's estimation of its quality, given his political activity. To be sure, much as he valued direct political activity, he saw his own vocation as focused mostly on helping people to think about politics and larger questions facing society, rather than directly on elections themselves. Still, he had abandoned thoughts of a Ph.D. at Yale, while pursuing his B.D. and M.A., because he had become impatient with metaphysics. Only thought connected with action would interest him. And he

---

61. Langdon Gilkey identifies the "dialectic of transcendence and relatedness" as "the central characteristic of Niebuhr's thought" (*On Niebuhr,* 16).

62. Fox, *Reinhold Niebuhr,* 349, 352; see also Ursula Niebuhr, *Remembering Reinhold Niebuhr: Letters of Reinhold and Ursula Niebuhr* (San Francisco: HarperCollins, 1991); and Elisabeth Sifton, *The Serenity Prayer: Faith and Politics in Times of Peace and War* (New York and London: Norton, 2003).

63. This is not to say that Niebuhr was not influenced by the American philosophical movement known as pragmatism. He wrote graduate papers on William James and carried on a lively, even vociferous public engagement with John Dewey. For quite different appraisals of Niebuhr's philosophical pragmatism, see Hauerwas, *With the Grain of the Universe,* Halliwell, *Constant Dialogue,* and also Cornel West, *The American Evasion of Philosophy: A Genealogy of Pragmatism* (Madison: University of Wisconsin Press, 1989).

would not settle for informing people, but aimed as well at motivating his audiences toward constructive response.

Niebuhr the clergyman and professor of ethics thus affirms politics itself as a worthy sphere of Christian work, despite the fact that, as Lovin quips, "politics seems not so much a field in which Christianity can be applied as one in which it is inevitably lost."[64] True, there is rarely an obviously "pure" choice available to be made. True, our motives also will never be pure. And true, there will likely be unintended, and unwelcome, consequences to whatever we decide. But we are not victims of either tragedy or fate: God is responsible and we are responsible, and the world requires well-intentioned, well-conceived, and well-executed action that nonetheless results in some evil. Larry Rasmussen offers this summary of Niebuhr:

> Political issues deal with complex problems of justice, every solution for which contains morally ambiguous elements. All political positions are morally ambiguous because, in the realm of politics and economics, self-interest and power must be harnessed and beguiled rather than eliminated. In other words, forces which are morally dangerous must be used despite their peril. Politics always aims at some kind of a harmony or balance of interest, and such a harmony cannot be regarded as directly related to the final harmony of love of the Kingdom of God.... The tendency to equate our political with our Christian convictions causes politics to generate idolatry.
>
> An action in the field of politics may be prompted by Christian motives and viewpoints, but it never overcomes the ambiguities indicated and can, therefore, never be regarded as clearly right or clearly wrong. It is the action which we believe to be relevant at the moment in order to bear our Christian witness in the cause of justice. There are no absolutely clear witnesses of faith and love in the political sphere, though there may be highly significant testimonies. It would seem, then, that the first duty of Christian faith is to preserve a certain distance between the sanctities of faith and the ambiguities of politics. This is to say that it is the duty of a Christian in politics to have no specific "Christian politics."[65]

We must press on, then, to conscientious and considered action. We seek forgiveness for the impurity of our motives and the evil results of our actions, but we must press on regardless to do what we can to increase justice and love. We must

---

64. Lovin, *Reinhold Niebuhr and Christian Realism*, 158.

65. Rasmussen here combines paragraphs from three different articles of Niebuhr's: see Niebuhr, *Reinhold Niebuhr*, 127.

not be fastidious in a broken, heaving world and seek to keep our hands clean. We join with our God, who himself has dirt and blood on his hands as he does what good he can within this complicated system he has made and maintains—for the ultimate good of the world:

> The Christian gospel which transcends all particular and contemporary social situations can be preached with power only by a church which bears its share of the burdens of immediate situations in which men are involved, burdens of establishing peace, of achieving justice, and of perfecting justice in the spirit of love. Thus is the Kingdom of God which is not of this world made relevant to every problem of the world.[66]

NIEBUHR'S LEGACY

Niebuhr found Christian symbols and stories to be necessary to explain the world we live in, to explain ourselves, and to explain our destiny. Early in his career, he averred that "adequate spiritual guidance can come only through a more radical political orientation and more conservative religious convictions than are comprehended in the culture of our era."[67] His challenge to those of other outlooks was simple, hardheaded, and confrontational on the shared turf of contemporary life: which view of things makes the most sense of all the pertinent data, leaving nothing out, and keeping things in proper relationship?

Niebuhr was sometimes called "neo-orthodox," thus placing him in a set that included mostly Europeans, such as Karl Barth and Emil Brunner. And, like Barth and Brunner, Niebuhr was very hard on liberals who refused an orthodox view of Christ (despite his own heterodoxy or, at best, agnosticism about crucial aspects of that view) and a realistic apprehension of evil. He did so, however, not as a watchdog on behalf of the tradition, but as one who had come to believe that at least some parts of the tradition did a better job in the real world than did the preferred pieties of his fellow liberals:

> The modern liberal Protestant interpretation of Christianity is...obviously informed by, and is an accommodation to, the general presuppositions of

---

66. Reinhold Niebuhr, "The Christian Church in a Secular Age," anthologized in *Essential Reinhold Niebuhr*, 86.
67. Quoted in Rasmussen, "Introduction," 11.

modern culture. The optimism of this culture makes the central message of the gospel, dealing with sin, grace, forgiveness and justification, seem totally irrelevant....

The effort is made [by such liberals] to maintain some contact with the traditional faith by affirming simply that Jesus was a very, very, very good man but that of course a better man might appear, at a future date, in which case the loyalty of the faithful would be transferred to him. These moderns do not understand that they cannot transcend the relativities of history by the number of superlatives which they add to their moral estimate of Jesus.[68]

Niebuhr nonetheless was himself basically a liberal—in both his own estimation and in the estimation of others.[69] And his disbelief in, or strategic rhetorical avoidance of, particular aspects of theological orthodoxy—particularly the literal, historical truth of the Biblical narrative—had, in fact, an ironic effect. This public language let him speak in places that likely would have resisted such explicit and traditional Christian emphases.[70] But it also robbed his speaking of the power of a strong expositional base in the Bible, as it ignored the traditional claim that the Christian Story does, in fact, describe the way things are, have been, and will be—historically and metaphysically, and not just morally.

Niebuhr seems never to have seriously wrestled with the possibility that Biblical "myths" were referring to actual events, however stylized these accounts might be according to the literary conventions and conceptual "furniture" available in the ancient Near East. We all appreciate that fictional stories can present things in a narrative even as some of these disparate elements defy attempts to correlate them all with the "real world" as we conceptualize it. Think of fairy tales that make a sort of narrative sense without every detail making metaphysical sense—at least, not to most readers today. Yet history and science also present us with happenings that, at

---

68. Niebuhr, *Nature and Destiny,* I:145, 146. This is, in my view, one of the most devastating passages ever written against liberal Christologies.

69. A particularly pithy description of Niebuhr in terms of neo-orthodoxy and liberalism is in Rasmussen, "Introduction," 22–29.

70. Larry Rasmussen offers some helpful observations in this regard: "Niebuhr was at his best in his ability to render a theological interpretation of events as a basis for common action for a wide audience. But precisely because of the audience's diverse beliefs, Niebuhr often cast his case in ways that left his Christian presuppositions and convictions unspoken. His theology was always the controlling framework, but his public discourse did not require knowledge of it, much less assent to it, in order to solicit response. Probably more than any other U.S. theologian, Niebuhr moved with utter ease between the language of Zion and that of regnant secular culture, and he made his choices as the occasion suggested. But the very felicity with which he communicated to pluralist audiences obscured the degree to which Christian symbols formed the thoughts he was winding into a stirring message" ("Introduction," 3).

least currently, defy our ability to draw them all together (whether the various competing narratives of the Big Bang or the incommensurate narratives of Einstein's relativity/gravity theories and Planck's quantum theories). Life fairly frequently presents us with narratives that are (temporarily, at least) not fully explicable. But we don't feel we have to discount them as not in any sense literally true.

Thus Niebuhr really was a modern liberal in the sense of one who just assumed that the tradition was wrong in the light of what science—whether historical/Biblical science or natural science—was (currently) saying. Yet the traditional claim to historical veracity, if properly nuanced and sustained (and I realize that is a big if), would actually have strengthened Niebuhr's own position and, indeed, would have done so in Niebuhr's own preferred way: by empirical validity. To put it simply, Niebuhr would have had a much more powerful case to make if he could have claimed, "We should see that this is the way things are today because this is what actually happened in the past, as the Bible says it did." But he seems never to have explored this position as a serious possibility.[71]

On a different axis, we can observe that Niebuhr offers almost no reflection on how the church as an institution could best involve itself in public life.[72] For all his voluminous writing and torrential speaking, Niebuhr has startlingly little to say about, and even to, the church as a social and political institution. He informs and exhorts individuals and occasionally addresses the collectivities of his fellow liberals and other ideologues. But he is utterly preoccupied with nations and their leaders.[73]

---

71. Gilkey raises a key, but quite particular, point about Niebuhr's refusal to take the Fall seriously as a historical event: "Niebuhr and other neo-orthodox deny (as did Pelagius) ...this role of Adam as a historical cause of our ills, and yet they seem unaware that this denial might push them into an ontological necessity, i.e., that the results of the fall are the consequences of creation" (*On Niebuhr*, 133; cf. Gilkey's account of Niebuhr's argument with Tillich over this matter, *On Niebuhr*, 93–94).

72. The issue of Niebuhr's (lack of) regard for the church surfaced at least as early as reviews of *Moral Man*, according to Fox, *Reinhold Niebuhr*, 142–43.

73. Niebuhr has his own distinctive locutions, of course, but he strikes themes quite similar to C. S. Lewis's in his recognition of the lasting importance of the individual versus communities that come and go in history, even as, characteristically, he points to the paradoxical relation of the individual and his or her communities:

The community is the frustration as well as the realization of individual life. Its collective egotism is an offense to his conscience; its institutional injustices negate the ideal of justice; and such brotherhood as it achieves is limited by ethnic and geographic boundaries. Historical communities are, in short, more deeply involved in nature and time than the individual who constantly faces an eternity above and at the end of the time process....
   ...The dimension of his freedom transcends all social realities. His spirit is not fulfilled in even the highest achievements of history....On the other hand the individual's life is meaningful only in its organic relation to historical communities, tasks, and obligations. (*Nature and Destiny*, II:310, 312)

Niebuhr does think about communities, of course. His first well-known book was titled *Moral Man and Immoral Society,* and in it he characteristically dealt with huge blocs of humanity in his analyses and exhortations, whether addressing universities, cities, governments, nations, or the World Council of Churches. But he tends to talk about "community" and "communities" in just those vague terms. One passage will serve for literally dozens of others:

> The individual and the community are related to each other on many levels. The highest reaches of individual consciousness and awareness are rooted in social experience and find their ultimate meaning in relation to the community. The individual is the product of the whole social-historical process, though he may reach a height of uniqueness which seems to transcend his social history completely. His individual decisions and achievements grow into, as well as out of, the community and find their final meaning in the community.[74]

The church-minded Christian will agree with all of this, and then will want Niebuhr to apply such a set of generalizations to how the *church* functions as such a community.[75] Furthermore, such a Christian will want Niebuhr to speak to congregations, denominations, and other groups of Christians as to what role, if any, they can and ought to play in society. But Niebuhr almost never gets this specific. He therefore fails both to apply these generalizations to church life and to show how churches might be importantly different in some respects from just any other human community, since, after all, the church claims to be uniquely led by Jesus Christ, indwelt by the Holy Spirit, and commissioned to make disciples of all nations.

The explanation for this lacuna might be quite simple. Niebuhr himself testified, at almost the end of his life,

> I had only one parish, in Detroit, where I served as pastor after my graduation from the Yale Divinity School in 1915 until my appointment to the faculty of

---

74. Niebuhr, *Children of Light*, 50.

75. Niebuhr seems on the verge of doing exactly this in a passage in which he chides both orthodox and liberal Christians for promoting too individualistic an ethic: "If ethical tension has been maintained, it has expressed itself, in both orthodoxy and liberalism, in too purely individualistic terms, so that the moral vigor, which is most relevant to the urgent moral problems of an era which must deal with the life and death of social systems, is expressed outside the churches" ("The Assurance of Grace," anthologized in *Essential Reinhold Niebuhr,* 69). But then Niebuhr goes on to say precisely nothing to the churches or about them. "Churches" turns out to be merely a synonym for "Christianity," not a set of social institutions to be addressed, challenged, and mobilized as such.

Union Seminary in 1928. But in subsequent years I was…a preacher in the universities and, of course, in our seminary chapel. The life of the local church was therefore terra incognita to me.[76]

Still, we might have expected at least some *theoretical* advice for the churches— especially given that, after all, the man did pastor a congregation for more than a dozen years, however busy he was in extra-congregational speaking and traveling. And this is guidance we need today, especially in regard to both the religious right and left in the United States and to politically active churches in many other places, such as in Latin America, China, and elsewhere. How should the church as an institution, and not just as well-intentioned individuals, function on behalf of justice and the highest ideal of love?

It may be that Niebuhr's lack of attention to the church was at least partly a function of his liberalism in that, as his brother Richard pointed out, "his God did not act in history."[77] As we have seen, quite what God was doing in the Biblical narratives, and even in the career of Jesus Christ, is not always clear in Niebuhr's writing in regard to what we might call its historical factuality. A further interpretive complication is that he seems considerably more orthodox in *The Nature and Destiny of Man* than in the earlier *Moral Man and Immoral Society,* so interpreting him on this score does depend on which phase of his career one examines.[78]

Orthodox Christians see the Bible's own ethical logic to be based on historical factuality. In the Old Testament, God says, "I am Yhwh your God who brought you out of Egypt, therefore you shall have no other gods but me" (Ex. 20:2–3). In the New Testament, the testimony is that God has raised Jesus from the dead and established him as Lord and Christ (Acts 2:32, 36). Since God has done *x*, then *y* follows as appropriate ethical response. In particular, the accounts of Jesus' commissioning of the nascent church indicate that he intended the church to perform the particular work of witnessing and disciple-making. And Christ intended the church to do so with the transformative power of the Holy Spirit.

So perhaps Niebuhr's lack of attention to the church indicates an implicit disbelief in all of this supernatural talk of a Spirit-empowered church engaged in

---

76. Reinhold Niebuhr, "A View of Life from the Sidelines," anthologized in *Essential Reinhold Niebuhr,* 254.

77. This is Fox's summary of Richard's views in the famous exchange between the Niebuhr brothers in the pages of *The Christian Century* in 1932 (Fox, *Reinhold Niebuhr,* 134).

78. Fox is among many who note that *Moral Man* is as far as Niebuhr would go in that brand of liberalism, and that he would return to draw upon the tradition more positively in later work (*Reinhold Niebuhr,* 147).

conversion. If God has set up the world and its order (rather deistically) and expects us to do the best we can to ameliorate evil and promote good, without hope of actualizing a perfect order until the end of history and Christ's return, then there is no reason to talk of the church as the distinctive locus of Jesus' ongoing ministry in the world. It is just one of a myriad of organizations that we can use to resist evil and do good. It therefore can be lumped in with "communities" in general.

Perhaps, however, we owe Niebuhr the benefit of an important doubt. At least in his Taylor Lectures at Yale in 1933, shortly after he published *Moral Man and Immoral Society,* he seems to recognize that the distinctive work of the church is, indeed, to bear witness and make disciples, and thus to call societies and their institutions to account for their departures from Biblical ideas.[79] Such work has political implications, to be sure, but it is mostly outside the realm of politics as Niebuhr—and most of his fellow moderns—understood politics. Thus the almost total absence of explicit political counsel within the horizon of the New Testament simply entailed that Niebuhr would, in turn, not talk much about the church as a political player.[80] I have not come across a passage in Niebuhr's own writings or in those of the Niebuhr experts I have consulted that discusses this particular point, so I can only speculate as to this gap in his exposition of Christian engagement in society. We must leave the question open, and pick up this theme in our own constructive discussion later in this book.

Reinhold Niebuhr's legacy is a rich and motivating one. Those of us who are Christians in particular need to recognize and engage in public theology today as a dimension of Christian mission to the world, a dimension of Christian citizenship, in which thoughtful Christians contribute what we can out of our particular tradition to our society's general conversation about our life together. We need to retrieve many of Reinhold Niebuhr's particular themes and emphases, including those outlined in this chapter. In particular, we must be both properly realistic and

---

79. Fox indicates that Niebuhr never published these lectures—indeed, he threw away the manuscript. The lectures "were a basis for *Reflections on an End of an Era*, but the book was a reformulation, not a revision" (310). Does the fact that Niebuhr, who published so much, did not publish these lectures show something (negative) of his interest in the church?

80. I am aware, as I trust the reader already recognizes, that the Anabaptist tradition, signified particularly by John Howard Yoder's *The Politics of Jesus* (Grand Rapids, MI: Eerdmans, 1972), reads this question quite differently. Indeed, it suggests that Jesus *does* teach and model a politics for Christians. I shall return to this question in the constructive part of this book. I am confident that Yoder, however, would agree that as Niebuhr and most of his contemporaries understood politics, the New Testament does not offer much in the way of programmatic advice. To agree with this point is, in fact, part of Yoder's agenda: to show that such a view of politics necessarily marginalizes Jesus' teaching as irrelevant, when Yoder thinks it isn't.

faithfully active. And we need to pray the prayer he composed that has inspired and directed millions: "God, grant me the serenity to accept the things I cannot change, courage to change the things I can, and the wisdom to know the difference."[81]

As Niebuhr himself recognizes, Christian prayer always has a corporate dimension: "*Our* Father, who art in heaven...." C. S. Lewis helps us see aspects of individual Christian faithfulness in society, while Reinhold Niebuhr provides us categories to examine both individual existence and the huge blocs of ideologies and institutions in conflict and cooperation. We turn now to Dietrich Bonhoeffer, who wrestled with both of these levels and also considered how the church—and other social forms of human life, such as the family—should figure in these matters as well.[82]

---

81. There are various versions of this prayer, and Niebuhr himself originally published, and continued to prefer, a different version of it. Alcoholics Anonymous is responsible for this, the more widely known version, the copyright to which was later bought by Hallmark Cards. Niebuhr provides this version in his reminiscences published in 1967: "God, give us grace to accept with serenity the things that cannot be changed, courage to change the things that should be changed, and the wisdom to distinguish the one from the other" ("A View of Life from the Sidelines," 251). We must note, in the light of the following paragraph, that Niebuhr's version contains the first person plural, while AA's is singular. On the (ironic) career of this prayer—it ended up being linked not only with AA and Hallmark but also with the West German army academy and Richard Nixon's "Silent Majority," see Fox, *Reinhold Niebuhr,* 290–91.

82. Robin Lovin wryly observes, "While the church is unimportant for Niebuhr, almost everything else is, too, apart from government and law. He is simply focused on a view of politics and history in which states (or the historical precursors of states) are the important actors, and he doesn't think a lot about any of Bonhoeffer's mandates except government—not the church, but also not culture, or the family, or work. This is really the point at which Bonhoeffer and Niebuhr, different as they are, can, I think, be brought together" (e-mail to author, 26 February 2007).

FOUR

DIETRICH BONHOEFFER

The Christian and the Church
in and for the World

To be a Christian does not mean to be religious in a
particular way, to make something of oneself (a sinner,
a penitent, or a saint) on the basis of some method or
other, but to be a man—not a type of man, but the man
that Christ creates in us.

—Dietrich Bonhoeffer

By the middle of the twentieth century, the term "theologian of crisis" had been
applied to Karl Barth, Emil Brunner, Reinhold Niebuhr, and Paul Tillich. But it
perhaps best suits Dietrich Bonhoeffer, for at least three reasons.

First, his adult life was shaped by the crisis that was Weimar Germany. Then he
endured the even more severe strictures of Nazi Germany, only to be killed by that
regime in a way that was itself theologically significant. Second, his theology was obviously and definitively shaped by the German situation of crisis, albeit in the light of his
contact with England, America, and parts of continental Europe via his ecumenical
work. And third, the word "crisis" doesn't just mean "a time of extreme upset," for
Krisis means a "point of decision."[1] Bonhoeffer's life and thought came to focus on
themes of transition, danger, and opportunity in matters of identity (especially of the
Christian individual and the church), of mission (again, of individual and church),
and even of language itself. In particular, Bonhoeffer was provoked to ask:

The epigraph for this chapter is drawn from Dietrich Bonhoeffer, *Letters and Papers from Prison*,
ed. Eberhard Bethge, trans. Reginald Fuller, Frank Clarke, and John Bowden (New York:
Macmillan, 1962 [1953]), 361.

1. Intriguingly, the Chinese word for crisis has two ideograms: one for "danger" and the other
for "opportunity."

- How am I to understand and speak, and how are we to understand and speak?
- Who am I, and who are we?
- What am I to do in the world, and what are we to do in the world?

Over his short but seminal career, Bonhoeffer spoke to a range of issues to do with the theology of culture. For him, however, all such discussion properly begins theologically, and that in a traditional way: with consideration of Jesus Christ, the Word of God. He criticized Reinhold Niebuhr and, indeed, most American theologians and ethicists he encountered during his brief tours of the United States in the 1930s for what he saw to be shallow theological grounding for what they professed.[2] So it is to basic theology that we first turn.

THE HEART OF BONHOEFFER'S THEOLOGY

Christ

Some of Bonhoeffer's earliest lectures focused on Jesus Christ and were published under the title *Christ the Center*. These lectures are structured in an intriguing pattern, one that puts in the foreground Luther's own concern to find a God *pro me*: first "The Present Christ—The Pro Me," then "The Historical Christ," and finally "The Eternal Christ" (the notes from which have been lost).[3]

---

2. Dietrich Bonhoeffer, "Protestantism Without Reformation," anthologized in *Dietrich Bonhoeffer: Witness to Jesus Christ,* ed. John de Gruchy (Minneapolis: Fortress, 1991 [1987]), 195–216.

3. *Christ the Center,* trans. Edwin H. Robertson (London: Harper, 1978 [1960]). It is remarkable how few of Bonhoeffer's books, in fact, represent completed works: almost all are fragmentary and incomplete to at least some extent. This fact has meant that his works are more open to interpretation, and thus are both more useful and more vulnerable to a wide range of theological agendas. A strong strand of Bonhoeffer scholarship has sought to compensate for this fact by emphasizing continuity in his writings, starting with the dissertations, but Bonhoeffer's own recorded ambivalence about *Discipleship* (his own title, *Nachfolge*, for what in English was called *The Cost of Discipleship*) complicates any sweeping generalizations about coherence ("Today I can see the dangers of that book, though I still stand by what I wrote" [*Letters*, 369]). Again, since my work is not intended as an original contribution to Bonhoeffer scholarship but rather as a harvesting of ideas from him, I pay attention to this interpretative question of continuity and development simply in hopes of getting Bonhoeffer as "right" as I can. For examples of the wide range of appropriation of Bonhoeffer, in addition to the works cited below, see: Stephen Williams, "The Theological Task and Theological Method: Penitence, Parasitism, and Prophecy," in *Evangelical Futures: A Conversation on Theological Method,* ed. John G. Stackhouse Jr. (Grand Rapids, MI: Baker Academic, 2000), 159–77; Stanley Hauerwas, *Performing the Faith: Bonhoeffer and the Practice of Nonviolence* (Grand Rapids,

Bonhoeffer affirms the Chalcedonian Definition implicitly in the first of these lectures and explicitly in the second: Jesus is God incarnate, fully God and fully human.[4] But he is not primarily concerned with such metaphysical matters, particularly given the modesty of the Chalcedonian formulation in all of its negations, balances, and paradoxes. Instead, Bonhoeffer is fundamentally concerned to encounter Jesus, to listen to him, to be changed by him, and to respond to him. Edwin Robertson comments,

> In these lectures on Christology, Bonhoeffer is not prepared to find a category for Christ. His questions are not, "How is it possible for Christ to be both man and God?" His question about Christ is never, "How?", but always, "Who?" He will not even have a disguised "What?" or "How?" in the form of a "Who?" Every avenue of his thinking leads him to confront Christ and ask, "Who art thou, Lord?" or to be confronted by Christ and hear his question, "Whom do you say that I am?"[5]

The lectures begin, in fact, with a powerful repudiation of academic theology's routine "science," in which one rolls up one's sleeves and gets to work analyzing data and testing hypotheses. "Teaching about Christ," Bonhoeffer asserts instead, "begins in silence.... The silence of the Church is silence before the Word." And then Bonhoeffer's paradoxes begin: "In so far as the Church proclaims the Word, it falls down silently in truth before the inexpressible."[6]

This "inexpressible" fundamentally is the person of Jesus Christ:

> "God revealed in the flesh," the God-man Jesus Christ, is the holy mystery which theology is appointed to guard. What a mistake to think that it is the task of theology to unravel God's mystery, to bring it down to the flat, ordinary human wisdom of experience and reason! It is the task of theology solely to preserve God's wonder, to understand, to defend, to glorify God's mystery as mystery.[7]

MI: Brazos, 2004); and Georg Huntemann, *The Other Bonhoeffer: An Evangelical Reassessment of Dietrich Bonhoeffer* (Grand Rapids, MI: Baker, 1993)—the last of which remarkably interprets Bonhoeffer through the categories of class and gender and finds him both aristocratic and patriarchalist, and commendably so. For a survey of views, see Stephen R. Haynes, *The Bonhoeffer Phenomenon: Portraits of a Protestant Saint* (Minneapolis: Augsburg Fortress, 2004).

4. Echoing the early church and its linkage of Christology and soteriology, Bonhoeffer asks, "If Jesus Christ is not true God, how could he *help* us? If Christ is not true man, how could he help *us*?" ("Letter to the Finkenwalde Brethren," in *Dietrich Bonhoeffer: Witness to Jesus Christ,* 219).

5. Edwin H. Robertson, "Translator's Preface," in Bonhoeffer, *Christ the Center,* 15.

6. Bonhoeffer, *Christ the Center*, 27.

7. Bonhoeffer, "Letter to the Finkenwalde Brethren," 217.

This revelation of the great Mystery of God (in both the modern and New Testament senses of "mystery": something we don't understand and something previously concealed that now is revealed), namely, "Christ in you, the hope of glory" (Col. 1:27), prompts Bonhoeffer to proclaim,

> The question, "Who?", is simply *the* religious question. It is the question about the other person and his claim, about the other being, about the other authority. It is the question of love for one's neighbour. Questions of transcendence and of existence become questions concerning the person.[8]

Bonhoeffer has no intention, to be sure, of rendering Jesus in the typical liberal mode of an abiding "presence," a divine "principle" or "influence," or some such thing. To combat this idea, he affirms the resurrection and ascension of Jesus:

> What is concealed behind this idea of the presence of Christ is the decision not to consider the resurrection, but to stop with the Jesus of the cross, with the historical Jesus. This is the dead Jesus Christ who can be thought of like Socrates and Goethe....
>
> ...Only the risen one, who has ascended to heaven, can be present with us, not one who is only within history. Ritschl and Herrmann put the resurrection to one side; Schleiermacher symbolizes it; in so doing they destroy the Church. "If Christ has not been raised, your faith is futile and you are still in your sins" (I Corinthians 15:17).[9]

In the succeeding chapters, Bonhoeffer affirms Christ's love for and presence in the church as word, as sacrament, and, indeed, as community itself. In fact, Bonhoeffer's previous writings—his doctoral dissertation, published as *Sanctorum Communio,* and his *Habilitationsschrift*, published in English as *Act and Being*—so emphasize the church as to run the risk of subjugating Christology to ecclesiology, so that Christ simply *is* the community.[10] This risk is averted in the Christology

---

8. Bonhoeffer, *Christ the Center*, 31.

9. Ibid., 44–45. He later distances himself from another characteristic teaching of the liberal tradition: "When Christ is called the Word of God today, it is usually with this sense of the idea. An idea is generally accessible, it lies ready to hand. Man can freely appropriate what he chooses from it. Christ as idea is timeless truth, the idea of God embodied in Jesus, available to anyone at any time" instead of the Word of God who addresses us personally, specifically, and concretely (50–51). See his discussion of liberal Christology as what he calls "the docetic heresy" in ibid., 76–82.

10. John de Gruchy comments that Bonhoeffer "set out to locate theology in the context of human social and ethical relations in history, rather than in the epistemological framework of post-Kantian philosophy or the individualism of existentialism. The individualism

lectures, however, as here Bonhoeffer affirms Christ as the center of human existence, the center of history, and the center between God and nature.[11] And he stoutly and repeatedly affirms that one must know Christ now and affirm *who* he is, whether or not, and no matter how much, one can explain *what* he is and what he does.

Note that only once he has affirmed Christ *pro me* does Bonhoeffer then look back to the historical Christ and then upward and onward, so to speak, to the eternal Christ. Existential, personal, and ethical concerns are foremost for him. At the end of his life, these concerns mark his thinking about God at the center again:

> Religious people speak of God when human knowledge (perhaps simply because they are too lazy to think) has come to an end, or when human resources fail—in fact it is always the *deus ex machina* that they bring on to the scene, either for the apparent solution of insoluble problems, or as strength in human failure—always, that is to say, exploiting human weakness or human boundaries. Of necessity, that can go on only till people can by their own strength push these boundaries somewhat further out, so that God becomes superfluous as a *deus ex machina*....It always seems to me that we are trying anxiously in this way to reserve some space for God; I should like to speak of God not on the boundaries but at the center, not in weaknesses but in strength; and therefore not in death and guilt but in man's life and goodness....God is beyond in the midst of our life. The church stands, not at the boundaries where human powers give out, but in the middle of the village.[12]

---

of both excluded the possibility of a true knowledge of God. For Bonhoeffer, the empirical existence of the church in history provided the place where such knowledge becomes possible" ("Introduction," in *Dietrich Bonhoeffer: Witness to Jesus Christ,* 4).

11. John de Gruchy sees Bonhoeffer making this shift in emphasis between the dissertations and the Christology lectures in his lectures on Genesis 1–3 (John de Gruchy, "Editor's Introduction," in Dietrich Bonhoeffer, *Creation and Fall,* ed. John de Gruchy, trans. Douglas Stephen Bax [Minneapolis, MN: Fortress, 1997], 10). Cf. Bonhoeffer's caution in *Discipleship*: "The unity between Christ and his body, the church, demands that we at the same time recognize Christ's lordship over his body....Christ is the Lord....Both the unity and the distinction are necessary aspects of the same truth" (*Dietrich Bonhoeffer Works,* vol. 4: *Discipleship*, ed. Geffrey Kelly and John Godsey, trans. Barbara Green and Reinhard Krauss [Minneapolis: Augsburg Fortress, 2001], 220).

12. Bonhoeffer, *Letters,* 282. Bonhoeffer returns to this theme a few months later—indeed, shortly before his death—and reaffirms explicitly his Christocentricity in another letter to Bethge: "How wrong it is to use God as a stop-gap for the incompleteness of our knowledge.... We are to find God in what we know, not in what we don't know; God wants us to realize his presence, not in unsolved problems but in those that are solved....God is no stop-gap; he must be recognized at the center of life.... The ground for this lies in the revelation of God in Jesus Christ. He is the center of life" (*Letters,* 311–12).

The Word of God

Whether in his activities of teaching, preaching, ecumenical relations, or community building, Bonhoeffer lived by the conviction that God has said Something, and continues to have Something to say. We can hear it, we *must* hear it, and then respond appropriately.

This conviction was in some respects a direct repudiation of the liberalism of his teachers who separated the "Jesus of history" from the "Christ of faith," and particularly their conviction that the Jesus of the Synoptic Gospels is other than the Pauline Christ.[13] Bonhoeffer cites Schweitzer and then Wrede in this regard: "Wrede makes quite clear than an historical Jesus in the sense of these researches into the life of Jesus is not feasible, because the Synoptic Gospels are written already under the presupposition of the 'faith of the Church'. One cannot get behind belief in the Christ as Lord (*Kyrios Christos*)."[14]

Still, Bonhoeffer was deeply influenced by higher criticism, by liberal theology, and by the force of his own thinking, and therefore records doubts about the Virgin Birth (because then Jesus would not be born *exactly* as we are, which he thinks is essential to his incarnation) and the historicity of the empty tomb. Indeed, he shows how deeply influenced he is by his German intellectual heritage as he alludes to Lessing's famous "ugly ditch" between history and the divine ideal:

> There is no way from history to the absolute. There is no absolute ground for faith derived from history. But from where does faith receive its sufficient ground to know that the uncertain is sure? There is only the witness of the risen one to himself, by which the Church bears witness to him as "in history." By the miracle of his presence in the Church, he bears witness to himself as there in history, here and now....
>
> ... When we have Christ witnessing to himself in the present, any historical confirmation is irrelevant....
>
> But does this not open the door to every kind of sentimentality? Such is not the case, because the witness of Jesus Christ to himself is none other than that which the Scriptures deliver to us and which comes to us by no other way than by the Word of the Scriptures....
>
> ... The Bible remains a book like other books. One must be ready to accept the concealment within history and therefore let historical criticism

---

13. Bonhoeffer, *Christ the Center,* 69.
14. Ibid., 70.

run its course. But it is through the Bible, with all its flaws, that the risen one encounters us. We must get into the troubled waters of historical criticism. Its importance is not absolute, but neither is it unimportant. Certainly it will not lead to a weakening, but rather to a strengthening of faith, because the concealment within the historical belongs to the humiliation of Christ.[15]

In all of this, Bonhoeffer reflects his times, particularly in German theology, as he emphasizes God's encounter with humanity through the figure of Christ and the text of the Bible despite whatever limitations or even flaws might be discerned in either. These themes recur in figures as theologically various as Barth, Bultmann, and Tillich. And they often emerge among such theologians under the rubric of "justification by faith," as if that soteriological slogan can be applied to all sorts of things, including epistemology—as in "we cannot know theological matters in the normal way, by inference from reliable data, but instead we trust that God is addressing us even through these rationally dubious media." This view was meant to champion the sovereign goodness of God, who reveals himself graciously as the great Subject, rather than as the object of religious investigation and rational apprehension.[16]

Bonhoeffer much earlier in these lectures had made his fundamental epistemological point about Christology, sounding themes more than slightly reminiscent of Karl Barth, who influenced him:

---

15. Ibid., 72–74. On the virgin birth, see 105; on the empty tomb, see 112–13. Bonhoeffer strikes me as needlessly and unhappily bound up with trying to emphasize the scandal of the Christian proclamation to both the "cultured despisers" *and* the "cultured defenders" of Christianity in his day by reveling in the apparently absurd claims of the gospel at the same time as he (properly) wants to claim no more for history (and thus of the Bible's accounts) than history can properly show. Bonhoeffer seems to me to be right to avoid the Scylla of naive and dogmatic realism, as he shuns claims of positive proof for orthodox Christological convictions (such as the virgin birth, the divinity and humanity of Jesus, and the resurrection), but he seems to take on water near the Charybdis of skepticism, as he fails to defend the historicity of these events as, in fact, both theologically important and rationally defensible.

16. Then and now, of course, it has been an outlook that both liberals and conservatives have found untenable, if not absurd. On what basis is *this* religious experience—for that is what is at the heart of this epistemology—identified as true versus all of the others one might have, or those of people of very different religious and philosophical convictions? It is a question that is posed today to the descendants of this epistemology, the so-called postliberals. See Alister E. McGrath, *The Genesis of Doctrine: A Study in the Foundations of Doctrinal Criticism* (Oxford: Basil Blackwell, 1990); Timothy R. Phillips and Dennis L. Okholm, eds., *The Nature of Confession: Evangelicals and Postliberals in Conversation* (Downers Grove, IL: InterVarsity, 1996); and William C. Placher, *Narratives of a Vulnerable God: Christ, Theology, and Scripture* (Louisville: Westminster John Knox, 1994), 126–27.

The incognito of the Incarnation makes it doubly impossible to recognize the Person by his Works:

1.   Jesus is man and the argument back from works to person is ambiguous.
2.   Jesus is God and the argument back from history to God is impossible.

If this way of understanding is closed there remains just one more chance to gain access to Jesus Christ. This is the attempt to be in the place where the Person reveals himself in his own being, without any compulsion. That is the place of prayer to Christ. Only by the Word freely revealing himself is the Person of Christ available and with that also his work.[17]

As we continue, then, to encounter Christ particularly in Scripture, in preaching, in the sacraments, and in church fellowship, we must construct theology in order to know better who Christ is and what he wants us to be and to do.[18] Bonhoeffer was no mystic: theology is to be worked up from Biblical and historical sources with care, and only then applied to contemporary challenges.[19] In his later *Ethics,* Bonhoeffer repudiates a typically liberal approach—indeed, a typically Niebuhrian and Tillichian approach—to the challenges that face us:

It is necessary to free oneself from the way of thinking which sets out from human problems and which asks for solutions on this basis. Such thinking is unbiblical. The way of Jesus Christ, and therefore the way of all Christian thinking, leads

---

17. Bonhoeffer, *Christ the Center*, 38–39.
18. So also in Bonhoeffer, *Discipleship*: "He is present with us today, in bodily form and with his word. If we want to hear his call to discipleship, we need to hear it where Christ himself is present. It is within the church that Jesus Christ calls through his word and sacrament.... To hear Jesus' call to discipleship, one needs no personal revelation. Listen to the preaching and receive the sacrament! Listen to the gospel of the crucified and risen Lord!" (202).
19. To be sure, Bonhoeffer has often been faulted on his exegesis in many of his lectures and sermons. His training and talents did not seem particularly fit for clear-eyed understanding of some of the texts he sought to exposit: often the verses ostensibly in question do not obviously support the theological point Bonhoeffer is making, whether in historical-critical perspective or in terms of sheer literary coherence. But his exegesis strikes most readers as sincere, rather than as mere window dressing or, worse, as eisegetical manipulation. John de Gruchy notes that Bonhoeffer's "theological exegesis" of Scripture was scorned by Biblical scholars much as Karl Barth's was—and I would go on to suggest that Barth's use of Scripture is subject to the criticisms I have listed of Bonhoeffer's (de Gruchy, "Editor's Introduction," 5–8). Still, one recognizes that Bonhoeffer's Scriptural exposition, and particularly of the Sermon on the Mount, in *Discipleship* has been widely acknowledged as a spiritual classic.

not from the world to God but from God to the world. This means that the essence of the gospel does not lie in the solution of human problems, and that the solution of human problems cannot be the essential task of the Church....

The Church's word to the world can be no other than God's word to the world. This word is Jesus Christ and salvation in His name.[20]

Finally, Bonhoeffer shows himself to be a product of his class, nation, church, and education in that he self-consciously works in the Lutheran tradition. He refers reflexively to Lutheran categories, such as "law and gospel" or "two kingdoms," even if he modifies or even disagrees with them, and regularly quotes Luther. Bonhoeffer proves himself to be a true child of Luther particularly, however, in his willingness to criticize both the received tradition and the church that embodies it on the basis of the Word of God about Jesus Christ, especially as he comes to view the tradition's contemporary expression in the German church as promoting subservience to the state, no matter how evil that state becomes.

Discipleship

Bonhoeffer's best-known book bears the English title *The Cost of Discipleship*. But "cost" is only one of its main themes, and Bonhoeffer's original title in German, *Nachfolge*, rendered "discipleship" in English, literally means just "following." The book he wrote, then, is not an exposition of what it costs to be a disciple, but a manual of how to be a disciple. It is far more than a warning: it is an invitation and an instruction.

Arguably the most quoted line in the Bonhoeffer canon comes from this book: "When Christ calls a man, he bids him come and die."[21] But Bonhoeffer assures us that Christ calls us to die in order to live again in life abundant: "Only Jesus Christ, who bids us to follow him, knows where the path will lead. But we know that it will be a path full of mercy beyond measure. Discipleship is joy."[22]

---

20. Dietrich Bonhoeffer, *Dietrich Bonhoeffer Works*, vol. 6: *Ethics*, ed. Clifford Green, trans. Reinhard Krauss, Charles West, and Douglas Stott (Minneapolis: Augsburg Fortress, 2005), 356.

21. *The Cost of Discipleship*, trans. R. H. Fuller (New York: Touchstone, 1995 [1959]), 89. The 2001 critical edition of this book, from which I will usually quote, renders this classic line in gender-inclusive language (which I generally use myself) that, alas, blunts its rhetorical force considerably: "Whenever Christ calls us, his call leads us to death" (*Discipleship*, 87). Cf. an equally powerful line in Bonhoeffer's earlier *Christ the Center*, speaking particularly of theologians who want to analyze Jesus but not really meet him: "There are only two ways possible of encountering Jesus: man must die or he must put Jesus to death" (35).

22. *Discipleship*, 40.

"Costly Grace" is, indeed, the title of chapter 1, and it opens thus: "Cheap grace is the mortal enemy of our church. Our struggle today is for costly grace."[23] Bonhoeffer goes on:

> Cheap grace means grace as doctrine, as principle, as system. It means forgiveness of sins as a general truth; it means God's love as merely a Christian idea of God.... Cheap grace means justification of sin but not of the sinner. Because grace alone does everything, everything can stay in its old ways.[24]

Then Bonhoeffer combines these themes:

> It is costly, because it calls to discipleship; it is grace, because it calls us to follow *Jesus Christ*. It is costly, because it costs people their lives; it is grace, because it thereby makes them live. It is costly, because it condemns sin; it is grace, because it justifies the sinner. Above all, grace is costly, because it was costly to God, because it costs God the life of God's Son...and because nothing can be cheap to us which is costly to God. Above all, it is grace because the life of God's Son was not too costly for God to give in order to make us live. God did, indeed, give him up for us. Costly grace is the incarnation of God.[25]

Why this emphasis?

> Is the price that we are paying today with the collapse of the organized churches anything else but an inevitable consequence of grace acquired too cheaply? We gave away preaching and sacraments cheaply; we performed baptisms and confirmations; we absolved an entire people, unquestioned and unconditionally; out of human love we handed over what was holy to the scornful and unbelievers. We poured out rivers of grace without end, but the call to rigorously follow Christ was seldom heard....
>
> ...It could not happen any other way but that possessing cheap grace would mislead weaklings to suddenly feel strong, yet in reality, they had lost their power for obedience and discipleship. The word of cheap grace has ruined more Christians than any commandment about works.[26]

---

23. *Discipleship*, 43.
24. Ibid.
25. Ibid., 45.
26. Ibid., 53–55.

Contrary to the liberal theology and church life of his day, then, Bonhoeffer subsumes the Christian life under the heading of "discipleship":

So the call to discipleship is a commitment solely to the person of Jesus Christ....

Discipleship is commitment to Christ. Because Christ exists, he must be followed. An idea about Christ, a doctrinal system, a general religious recognition of grace or forgiveness of sins does not require discipleship. In truth, it even excludes discipleship; it is inimical to it.[27]

Later, this theme will dominate his *Ethics:*

Those who wish even to focus on the problem of a Christian ethic are faced with an outrageous demand—from the outset they must give up, as inappropriate to this topic, the very two questions that led them to deal with the ethical problem: "How can I be good?" and "How can I do something good?" Instead they must ask the wholly other, completely different question, what is the will of God?[28]

These reflections lead Bonhoeffer to the nexus of belief and action, of faith and works—and to one of his more controversial claims: "Only the believers obey, and only the obedient believe."[29] This claim, which to many ears would sound simply like the New Testament, nonetheless would have pricked the conscience of many German believers as they came to see themselves as collaborating with evil in the National Socialist regime, particularly in the laws against Jews—which compunction was exactly Bonhoeffer's aim. The Lutheran emphasis on justification by faith alone, through grace alone, had been set adrift from Luther's own concern for holiness and rectitude. The *solas* had come to give dangerous comfort to many of Bonhoeffer's contemporaries who had no demonstrable interest in following Christ but rather were content to be saved by him—eventually.

This emphasis on following the person of Christ, who reveals himself and is not simply an example of a general religious principle nor a mere factor in a general religious system, also means that Christ might confront a disciple, or a community of disciples, with unexpected demands. Just as Jesus often startled his disciples in the Gospels with his words and deeds, so he might do the same today. Thus did

---

27. Ibid., 59.

28. Bonhoeffer, *Ethics*, 47.

29. Bonhoeffer, *Discipleship*, 63.

Bonhoeffer see the disciple as radically free from the constraints of any tradition or institution to do what needed to be done in a particular moment. Just how radical that freedom might be, he would see in his efforts against the Nazis at the end of his brief life.

This radically free disciple is called by Christ as an individual. Bonhoeffer went further: "Jesus' call to discipleship makes the disciple into a single individual. Whether disciples want to or not, they have to make a decision; each has to decide alone." And then the paradox: "It is not their own choice to desire to be single individuals. Instead, Christ makes everyone he calls into an individual. Each is called alone [out of his family, his clan, his club, his class, and his nation, we might say]. Each must follow alone."[30]

Bonhoeffer goes on:

> He has deprived those whom he has called of every immediate connection to those given realities. He wants to be the medium; everything should happen only through him. He stands not only between me and God, he also stands between me and the world, between me and other people and things. *He is the mediator,* not only between God and human persons, but also between person and person, and between person and reality. Because the whole world was created by him and for him…he is the sole mediator in the world. Since Christ there has been no more unmediated relationship for the human person, neither to God nor to the world. Christ intends to be the mediator.[31]

This is a crucial motif for Bonhoeffer, therefore: the individual, called by Christ as such, who then is related to everything else in creation by way of Christ, who is the center. It shows up in *Life Together* as the fundamental dynamic of Christian fellowship. It also lies at the heart of Bonhoeffer's more mature writing about Christian life in the world. Such individualism focused on such radical Christocentrism does, as we have seen and will see again below, mean a radical call to individual faith and obedience, in the face of much pressure to conform to group norms—whether Nazi pressure or even Christian pressure.

Yet the life of a disciple, for Bonhoeffer, could not *normally* be lived without robust Christian community. He explored some dimensions of Christian community

---

30. Bonhoeffer, *Discipleship*, 92.
31. Ibid., 94–95; emphasis in original.

in his two dissertations, *Sanctorum Communio* and *Act and Being*. These works have received little attention beyond the considerable coterie of Bonhoeffer scholars.[32] But many more readers encountered his thought in the slim volume *Life Together*.

This popular book is based primarily on his experience of teaching and living in the Finkenwalde seminary community. Some passages quite clearly depend, however, on his experience in the Bonhoeffer family and in churches he had attended and pastored. It therefore is not as extreme as it might have been had it been confined to the highly unusual and isolated life of the seminary and its single men living together. Some readers have seen it, and the Finkenwalde seminary itself, as almost a "type" of ideal Christianity, and therefore *Life Together* has been a bit dangerous to those who might focus exclusively on this sort of (temporary) Protestant monasticism. But it offers instructions for family devotion, as well as for the church: Monasticism is not its intent.

Our identity, Bonhoeffer asserts, is found in, and formed by, life in community, and our Christian identity—our true self—takes shape in the church. The church itself is both the agent of God's will and a realization of God's will:

> Ethics as formation is possible only on the basis of the form of Jesus Christ present in Christ's church. *The church is the place where Jesus Christ's taking form is proclaimed and where it happens.* The Christian ethic stands in the service of this proclamation and this event.[33]

To be sure, the church is still a *peccatorum communio*—a communion of sinners—and thus not to be equated with the Kingdom of God. Yet, Bonhoeffer goes on, it is wonderfully true that we are "in him" and he is "in us." The church is the Body of Christ. Indeed, as Bonhoeffer later writes in his *Ethics*, "the church is not a religious community of those who revere Christ, but Christ who has taken form among human beings."[34] Thus the church utters "the joyful cry of those who have been granted a share in a great, astonishing gift, 'Here is the gospel!' 'Here are the pure sacraments!' 'Here is the church!' 'Come here!'"[35]

---

32. De Gruchy cites a letter of Bonhoeffer in which, already by 1932 (he is but twenty-six years old at the time), he himself calls his *Habilitationsschrift* a "product" with which he no longer felt much empathy—having completed it not three years previously (de Gruchy, "Editor's Introduction," 13).

33. *Ethics*, 102; emphasis in original.

34. Ibid., 96.

35. Dietrich Bonhoeffer, "The Question of the Boundaries of the Church and Church Union" (1936), anthologized in *Dietrich Bonhoeffer: Witness to Jesus Christ*, 149.

Bonhoeffer's commitment to the church—the actual church, the congregations and denominations of his time—was abundantly evident, in what we might see as concentric circles. At the outermost edge, he devoted great energy to ecumenical work beyond Germany. (He was so well traveled and connected, in fact, that—in one of several deep ironies in his life—he was able to use this work as both a cover and a communications network for his intelligence service to the anti-Hitler conspiracy.)[36] Bonhoeffer also worked hard within Germany in trying to purify and bind together the church against Adolf Hitler and for Jesus Christ, through preaching and public speaking (until the Reich silenced him) as well as through denominational politics. He served the church by teaching humbly at the tiny seminary at Finkenwalde. He served individuals through voluminous correspondence. And then, in the extraordinarily restricted situation of prison, he refused any status as a pastor but attempted frequently to improve conditions on behalf of less privileged inmates, particularly during the air raids.

With Bonhoeffer's pronouncement that "Christ is the church" and his ecclesiastical ministry briefly sketched, we thus come to questions of "Christ and culture" in almost a literal way. Bonhoeffer takes individual responsibility very seriously, as we shall see, and his vision is as wide as international politics and global ecumenism. But he also insists on the corporate nature of Christian discipleship, and calls the church—not just "the church" in general as a synonym for "Christianity," but congregations and denominations in all their concrete particularity—to faithful action.

THEMES IN A THEOLOGY OF CULTURE

Christ as Lord of the World

Bonhoeffer's great work was his *Ethics*—the one book he himself wanted earnestly to complete, although he was prevented from doing so by his untimely death.[37] Written between 1940 and 1943, it remains fragmentary, and yet so very

---

36. Indeed, it was a double irony: the ecumenical work served as a cover for his official work in the Abwehr, within which he was working for the conspiracy against Hitler; see Eberhard Bethge, *Dietrich Bonhoeffer: A Biography,* rev. and ed. Victoria J. Barnett (Minneapolis: Fortress, 2000), 702.

37. Bonhoeffer wrote to his friend Eberhard Bethge: "I've reproached myself for not having finished my *Ethics* (parts of it have probably been confiscated), and it was some consolation to me that I had told you the essentials, and that even if you had forgotten it, it would probably emerge again indirectly somehow. Besides, my ideas were still incomplete" (*Letters*, 129).

rich and suggestive. Eberhard Bethge comments, "The exclusiveness of Christ's lordship—that is the message of *Discipleship,* the wide range of his lordship—that is the new emphasis of *Ethics.*"[38]

Its theme is this powerful claim: "The reality of God is disclosed only as it places me completely into the reality of the world."[39] Bonhoeffer repudiates any strong sense of "two spheres" or "two kingdoms" as opposing realities:

> There are not two realities, but *only one reality,* and that is God's reality revealed in Christ in the reality of the world. Partaking in Christ, we stand at the same time in the reality of God and in the reality of the world.... Because this is so, the theme of two realms, which has dominated the history of the church again and again, is foreign to the New Testament. The New Testament is concerned only with the realization [*Wirklichwerden*] of the Christ-reality in the contemporary world that it already embraces, owns, and inhabits. There are not two competing realms standing side by side and battling over the borderline, as if this question of boundaries was always the decisive one. Rather, the whole reality of the world has already been drawn into and is held together in Christ. History moves only from this center and toward this center.[40]

Even more pointedly, Bonhoeffer continues,

> The world is not divided between Christ and the devil; it is completely the world of Christ, whether it recognizes this or not.... The dark, evil world may not be surrendered to the devil, but [must] be claimed for the one who won it by coming in the flesh, by the death and resurrection of Christ.... Every static distinction between one domain [*Bereich*] as belonging to the devil and another as belonging to Christ denies the reality that God has reconciled the whole world with himself in Christ.[41]

---

38. Bethge, *Dietrich Bonhoeffer,* 718.

39. Bonhoeffer, *Ethics,* 55.

40. Ibid., 58.

41. Ibid., 65–66. Bonhoeffer provides virtually his own counterpart to H. Richard Niebuhr's typology in this passage—and note that he calls the second one *pseudo*-Lutheran: "In the high scholastic period the natural realm was subordinated to the realm of grace. In pseudo-Lutheranism the autonomy of the orders of this world is proclaimed against the law of Christ. Among the Enthusiasts the church-community of the elect sets out to struggle against the enmity of the world in order to build the kingdom of God on earth. In all this the concern of Christ becomes a partial, provincial affair within the whole of reality. One reckons with realities outside the reality of Christ. It follows that there is separate access to these realities, apart from Christ" (*Ethics,* 56–57).

In yet another passage of the *Ethics,* Bonhoeffer might seem to contradict himself by retaining the language of "two kingdoms," but in fact he uses this term to reinforce his theme of the Lordship of Christ over the one reality there is:

> There are two kingdoms [*Zwei Reiche*], which, as long as the earth remains, must never be mixed together, yet never torn apart: the kingdom of the proclaimed word of God and the kingdom of the sword, the kingdom of the church and the kingdom of the world, the kingdom of the spiritual office and the kingdom of worldly authority. The sword can never bring about the unity of the church and of faith; preaching can never rule the peoples. But the lord of both kingdoms is God revealed in Jesus Christ. God rules the world by the office of the word and the office of the sword. The bearers of both of these offices are accountable to God.[42]

We note in these ethical reflections, then, the recurrence and the foundational position of the theological themes of the Incarnation itself, the union of the divine and the human, and also of the centrality of Christ. These themes characterize Christian discipleship *because* they are established in the nature of things: in ontology and experience, and thus in theology. (This kind of theological groundwork for ethics is what Bonhoeffer found lacking in his American colleagues at Union Seminary.) Bonhoeffer says in his *Ethics,*

> The *subject matter of a Christian ethic is God's reality revealed in Christ becoming real [Wirklichwerden] among God's creatures,* just as the subject matter of doctrinal theology is the truth of God's reality revealed in Christ. The place that in all other ethics is marked by the antithesis between ought and is, idea and realization, motive and work, is occupied in Christian ethics by the relation between reality and becoming real, between past and present, between history and event (faith) or, to replace the many concepts with the simple name of the thing itself, the relation between Jesus Christ and the Holy Spirit. The question of the good becomes the question of participating in God's reality revealed in Christ.[43]

---

42. Bonhoeffer, *Ethics*, 112. Bonhoeffer says later, "Christianity must be used polemically today against the worldly in the name of a better worldliness; this polemical use of Christianity must not end up again in a static and self-serving sacred realm. Only in this sense of a polemical unity may Luther's doctrine of the two kingdoms [*Zwei Reiche*] be used. That was probably its original meaning" (60).

43. Ibid., 49–50.

In *Christ the Center,* Bonhoeffer anticipates some of this teaching and makes some startling claims:

> Because Christ, since the cross and resurrection, is present in the Church, the Church also must be understood as the centre of history. It is the centre of a history which is being made by the state. Again this is a hidden and not an evident centre of the realm of the state. The Church does not show itself to be the centre by visibly standing at the centre of the state or by letting itself be put at the centre, by which it is made a state Church.... The meaning and the promise of the state is hidden in it, it judges and justifies the state in its nature....
>
> So, just as the Church is the centre of the state, it is also its boundary. It is the boundary of the state in proclaiming with the cross the breaking-through of all human order....
>
> Christ is present to us in the forms both of Church and State. But he is this only for us, who receive him as Word and Sacrament and Church; for us, who since the cross must see the state in the light of Christ. The state is God's "rule with his left hand" (Luther [various citations]). So long as Christ was on earth, he was the kingdom of God. When he was crucified the kingdom broke up into one ruled by God's right hand and one ruled by his left hand. But the complete Christ is present in his Church. And this Church is the hidden centre of the state.[44]

Thus the state ought to recognize the church's claim to, and right to, enough space in which it can perform its central task of proclaiming "the reign of Jesus Christ over the whole world."[45] The state—for its own sake, as a servant of God that needs a healthy, functioning church for its own healthy functioning—must not encroach on the church's territory and role (as the Nazis were doing).[46] Without the church and its proclamation of Jesus as Lord, the state becomes, ironically, something other than truly and properly worldly. Lacking a divine reference

---

44. Bonhoeffer, *Christ the Center,* 63–64. Bonhoeffer is similarly straightforward in the *Ethics:* "The renewal of the West lies completely in God's renewal of the church, which leads it into community with the resurrected and living Jesus Christ" (142).

45. Bonhoeffer, *Christ the Center,* 63.

46. Ibid., 63–64; see also Dietrich Bonhoeffer, *Dietrich Bonhoeffer Works,* vol. 16: *Conspiracy and Imprisonment: 1940–45,* ed. Mark Brocker, trans. Lisa Dahill (Minneapolis: Augsburg Fortress, 2006), 548–50. One recalls Hitler's demand that Germans have enough *Lebensraum* ("living space" in Europe), as one listens to Bonhoeffer speak of the state respecting the church's "space."

point, it becomes idolatrous instead, as "the worldly will always seek to satisfy its unquenchable desire for its own deification."[47]

At the same time, the church is careful not to dictate politics to the state:

> The rule of Christ's commandment over all created being is not synonymous with the rule of the church....
>
> The law within this "corporate entity" can never and may never become the law of the worldly orders lest an alien rule be established. Conversely, the law of a worldly order can never and may never become the law of this corporate entity.[48]

Bonhoeffer thus recommends a conservative approach to the law and to government:

> The Christian is not obliged and not able to prove in every single case the right of the governmental demand. The duty of Christians to obey binds them up to the point where the government forces them into direct violation of the divine commandment, thus until government overtly acts contrary to its divine task and thereby forfeits its divine claim. When in doubt, obedience is demanded, for the Christian does not bear the governmental responsibility.[49]

Bonhoeffer is recognizing that citizens in a representative democracy are not privy to the information their leaders have in any given situation, and rarely see all of the relevant issues in play. So they must be slow to second-guess, much less disobey.

Even bad governments are still governments, and so Bonhoeffer concludes, "It would therefore not be permissible to refuse to pay taxes to a government that was persecuting the church."[50] It would take a very bad government indeed—Bonhoeffer says it would have to be a diabolical, apocalyptically bad government—to warrant revolt. The careful Christian therefore will focus any outright resistance on those elements that have forfeited their mandate.[51] (Bonhoeffer and his

---

47. Bonhoeffer, *Ethics,* 401.

48. Ibid., 403–4.

49. Bonhoeffer, *Conspiracy and Imprisonment*, 516–17.

50. Ibid., 517.

51. See ibid., 517, for "diabolical" and "apocalyptic"; see 525 for "According to scripture there is no right to revolution..."

co-conspirators thus sought the assassination of Hitler particularly, without seeking the overthrow of Germany itself or even of the German government *holus bolus*.)

Bonhoeffer affirms this revelation of the basic unity of things, despite the divisive and upsetting presence of evil in the world. And let us recall that Bonhoeffer is writing about church and state in the context of Weimar and then Nazi Germany, and that it is Bonhoeffer who is doing so: the one who, more than anyone else, challenged the church to stand up against the Nazi regime as perverters of the state. The Christian individual and the Christian church thus order life as a response to the Lordship of Christ, who personally calls us to obedience and joy. "The ethical is not essentially a formal principle of reason [whether understood in a Kantian or secular existentialist manner] but a concrete relationship based on commands."[52] This theme coheres with the conviction of Eberhard Bethge, Bonhoeffer's nephew-in-law and biographer, that *Discipleship* really is the first part of Bonhoeffer's ethics—but, as we have seen, the unity extends back even further in Bonhoeffer's writings.[53]

Bonhoeffer does not believe, however, in a kind of religious mania that prays for divine guidance in every decision of the day.[54] Quite the contrary: "I myself affirm the given realities of parents, marriage, life, and property that I find in the center and fullness of life as God's holy institution."[55] He goes on:

> God's commandment allows human beings to be human before God. It lets the flow of life take its course, lets human beings eat, drink, sleep, work, celebrate, and play without interrupting those activities, without ceaselessly confronting them with the question whether they were actually permitted to sleep, eat, work, and play, or whether they did not have more urgent duties.... The self-tormenting and hopeless question about the purity's of one's motives, suspicious self-observation, the blazing and wearisome light of ceaseless conscious awareness—all this has nothing to do with God's commandment, which grants freedom to live and act....
>
> The commandment's goal is not avoiding transgression, not the agony of ethical conflict and decision, but rather the freely affirmed, self-evident life in church, marriage, family, work, and state.[56]

---

52. Bonhoeffer, *Ethics,* 374.

53. Eberhard Bethge, "Editor's Preface to the Sixth German Edition," in Dietrich Bonhoeffer, *Ethics,* ed. Eberhard Bethge, trans. Neville Horton Smith (New York: Simon & Schuster, 1995 [1949]), 17.

54. He chides moralists in exactly these terms in *Ethics,* 365–66.

55. Ibid., 382.

56. Ibid., 384–86.

Thus Bonhoeffer sees life whole.[57] Yes, life is deeply affected by the Fall, but not hopelessly dominated by it. In the *Ethics,* Bonhoeffer speaks of the created order as now the arena in which the "natural" and "unnatural" contend. The natural is "the form of life preserved by God for the fallen world that is directed toward justification, salvation, and renewal through Christ." The unnatural resists all that, and serves to impede and destroy the redemption God is accomplishing in the world.[58] God then works with the natural and, in the *super*natural power of the Holy Spirit, effects salvation.[59] That salvation is *not* a rendering of the human into the spiritual, much less the divine. In implicit contradiction to the emphases of Athanasius, and of the Eastern churches and most mystics ever since, Bonhoeffer writes: "Human beings become human because God became human....God changes God's form into human form in order that human beings can become, not God, but human before God."[60]

In a passage remarkably reminiscent of C. S. Lewis, Bonhoeffer celebrates "the right to bodily life." The body, he contends, is "both a means to an end and an end in itself." It is part of the "natural," what is yet good after the Fall and oriented toward our eventual salvation. Indeed, "within natural life, the joys of the body are a sign of the eternal joy that is promised human beings in the presence of God."[61]

Unlike an animal shelter, a human dwelling is not intended to be only a protection against bad weather and the night, as well as a place to raise offspring. It is the space in which human beings may enjoy the pleasures of personal life in the security of their loved ones and their possessions. Eating and drinking serve not only the purpose of keeping the body healthy, but also the natural joy of bodily life. Clothing is not merely a necessary covering for the body, but is at the same time an adornment of the body. Relaxation not only serves the purpose of increasing the capacity for work, but also provides the body with the measure of rest and joy that is due to it. In its essential distance from all purposefulness, play is the clearest expression that bodily life is an end in itself.

57. "The Christian is no longer the person of eternal conflict. As reality is *one* in Christ, so the person who belongs to this Christ-reality is also a whole. Worldliness does not separate one from Christ, and being Christian does not separate one from the world. Belonging completely to Christ, one stands at the same time completely in the world" (ibid., 62).

58. Ibid., 171–85.

59. Bonhoeffer makes this distinction between the natural and the supernatural in ibid., 59.

60. Ibid., 96.

61. Ibid., 186–87.

Sexuality is not only a means of procreation, but, independent of this purpose, embodies joy within marriage in the love of two people for each other.[62]

Not for Bonhoeffer, then, any asceticism that demeans the body in order to privilege the spirit, nor an otherworldliness that suppresses any interest in the present life. Indeed, a youthful sermon contains this telling declaration: "God wants to see human beings, not ghosts who shun the world."[63] Instead, Bonhoeffer seeks to relate the body and the spirit and to relate this world and the next in ways that both give proper value to each and to order them all toward the goal of God's mission: the eventual salvation of the world.[64]

Bonhoeffer pours out much wisdom in a letter to his friend Bethge:

I believe that we ought so to love and trust God in our *lives,* and in all the good things that he sends us, that when the time comes (but not before!) we may go to him with love, trust, and joy. But, to put it plainly, for a man in his wife's arms to be hankering after the other world is, in mild terms, a piece of bad taste, and not God's will. We ought to find and love God in what he actually gives us; if it pleases him to allow us to enjoy some overwhelming earthly happiness, we mustn't try to be more pious than God himself.... God will see to it that the man who finds him in his earthly happiness and thanks him for it does not lack reminder that earthly things are transient, that it is good for him to attune his heart to what is eternal, and that sooner or later there will be times when he can say in all sincerity, "I wish I were home." But everything has its time, and the main thing is that we keep step with God, and do not keep pressing on a few steps ahead—nor keep dawdling a step behind. It's presumptuous to want to have everything at once—matrimonial bliss, the cross, and the heavenly Jerusalem.[65]

Bonhoeffer sees life now as ordered by God through institutions that give it shape, that give it guidance toward the good and protection against evil:

The commandment of God revealed in Jesus Christ embraces in its unity all of human life. Its claim on human beings and the world through the reconciling

---

62. Ibid., 187–88.

63. Quoted in Bethge, *Dietrich Bonhoeffer,* 114.

64. Bonhoeffer did not finish this section, but he had planned complementary reflections on "the natural rights of the life of the mind" and "the natural right to work and property" (see Bethge, "Editor's Note," 184 n. 22).

65. Bonhoeffer, *Letters,* 168–69.

love of God is all encompassing. This commandment encounters us in four different forms that find their unity only in the commandment itself, namely, in the church, marriage and family, culture and government.[66]

These institutions are not to be at odds, as they often are:

Only insofar as church, family, work, and government mutually limit each other, insofar as each is beside and together with the others, upholding the commandment of God each in its own way, are authorized to speak from above to speak. None of these authorities can identify itself alone with the commandment of God. The sovereignty of the commandment of God proves itself precisely in ordering these authorities in a relationship of being with each other, beside each other, together with each other, and over against each other so that the commandment of God as the commandment revealed in Jesus Christ is upheld only in these multifaceted concrete relationships and limitations.[67]

The Christian receives and participates in these institutions, therefore, as gifts of God, when they are functioning according to their divine mandate, as necessary structures of society under the Lordship of Christ.

Bonhoeffer is no utopian. He recognizes that the church is not perfect. He had been raised in the church (albeit in a family that was not particularly pious, disaffected with the church as many Germans were after the ecclesiastical jingoism of the First World War) and had pastored churches, including a stint as a youth worker—a form of ministry guaranteed to inculcate realism in any fledgling clergyperson. Then he had wrestled with the German Christians and finally even with the Confessing Church over fidelity to the gospel. He had enjoyed a loving family—by all accounts the Bonhoeffer clan was unusually affectionate and loyal—but had no illusions about family life, either. He was a well-educated young man, familiar with the culture of his day, and through his family was aware of the inner workings of government. Bonhoeffer knew that none of these institutions would provide sheer goodness and happiness.

Early on (in *Creation and Fall*), Bonhoeffer described these institutions as "orders of preservation," instituted by God *after* the Fall in the light of its implication that means were needed to promote good and particularly to restrain evil. He thus rejected the traditional Lutheran term "orders of creation," particularly

---

66. Bonhoeffer, *Ethics*, 388.
67. Ibid., 380–81.

because it was being used by contemporary theologians to justify war—and the Nazi regime—as if "what is, is good." Elsewhere he wrote that

> the danger of the argument [from "orders of creation"] lies in the fact that just about everything can be defended by it. One need only hold out something to be God-willed and God-created for it to be vindicated for ever, the division of man into nations, national struggles, war, class struggle, the exploitation of the weak by the strong, the cut-throat competition of economics. Nothing simpler than to describe all this—because it is there—as God-willed and therefore to sanction it....It is not realized in all seriousness that the world is fallen and that now sin prevails and that creation and sin are so bound up together that no human eye can any longer separate the one from the other.[68]

In *Creation and Fall,* Bonhoeffer also draws this clear line to separate the pronouncement of "very good" in Genesis 1 from what emerges in God's providence to order human life after the Fall—he exposits these "orders" in his discussion of God providing cloaks of skin for the fallen Adam and Eve at their expulsion from Eden.[69] And these "orders of preservation," he argues, "find their end and meaning only through Christ"—indeed, "all orders of our fallen world are God's orders of preservation that uphold and preserve us for Christ."[70] He put it elsewhere as a question: "Which orders can best restrain this radical falling of the world into death and sin and hold the way open for the gospel?"[71]

My sense is that Bonhoeffer posits here an understanding of the orders that is more focused on (eventual) salvation in Christ than what is implied in "orders of creation," yes, but also more than what he later teaches as "divine mandates" in the *Ethics.* The "orders of preservation" as such are only temporary measures, intrinsic neither to creation nor to the world to come. As such, they are particularly open to Christ's supervention at any time—and therefore to the disciple's contravention under Christ's command.

Bonhoeffer's later terminology of "divine mandates," however, seems to nudge the theological balance between creation and redemption back toward creation, resulting in what we might call "redeemed and redeeming" versions of the

---

68. Dietrich Bonhoeffer, "A Theological Basis for the World Alliance," in *Dietrich Bonhoeffer: Witness to Jesus Christ,* 104–5.

69. Bonhoeffer, *Creation and Fall,* 139–40.

70. Ibid., 140.

71. Bonhoeffer, "A Theological Basis for the World Alliance," 106.

"orders of creation": structures that God ordains not merely to preserve us until Christ returns, but also to bless us in the meanwhile and to prepare us for that return. For that return will entail not the mere discarding of these orders but the fulfillment of them, as current family life and government, for example, are taken up into the one people of God under the direct Lordship of Christ.[72] Drawing together several of his key themes, Bonhoeffer defines "mandate" as follows:

> The concrete divine commission grounded in the revelation of Christ and the testimony of scripture; it is the authorization and legitimization to declare a particular divine commandment, the conferring of divine authority on an earthly institution. A mandate is to be understood simultaneously as the laying claim to, commandeering of, and formation of a certain earthly domain by the divine command. The bearer of the mandate acts as a vicarious representative, as a stand-in for the one who issued the commission. Understood properly, one could also use the term "order" here, if only the concept did not contain the inherent danger of focusing more strongly on the static element of order rather than on the divine authorizing, legitimizing, and sanctioning, which are its sole foundation. This then leads all too easily to a divine sanctioning of all existing orders per se, and thus to a romantic conservatism that no longer has anything to do with the Christian doctrine of the four mandates.[73]

Bonhoeffer thus distinguishes between the life we now live as ordered by these institutions and the life to come in which Christ's Lordship is direct and unimpeded. Yet he also sees that this life, what he calls the "penultimate," is also given shape by, judged by, and inspired by the life to come, what he calls the "ultimate."[74] He therefore eschews both radicalism, which despises the penultimate, and capitulative compromise, which despairs of the ultimate.[75] Instead, he recommends

---

72. Bonhoeffer, *Ethics*, 68–75.

73. Ibid., 389.

74. Dietrich Bonhoeffer, "Ultimate and Penultimate Things," in *Ethics*, 146–70.

75. We must not elide important differences in Bonhoeffer's writing, even in this brief discussion. *Discipleship* is a radical book on just this theme: "Christians are to remain in the world, not because of the God-given goodness of the world, nor even because of their responsibility for the course the world takes. They are to remain in the world solely for the sake of the body of the Christ who became incarnate—for the sake of the church-community. They are to remain in the world to engage the world in a frontal assault. Let them 'live out their vocation in this world' in order that their 'unworldliness' might become fully visible" (244; see both the passages preceding, exposing Romans 13 in a virtually Anabaptist mode, and also those following, particularly those invoking Luther).

the way of Christ, which means traveling through the world, doing what one can in the world, and confronting the world—informed and encouraged by the Christian Story (creation, Fall, redemption, and consummation) and especially by the story of Christ.[76] These stories, of course, have at their heart the divine project of redemption, and thus we live in the penultimate with the ultimate ever in view.[77] Bonhoeffer makes this clear:

In the *Ethics,* Bonhoeffer seems to rework this very passage of *Discipleship* to say something similar, but also importantly modified: "People do not fulfill the responsibility laid on them by faithfully performing their earthly vocational obligations as citizens, workers, and parents, but by hearing the call of Jesus Christ that, although it leads them also into earthly obligations, is never synonymous with these, but instead always transcends them as a reality standing before and behind them. Vocation in the New Testament sense is never a sanctioning of the worldly orders as such. Its Yes always includes at the same time its sharpest No, the sharpest protest against the world. Luther's return from the monastery into the world, into a 'vocation,' is, in the genuine spirit of the New Testament, the fiercest attack that has been launched and the hardest blow that has been struck against the world since the time of earliest Christianity. Now a stand against the world is taken *within* the world. Vocation is the place at which one responds to the call of Christ and thus lives responsibly. The task given to me by my vocation is thus limited; but my responsibility to the call of Jesus Christ knows no bounds" (290–91).

Bonhoeffer never repudiates *The Cost of Discipleship,* but at the end of his life he indicates that he has moved on from it: "I thought I could acquire faith by trying to live a holy life, or something like that. I suppose I wrote *The Cost of Discipleship* as the end of that path. Today I can see the dangers of that book, though I still stand by what I wrote" (*Letters,* 369). I think it is fair to say that when one considers this area of change, plus the agonized, emergency setting aside of pacifism to take up resistance to Hitler, Bonhoeffer moves from one stance to another in regard to life in the world—a movement from a version of "Christ against culture" to some version of "Christ in paradox with culture" or "Christ transforming culture." On the theme of the church keeping separate from the world, see "The Saints," in *Discipleship,* 253–80.

Larry Rasmussen comments, "In *The Cost of Discipleship* the key word is single-minded obedience....But in *Ethics* it is freedom, permission, liberty that are commanded. Bonhoeffer certainly does not drop obedience as a key term for Christian ethics, but...he now speaks of a real tension between obedience and freedom" (Larry L. Rasmussen, *Dietrich Bonhoeffer: Reality and Resistance* [Nashville: Abingdon, 1972], 50; quoted in de Gruchy, "Introduction," 34). This development dovetails with Bonhoeffer's increasing sense of the "world come of age" in his later writings. It might prompt one to think of *Discipleship* as a young man's book—full of sharp distinctions and clear instructions—and the later books as those of a man maturing into middle age who has found the world, and Christian discipleship, both more complicated than he had earlier thought and yet more simple: life still is about heeding the word of Jesus Christ, but one might not be able to predict what that word will be or be blithely certain of it when it comes.

76. Bonhoeffer, *Ethics,* 151–59.

77. Thus Bonhoeffer steers a course that both combines the emphases while avoiding the extremes of the this-worldly emphasis of his liberal professors, which so easily lent support to the German military regimes of kaiser and Führer, the transcendent emphasis of Barth, whose God revealed things only from the "outside" and not "within" history, and the experiential emphasis of his mother's Pietism, which tended to quietism and anti-intellectualism. It is a remarkable synthesis.

From this follows now something of decisive importance, that the penultimate must be preserved for the sake of the ultimate. Arbitrary destruction of the penultimate seriously harms the ultimate. When, for example, a human life is deprived of the conditions that are part of being human, the justification of such a life by grace and faith is at least seriously hindered, if not made impossible. Concretely stated, slaves who have been so deprived of control over their time that they can no longer hear the proclamation of God's word cannot be led by that word of God to a justifying faith.... Those who proclaim the word yet do not do everything possible so that this word may be heard are not true to the word's claim for free passage, for a smooth road. The way for the road must be prepared. The word itself demands it.[78]

Bonhoeffer lived this way. He thrived in the university world and paid close attention to politics. His life was characterized by active sports (he led his students on camping trips and enjoyed games) and music (classically trained, he thrilled to African American gospel and pop music when he encountered it in New York), and he enjoyed nature, food, and drink. Indeed, late in his young life and in a Nazi prison cell, he reflected on the four mandates as too constrictive:

Marriage, work, state, and church all have their definite, divine mandate; but what about culture and education? I don't think they can just be classified under work....

They belong, not to the sphere of obedience, but to the broad area of freedom, which surrounds all three spheres of the divine mandates. The man who is ignorant of this area of freedom may be a good father, citizen, and worker, indeed even a Christian; but I doubt whether he is a complete man and therefore a Christian in the widest sense of the term....I wonder whether it is possible (it almost seems so today) to regain the idea of the church as providing an understanding of the area of freedom (art, education, friendship, play), so that Kierkegaard's "aesthetic existence" would not be banished from the church's sphere, but would be re-established within it? ... Who is there, for instance, in our times, who can devote himself with an easy mind to music, friendship, games, or happiness? Surely not the "ethical" man, but only the Christian.[79]

---

78. Bonhoeffer, *Ethics*, 160.
79. Bonhoeffer, *Letters,* 192–93.

Even in prison, Bonhoeffer did not read and think theology all the time, but instead read a considerable number of histories and novels—although he never compartmentalized his theological ruminations: "One often learns more about ethics from such books as these than from textbooks," he wrote to his parents.[80] And, despite his reputation for an "aloof " and even "aristocratic" demeanor, he relished life best in company, where he proved himself a warm and generous friend or relative over and over. Indeed, Bonhoeffer rejoiced in his family, throughout its own multiple living generations and through marriage with others: he seems to have delighted in his in-laws. And when romantic love finally blossomed for him in his thirties, this brilliant theologian and self-disciplined pastor did not spiritualize it, but embraced it all, as even his published letters make clear.[81] Yet he never ignored the limitation and sin in himself, in others, or in the world, and, in the truly *ultimate* test, was willing to let go of this world in hope of the world to come.

Religionless Christianity

Bonhoeffer's *Letters and Papers from Prison* has been mined by all sorts of Christian thinkers because its provocative suggestions are vulnerably offered in these small packets (letters and papers), rather than being both restrained and solidified within a coherently framed whole. Thus even death-of-God theologians have invoked Bonhoeffer's famous call for "religionless Christianity," as if he meant anything like what they meant—which he didn't.[82]

So what did Bonhoeffer mean by "religionless Christianity"? To begin, we should ask what religion is, and how has it failed.

---

80. Ibid., 88. Indeed, Larry Rasmussen suggests that Bonhoeffer's reading in what he calls various forms of "cultural criticism" suggests that Bonhoeffer "senses a crisis in civilization centuries deep" (Larry Rasmussen, "The Ethics of Responsible Action," in *The Cambridge Companion to Dietrich Bonhoeffer,* ed. John W. de Gruchy [Cambridge, UK: Cambridge University Press, 1999], 215).

81. Dietrich Bonhoeffer, *Love Letters from Cell 92: The Correspondence Between Dietrich Bonhoeffer and Maria von Wedemeyer,* ed. Ruth-Alice von Bismarck and Ulrich Kabitz (Nashville, TN: Abingdon, 1992). He also wrote to his fiancée after a prison visit: "Our marriage shall be a yes to God's earth; it shall strengthen our courage to act and accomplish something on the earth. I fear that Christians who stand with only one leg upon earth also stand with only one leg in heaven" (*Letters*, 415).

82. For a helpful account, see John W. de Gruchy, "The Reception of Bonhoeffer's Theology," in *Cambridge Companion,* ed. de Gruchy, 93–109. Peter Selby puts the matter eloquently: "This apostle of secular Christianity turns out to be remarkably attached to its central doctrinal inheritance; this protagonist of what came to be celebrated as 'religionless Christianity' is clearly immersed in a tradition of piety and devotion from which he derived enormous sustenance and which echoes with the sounds of a lifetime's spiritual formation; this determined

Religion for Bonhoeffer meant at least two things that overlapped in his experience. Sociologically speaking, religion was the condition of official, mainstream German Christianity by the turn of the twentieth century. Christianity had been reduced to a birthright of Germans, an identity and ethic that had themselves been reduced to nationalism, convention, perhaps some personal spiritual experience, and communal solidarity. Such religion was what was necessary to be a good German, and all that was necessary to be a good Christian.

Theologically speaking, according to Bonhoeffer's liberal teachers, religion was the general quest for, apprehension of, and response to the divine among human beings around the world (sometimes termed the "religious a priori," meaning a kind of religious given) that was then thematized and formalized in the various world religions. Thus the teachings of Christianity were simply a particular culture's way of articulating and practicing the timeless and universal truths that were also, if differently, articulated and practiced by Hindus, Muslims, or Daoists.

In the face of this doubly "automatic" and circumscribed religion, Bonhoeffer called for a Christianity—note that he retains this term for what he wants because it is a term that places Christ at the center—that was freed of religion. For he had seen religion implicated with what we might call the "old regime" of German culture, a subjugated religion that had resulted in acquiescence, servitude, and even willing collaboration with a militarist Wilhelmine regime, a desperately confused Weimar interregnum, and then a diabolical Nazi Reich.

The series of disasters that had befallen Germany—and all of Europe—in the three decades since 1914 had definitively shown such religion to be both unintelligible and irrelevant to the "common man." Decent, ordinary people, we might hear Bonhoeffer say, have seen through the sham and will be satisfied only with clarity, radical authenticity, and usefulness in building a good life—and, indeed, in rebuilding after the war. Such people will want a Christianity that works in the real world, a "secular" or "worldly" Christianity that neither surrenders to evil in this world nor merely waits for the good of the next. And Bonhoeffer already made clear in his *Ethics* that Christ himself unites what is

---

advocate of human autonomy and secular strength is constantly searching for the way of obedience to Christ's claim upon his life; and Bonhoeffer the disciple determined to share the fate of God who suffers at the hands of a godless world shows no sign of the disdain for life and its beauty and delight which sometimes characterizes those willing to suffer and die for their faith" ("Christianity in a World Come of Age," in *Cambridge Companion*, ed. de Gruchy, 228).

"secular" and what is "Christian" into the one world over which he reigns.[83] Thus he writes,

> Our whole nineteen-hundred-year-old Christian preaching and theology rest on the "religious a priori" of mankind.... But if one day it becomes clear that this a priori does not exist at all, but was a historically conditioned and transient form of human self-expression, and if therefore man becomes radically religionless—and I think that that is already more or less the case (else how is it, for example, that this war, in contrast to all previous ones, is not calling forth any "religious" reaction?)—what does that mean for Christianity?... How can Christ become the Lord of the religionless as well? ...
>
> ... What do a church, a community, a sermon, a liturgy, a Christian life mean in a religionless world? How do we speak of God—without religion, i.e., without the temporally conditioned presuppositions of metaphysics, inwardness, and so on? How do we speak ... in a "secular" way about "God"? In what way are we "religionless-secular" Christians, in what way are we the ἐκ-κλησία, those who are called forth, not regarding ourselves from a religious point of view as specially favoured, but rather as belonging wholly to the world? In that case Christ is no longer an object of religion, but something quite different, really the Lord of the world. But what does that mean?[84]

Bonhoeffer pushes his concepts and language to the limit as he muses late in his life about living in the world as if God doesn't exist—*etsi deus non daretur.* In this reflection Bonhoeffer is, I think, returning to his theme of living fully in the world and for the world, under God. "God himself compels us to recognize it."[85] And we are to live as God has lived among us, as suffering with and for the world, not as rescuers of the world who can immediately solve all of its problems and relieve all of its agonies:

> Here is the decisive difference between Christianity and all religions. Man's religiosity makes him look in his distress to the power of God in the world:

---

83. "Because in Jesus Christ God and humanity became one in the action of the Christian. They are not opposed to each other like two eternally hostile principles. Instead, the action of the Christian springs from the unity between God and the world, and the unity of life that have been created in Christ" (Bonhoeffer, *Ethics,* 253).

84. Bonhoeffer, *Letters,* 280–81.

85. Ibid., 360.

God is the *deus ex machina*. The Bible directs man to God's powerlessness and suffering; only the suffering God can help.[86]

Thus we can understand Bonhoeffer's famous dictum: "Before God and with God we live without God."[87] We live without the God that most people want in their religion, a deity who answers their questions, soothes their anxieties, and guarantees their well-being.[88] Instead, we are to live fully in the world that the true God has made according to the way that he has made it and according to the way it has fallen. Thus we suffer along with God, yes, but suffering as God does: in the knowledge that such work is not in vain but is right and good and effective, and with the certain hope of the eventual redemption of the world. To interpret Bonhoeffer, as the death-of-God theologians and other extremists have done, as despairing of orthodox faith and moving into some weird zone of secularity in which God simply *is* the world, is to posit a total break in Bonhoeffer's thought in the last couple of years of his life. It is more plausible to see instead these provocative speculations as emerging out of what he had written clearly before and into the as-yet-unseen world of postwar Europe and its needs.

What, then, is Christianity in this new/old mode? It is, as ever, discipleship to Jesus. It focuses upon Jesus and his Word.[89] It is a community of worship, fellowship, and mission. It is proclamation of Christ as the center, and service radiating out to all: family, neighbors, society, the state, and the rest of the world,

---

86. Bonhoeffer, *Letters*, 361.

87. Ibid., 360.

88. Bonhoeffer later writes: "The God of Jesus Christ has nothing to do with what God, as we imagine him, could do and ought to do. If we are to learn what God promises, and what he fulfils, we must persevere in quiet meditation on the life, sayings, deeds, sufferings, and death of Jesus" (*Letters*, 391). Peter Selby observes that Bonhoeffer's declarations about this life "without God" comes after a brief survey of intellectual history that concludes with Grotius's positing of law "as if God were not a given" ("Christianity in a World Come of Age," 235). All "automatic" conceptions of God, as we have seen in other contexts, Bonhoeffer repels.

89. And by "his Word" Bonhoeffer meant not only the Gospels, nor even just the New Testament, but the whole Bible—contrary to the various forms of prejudice against the Old Testament that mark German liberal theology at least as far back as Reimarus. As late as December 1943, Bonhoeffer tells his friend Bethge that "my thoughts and feelings seem to be getting more and more like those of the Old Testament, and in recent months I have been reading the Old Testament much more than the New. It is only when one knows the unutterability of the name of God that one can utter the name of Jesus Christ" (*Letters*, 156–57). John de Gruchy points out that Bonhoeffer's convictions about "the 'worldliness' of Christianity in a 'world come of age' is also rooted in his understanding that the New Testament must be read in the light of the Old" ("Editor's Introduction," 10; see Bonhoeffer, *Letters*, 282).

although Bonhoeffer says little about ministry beyond Germany.[90] And it is about undertaking the responsibility to live in this world as faithfully as one can—about which Bonhoeffer had much more to say, as we shall now see.

Ambiguity, Paradox, and Responsibility

The world is deeply troubled. And it is troubled in ways that defy easy analysis, let alone solution. The church needs to recognize these facts soberly and modestly:

> If one implies that Christianity has an answer to *all* social and political questions of the world, so that one would only have to listen to these answers to put the world in order, then this is obviously wrong....
>
> Jesus is hardly ever involved in solving worldly problems....Since Jesus brings the redemption of human beings, rather than the solution to problems, he indeed brings the solution to all human problems....
>
> Who actually says that all worldly problems should and can be solved? Perhaps to God the unsolved condition of these problems may be more important than their solution, namely, as a pointer to the human fall and to God's redemption. Human problems are perhaps so entangled, so wrongly posed, that they are in fact really impossible to solve.[91]

Paradox, irony, and obscurity recur in Bonhoeffer's account of things. He reflects on Luther's own career on 31 October 1943, in his prison cell at Tegel:

> Today is Reformation Day, a feast that in our time can give one plenty to think about. One wonders why Luther's action had to be followed by consequences that were the exact opposite of what he intended, and that darkened the last years of his life, so that he sometimes even doubted the value of his life's work. He wanted a real unity of the church and the West—that is, of the Christian peoples, and the

---

90. Thus Bonhoeffer refers to Jesus as "the man for others" and declares that "the church is the church only when it exists for others" (*Letters*, 382). Indeed, he offers these recommendations to the church—the state-funded, state-sanctioned church of his heritage: "To make a start, it should give away all its property to those in need. The clergy must live solely on the free-will offerings of their congregations, or possibly engage in some secular calling. The church must share in the secular problems of ordinary human life, not dominating, but helping and serving. ... It must not underestimate the importance of human example (which has its origin in the humanity of Jesus and is so important in Paul's teaching); it is not abstract argument, but example, that gives its word emphasis and power" (ibid., 382–83).

91. Bonhoeffer, *Ethics*, 354–55.

consequence was the disintegration of the church and of Europe; he wanted the "freedom of the Christian man," and the consequence was indifference and licentiousness; he wanted the establishment of a genuine secular social order free from clerical privilege, and the result was insurrection, the Peasant's War, and soon afterwards the gradual dissolution of all real cohesion and order in society.[92]

Bonhoeffer recognizes that a fundamental ambivalence marks the Christian life itself, in an extended reflection on the simultaneous "yes" and "no" of discipleship:

> The No spoken over our fallen life means that it cannot become the life that is Jesus Christ without its own end, annihilation, and death. The No that we hear brings about this death. However, by killing us, the No becomes a hidden Yes to a new life, to the life that is Jesus Christ.[93]

The world, therefore, is "loved, judged, and reconciled by God," and "is thus the *domain of concrete responsibility* that is given to us in and through Jesus Christ."[94] In this world, in which we live out a "yes" and a "no" that are unified in discipleship to Jesus, we thus take on our role as "deputies" of his, working with him in his extraordinary work of salvation.[95]

The world is misshapen by evil, broadly and profoundly. It is so marked, in fact, that as we follow Christ over this tortured terrain, we may encounter ethical choices that include no option that is both obvious and pure—no "straight paths."[96] God's ways themselves are transcendent and therefore not always, or even often, apparent to us—indeed, they can appear evil to us. Thus we must be careful what lessons we draw from the Biblical narrative and from our experience of God's providence, recognizing that even with great care we may well

---

92. Bonhoeffer, *Letters*, 123.

93. Bonhoeffer, *Ethics*, 251.

94. Ibid., 267.

95. The term "deputy" comes from Bonhoeffer, *Ethics*, 257–60. It is a perhaps too-terse rendering of a key term for Bonhoeffer, "*Stellvertretung*," which means "responsible action on behalf of [literally in the place of] others," and which characterizes the ministry of Christ himself. The more recent Fortress Press edition uses "vicarious representative action" instead of "deputyship" and the like.

96. "Responsible human beings, who stand between obligation [*Bindung*] and freedom and who, while bound, must nevertheless dare to act freely, find justification neither by their bond nor by their freedom, but only in the One who has placed them in this—humanly impossible—situation and who requires them to act. Responsible human beings surrender themselves and their action to God" (Bonhoeffer, *Ethics*, 288).

mistake what it is we are to conclude and then do. Bonhoeffer speaks to this ambiguity in his *Ethics*:

It is now necessary to actually discern what the will of God may be, what might be right in the given situation, what may please God; for one must, of course, live and act concretely. Intellect, cognitive ability, and attentive perception of the context come into lively play here. All of this discerning will be encompassed and pervaded by the commandment. Prior experiences will raise encouraging or cautionary notes. Under no circumstances must one count on or wait for unmediated inspirations, lest all too easily one fall prey to self-deception. Given the matter at hand, an intensely sober attitude will govern the discerning. Possibilities and consequences will be considered carefully. In short, in order to discern what the will of God may be, the entire array of human abilities will be employed. But in all of this there will be no place for the torment of being confronted with insoluble conflicts, nor the arrogance of being able to master any conflict, nor also the enthusiastic [*schwärmerisch*] expectation and claim of direct inspirations. There will be faith that, to those who humbly ask, God will surely make the divine will known. And then, after all such serious discernment there will also be freedom to make a real decision; in this freedom there will be confidence that it is not the human but the divine will that is accomplished through such discernment. The anxiety about whether one has done the right thing will turn neither into a desperate clinging to one's own good, nor into the certainty of knowing about good and evil. Instead, it will be overcome in the knowledge of Jesus Christ, who alone exercises gracious judgment; this will allow one's goodness to remain hidden in the knowledge and grace of the judge until the proper time.[97]

All we can do, therefore, and what we must do, therefore, is to discern our responsibility as best we can and then fulfill it.[98] We do so, as Bonhoeffer put it in a poem, with "sorrow and joy."[99] And this is true not only of individual Christians

---

97. Ibid., 323–24.

98. "Responsible action renounces any knowledge about is ultimate justification. The deed that is done after responsibly weighing all personal and factual circumstances, light of God becoming *human* and *God* becoming human, is completely surrendered to God the moment it is carried out. Ultimate ignorance is one's own goodness or evil, together with dependence upon grace, is an essential characteristic of responsible historical action. Those who act on the basis of ideology consider themselves justified by their idea. Those who act responsibly place their action into the hands of God and live by God's grace and judgment" (ibid., 268–69; emphasis in original).

99. Bonhoeffer, *Letters*, 334–35.

but of churches as well. Bonhoeffer has in mind, of course, the German church of his day and its widespread capitulation to German nationalism, if not National Socialism itself. (Indeed, it is instructive for us to recall that many Germans were not convinced Nazis but were convinced nationalists, and thus cooperated with the regime in power. Bonhoeffer recalls that "the very neutrality [note: not the outright idolatry] of many Christians was the gravest danger that would lead to the disintegration and dissolution of the church, indeed, that it was essentially hostility toward Christ.")[100] Thus Bonhoeffer calls the church to freedom from all such secondary and intermediate, if not actually perverted, loyalties. Christ places us in the world and thus in a variety of institutional contexts in order to glorify him, not to forget him and make idols of those institutions—nor even merely to cooperate with them. The Church in general, and churches in particular, are free to follow Christ, and are commanded to do so—whatever be the commands of principalities and powers.

Again, this freedom is not freedom to make up one's own mind as to what is best: it is not "situational ethics" (*pace* John A. T. Robinson's *Honest to God,* which has done much to confuse people as to Bonhoeffer's views).[101] It is freedom to listen to Christ's word and then to do it. Indeed, the German word for responsibility, *Verantwortlichkeit,* means "answerability": to answer the address of someone else, in this case, the Lord Christ.[102] Bonhoeffer himself warns us against any individualistic freedom that fails to be true discipleship:

> Those, however, who take their stand in the world in their *very own free-dom,* who value the necessary action more highly than their own untarnished conscience and reputation, who are prepared to sacrifice a barren principle to a fruitful compromise or a barren wisdom of the middle way to a fruitful radicalism, should take heed lest precisely their presumed freedom ultimately cause them to fall. They will easily consent to the bad, knowing full well that it is bad, in order to prevent the worse, and no longer be able to recognize that precisely the worse choice they wish to avoid may be the better one. Here lies the raw material of tragedy.[103]

100. Bonhoeffer, *Ethics,* 343.

101. John A. T. Robinson, *Honest to God* (Philadelphia: Westminster, 1963).

102. Clifford Green, "Human Sociality and Christian Community," in *Cambridge Companion,* ed. de Gruchy, 115–16.

103. Bonhoeffer, *Ethics,* 79–80. Bonhoeffer later explains this fatal confusion: "The essence of Greek tragedy is that human beings are destroyed by the clash of incompatible laws" (ibid., 264).

All the while we are trying to follow Christ, then, we will recognize the concomitant realities—realities that will discomfit not only pacifists (as Bonhoeffer formerly was himself) but all conscientious Christians:

- We will never fulfill our responsibility perfectly, but will surely fall short.[104]

- We may have to undertake duties that are not recognized or undertaken by others—indeed, we must decide as individuals about our vocation.[105]

- Our responsibility may lie in undertaking what is apparently, and what would normally be, evil in order that good may come, versus maintaining an immature hope that God will rescue us from our responsibility to work alongside him in the real world.[106]

- We must therefore confess our sins—even before we commit them, even as we intend to commit them for God's glory and our neighbor's good. The paradox here is that "responsible action involves both *willingness to become guilty* [*Bereitschaft zur Schuldübernahme*] and *freedom*."[107]

To be sure, the immediate context from which this last quotation comes is murky. Its main point seems to be to call us to solidarity with our fellow (guilty) human beings just as Christ, the sinless one, took on our guilt—which isn't the point I am making here and isn't always the point Bonhoeffer makes about incurring guilt. Yet it seems to me consistent with Bonhoeffer's thought on these quite paradoxical and difficult matters to say what I have said, namely, that Bonhoeffer affirms that the free Christian, in extraordinary circumstances, properly does something that is, by normal standards, wrong because it yet is God's will in that (highly abnormal) moment. Indeed, only a few pages later in the same chapter

---

104. Even in the demanding context of *Discipleship,* Bonhoeffer concludes: "We journey under God's grace, we walk in God's commandments, and we sin" (279). In his *Letters,* he strikes a somewhat more positive note, with a trace of wry humor: "I believe that even our mistakes and shortcomings are turned to good account, and that it is no harder for God to deal with them than with our supposedly good deeds" (11).

105. "Jesus' call to discipleship makes the disciple into a single individual. Whether disciples want to or not, they have to make a decision; each has to decide alone. It is not their own choice to desire to be single individuals. Instead, Christ makes everyone he calls into an individual. Each is called alone. Each must follow alone" (Bonhoeffer, *Discipleship,* 92).

106. "The world *is,* in fact, so ordered that a basic respect for ultimate laws and human life is also the best means of self-preservation, and that these laws may be broken only on the odd occasion in case of brief necessity" (Bonhoeffer, *Letters,* 11).

107. Bonhoeffer, *Ethics,* 275.

Bonhoeffer takes up Kant's scenario of a murderer who breaks into one's house and asks whether one is sheltering a friend whom the murderer is hunting. Bonhoeffer writes,

> Responsibility is the entire response, in accord with reality, to the claim of God and my neighbor, then this scenario glaringly illuminates the merely partial response of a conscience bound by principles. I come into conflict with my responsibility that is grounded in reality when I refuse to become guilty of violating the principle of truthfulness for the sake of my friend, refusing in this case to lie energetically for the sake of my friend—and any attempt to deny that we are indeed dealing with lying here is once again the work of a legalistic and self-righteous conscience—refusing, on other words, to take on and bear guilt out of love for my neighbor. Here, as well, a conscience bound to Christ alone will most clearly exhibit its innocence precisely in responsibly accepting culpability.[108]

This paradoxical, dialectical ethic concludes thus: "Those who act out of free responsibility are justified before others by dire necessity; before themselves they are acquitted by their conscience, but before God they hope only for grace."[109]

I am not sure why Bonhoeffer feels such a person needs mercy from God, since he is doing what he understands God's will to be. Indeed, Bonhoeffer writes that "those who act in the freedom of their very own responsibility see their activity as flowing into God's guidance. Free action recognizes itself ultimately as being God's action, decision as God's guidance, the venture as divine necessity."[110] I conclude that Bonhoeffer is acknowledging the deep ambivalence of some of our actions in obedience to Christ: things that are in themselves not good (such as the infliction of suffering or death on another or on ourselves), which count as *objective* sin in the Biblical sense of deviating from what would normally be good according to God's general commands, but that also are, in the particular circumstances, the right things to do as they are God's will in that moment—and thus not what we would call *subjective* sin. And he invokes Christ's Lordship over the law to set the disciple free from the law to do what must be done:

---

108. Ibid., 280.
109. Ibid., 282–83.
110. Ibid., 284.

For the sake of God and neighbor, which means for the Christ's sake, one may be freed from keeping the Sabbath holy, honoring one's parents, indeed from the entire divine law. It is a freedom that transgresses this law, but only in order to affirm it anew. The suspension of the law must only serve its true fulfillment. In war, for example, there is killing, lying, and seizing of property. Breaking the law must be *recognized* in all its gravity.... Whether an action springs from responsibility or cynicism can become evident only in whether the objective guilt one incurs by breaking the law is recognized and borne, and whether by the very act of breaking it the law is truly sanctified. The will of God is thus sanctified in the deed that arises out of freedom. Precisely because we are dealing with a deed that arises from freedom, the one who acts is not torn apart by destructive conflict, but instead can with confidence and inner integrity do the unspeakable, namely, in the very act of breaking the law to sanctify it.[111]

It seems to me, then, that in this ethical reflection Bonhoeffer has retained the emphasis upon discipleship from his earlier writings, but he also has moved well beyond the model of discipleship as simple obedience to Christ's commandments he advocates particularly in *Discipleship*. He moves beyond what sometimes appears to be a "look it up in the Book and do it" model—what I would call a Torah-like approach—to an appreciation of the ambiguity and paradox of Christian faithfulness that sounds more like the Wisdom literature of the Bible. Bonhoeffer thus sees the Christian individual and, indeed, the Christian church as guided by Biblical law, yes, but as a resource for producing wisdom—which is always about determining and obeying what God says *right now*. Indeed, the simplicity Bonhoeffer emphasizes over against endless ethical deliberation is one of hearing *and then doing*. Thus Bonhoeffer offers finally what I would see to be an existentialist mode of ethics, as long as it is understood to be a fundamentally Christian—literally, Christ-focused—existentialism.

I must note that Bonhoeffer's typical failure to mention the Holy Spirit—typical of him but also typical of his theological tradition at the time—is crucial here. For without a strong and articulate sense of the Holy Spirit's immediate guidance, Bonhoeffer's view of Christian discipleship remains vague precisely where it most needs to be clear. If we are not to follow merely the Bible, or tradition, or conscience, or high ideals, or whatever—and, as I shall note in the next paragraph, Bonhoeffer ruthlessly strips us of any or all of these if they substitute for the governing mode of personal obedience to Jesus Christ—then is the Christian simply to decide on

---

111. Bonhoeffer, *Ethics,* 297.

some sort of cumulative basis what Christ's will is in any given situation? Or can he expect immediate guidance by the Holy Spirit to direct him to Christ's will? I think Bonhoeffer settles for the former; I think it is all that is available to him in his theological context, and one also detects a revulsion toward "enthusiasm" and "inspirations" (typical of Luther himself) in Bonhoeffer's comments quoted above. Thus he really must venture into the darkness of the uncertain future and trust God's mercy upon his best guess as to how to follow Jesus in this situation. Those Christians with a more vivid sense of the Holy Spirit's work among us might well agree with everything Bonhoeffer recommends and then rejoice in the additional confidence—although not, to be sure, a strict epistemic certainty—that comes from trusting God's Spirit precisely in this existential moment of decision.[112]

Bonhoeffer's wrestling theologically and practically with the Nazi horror produced these difficult conclusions—difficult to sort out intellectually, and especially difficult to perform. Yet after cataloguing the failures of a wide range of Christian alternatives—reasonable people, moral fanatics, those following (mere) conscience, those doing their duty to superiors, those who assert freedom, and those of private virtuousness—Bonhoeffer concludes,

> Who stands fast? Only the man whose final standard is not his reason, his principles, his conscience, his freedom, or his virtue, but who is ready to sacrifice all this when he is called to obedient and responsible action in faith and in exclusive allegiance to God—the responsible man, who tries to make his whole life an answer to the question and call of God....
>
> Free responsibility...depends on a God who demands responsible action in a bold venture of faith, and who promises forgiveness and consolation to the man who becomes a sinner in that venture....
>
> The ultimate question for a responsible man to ask is not how he is to extricate himself heroically from the affair, but how the coming generation is to live.[113]

Looking to the Future in Realism and Hope

Bonhoeffer thus maintained that he and his fellow Christians must not only focus on resolving the current crisis and alleviating their current distress but also build

---

112. John G. Stackhouse Jr., "Why Christians Should Abandon Certainty," in *Living in the LambLight: Christianity and Contemporary Challenges to the Gospel,* ed. Hans Boersma (Vancouver: Regent College Publishing, 2001), 33–42.

113. Bonhoeffer, *Letters,* 5–7.

for the future on behalf of those who would succeed them: "living every day as if it were our last, and yet living in faith and responsibility as though there were to be a great future."[114] And they were to do so with hope (what Bonhoeffer sometimes called "optimism," as in the next passage), for they were to undertake their duties in cooperation with God, who means well and does well:

> It is wiser to be pessimistic; it is a way of avoiding disappointment and ridicule, and so wise people condemn optimism. The essence of optimism is not its view of the present, but the fact that it is the inspiration of life and hope when others give in; it enables a man to hold his head high when everything seems to be going wrong; it gives him strength to sustain reverses and yet to claim the future for himself instead of abandoning it to his opponent. It is true that there is a silly, cowardly kind of optimism, which we must condemn. But the optimism that is will for the future should never be despised, even if it is proved wrong a hundred times; it is health and vitality, and the sick man has no business to impugn it. There are people who regard it as frivolous, and some Christians think it impious for anyone to hope and prepare for a better earthly future. They think that the meaning of present events is chaos, disorder, and catastrophe; and in resignation or pious escapism they surrendered all responsibility for reconstruction and for future generations. It may be that the day of judgment will dawn tomorrow; in that case, we shall gladly stop working for a better future. But not before.[115]

This work in the meanwhile, then, is encouraged by a clear vision of the future, a vision given by Christ's Word in the Bible:

> As long as the earth exists, Jesus will always be at the same time the Lord of all government and the head of the church-community, without government and church-community ever becoming one, But in the end there will be a holy city (polis) without a temple, for God and the Lamb will themselves be the temple (Revelation 21), and the citizens of this city will be believers from the community of Jesus in all the world, and God and the Lamb will exercise dominion in this city. In the heavenly polis, state and church will be one.[116]

---

114. Ibid., 15.
115. Ibid., 15–16.
116. Bonhoeffer, *Conspiracy and Imprisonment,* 512.

We can make sense, then, of Bonhoeffer's apparently contradictory assertion in his *Letters* that "what is above this world is, in the gospel, intended to exist *for* this world."[117] Bonhoeffer immediately makes clear that he doesn't mean "in the anthropocentric sense of liberal, mystic pietistic, ethical theology" that makes everything focus on our experience here and now, as if that is all that matters. Instead, we understand it "in the Biblical sense of the creation and of the incarnation, crucifixion, and resurrection of Jesus Christ."[118] By these latter references, I think Bonhoeffer is emphasizing the *one* Story of the Bible: one world, created by God, that fell into evil and has been redeemed by God through Jesus Christ. This world is the world there is, and that will be—albeit renewed (resurrected) in eternal life. Thus we must not neglect this world in honor of the next, for there is no "next" in distinction from this one: "With respect to its origin this indivisible whole is called 'creation.' With respect to its goal it is called the 'kingdom of God.'"[119] Thus what is "above"—that is, the blessings of heaven—is indeed given to us by grace "*for* this world."[120]

Direct Action

Bonhoeffer—the opponent of "cheap grace"—clearly believed that action was crucial to discipleship, not simply correctness of ideas and warmth of piety. This is a rather impressive conviction coming from a lifelong pastor and professor. In *Discipleship* Bonhoeffer makes this clear:

Not everyone who says it will enter the kingdom of heaven. The separation will even take place within the confessing community. The confession alone grants no claim on Jesus. On that day no persons can justify them-

---

117. Bonhoeffer, *Letters,* 286.

118. Ibid.

119. Bonhoeffer, *Ethics,* 53.

120. A later letter takes up this theme: "The difference between the Christian hope of resurrection and the mythological hope is that the former sends a man back to his life on earth in a wholly new way which is even more sharply defined than it is in the Old Testament. The Christian, unlike the devotees of the redemption myths, has no last line of escape available from earthly tasks and difficulties into the eternal, but like Christ himself ('My God, why hast thou forsaken me?'), he must drink the earthly cup to the dregs, and only in his doing so is the crucified and risen Lord with him, and he crucified and risen with Christ. This world must not be prematurely written off; in this the Old and New Testaments are at one. Redemption myths arise from human boundary-experiences, but Christ takes hold of a man at the center of his life" (Bonhoeffer, *Letters,* 336–37). And Bonhoeffer writes of "blessing" in the Bible as "the intermediate theological category between God and human fortune" in a late letter to Bethge (374).

selves on the basis of their confession. Being members of the church of the true confession is nothing we can claim before God. Our confession will not save us. If we think it will, then we commit Israel's sin of making the grace of our calling into a right before God. This is sin against the grace of the one who calls us. God will not ask us someday whether our confession was evangelical, but whether we did God's will. God will ask that of everyone, including us.[121]

In terms of action, then, we begin by noticing that Bonhoeffer did resist entering the political arena because he correctly recognized that such activity would limit his academic work. But he answered the call he heard to take a range of dramatic actions—many of them political—in a time of crisis for his country and his church.[122]

Despite his family's connections with German politicians, Bonhoeffer himself had little involvement in official politics. He certainly approved, however, of those who sought political and diplomatic solutions to the rising problem of Nazism in the 1930s. Furthermore, if "war is the continuation of politics by other means," as Clausewitz said, then Bonhoeffer fully engaged in politics by finally waging direct war against Hitler. One of his acquaintances testifies, "He used to say: it is not only my task to look after the victims of madmen who drive a motorcar in a crowded street, but to do all in my power to stop their driving at all."[123] And in his *Ethics* he poses a crucial question:

Is it the sole task of the church to exercise love within the given worldly orders, i.e., to animate them as far as possible with a new way of thinking, to compensate for hardships, to care for the victims of these orders, and to establish *within* the *church-community* its own new order; or does the church have a mission in regard to the given worldly orders themselves, in the sense of correction,

---

121. Bonhoeffer, *Discipleship*, 178–79.

122. Bonhoeffer writes to others, but he could also have been prophesying to himself:

All of the activity of the disciples is subject to the clear precept of their Lord. They are not left free to choose their own methods or adopt their own conception of the task. Their work is to be Christ-work, and therefore they are absolutely dependent on the will of Jesus. Happy are they whose duty is fixed by such a precept, and who are therefore free from the tyranny of their own ideas and calculations.

...The choice of field for their labours does not depend on their own impulses or inclinations, but on where they are sent. This makes it quite clear that it is not their own work they are doing, but God's. (*Letters*, 206)

123. G. Leibholz, "Memoir," in Bonhoeffer, *The Cost of Discipleship* (1995), 28.

improvement, that is, of working toward a new worldly order? I.e., is the church merely to pick up the victims, or must the church take hold of the spokes of the wheel itself?[124]

Bonhoeffer came to this latter conviction with some anguish. After all, he had earlier written the following in *Discipleship*:

> The overcoming of others now occurs by allowing their evil to run its course. The evil does not find what it is seeking, namely, resistance, and therewith, new evil which will inflame it even more. Evil will become powerless when it finds no opposing object, no resistance, but, instead is willingly borne and suffered. Evil meets an opponent for which it is not a match.[125]

Yet Bonhoeffer's Lutheran heritage of the "two kingdoms" seems evident in this same chapter (titled "Revenge") as he writes: "Nonresistance as a principle for secular life is godless destruction of the order of the world which God graciously preserves." And then, in language reminiscent of, say, John Howard Yoder, he continues, "But it is not a programmatic thinker who is speaking here. Rather, the one speaking here about overcoming evil with suffering is he who himself was overcome by evil on the cross and who emerged from that defeat as the conqueror and victor."[126] God and the world, so to speak, would have to restrain the evil in the world: Christians were to demonstrate an alternative ethic and be willing to tire and even exhaust evil by their non-resistance.

---

124. Bonhoeffer, *Conspiracy and Imprisonment*, 541. Lest anyone suspect Bonhoeffer of becoming a sort of neo-Calvinist, he writes: "Here one should note that this is not a matter of a 'Christian state' or 'Christian economy,' but rather of the just state, the just economy as a worldly order for the sake of Christ" (543; see also 509–10 and 521–24 on the state). He also suggests that the Church can render two kinds of service to the state and, indeed, to the economy: "*on the one hand,* it must declare as reprehensible, by the authority of the word of God, such economic attitudes or systems that clearly hinder faith in Christ, thereby drawing a negative boundary. *On the other hand,* it will not be able to make its positive contribution to a new order on the authority of the word of God, but merely on the authority of responsible counsel by Christian experts" (*Ethics*, 361). The more frequently quoted version of Bonhoeffer's last line in the quotation is as follows: "not just to bandage the victims under the wheel, but to put a spoke in the wheel itself"—an extraordinarily provocative image, especially when one considers that it occurs in Bonhoeffer's early paper "The Church and the Jewish Question," written in direct response to the Aryan Clause of 1933 (excerpted in *Dietrich Bonhoeffer: Witness to Jesus Christ*, 127).

125. Bonhoeffer, *Discipleship*, 133.

126. Ibid., 136.

Bonhoeffer thus was a pacifist for much of his adult life.[127] He also has been criticized, even by those who admire him, for saying too little about how a theologically grounded concern for peace, manifest especially in the ecumenical movement, would accomplish anything without actual political work, likely including alliances with other international peace movements, such as those centering on labor or, after his death, human rights. Bonhoeffer, unlike, say, Niebuhr, did not naturally think in terms of institutional politics—of banks and companies and political parties and armed forces—and so did not make any programmatic suggestions in this regard.[128]

Still, when it came time for him to decide about the most direct political action of all—tyrannicide—he agreed. He did so, to be sure, only with the strongly conflicted sense that this was the thing God wanted him to do and yet he was doing something evil for which he needed—and hoped for—forgiveness.

He joined the Abwehr (military intelligence) originally in order to assist surreptitiously in the rescue of Jews and also to engage in political and diplomatic work on behalf of his country. In particular, he tried to cultivate goodwill abroad to show that not all Germans were Nazis and thus to secure assurances from Britain that the Allies would not take advantage of a German coup d'état to devastate the whole German nation.

Bonhoeffer played this dangerous game fully. In 1940, upon the fall of France, Eberhard Bethge recalls an announcement being made in a café in a small German town. Everyone leapt to their feet, began singing, "Deutschland, Deutschland über alles," and raised their arms in the Nazi salute. To Bethge's perplexity, Bonhoeffer raised his arm as well, and then whispered to his friend, "Raise your arm! Are you crazy?" Afterward he said, "We shall have to run risks for very different things now, but not for that salute!" This kind of pragmatism, for Bonhoeffer, is what it meant to serve Christ in the real world.[129]

It is well known, of course, that he was aware of more than one plot to assassinate Hitler, but he played no large part in any of them. Once arrested as an agitator and as a suspected conspirator, however, he lied to the Gestapo in order to protect his fellow conspirators. When an escape plan for him was put into effect,

---

127. John de Gruchy, in his introduction to *Dietrich Bonhoeffer: Witness to Jesus Christ*, nuances this claim: "Whether Bonhoeffer was ever a strict pacifist is a matter of debate, but during the next few years [that is, the mid-1930s] he was as near to being one as really makes little difference" (12).

128. See Keith Clements, "Ecumenical Witness for Peace," in *Cambridge Companion,* ed. de Gruchy, 168–71.

129. Bethge, *Dietrich Bonhoeffer,* 681.

he refused to join it, for fear of imperiling others—particularly to protect them from Nazi reprisals. And he offered pastoral comfort and advice to his fellow inmates, and even some troubled guards. Bonhoeffer believed all of these actions to be of a piece. All of this was to follow Christ in particular circumstances, even when the way was murky and the options all unpalatable. Bonhoeffer refused to allow others to call him a martyr.[130] He recognized that he was not merely an innocent destroyed for his faith, but an active enemy of the Reich who was caught and killed. Yet, whatever one makes of his decisions and actions, he was indeed a martyr in the strict sense: he was a witness to what he believed about what it meant to follow Jesus Christ today.[131]

Less than a year before his death, he wrote to Bethge:

> Not only action, but also suffering is a way to freedom. In suffering, the deliverance consists in our being allowed to put the matter out of our own hands into God's hands. In this sense death is the crowning of human freedom. Whether the human deed is a matter of faith or not depends on whether we understand our suffering as an extension of our action and a completion of freedom. I think that is very important and very comforting.[132]

STATIONS ON THE WAY TO FREEDOM

As a disciple of the Word, words mattered to Bonhoeffer, both good and evil ones. He shared what good words he could in every medium available to him, which was quite a range: preaching, teaching, and writing (both popular and academic) theology and ethics, plus poetry, drama, fiction, letters, songs, and more.

Many themes in Bonhoeffer's thought and life come together, then, in one of his prose poems, and it offers us, in its four sequential meditations, a poignant summary of his legacy to all of us:

Self-Discipline

If you set out to seek freedom, you must learn before all things
Mastery over sense and soul, lest your wayward desirings

---

130. See ibid., 834, 931.

131. See Craig J. Slane, *Bonhoeffer as Martyr: Social Responsibility and Modern Christian Commitment* (Grand Rapids, MI: Brazos, 2004).

132. Bonhoeffer, *Letters,* 375.

Let your undisciplined members lead you now this way, now that way.
Chaste be your mind and your body, and subject to you and obedient,
Serving solely to seek their appointed goal and objective.
None learns the secret of freedom save only by way of control.

Action

Do and dare what is right, not swayed by the whim of the moment.
Bravely take hold of the real, not dallying now with what might be.
Not in the flight of ideas but only in action is freedom.
Make up your mind and come out into the tempest of living.
God's command is enough and your faith in him to sustain you.
Then at last freedom will welcome your spirit amid great rejoicing.

Suffering

See what a transformation! These hands so active and powerful
Now are tied, and alone and fainting, you see where your work ends.
Yet you are confident still, and gladly commit what is rightful
Into a stronger hand, and say that you are contented.
You were free [for] a moment of bliss, then you yielded your freedom
Into the hand of God, that he might perfect it in glory.

Death

Come now, highest of feasts on the way to freedom eternal,
Death, strike off the fetters, break down the walls that oppress us,
Our bedazzled soul and our ephemeral body,
That we may see at last the sight which here was not vouchsafed us.
Freedom, we sought you long in discipline, action, suffering.
Now as we die we see you and know you at last, face to face.[133]

---

133. Ibid., 370–71. I have substituted "for" for "from" in the original, which seems a likely typo-
graphical error.

PART III

MAKING THE BEST OF IT

It might seem rather laborious to trace ethical ideas through three successive thinkers, C. S. Lewis, Reinhold Niebuhr, and Dietrich Bonhoeffer. It might also seem precious to discuss the fine-tuning of H. Richard Niebuhr's typology. Why not simply present a "corrected" version of "Christ and culture"? Why not simply present a digest of Lewis, Niebuhr, and Bonhoeffer? Indeed, why not skip all of that entirely and present my own offering of ethical ideas straightaway?

I have chosen this less direct course partly because, while I do intend in what follows to conclude what I can as directly as I can, I fear coming to those conclusions too easily. My hope is that this exercise in tracing out the convictions of my eminent predecessors at even this relatively brief length will help us understand better the true character of their affirmations and help us avoid triggering our reflexes to overlook, repress, or misrepresent—even to ourselves, even without consciously intending to do so—any complex, odd, or even initially repellent thing they might say that we need to hear. I also frankly admire their ways of raising certain questions, setting out certain categories, and offering certain answers, so it is a pleasure to analyze these rich resources before I attempt to address some of the basic themes they bring into view.

These resources are sufficiently variegated, however, that it would be needlessly complicated, if not impossible, to construct a single, comprehensive framework of questions and answers from the foregoing to which I would then systematically connect my own reflections. So I shall not attempt to tie what follows to the preceding discussions at every point, or even at many. Instead, I trust that the previous expositions will have prepared us, each in its particular way, for the proposals that follow. (And readers interested in intellectual genealogy will see pretty plainly, I think, how I have been influenced by—and how I sometimes disagree with—Lewis, the Niebuhrs, Bonhoeffer, and others.)

Paying due regard to the variegation among the Niebuhrs, Lewis, and Bonhoeffer leads us to consider the more general danger of oversimplification in ethics. Such a danger looms large partly because ethics is a field of human thought and behavior that of necessity must be encodable in short, memorable phrases: proverbs, maxims, rules, and the like. If an idea is too complicated, it is too difficult to "carry" in one's mind or in the collective memory of a group. Thus we properly try to reduce ethical complexity to simplicity.

As Albert Einstein is supposed to have said, however, we should simplify as far as possible—and no farther. It is bad both in physics and in ethics to oversimplify. Reality is not *represented* properly, and therefore is not *understood* properly, and therefore is not *negotiated* properly. Arguments, bridges, relationships, and societies all collapse from oversimplification.

The history of ethics offers us numerous examples of dangerous oversimplification. We recall Clausewitz's affirmation, "War is the continuation of politics by other means." That phrase can serve to justify war as "merely" the continuation of politics. Ironically, to be sure, it could also work exactly oppositely to invalidate all politics because of its connection with war (which is now presumed to be evil). To select a more venerable example, "Thou shalt not kill" (Ex. 20:13) has been deployed against warfare, yes, but also against capital punishment, euthanasia, abortion, and meat eating. Between these examples from modern Europe and ancient Israel lie the Crusades, with their self-justifying invocation of Jeremiah 48:10: "Cursed is he who keeps back his sword from bloodshed." Indeed, the Crusades give us perhaps the most simple and awesome simplification in Western ethics: *deus vult,* "God wills it!"

If the menace looms of reducing reality to a thin residuum by oversimplification, a second peril threatens to take that residuum and distort it. Freud warned us of the phenomenon of *rationalization*, in which one presents to others, and perhaps to oneself, a praiseworthy reason (a rationale) for an action in order to justify it and thus to disguise its true, evil intention. The Lothario who declaims that he never tells his lovers about his romantic past, his current multiple liaisons, or his future intentions "because I don't want to hurt their feelings" is rationalizing. Perhaps, as we say, he even believes it himself.

Marx earlier warned us of the phenomenon of *ideology*, which is rationalization writ large on a societal scale. Those in power evolve an explanation of how they got to be in charge and how it is therefore proper for everyone else to respect the order of things and to play their respective parts with compliance and even diligence. The divine right of kings, the universally beneficial "rising tide" of capitalism, nationalist myths, and communist utopias all have been formulated as persuasive accounts of the inherent goodness of the status quo. Again, perhaps those in power have believed it themselves.

One does not need to consult Freud and Marx and other nineteenth-century masters of suspicion, of course, for such insight into this sort of human behavior. The Bible is replete with tales of self-justification, from Adam and Eve pointing fingers after the Fall, to King Saul wrapping his disobedience in piety, to Judas betraying Jesus, to the Antichrist attacking God's people. "The heart is devious above all else; it is perverse—who can understand it?" (Jer. 17:9).

Therefore, a somewhat longer way round might bring us more nearly to home. I have no magisterial command of the history of ethics upon which to draw. Yet I can at least be aware of how easy it is to offer passionate but glib pronouncements in this discourse and to discipline myself by paying careful attention to some other worthy and complex sources before speaking on my own. That I have tried to do.

It is now time, however, to do that speaking. So let us begin with a discussion of how we are to discern God's will and formulate ethics. Then we will establish some ethical basics, go on to formulate some procedural principles, and finally apply all this theory to various modes of life and particularly to concrete practice.

FIVE

METHOD IN ETHICS
A Sketch

If our fundamental question is *Who are we, for Jesus Christ, today?* then we need to be clear about how to go about answering this question. In a subsequent book, I intend to set out a full-fledged Christian epistemology. Here I can only sketch—with minimal detail and apologetic—how I think Christians should think about what it means to be Christian: to follow Jesus, here and now.[1]

ATTENDING TO JESUS

I take discipleship to be the fundamental concept in the Christian ethos. It is the concept at the heart of the Great Commission, the one thing Jesus calls his disciples particularly to do upon his ascension: to bear witness to his revelation and thus to make (more) disciples (Mt. 28:19–20; Lk. 24:48; Acts 1:8).

It is true—wonderfully true—that God has called us into friendship, not just servanthood (Jn. 15:15), and from there into actual adoption into his family. Precisely as adopted children, however, we must learn how to fit into this new family and play our proper parts. Yes, God has granted us his Holy Spirit to indwell us and to connect us with himself. Yes, the main work of renewal is done by his own transforming power; we certainly cannot transform ourselves into godliness. And yes, our fundamental posture is that of faith: trustful receiving of that which we cannot possibly earn or achieve on our own.

This faith, however, is to be worked out. In the basic dialectic of Christian development, Christians are to "work out your own salvation with fear and trembling; for it is God who is at work in you, enabling you both to will and to work

---

1. I have elaborated on some of the following epistemological matters already in my "Deciding About Religion," in *Humble Apologetics: Defending the Faith Today* (New York: Oxford University Press, 2002), 86–113.

for his good pleasure" (Phil. 2:12–13). The best way to do that, to work out our salvation into every corner of our lives and to the end of our days unto eternal life, is to follow the pattern of the firstborn, Jesus Christ, to be "conformed to the image of his son" (Rom. 8:29). Thus to actualize our status as sons and daughters, we can do no better than to apprentice ourselves to Jesus.

The fundamental posture of the disciple is that of attention to the master. The disciple wants to be like the master as much as possible, so the disciple listens, but also watches, ponders, and does everything else she can to receive whatever the master will give by word and deed. The disciple then tries to emulate the master—as is appropriate. She does not literally mimic him, of course. She does not act like a master herself and set up her own, separate band of disciples. She does not teach as if she has his authority, nor does she act as if she has his power. But inasmuch as it is appropriate to her station, and also to her gifts and opportunities, and especially to any assignment he has given to her, she acts like him: talks like him, works like him, feels like him, *imitates* him.

We therefore see three basic components to her sense of discipleship, not merely the idea of imitating Jesus: the revelation of Christ (about who he is, what he does, and what he proclaims), her sense of herself as a particular individual, and then the call of Christ upon her (particular) life. Moreover, this threefold scheme is true for any group of Christians, from a small fellowship to the church universal. In what follows, then, we will continue, for simplicity's sake, with the model of the individual disciple. But we will regularly remind ourselves that these ideas apply also, at least in most cases, to groups.

We will explore the nature of vocation in the next chapter. For now, however, we can trace some basic ideas about how a disciple properly discerns her calling—ethical method—from the nature of discipleship itself.

Let us posit two axioms about Christian discipleship: (1) the primary calling of Christians is to increase in knowledge and love of God and to do what he wants us to do, and (2) God will provide Christians with all we need to fulfill that calling, namely, to increase in knowledge and love of God and to work with him in his mission to the world.

Now, among those things necessary to fulfill that primary calling is knowledge. More particularly, we need to know those three components of discipleship: Christ, ourselves, and our particular calling. We do not need to know any of those three exhaustively. Indeed, it seems certain that we could not know any of those three exhaustively. But we need to know enough of all three in order to fulfill our calling. Since we do need to know enough of all three, therefore, we can trust God to provide us with that knowledge to the degree necessary for the fulfillment of that calling. This confidence is one aspect of "faith seeking understanding": we seek understanding with the assurance that God will grant us whatever under-standing we truly need—that is, the understanding he knows we need, rather than the understanding that we happen to think we need.

This last caveat is important. Christians cannot expect that they will under-stand everything better than their non-Christian neighbors. True, all other things being equal, a Christian worldview does position one to see reality more clearly, coherently, and comprehensively than do alternative worldviews. Moreover, being indwelt by the Holy Spirit does provide assistance to overcome at least some of the distortions in our apprehension and comprehension of things caused by sin—our tendencies, so to speak, to see what we want to see and to believe what we think is in our best interest to believe. So we can agree with a wide range of Christian thinkers that Christian belief and community do make a positive difference in our apprehension of things. John Howard Yoder writes,

> The church precedes the world epistemologically. We know more fully from Jesus Christ and in the context of the confessed faith than we know in other ways. The meaning and validity and limits of concepts like "nature" or of "science" are best seen not when looked at alone but in light of the confession of the lordship of Christ. The church precedes the world as well axiologically, in that the lordship of Christ is the center which must guide critical value choices, so that we may be called to subordinate or even to reject those values which contradict Jesus.[2]

Still, it is clear that God's gracious providence rains down intelligence on the just and the unjust—and, I should add, on the justified and on the unjustified—such that non-Christians frequently have better ideas than Christians. The dis-tinctive assurance Christians have, therefore, is that God can be trusted to grant us epistemic success precisely in the areas necessary to accomplishing his will.

Immediately, however, we confront a paradox. We must understand that the will of God in our day-to-day lives ought to be defined as "what is consonant with God's overarching and ultimate purposes as working out in this particular situa-tion," rather than as "what God would like to happen if the world had not fallen and nothing else were wrong." For lots *is* wrong in our world since the Fall. In such a world, we must see that it might well be the will of God for a Christian indi-vidual (or, again, a group of Christians) not only to be limited in knowledge but actually mistaken—even about something important. God humbles the proud,

---

2. John Howard Yoder, *The Priestly Kingdom: Social Ethics as Gospel* (Notre Dame, IN: Univer-sity of Notre Dame Press, 1985), 11.

and that includes proud believers. It might do someone who has invested too much in her intellectual prowess a great deal of good to fail at an academic task. It might do someone who flatters himself over his entrepreneurial ability a great deal of good to face bankruptcy. It might do a denomination that has assured itself of its doctrinal sophistication a great deal of good to confront a theological movement in its midst that evidences even greater clarity and subtlety.

The focus of the Christian's reliance is therefore on God and not on the gifts of God, including the gifts of knowledge.[3] To be sure, faith and knowledge are not separate: we confide in God, after all, because we think we know enough about him to warrant that trust, just as we commit our welfare to this automobile or that physician on the basis of what we think we know about each. Still, as modern philosophy has gone to great pains to tell us, we cannot find a neutral, high vantage point from which to look down on reality and make up our minds about it. We are entirely enswirled by it, and our thinking/believing/trusting is inescapably a sort of ecological system in which particular beliefs depend on particular facts that were selected and interpreted according to particular presuppositions that we retain because they seem to help us to make sense of what we perceive and to negotiate life well. Our minds carry around a "web of belief," as W. v. O. Quine famously put it, but that web is ever in four-dimensional motion as facts, beliefs, and presuppositions continue to move in and out of it, and to shift places within it, over time.

Amid this swirl, Christianity affirms faith in God as the one who sits in the heavens and who enjoys the perfect vantage point from which to show and tell us what we need to know. We believe that we have good grounds to trust God. Indeed, we believe that God has granted us the spiritual and intellectual ability to do so (faith) as a gift. For it is easy to construe reality in other ways (hence other religions and philosophies), both because of our limitations as knowers and because of our penchant for construing reality in a manner convenient to ourselves. God has kindly helped us, then, to "pick him out" from the roster of available deities and first principles, and has taken us into personal relationship with him.

Again, our epistemic confidence is in God himself, and not finally in any of the epistemic means he has provided to us: reason, experience, Scripture, tradition, and so on. We do, however, recognize a certain ineluctable epistemic circle here: we believe in God because of what he has taught us through this or that means,

---

3. "Discipleship is less a matter of what we know, or of knowing the right things, and more of being actively and rightly related to God, people, and creation" (William A. Dyrness, *The Earth Is God's: A Theology of American Culture* [Maryknoll, NY: Orbis, 1997], 24).

and those means we affirm to be valid because we believe those are gifts of the God we trust.

What keeps this from being a vicious—or perhaps just silly—epistemic circle is that we do not actually think in this way, as Alvin Plantinga, Nicholas Wolterstorff, and others have shown.[4] We simply grow up with certain epistemic abilities and techniques, and as we mature we refine them by trial and error and by the guidance we receive from human culture (our parents, our schools, and so on). God meets us through those abilities and techniques in such a way as to convince us of his reality and his goodness, prompting us to put our faith in him. As we go on in life, we might reflect on our thinking processes (if we are so inclined) as they more or less successfully help us apprehend and negotiate our experience, and thus we come to new understandings of their relative trustworthiness as gifts God has granted us. But to reiterate, we do not make up our minds about God in the circular way I originally suggested: as if we come to believe things by means that we trust because they are given by God, whom we have learned to trust by these means that he has authorized! (One thinks of certain Protestants who declare their beliefs to be true because they come from the Bible, which is, they say, the Word of God—yet it is the divine status of the Bible, of course, that is among the crucial matters in question.) God equips human beings with means to apprehend reality in a reliable and useful way, and through those means, as people test them in practice, God then draws people to faith in him as the ultimate source of knowledge.

We must question those means and sort through their relative validity, however, if we would refine our ability to know God and the world, especially in the light of the occasional failure of these means to deliver truth—whether in the relatively trivial case of mistaking one acquaintance for another at a party or in the significant case of finding that one's inherited interpretation of Genesis 1 and 2 as scientifically precise is not the best way to view those texts. We will also have occasion to consider our epistemology if we are faced with competing claims from other means (such as ESP from a medium or spirit channeling via a shaman) or other worldviews (such as various forms of secularism that rule out anything supernatural).

Since we do not dwell in an epistemic Eden, therefore, but rather live in a somewhat inconstant, pluralized, and conflictual epistemic environment, let's consider carefully how we are to form (and re-form) our ethics.

---

4. Nicholas Wolterstorff, *Reason Within the Bounds of Religion,* 2nd ed. (Grand Rapids, MI: Eerdmans, 1984); Alvin Plantinga and Nicholas Wolterstorff, eds., *Faith and Rationality: Reason and Belief in God* (Notre Dame, IN: University of Notre Dame Press, 1983); and Alvin Plantinga, *Warranted Christian Belief* (New York: Oxford University Press, 2000).

A (PROTESTANT) CHRISTIAN
TETRALECTIC

Traditionally, Christians have drawn upon four main resources in the construction of theology in particular, and in their thinking in general: scripture, tradition, reason and experience. Roman Catholics, Orthodox, and Protestants have differed about how to understand, weight, and coordinate these resources. What I will offer here is what I think *ought* to be the generically Christian case, but it clearly is a Protestant scheme that I hope nonetheless will be of some help to my Orthodox and Catholic siblings *mutatis mutandis*.

Moreover, various Protestant individuals and groups have not affirmed explicitly all four of these resources. Some Protestants have claimed no authority but the Bible (so most Baptists and modern fundamentalists); others have claimed to be led directly and entirely by the Holy Spirit (so some Quakers and Pentecostals/charismatics); experience and reason dominate the thinking of liberals and modernists of all stripes; and still other Christians have invoked Scripture, tradition, and reason without naming experience (so Richard Hooker and the Anglican tradition).

It was the Anglican-trained and -ordained John Wesley, however, who worked out theology according to these four sources, prompting the historian Albert Outler to refer to Wesley's theological method as the "Wesleyan Quadrilateral."[5] What was true explicitly of Wesley I contend has always been true of most Protestants. Hence I have shifted the bracketed adjective to "Protestant" from "Wesleyan."

I have also shifted the noun from "Quadrilateral" to the neologism "tetralectic," for reasons that will emerge in the following discussion. To begin with the Quadrilateral, the four resources of scripture, tradition, reason, and experience each form a side of the figure. Each is accessed by the Christian individual or community as he, she, or they consider a theological matter. Scripture, however, typically plays both a foundational and adjudicatory role. That is, the Bible provides the fundamental written revelation of God that grounds and frames our consultation of tradition, reason and experience. And then, once we have canvassed these other resources, the Bible judges what of their deliverances we ought to take as truth.

---

5. Albert C. Outler, *The Wesleyan Theological Heritage: Essays of Albert C. Outler,* ed. Thomas C. Oden and Leicester R. Longden (Grand Rapids, MI: Zondervan, 1991); cf. Donald A. D. Thorsen, *The Wesleyan Quadrilateral: Scripture, Tradition, Reason and Experience as a Model of Evangelical Theology* (Grand Rapids, MI: Zondervan, 1990).

Before we analyze this scheme, however, let's be clear on its elements. Wesley and other theologians naturally confined these categories to whatever would be useful for theology per se. But our interest is broader than that, and we can broaden the categories in turn.

Scripture itself remains the same: the canon of sixty-six books recognized by the church since ancient times as the Word of God written—the book, so to say, that God prompted and God wants us to have with his authority.[6] Yes, Roman Catholics have recognized additional books as Scripture since Jerome translated the apocryphal books along with the others in the fourth century. In that project Roman Catholics have seen the authoritative work of God, while Protestants and Orthodox have not. Yes, the canon of twenty-seven New Testament books was not agreed upon widely until several centuries after the books were written, but it is pretty evident that the vast majority of Christians recognized all of the major books of the New Testament as Holy Scripture very early on—the gospels and the major letters of Paul. So for Protestants standing anywhere in the mainstream of Christianity, the category of "Scripture" is not in doubt.

Tradition is that which one generation deems worthwhile to pass on to the next. Again, for theologians this category tends to be occupied by the creeds, other conciliar formulations, and the works of great theologians and church hierarchs. But it also properly includes liturgies, rituals, hymns, ethical teachings, and other encodings of Christian thought, behavior, and value. The actual content of "tradition," therefore, will vary with each Protestant individual and group: some will revere the Augsburg Confession, while others follow the Westminster Standards, and so on.

To value tradition does not mean to follow it slavishly. Our forebears were not necessarily wiser than we are, nor were they facing always the same challenges that we do. Yet some of them *were* wiser than at least most of us, and many challenges are generically human and thus perennial. Therefore we do well to listen to the voices of the past, and especially those voices whose testimonies have been validated by successive generations of Christians. As G. K. Chesterton says, tradition means giving one's ancestors a vote—not all the votes, but at least some of them.[7]

Reason means two things when it comes to Christian thinking. Formally, it means simply rigorous thinking: industrious, disciplined, honest, patient, consistent,

---

6. I align myself particularly with two contemporary statements on these matters: John Webster, *Holy Scripture: A Dogmatic Sketch* (Cambridge, UK: Cambridge University Press, 2003); and Nicholas Wolterstorff, *Divine Discourse: Philosophical Reflections on the Claim That God Speaks* (Cambridge, UK: Cambridge University Press, 1995).

7. G. K. Chesterton, *Orthodoxy* (Garden City, NY: Image, 1959), 48; see also Jaroslav Pelikan, *The Vindication of Tradition* (New Haven: Yale University Press, 1984).

and thorough. To be sure, the standards for "rigorous thinking" vary from culture to culture—recognizing "culture" to denote even particular academic disciplines or ethnic subgroups. Some cultures will rely heavily on analogy from observations of the natural world. Other cultures depend on mathematical or quasi-mathematical modes of inquiry and expression. Still others see the highest form of reason to be the reconciliation of the various teachings of traditional authorities. Thus we see unavoidable variety again in Christian thought: not only different understandings of what counts as "tradition," but also different understandings of what counts as "rational." We also recognize, however, that these understandings are not totally different: the law of non-contradiction seems universal, as do a number of other basic principles of sound thinking. Thus members of various groups can, and do, think together, recognizing useful processes and conclusions in each other's work. The Christian, then, thinks as carefully as she can, according to the standards of her culture—in trust that, under the providence of God, such thinking will be adequate to fulfilling her vocation.

Materially, reason means the full panoply of human inquiry: natural sciences, social sciences, applied sciences, humanities—the lot. Christian thought ought to welcome all the knowledge that is available, since the Christian has nothing to fear from reality properly construed. The Bible and church tradition certainly don't answer all the questions human beings have to ask, whether about animal husbandry, astronomy, plumbing, economics, musical composition—or politics. (I emphasize the last category not because I think it is different but because I think it is *not* different from the others. Yet some Christians who would readily agree that Scripture has little to say about the other subjects believe that the Bible and tradition do offer a clear and authoritative politics, whether of cultural conquest and hegemony or of selective cultural engagement while maintaining a separate, powerless, pure community—and I maintain that neither one can be simply read right out of the Bible.)

To be sure, the Christian will do well to appreciate the limitations and distortions in human apprehension and comprehension of the world that affect each of these disciplines, just as they affect Christian tradition and even Scripture itself. (In the case of the Bible, I do not see how God's inspiration allows for human sin in its writing, but the limitations of the human [co-]authors certainly are evident, even at the level of grammar.) Yet she gratefully learns all she can from these means of understanding the world, the world she is negotiating as best she can in order to fulfill her vocation as best she can.

We can pause over the category of reason a moment longer to note that it is made up of both constructive and critical modes. Thus imagination belongs here, as it takes what experience and reflection provide it and then works to solve mathematical problems, devise political strategies, invent machines, or compose music. We create and we critique in hopes of producing the best version of our ideas.

Finally, there is the realm of *experience*. The Christian individual (and group) properly takes into account all of experience. Christians thankfully receive special spiritual experiences of God's guidance, reassurance, comfort, warning, and so on. They also, however, are glad to sense what others sense in normal human life, whether the beauties, terrors, oddities, and ordinary regularities of nature, or the horrors, frustrations, mysteries, and joys of human society. All of this is access to reality; all of this is grist for the mental mill.

Christian thought draws on all four of these resources. There are some problems with this way of seeing theology, however, that are implicit in the metaphor of a quadrilateral. For one thing, the image is static, while theology, and Christian thinking in general, is dynamic. The conclusions of one age become the tradition that guides the next, but they do not provide all that the next age needs in exactly the formulation it needs. The Nicene Creed, for example, provides guidance that churches all over the world receive gratefully to this day, but its categories are ancient and its concepts need restatement, as well as expansion, to help us think adequately about the triune God according to the demands of our particular time and place, whether that is New York City, Nairobi, or New Delhi.

For another thing, the quadrilateral image can suggest that one circuit of the four resources is enough. Let's start with Scripture, proceed to listen to tradition, reason, and experience, then conclude with another consultation of Scripture, and we're done—here is the truth. But there are at least three problems with this procedure.

First, we do not start simply with Scripture. Our knowledge of Scripture comes to us in mediated form, via some combination of family, friends, enemies, schooling, cultural flotsam and jetsam, church, reading, movies, and the like. Tradition, reason, and experience, that is, are not accessed at some point after our pristine reading of Scripture, but already shape our reading of Scripture. Thus our reading of Scripture is always in a tetralectic, a *four-way conversation* among these four resources.

Second, we never have at our disposal simply Scripture, tradition, reason, and experience. In the case of the Bible, for example, the actual Bible that we have on hand in any given case is just those portions of the Bible that we can remember, that we are bringing to bear on the question, and that operate in the background shaping our presuppositions. But it isn't the entire canon. Furthermore, those Bible portions that *are* operative in a given moment are themselves interpreted by us. So we do not have access to the Bible per se when we are thinking, but only a Bible that is both partial and interpreted. The same is true, of course, for tradition, reason, and experience. The tetralectic thus takes place not among Scripture, tradition, reason, and experience but among *our interpretations* of Scripture, tradition, reason, and experience.

Third, it is unlikely that a single pass through the resources or—better—one round of conversation among them will be enough. The hermeneutical circle is better seen as a hermeneutical spiral, in which successive readings of each resource and successive syntheses of the four resources bring us to what we hope are progressively better understandings. And for many issues, only a series of such conversations will bring us to the place in which we believe we have a sufficiently coherent and warranted view upon which to base an opinion and take an action.

Here we must confront a dirty little secret about hermeneutical spirals. We engage in them in the hope—indeed, usually simply the expectation—that they will bring us closer and closer to the truth, by which we mean closer and closer to a perfect representation of reality. Passing through successive spirals is rather like watching an image load slowly on a computer screen as it becomes more and more definite, thus becoming a truer and truer likeness of the original. The problem with such expectations, however, is that they are sometimes not met. In fact, sometimes the spirals work the other way, drawing an individual or a group farther and farther away from reality and deeper and deeper into error and lies. What begins as a suspicion in one's mind can become confirmed, it can seem, in a raging paranoia. Racist and nationalist tendencies sometimes can begin small and then blossom into full-blown ideologies with impressive apologetics and widespread subscription, whether in the Reconstructionist American South, apartheid South Africa, or Nazi Germany.

A related problem must also be acknowledged. At least as far back as John Locke, epistemologists have urged us to beware what we might today call "binary thinking," either assenting to or denying a belief: yes or no, right or wrong, true or false. Instead, they have told us to proportion our assent to the warrants we have for believing x: if strong warrants, then strong but not total assent; if weak warrants, then weak but not negligible assent. This recommendation seems entirely sensible and forms a basic part of any discussion of critical thinking.

Lurking in the shadows, however, is the realization that we can never be sure that we have rounded up all of the pertinent data *and* interpreted them properly so that we have a reliable sense of the whole by which to proportion our assent. Suppose dark matter does make up most of the universe, as some currently suggest, so that our theorizing on the basis only of the matter we can perceive is doomed to error. Or suppose the physical constants we take for granted—the speed of light, Planck's constant, and the like—are not constant, as some are suggesting.

Those who know physics (and I am only an interloping amateur) recognize that even in this realm, which laypeople consider highly precise and based on exact observation, there is very much we do not know—including what there is even to take into account. How much more, then, are we in doubt when it comes to explaining a war, or a new movement in literature, or the behavior of insects? Yes, proportioning our assent is still prudent advice, but it's really simply the best we can do in our fundamentally limited situation in which we can never be sure that we know even what the total is against which we are to measure our proportion of data and interpretation.

Once again, therefore, we must confront the lack of an epistemic guarantee outside the person of God himself to guide us. No method can be trusted to deliver us the truth. More radically still, even God cannot be trusted in that sense. He is not an epistemological patron, much less a celestial Web site, from whom various intellectual favors can be requested and then received with certainty. He is the gracious God who has revealed much to us for our good and on whose revelation we gratefully rely. But he remains the Lord who grants us what he pleases in order to accomplish what he pleases: *that* is the Christian epistemic hope.

Before we move on to locate the tetralectic in a broader context, we recognize that the Christian properly will privilege the Bible among the four resources, just as her forebears did in the Quadrilateral. (Her orthodox Roman Catholic friends will differ from her, as they see tradition as a co-equal resource for theology alongside the Bible.) She privileges it, however, in a way appropriate to her scheme. She has recognized that she does not simply have the authority of the Bible to bring to bear on her deliberations because she can never have the whole Bible, and that properly interpreted, in her finite, fallen mind. But she can still respect the authority of the Bible, and of her God who gave it to believers and promised to bless believers through it. Thus she never goes against what she thinks it says. She recognizes full well that her interpretation of Scripture on this matter might be erroneous. But she respects the provision of God's Word such that she maintains the Christian practice of refusing to set aside anything she believes it says.

She might well face the situation in which one or more of the other resources call her Biblical interpretation into question. Perhaps she was raised in a creation science tradition and believes Genesis 1 and 2 provide literal descriptions of creation that are now being questioned by her high school biology class. She recognizes this contradiction, but she does not discard her Biblical views. Nor, however, does she dig in her heels in class and denounce the curriculum as ungodly. Instead, she learns what her science teacher wants to teach her, meanwhile also paying attention to her pastor and to other Christian resources (such as books in her parents' home library or Web sites of other Christian organizations on science and faith) to see if Genesis and evolution can somehow be reconciled. Perhaps one day she will find a way to do so, in which case the tension will be eased. In the meanwhile, it is appropriate for her to defer making up her mind at all about just what happened at the origin of the world. (One might add that a little of this humility would behoove certain strident experts in the fields of both paleontology and Biblical studies as well.)

Her fidelity to the Bible does not mean that she must hold fast, come what may, to whatever her current interpretation happens to be; that would mean confusing the relatively unimportant status of her own interpretation with the authority of the Word of God itself. Instead, her fidelity to the Bible entails not going against what God has been pleased so far in her life to provide her as the interpretation of this or that verse or theme or doctrine. But such a stance might well entail a suspension of assent in the face of contradictions between two or more of the epistemic resources she possesses (say, science and Scripture), all of which she receives and treats gratefully as gifts of God.

So far, then, we have discussed Christian thinking in terms of the solitary Christian drawing together her findings from Scripture, tradition, reason, and experience in a hermeneutical spiral that she hopes will eventuate in knowledge sufficient for her to know and love God better and to do his will in the world. More, however, needs to be said about this model of Christian thought. It remains improperly restricted to the individual.

For one thing, God normally locates believers in a community. Whether ancient Israel or the later Christian church, God calls Christians into fellowship within which they conduct every part of their lives, including thought. The New Testament books are written mostly to churches, and the governing expectation is that individual Christians are members of congregations. Indeed, it is impossible to read the New Testament in an individualistic way in the face of the plural addresses to "you" and the plethora of terms of corporate identity ("body," "house," "temple," "priesthood," "family," "people"), let alone all of the explicit teaching regarding Christian community.

We can note immediately that a social context for thinking is hardly unique to God's people; rather, it is simply the normal human experience. Babies grow up in communities and learn not only from them but within them: shaped by their ways, their limitations, their controversies, their discoveries, their evils, and their opportunities. So a social dimension to our thinking is simply given, and the wise person takes that context as thoroughly and clearly into account as she can: "I'm from rural Alberta, and my large Dutch-Canadian family of origin farmed wheat and attended a Presbyterian church in a small town, and..." Schools and teachers, teams and coaches, bands and directors, workshops and leaders, sweethearts and rivals, friends and enemies, mass media and local pundits—all of these social influences affect our thinking somewhat, whether in the influence they exerted on us in the past or in that they exert on us in the present.

The prudent Christian not only tries to analyze her own thinking in terms of these influences so as to understand and compensate for these influences, but also recognizes and seeks out positive social influences by which she can improve her cognition. She knows that if she wants to make a decision better informed by the relevant data, she should find the social communities that can provide that information, whether in person through the appropriate university departments, community discussion groups, and the like, or virtually, through print and electronic media. She knows that if she wants to make a decision better informed by the best moral principles, she will immerse herself in the most noble company she can find.

In particular, she will seek out and function fully in a local church. The Christian church, among all other groups, is the one founded by Jesus and indwelt by the Spirit. Christ is Lord of the whole earth, to be sure, and he works out his good purposes in many groups beyond the church. But the church is the one community in the world that is centered on Jesus Christ. It is the one group in the world that fervently worships the triune God, authoritatively preaches the gospel of Christ, faithfully preserves the tradition, and devotedly nurtures growing disciples. It is the key community in which Christians learn the practices—theological, moral, liturgical, missional, and more—by which they are progressively shaped into the image of Christ and through which they may more faithfully do his will. It is the place in which the Christian can count on finding the Word of God proclaimed by "apostles,...prophets,...evangelists, [and] pastors and teachers, to equip the saints for the work of ministry, for building up the body of Christ" (Eph. 4:11–12). Therefore a good church is fundamental as the context for Christian thinking and living, and each individual Christian is wise to find his or her place in such a body.

With this recognition of both the inevitable givenness and the prospective goodness of community, the realistic Christian also acknowledges the dark side of all human associations. She eschews all sentimentality about "community" as it sometimes is touted, even by intelligent theologians and preachers who ought to know better, as the great, beneficent alternative to "individualism," the putatively wretched product of the modern West. She knows people from various religious and ethnic communities, including Christian ones, who have spent much of their lives trying to extricate themselves from the stifling effects of certain communities—including Christian communities of family or congregation. She knows, whether she has read Reinhold Niebuhr or not, that communities can be even more evil than the individuals that constitute them—that corporations and churches, as well as mobs, often commit sins that their constituents would not normally even consider on their own. She would agree with political scientist Glenn Tinder that "maintaining a prophetic attitude means looking beyond every historical relationship and remembering that nothing in history, nothing human, can be absolutely relied upon"—not even the church.[8] So she does not see community as anything other than a God-given mode of human existence with which she properly reckons as she sorts out ethics as a responsible individual—*for* herself, but not *by* herself.[9]

THE HOLY SPIRIT AND SPIRITUAL RECEPTIVITY

In, with, and under these resources and the Christians who investigate them works the Holy Spirit of God. Indeed, the allusion to prepositions regarding the elements of the Lord's Supper ("in, with, and under") prompts us to consider the tetralectic under a category not normally employed in epistemology, namely, the means of grace. Yet the use of more typical means of grace—Bible reading, preaching, prayer, confession, baptism, communion—shares some important similarities with epistemology. However perfect the Bible itself might be, our reading and preaching of it certainly isn't perfect, and yet we count on God to bless us through those experiences as believing communities have long counted on him to do. Prayer doesn't seem always to work as we expect or hope, but we trust God to answer it well. Baptism doesn't magically transform people into moral paragons, communion doesn't imbue us with invincible spiritual power, and so on—yet the testimony of the church through the ages is that the proper, faithful, and regular use of these means does result in the receipt of grace from God who has sovereignly chosen to institute and use such means to convey his gifts.

The same dynamic, I argue, is the case in the proper, faithful, and regular use of scripture, tradition, reason, and experience. These resources also have been

---

8. Glenn Tinder, *The Political Meaning of Christianity: An Interpretation* (Baton Rouge: Louisiana State University Press, 1989), 9.

9. Glenn Tinder is correct to observe the following fact, which pertains to the church as much as it does to any other group: "Determining the direction of God's leadership is, in the final analysis, the responsibility of each individual, singly. The initiative of God can never be equated with the initiative of any human leader or any historical party, nation, or movement. There is therefore an ineradicable element of solitary reflection and choice in our political lives. Although an individual is no more infallible than a group, an individual cannot allow a group to exercise any unconditional and uncritical authority. Each person must decide alone concerning his responsibilities in history" (ibid., 15; cf. 90–99 specifically on the church).

given to us by God in order to convey God's grace to us. It is therefore not pious but disobedient to shirk their use in the name of the Bible alone, the Spirit alone, the Church alone, the law of love alone, or whatever else might stand in the place of responsible ethical discernment. Instead, we ought to receive and use these gifts as the equipment God has provided for us in order to grow in knowledge and love of him and to work with him in his mission to the world.

Several implications follow from this understanding. First, we should recognize that it is God who leads us through these means. They are not authoritative in themselves. The Christian way must not devolve into a textualism in which exegesis and application of the Bible become the sole mode of ethical reasoning. The Christian way must not devolve into a traditionalism in which maintenance of the "ancient paths"—or even the recently established patterns—becomes the sole mode of Christian living. The Christian way must not devolve into a rationalism in which even the best of human reasoning becomes the sole content of our thought and life. And the Christian way must not devolve into an experientialism in which spiritual impulse becomes the sole norm of our belief and conduct. We follow the living God who meets us in these means as we work with him to investigate and coordinate them into a useful pattern of thought and service.

Second, God does meet us in these means, and yet he is sovereign to go beyond them in special circumstances. God normally works through normal means— that's why they are normal. But he occasionally works through unusual means (to keep this string of tautologies running). In the physical world, these events, at least when they are obvious enough to be recognized as such, are called miracles. In the epistemological realm, they are called "intuitions," "a word from the Lord," or even a "vision" or "voice."

(There is another sense of "intuition," namely, a kind of rationality that works beneath articulate consciousness to come up with surprising, but not supernatural, conclusions. Consider a small-engine repairman who just "knows" what is wrong with one's lawn mower, or a surgeon who just "senses" that there is a problem lurking behind that apparently healthy organ. This kind of intuition we can categorize as part of what God normally grants through the epistemic means of grace. The kind of intuition we are discussing now we are seeing instead as special.)

Precisely because these events are not normal, and therefore are not routinely evaluated according to the critical programs our minds always run, they must be carefully weighed to sort them out from deceptions issuing from our own minds or perhaps even from diabolical sources. Wise Christians do in fact seek to sort them out, checking them against what is already known about God, his ways, his calling of the individual or group in question, the likelihood that this extraordinary means of grace was necessary in the circumstances (rather than a personally convenient way of avoiding the clear implication of those circumstances), and so on. These checks are indeed prudent. And they are checks meant not to quench the Spirit when he does something unusual, but to recognize him when he does.

Third, since it is God who is teaching us through these means and, again, not we ourselves simply exerting ourselves in various epistemic disciplines dealing with various data we have gathered, it becomes obvious that our spiritual health is vital to the ethical enterprise at this level, the cognitive, as well as at the more obvious level of the volitional. We literally will not see the truth if we are spiritually impaired or impeded, well before we encounter the question of whether we will do it.

Furthermore, by "spiritually impaired or impeded" we must mean something relational, not just some quality in ourselves. Since the underlying dynamic and model here is that of discipleship to Jesus, we must strive not only to be as holy as possible in some abstract sense but also to be as rightly related to him as possible. Indeed, too great a focus on our own ostensible goodness becomes perverted into something other than that. It becomes an inwardly curved, thus isolated, thus curdled "sanctity" that results in the grotesque distortion of the Pharisee who "prayed with himself," not with the God he so ostentatiously presumed to address (Lk. 18:11).

Again, given that this model of epistemology relies fundamentally on the motif of "means of grace," Christians recognize that we must attend to our spirit and our relationship with Christ precisely in order to do what needs to be done epistemically, as in every other dimension of life: to grow in knowledge and love of God and to work with him in his mission to the world.

Thus does ethical method arise naturally out of the basic relationships of the believer with the church, with the world, and with God, in the basic mode of discipleship to Jesus. From method, then, let us proceed to the *contents* of the Christian outlook, from which, with that method, Christians can proceed to ethical deliberation and action with confidence.

SIX

THE STORY AND THE MISSION

What does it mean to be Christian in the world? What are Christians to do in the world? *Who are we, for Jesus Christ, today?* These are our guiding questions, and we shall begin to answer them in this chapter in terms of the great themes of *shalom*, mission, and vocation.

The Christian Scripture, however, does not present the ethos of Christianity primarily in the form of questions and answers. It is not a catechism—or, at least, not a catechism in the form we expect. The Bible is fundamentally a story. While it does contain a wide range of other genres, including poems, laws, prophecies, lyrics, proverbs, letters, apocalypses, and more, at base the Bible is a narrative with a beginning, a middle, and an end. And that's good. As David Martin writes,

> We need a good story, a moral landscape of admonition and promise, for people who have sustained a bad Fall, but nevertheless seek a better city; and en route that story should tell them who is their neighbour, how to find a way home after prodigal expenditure in a waste land, and how to recognize a pearl of great price when they see it.[1]

Sylvia Keesmaat and Brian Walsh make the point even more sharply: "What basis will you have for either a sustained critique or a subversive lifestyle if you are unable to appeal to an alternative narrative as better than the lies of the market?"[2]

1. David Martin, *Christian Language in the Secular City* (Aldershot, UK: Ashgate, 2002), 177.

2. Brian J. Walsh and Sylvia C. Keesmaat, *Colossians Remixed: Subverting the Empire* (Downers Grove, IL: InterVarsity, 2004), 170. This principle lies at the heart of Victoria Barnett's analysis of those Germans who resisted the Nazis, and particularly the Holocaust, and those who did not—the latter of whom she calls "bystanders." The main difference between the two groups, she found, is that those who rescued Jews maintained a different *vision* of what Germany was and could be from that which the Nazis promoted, while those who stood by felt *machtlos*—helpless—to do anything other than comply because they saw the situation as irremediable. They could not imagine things otherwise than they were. See Victoria J. Barnett, *Bystanders: Conscience and Captivity during the Holocaust* (Westport, CT: Praeger, 1999).

The narrative of the Bible, moreover, is told as being true: not only true to life as a series of illustrations of timeless moral and spiritual realities, but true also as in what happened, what is happening, and what is going to happen in *history,* however pictorially represented.

This historicity, finally, is presented as being important. Indeed, it is crucial to Biblical religion in two respects. First, the most basic posture of the believer is that of faith, of trusting in God. And the logic of both the Old and the New Testament is that this personal trust in God rests on one's believing that God performed certain actions in the past, actions that sufficiently reveal both God's power and God's benevolence such that they prove him trustworthy in the present and for the future.[3] In the Old Testament: "I am Yhwh your God who brought you out of the land of Egypt, out of the house of bondage," and therefore "you shall have no other gods before me" (Ex. 20:2–3). In the New Testament, the exodus is out of the bondage to sin and death. Thus Jesus is trusted as Lord because he has rescued us through his cross and raised us through his resurrection. Such a confidence in the historicity of the Christian Story does not entail believing that every story in the Bible is given to us as accurate historical description. Again, the Bible is a congeries of various genres. But the overall narrative, and certainly key elements in it, are taken as historically veracious by Christians fundamentally because our following Jesus depends on our believing in what God has done as the basis for trusting what he is doing now and will do in the future.

Second, historicity matters to Christians in that we will understand and live out our ethos best if we understand where we are in the great narrative of the Bible and thus understand our parts in God's plan. In the early days of shopping malls, painted plywood signs were located at each entrance to guide shoppers to their desired destinations. Invariably, however, some unhelpful youngster would soon scrape off a crucial datum on that map: the circular Day-Glo orange sticker that told a shopper, "You are here." Without this crucial orientation, the rest of the map was virtually useless, open to a wide range of misinterpretations and thus misguided shoppers. Fundamental errors in Christian ethics, likewise, have been made by failing to take seriously the narrative shape of the Christian scheme of things, and also by failing to locate oneself properly within that story. We need to comprehend our context as a condition for deciding properly about how to act in this context.[4]

---

3. Walter Brueggemann makes the point that the Old Testament prefers to describe God in terms of verbs, then adjectives, and only finally and derivatively nouns (*Theology of the Old Testament: Testimony, Dispute, Advocacy* [Minneapolis: Augsburg Fortress, 1997], 229–30).

4. Oliver O'Donovan recognizes the importance of a narrative description of Christian ethics and comments, "The world-shaping, cultural sins have to do with bad descriptions: of sexual

THE CHRISTIAN STORY—AND
US WITHIN IT

A common summary of the Biblical narrative runs thus: creation, Fall, redemption, and consummation.[5]

"In the beginning, God created the heavens and the earth" (Gen. 1:1). In this primeval narrative, however stylized its depiction, we encounter theological truths entailed by God's words and deeds.[6]

God creates the world and it is pronounced "very good" (1:31). We shall have more to say about God's commissioning of human beings in that account. For now, however, we can pause over the quality attributed to creation at that time: "very good." The world is very good, in all its materiality, temporality, and finitude—qualities that in some philosophies and cultures mark it *not* as good but as something to be traversed, endured, "seen through," or even despised. Christianity, like the ancient Israelite religion whose scriptures Christianity incorporated into its own canon, revels in the goodness of the world. Animals matter; plants matter, the oceans and rivers and lakes matter; the air matters: God intended them all to exist and he made them good.

Human beings matter, too, and God made us for one express purpose: to garden the rest of the planet. Again, we will explore this commissioning (Gen. 1:26–28) in more detail presently. We should notice here, however, that not only is what we sometimes call the "natural world" good, but human *culture* is instituted as part of the cosmos God calls "very good." We can trace out the implications of this idea at two levels, the epistemological and the ethical. First, for human beings

---

intercourse as a merely physical encounter; of deterrence as a threat that does not commit one to consequent action; of a foetus as a piece of maternal tissue; of justice as the will of the majority, and so on. Serious moral debate cannot avoid arbitrating questions of description and so enquiring into the structures of reality" (*The Desire of the Nations: Rediscovering the Roots of Political Thought* [Cambridge, UK: Cambridge University Press, 1996], 14).

5. Richard Bauckham cautions us that "the Bible itself offers no summary of the whole story from beginning to end" (*Bible and Mission: Christian Witness in a Postmodern World* [Grand Rapids, MI: Eerdmans, 2003], 93), and elaborates on the "profusion and sheer untidiness of the narrative materials" (92). Such richness defies all attempts at comprehensive schematization, including all attempts at a comprehensive theology of culture. But I expect that Bauckham, and at least most Christian readers, would agree on the basic outline offered here.

6. Happily, I do not need to pause here to detail my views of the literary nature of the Genesis creation accounts. For the purpose of this level and kind of theological and ethical reflection, Christians can and should take the story on its own terms: this is a picture of God creating the world. Indeed, I am content to defer the question of precisely what happened at the origin of the planet until both Old Testament studies and paleontology come to more definitive conclusions than they have heretofore.

to subdue/cultivate/garden the earth means that reason is blessed by God and meant by him to be used by us. Humans were not meant to stroll through Eden merely picking up fallen fruit to munch on our way to swim or sunbathe or sleep in some truly animalistic paradise. Those are all good things, to be sure, but to confine ourselves to them would be to remain subhuman. We were meant to take what God created and work it, cultivate it, do something with it. Such activity entails reason, of course, in the broad sense in which I defined it earlier (and not merely formal logic). So the commissioning of human beings at creation validates both the use of reason and its employment in culture.

Second, the creation story must be understood as the beginning of a larger story that unfolds in the subsequent chapters. Yet nowadays some ethical consideration is conducted as if we are still in Eden. No one seriously argues that we dwell in Arcadia, of course. What some people do seriously argue, however, is that the world as we find it is, in itself, simply and unqualifiedly good. If something can be shown to be "natural"—that is, unaffected by and not a product of human action—then it is pronounced "good." Advertisers have touted the adjective "natural" for a bewildering array of products for a generation or more, with "organic" the more recent version of it. The most common ethical use of this argument currently is in the realm of sexuality. If homosexuality in particular, but other forms of sexuality also, can be shown to be the direct result of, say, brain development, and thus perfectly natural (note how loaded both of those terms are: "perfectly" and "natural"), then they ought to be validated as being just as good as heterosexuality. This type of argument is the current form of "What is, is good," and in Christian terms we can see its fallaciousness in its failure to recognize that we haven't lived in Eden for a long, long time. Much has happened since then, and some of it pretty bad, as we recall from the story of the Fall and its implications. To argue ethically from "is" to "ought," therefore, is not immediately wrong from the Christian point of view, but it is not immediately right, either. The whole story has to be taken into account to decide whether, and to what extent, the matter in question is properly seen solely in terms of the goodness of the pristine world.

Another ethical mistake in our day stems from failing to see the hierarchy instituted in both Genesis accounts of creation (chapters 1 and 2). Human beings are given dominion over the rest of the world. Despite the assertions of "deep ecology" and similar ideologies that place human beings on the same level as all other animals (in Peter Singer's brilliant phrase "a boy is a dog is a rat"), the Bible says that human beings are literally the lords (*domini*) of creation.

Such language in our society resonates negatively with fearsome words such as "dominate" and with ugly ideas such as human exploitation and despoliation of the rest of creation. Does Genesis provide a rationale for such rapacity? Quite the contrary. Human beings are created in the image of God, and therefore are literally to look like and act like God in regard to the rest of creation.

Indeed, we are "lords" under the express authority of God, *the* Lord: " 'The world is mine,' declares the Lord, 'and all that is in it' " (Ps. 50:12). The formal term for my country, the Dominion of Canada, helps us here, for in this case, "dominion" means "a self-governing nation of the Commonwealth of Nations other than the United Kingdom that acknowledges the British monarch as chief of state."[7] "Dominion" has nothing to do with the act of domination, but rather with the status and responsibility of authority—in this case, authority that is wielded under the authority of another, as the Canadian Parliament governs Canada under the authority of the Queen. So human beings are "lords" in the feudal sense, we might say, under the authority of the Great King who gives us our lands and our authority to govern them, and to whom we owe fealty and obedience in all we do. John Paul II warns us well:

> Humankind, which discovers its capacity to transform and in a certain sense create the world through its own work, forgets that this is always based on God's prior and original gift of things that are. People think that they can make arbitrary use of the earth, subjecting it without restraint to their wills, as though the earth did not have its own requisites and a prior God-given purpose, which human beings can indeed develop but must not betray.[8]

And how does God, this Great King, act toward the world he made? With care; with sustenance and creativity. David Martin avers, "Providence...is about God's consistent and persistent sustaining provision, power, and purpose for us and the world."[9] Human beings likewise are the gardeners under God's commission, and in that image we see the reciprocity of relation between humans and their fellow creatures. For who benefits from the gardener doing his work well, the gardener or the garden? Clearly they both do. The gardener is "in charge" in both senses of that term: he decides what is to be done with the garden because he has been charged by God to make those decisions, precisely in order to benefit both himself and the garden under his care.

---

7. *Unabridged Merriam-Webster Dictionary*, s.v. "dominion"; http://unabridged.merriam-webster.com/cgi-bin/unabridged?va=dominion&x=0&y=0; accessed 22 December 2006.

8. John Paul II, *Centesimus Annus, Encyclical Letter on the Hundredth Anniversary of Rerum Novarum* (Boston: St. Paul Books, 1991), 54; quoted in Jean Bethke Elshtain, *Who Are We? Critical Reflections and Hopeful Possibilities* (Grand Rapids, MI: Eerdmans, 2000), 53.

9. Martin, *Christian Language*, 139.

Andy Crouch thus observes that Singer and his ilk miss a fundamental point when they accuse human beings of "speciesism." Yes, we humans think we are special. But this dominion we Christians believe we have from God is an oversight *on behalf of others*. For "in the whole known universe we are the only species that takes responsibility for the others; the only species that demonstrates the slightest interest in naming, tending, and conserving the others; [the only species] that indeed is accountable for the stewardship of the others; and the only species that feels guilt (however fitfully and hypocritically) when its stewardship fails."[10] We are the only species that is to *care for* everything else because we are the only species that, at our best, *cares about* everything else.

Culture, then, is something in which human beings engage in their very essence, as "image of God." Culture, moreover, is an activity that properly benefits all involved: the gardener and his garden. From this happy origin, however, humanity fell. And when the gardener goes awry, the garden suffers, too.

In the Fall, depicted in Genesis 3—although its implications trail out for the rest of the Bible, to almost its last page—humanity disobeys God. Not content to be created in the image of God, humans decide to "be like God" in some other sense, abandoning moral innocence for the knowledge of good and evil—knowledge gained, alas, by experience and by willfulness. Having already known good, they now know evil by the paradigmatic sin of deciding for themselves rather than humbly obeying God, by proceeding then to disobey, and by bearing the consequences of that sinful action.[11]

The consequences of sin do show up in both of our categories again: the epistemological and the ethical now seen to be closely intertwined. In the woman's conversation with the serpent, in which God's express words are altered to make them both more severe ("Don't *touch* it") and less definite ("*in case* we *might* die"), we see a weird clouding of the cognitive that leads to immorality. She literally doesn't get God's proscription quite right, as if to leave open a deceitful alternative that the serpent is only too happy to provide. And then when God calls the human pair to account, the finger-pointing away from oneself is not only morally wrong but cognitively wrong: It literally isn't the truth—the whole truth—of the matter. I don't mean to overemphasize this point about rationality, but in the very next story, in Genesis 4, Cain seems to be confused about how to honor God in sacrifice and then, rather than alter his behavior in the light of God's correction, he proceeds to kill Abel. This is a story so familiar to us that we must not fail to

---

10. Andy Crouch, "Feeling Green," *Books and Culture,* March/April 2007, 33.

11. I thank Gerry McDermott for the phrase "paradigmatic sin" (correspondence with the author).

see how *irrational* is Cain's action, quite apart from its being immoral. For how can killing Abel possibly improve Cain's situation, which is a situation of God's dissatisfaction with him? "What was Cain thinking?" we might cry. It is an act of both wickedness (morality) and derangement (epistemology).

We must be careful, however, to see the Fall also in its context as just one part of the story. Some Christians instead have interpreted our current existence as if we are in a world utterly fallen, corrupted beyond repair, a valley of the shadow of death through which we must travel as expeditiously as possible in order to reach the sunlit lands of the next life. In particular, culture itself is seen as a bad thing in the form of the *city*—the antipode to Eden (which is, to make this contrast work best, depicted as a "natural" place, not the garden it was, which of course implies culture). The first city was founded by Cain. Aha! That means cities are bad, and thus all human culture downstream of the Fall is bad.[12]

Yet long before the Bible sets up its ongoing dialectic between the evil city (Babel/Babylon) and the good city (Jerusalem/Zion), even a little study of the immediate Biblical context suggests an interweaving of the good and the bad after the Fall. Genesis 4 proceeds from the story of Cain and Abel to show us at least two forms of cultural decline in the person of Lamech, who marries two wives and then boasts to them of his disproportionate violence, killing a man who had (merely) hurt him. Yet this Lamech fathers three sons, one of whom is the ancestor of nomads, those who dwell in tents and herd livestock; another of whom is the first musician; and the third of whom is the archetypal metalsmith. However much one might be suspicious of cities, and however much one might disdain loutish Lamech, in the gracious providence of God even *this* family produces cultural advancement through three creative and productive sons.

Despite these good developments, however, the world and its human gardeners clearly are doomed by the spreading stain of sin. Thus the Bible shows us a relatively quick decay of humanity into a state so awful that God wipes them off the face of the earth in the great flood, sparing only the righteous remnant of Noah and his family to restart the garden. This narrative takes up only a handful of chapters in Genesis, and then what we might call the time-lapse pace of the narrative slows down to focus on one man, Abram (later called Abraham), and his descendants—both physical and spiritual, Israelite/Jewish and Christian—who take up the rest of the narrative of the Bible until the final apocalypse. And none

12. Jacques Ellul is of course a careful and penetrating thinker about many things, but on the subject of the city, he is prone to gloomy oversimplification. See his *The Meaning of the City* (Grand Rapids, MI: Eerdmans, 1970). A helpful alternative viewpoint to Ellul's is found in Eric Jacobsen, "Learning to See Our Cities," *Radix* 29, 1 (2001): 12–15, 26–28, 31.

of those characters—including Noah and Abram themselves—are depicted as free from sin. Thus the vast majority of the Christian Story focuses on the third stage, redemption.

This era is ours. But the Bible's richness of narrative about this era leads us to see that it is too simple to say only that we live in the era of redemption. For this era itself divides up into at least three discrete eras, and it makes a crucial difference for ethics as to which era is the pertinent one. Further subdivisions are important for understanding how this or that part of the Bible pertains to us, but we ought to begin with the fundamental distinction between the Old Testament and the New, with the earthly career of Jesus as the bridge between them. The question of the relations among these three eras is fundamental to Christian ethics.

If the Old Testament is taken as directly regulative for all believers at all times, then we Christians should be applying it today in all its particulars—ceremonial, civil, liturgical, and so on.[13] Few Christian groups advocate such a position today. (Christian Reconstructionism, also known as "Theonomy," a deviant form of Calvinism, perhaps comes closest.) But whenever Christians simply draw out a text from the Old Testament and apply it directly to a current question, we are faced with the possibility of an important ethical anachronism, a failure to see that today is not 1000 B.C., here is not the ancient Near East, and we are not the people of Israel. The American religious right trades in this sort of proof texting perhaps more than any other contemporary Christian community, with its advocacy of the current state of Israel as if it is directly fulfilling Old Testament prophecy and is entitled to the regard expected of Gentiles for God's chosen people. They maintain this equation despite the manifest secularity of the vast majority of Israelis (which would disqualify them as "true Israel," according to the Biblical prophets), quite apart from what one thinks of Israeli policies toward Palestinians. "Health and wealth" preachers, for their part, also claim promises of earthly prosperity that make some sense in an Old Testament situation but do not so obviously fit in the very different economy of the New (Deut. 7:13; 8:7–13; II Chr. 7:14; cf. II Cor. 11:23–28).

To notice the difference between the Old Testament and the New is not to disparage the Old, much less to dismiss it as irrelevant. I myself have already drawn

---

13. Richard Bauckham writes thus about the Old Testament laws: "They are not sufficient to form a code of law for regular consultation by the judicial authorities. They are *examples* of laws rather than an exhaustive collection.... Neither the Old Testament law as a whole, nor specific parts of it, should be regarded as a statute-book for use in the courts. Rather its purpose is to educate the people of God in the will of God for the whole of their life as his people, to create and develop the conscience of the community" (*The Bible in Politics: How to Read the Bible Politically* [Louisville, KY: Westminster/John Knox, 1989], 26).

on the first few chapters of Genesis to make some points that I think are crucial in a Christian understanding of things, and I will continue to draw on it as Holy Scripture in what follows. The correct "use of the Law" is, to be sure, a perennial subject of controversy among Christians, but all of the major traditions affirm *some* use of it as God's abiding Word. We must therefore be careful not to simply lop off the Old Testament as irrelevant for Christian ethics, even as no Christian should fail to observe that we do not live in the Old Testament and that correct and fruitful reading of the Old Testament is a skill acquired only carefully.

When we come to the next era, then, the career of Jesus, many Christians happily set up ethical camp, so to speak, longing to follow Jesus as the first disciples did. Whatever the charms be of such nostalgia (for that is what it is), we must not succumb to them. We are not Jesus, and we are not the first disciples listening to him on a Galilean hillside—just as we are not Israel during the Exodus, conquest, monarchy, exile, or return.

Jesus himself is the great bridge between God and creation via the lords of creation, human beings. Jesus is also the center of God's great plan of redemption, through his incarnation, public ministry, crucifixion, resurrection, ascension, and second coming. In the light of this great work, the church's earliest and most central confession was that Jesus is Lord. In the logic of the Story and in the logic of salvation, therefore, the gospels that narrate the life of Jesus are positioned at the beginning of the New Testament.

From these facts, however, some Christians have drawn some improper conclusions that affect Christian ethics both materially and formally. Materially, we must deal with the tradition of *imitatio Christi,* the "imitation of Christ," as the fundamental model for Christian life. Thomas à Kempis's spiritual classic is but the most famous work in a long line of literature commending the life of Christ as the model for our own. (In our own culture, this tradition has been radically simplified and popularized in the slogan, "What would Jesus do?"—a slogan that is now more than a century old, stemming as it does from Charles Sheldon's bestselling book of 1897, *In His Steps*.)[14] This tradition of imitation does have strong Biblical warrant, of course. In his Upper Room Discourse, Jesus says that he is setting his disciples an example of loving service (Jn. 13:15). Moreover, his new commandment explicitly binds them to imitation: "I give you a new commandment, that you love one another. Just as I have loved you, you also should love one another" (John 13:34). Paul urges his churches to imitate Christ (Eph. 5:1–2; I Thes. 1:6)—although often he says instead to imitate more senior Christians who are themselves imitating

---

14. Charles M. Sheldon, *In His Steps: What Would Jesus Do?* (New York and Toronto: Revell, 1897).

Christ, such as himself (I Cor. 4:16; 11:1; Phil. 3:17; I Thes. 2:14; II Thes. 3:7–9; cf. Heb. 6:12; 13:7). And the Epistle to the Hebrews points to Jesus as the great example—the "Author and Finisher of our faith" (Heb. 12:2–3, KJV).

It has been an important mistake, however, to construe Christian discipleship to mean following Christ as if that meant simply "imitating." For one thing, we are not Jesus, and Jesus was who he was and did what he did in order to accomplish his distinctive mission. We are not called to fulfill the promises to Israel and to inaugurate the Kingdom of God. We are not called to be the Savior of the world and the Lord of resurrection life. Thus we are not all called to be Jewish, or male, or single; no one reading this book has been called to live two thousand years ago in the Levant under Roman oppression; and few of us are called to a trade, only to give it up for public religious teaching ministry. There is much about Jesus that we are not called to imitate, for there is much that is particular to his particular identity and vocation.

For another thing, Jesus calls us not to do his work but to extend his work—indeed, to perform "greater works than these" (Jn. 14:12). We must take this point seriously: Jesus' work was limited, as he played his particular role in the divine drama. That work was meant to inspire us outward and onward, not to confine us within limits that were proper for Jesus' calling but not for ours. Imbued with the Spirit of Jesus, and as the Body of Christ, we are to bear witness to Jesus Christ far beyond the extent of his own quite limited preaching tours in Israel (with only the occasional venturing beyond to the Gentiles) and to make disciples of all nations, which the church is in the process of doing today, after two thousand years of labor. Beyond this direct extension of his work, furthermore, Christians are called—as we shall see in more detail presently—to continue in the generic human work of gardening the world, albeit with the distinctive mark of those who know the Great Gardener and who work in conscious and delighted cooperation with him.

Thus it is crucial that we see that we are not living as if Jesus were present now in his earthly ministry, but *after* that: after the crucifixion, the resurrection, and the ascension; after Pentecost and the giving of the Holy Spirit; after the gospels and the Book of Acts, which record the launching of the church's distinctive era and mission. We live after the Old Testament and after the career of Jesus in a third era of redemption, the age of the church before the return of Christ in the consummation of history. "It is for your benefit that I go away," Jesus told his disciples (Jn. 16:7), and we must take him at his word. We must not live as if he hadn't gone away and is present for us now as he was then, to follow in that particular mode of ministry.

"What would Jesus do?" therefore is the wrong question for Christian ethics. If we keep asking it, moreover, we will keep making the perennial mistakes many have made, such as prioritizing church work over daily trades ("because Jesus gave up carpentry for preaching the gospel"); valorizing singleness, at least for clergy ("because Jesus didn't marry"); and denigrating all involvement in the arts, politics, or sports ("because we never read of Jesus painting a picture or participating in political discussions, much less kicking a ball"). Instead, "What would Jesus want me or us to do, here and now?" is the right question—or, if I may, *Who are we, for Jesus Christ, today?*

Connected with this material issue, the issue of the imitation of Christ as the main motif of Christian discipleship, is a formal issue for ethical method. Many Christians, including some quite sophisticated theologians, seem to equate the priority of Christ himself versus other figures with the priority of the gospels versus other books of the Bible, such as the prophets or the epistles. But this is an important hermeneutical error (bemusingly reminiscent of I Cor. 1:12: "I belong to Paul" or "I belong to Cephas" or "I belong to Christ"), and in at least four respects.

First, even though the gospels come first in the canon of the New Testament, they are probably not the earliest testimonies to Jesus in the Bible. Paul's early letters, most scholars agree, predate most or all of the four gospels. So if we are seeking access to the most primitive layer of "Jesus tradition," in terms of whole books (rather than this pericope or that saying or this hymn or that parable in the gospels), Paul's work would deserve priority.

Second, we should not be privileging whatever we guess is the earlier material of the New Testament versus the later, because all of it is inspired by God and therefore has the same status: Holy Scripture. Any historian knows that sometimes later accounts are better than earlier ones precisely because the later accounts can have benefited from access to several earlier accounts plus perspective that only time can bring. So there is neither theological nor historical ground for preferring "earlier" to "later"—and that goes for preferring Mark's gospel to John's, too.

Third, privileging the gospels in the name of privileging Jesus would make sense in terms of the relative status of the Lord Jesus versus his disciples, the epistle writers Paul, Peter, John, and others. But the gospels are authored not by Jesus but by other Christians: traditionally, Matthew, Mark, Luke, and John. So to privilege them is simply to prefer Matthew to Paul, or Mark to Peter, or John to, well, John (I–III John)—which reduces to a preference of genre, of gospels versus epistles.[15] Such a preference hardly has literary or theological merit. (Indeed, the championing of the gospels over the rest of the New Testament is particularly odd

---

15. I do hold to the traditional ascriptions of authorship in the New Testament, including the conviction that the same author, John, wrote the gospel and the epistles that bear his name. But my point stands even if one doesn't hold to this position.

coming from educated Christians, who sound as if they have discovered a red-letter edition of the Bible, except that their new version prints all of the gospels in red ink, while the rest of the Bible remains in black.)[16]

Finally, the story of Jesus is, of course, the key to history. But to emphasize the gospels over the rest of the New Testament is to forget that Jesus is Lord over all of history, Head of the church that succeeds him in earthly ministry, and in fact Author of the whole New Testament via the inspiration of the Holy Spirit— as he is the God who inspired the whole Bible. The better hermeneutical path, therefore, is to keep clearly in view what each of the books of the Bible has to offer us and to draw upon them according to their distinctive natures, regarding not only their genre strengths and limitations but also the place of their subject matter in the Christian Story. We Christians are not to be forever repristinating the experience of the disciples trooping about with Christ in ancient Judea—nor, for that matter, the experience of the disciples in the early chapters of Acts. For there are more chapters in Acts, and the unfinished nature of that book has itself prompted many readers to the conclusion that God intends the rest of the church to keep writing it, generation by generation, until the Lord of the church returns, to fulfill the promise made at that book's beginning (Acts 1:11).

Richard Bauckham offers some crucial reflections in this vein that are well worth listening to at length:

---

16. This, to me, is one of the most fundamental mistakes typically made in the Anabaptist tradition and thus by such important exemplars of it as John Howard Yoder: "For the radical Protestant there will always be a canon within the canon; namely, that recorded experience of practical moral reasoning in genuine human form that bears the name of Jesus" (*The Priestly Kingdom: Social Ethics as Gospel* [Notre Dame, IN: University of Notre Dame Press, 1985], 37). It must be exposed as such, particularly because of that tradition's frequently overbearing rhetoric of being more Christian than thou, as in the following typical phrasing of Yoder: "Since Constantine, one tradition has assumed that it is the duty of Christians to be the chosen organs of God to guide history in the right direction,... it has been decided on a priori grounds that the teachings of Jesus with regard to Mammon and Mars were not meant to be obeyed, [and] that we have in 'nature' or 'common sense' or 'culture' or somewhere else a body of ethical rules which outrank the teachings and example of Jesus" (ibid., 119). I believe that Christian thinking should be Christological and Christocentric, but, as I am arguing here, that means neither that the earthly career of Jesus is normative in Yoder's sense nor that the gospels themselves are privileged above other Biblical literature. For affirmation of how Christ ought to figure in theology, see my "Evangelical Theology Should Be Evangelical," in *Evangelical Futures: A Conversation on Theological Method,* ed. John G. Stackhouse, Jr. (Grand Rapids, MI: Baker Academic, 2000), 39–58.

As for Yoder's occasional sarcasm in ethical disputation, David Martin responds for the other side, as he characterizes Yoder and his ilk as the sort of Christian "who neatly bypasses all the real elements in the world, like force and hierarchy, by giving them a brief moral scolding" (*Christian Language,* 139). But as my friends and family would attest, I myself would never say such a thing.

The difference between the testaments might be better expressed in terms of a difference of political context. Much of the Old Testament is addressed to a people of God which was a political entity and for much of its history had at least some degree of political autonomy. The Old Testament is therefore directly concerned with the ordering of Israel's political life, the conduct of political affairs, the formulation of policies, the responsibilities of rulers as well as subjects, and so on. The New Testament is addressed to a politically powerless minority in the Roman Empire. Its overtly political material therefore largely concerns the responsibilities of citizens and subjects who, though they might occasionally hope to impress the governing authorities by prophetic witness (Mt. 10:18), had no ordinary means of political influence....

The difference between the testaments explains why, from the time of Constantine onwards, whenever the political situation of Christians has moved towards more direct political influence and responsibility, the Old Testament has tended to play a larger part in Christian political thinking than the New Testament. This has been the case not only in the classic "Christendom" situation of much of Western Christian history, where the confessedly Christian society bore an obvious resemblance to political Israel. It can also quite often be seen in situations where Christians have supported revolutionary movements and in modern pluralistic democracies.[17]

The proper theological aim, therefore, is to make the best sense of the whole Bible for inspired instruction on how to be God's people in the world.

Indeed, good theology also takes into account the ongoing work of the Holy Spirit in the life of the church. As Oliver O'Donovan writes,

---

17. Bauckham, *The Bible in Politics*, 3–4. Bauckham later adds: "The Bible's political teaching is in some degree *conditioned* by the social and political context in which it arose....For example, the political wisdom of the book of Proverbs, with its emphasis on the stability of a fixed social order (Prov. 19:10; 30:21–23) and its sometimes deferentially uncritical attitude to the monarchy (Prov. 16:10–15; 25:3), reflects the outlook of the court circles from which it derives. This makes it not a mistaken but a *limited* viewpoint, and therefore one which needs to be balanced by other aspects of biblical teaching" (13). Finally: "The most difficult hermeneutical task is probably that of relating the Bible to the really novel features of the modern world which the Bible does not directly address. All too often Christians who try to see the world in a Biblical perspective end up forcing the modern world on to the Procrustean bed of the Biblical world (i.e., the world within which and to which the Bible was originally written). Genuinely novel features of the modern world are either reduced to some feature of the Biblical world, so that their novelty is not really admitted, or else they are not seen as really important features of the modern world, so that their novelty can be admitted but trivialized" (131).

There was no revealed political doctrine in the New Testament, prescribing how the state was to be guided. The early church had simply to proclaim God's Kingdom come in Christ. The political doctrine of Christendom was discovered and elicited from the practical experience of Christian political discipleship.[18]

The Christian therefore has to be suspicious of any theology, and particularly any Christian ethics, that effectively shrinks the canon to a few, favorite books, whether gospels, epistles, torah, apocalyptic, or what have you. And we wisely pay critical attention to the experiences and reflections of our forebears in various cultural situations since the apostolic period. Or do we believe that the Holy Spirit did not, in fact, lead the church into any more truth—including truth about how to participate in society when society was willing for Christians to do so—once the canon was completed?[19]

We have implicitly circled around a fundamental point of dispute in Christian ethics, so let us now take it on: what are Christians today to make of the deeds and words of Jesus in his earthly career? At one extreme, Jesus' example and instruction is encapsulated in a dispensationalist scheme that removes most of what he did and said to a bygone episode: Jesus came to offer the Kingdom to Israel, but Israel refused it, so now God moves on to deal with the church. Thus the Sermon on the Mount is to be seen as legislation for an economy that was never actualized, and is more or less instructive for us now in a manner similar to the way the Torah is more or less instructive for us now. I doubt that many readers of the present book are seriously considering this approach, so I will move on to the other extreme, which does have considerable purchase in ethical discussions today.

---

18. O'Donovan, *Desire of the Nations,* 219.

19. Some theological readers are alert to the category of "Trinity" in theology, such that authors are scored, sometimes quite mechanically, on how often they mention the several members of the Godhead ("Ah, author X mentions God and Christ most of the time, and thus must be deprecating the Holy Spirit"). I acknowledged that this paragraph marks one of the relatively few times in which I mention the Holy Spirit in this volume. Usually I refer to either (the triune) God or to Jesus. I do so because this paragraph is one that I think makes the most sense of the particular subjects I discuss herein. (It also happens to correspond to the pattern of the Bible, which does not routinely mention all three members of the Godhead, but rather refers to God and Christ much more often.) I am indeed a traditional Trinitarian and I rejoice in the gift of the Holy Spirit. I do not think, however, that it follows that on every topic I must mention all three persons of the Trinity and with equal emphasis (as some contemporary theologians seem to believe we must—and thus they often run into either an implicit modalism or tritheism). I trust, instead, that readers will not take offense at this pattern—or at least will point out where it would make a material difference to refer directly to the Holy Spirit in given instances. That is what the Bible does—talk about the one God or the various members of the Godhead in a way pertinent to the topic under discussion, rather than constantly speak of one-in-three-and-three-in-one.

This view affirms that Jesus meant literally what he said and intended us to do what he did. The Sermon on the Mount is meant to be applied directly, as is everything else in the gospels. Any ethical alternatives to this literalism are then scorned as disobedient compromises with the world, as failures to take up the cross with vigor and courage, as substandard and ultimately sinful.

This position has an enduring attraction for any serious Christian, of course. Its clarity and radicalism combine to portray a heroic Christianity that rises impressively high above our actual attempts to follow Christ. But is this clear and radical model actually coherent—with itself, with the Christian Story, and with Christian history? I suggest it is not, and it is important that it be exposed as such so that we may embrace instead an ethic that is more truly and fully Biblical, untroubled by the accusations of infidelity that are so frequently hurled at those who abandon the extreme version for something more realistic.

First, this "clear and radical" version, as I am calling it, is incoherent with itself. We need proceed no farther than to examine the Sermon on the Mount, the usual test case for such discussions. It is common for advocates of this position to tell us to do just what Jesus said in this sermon. But they do not really mean that.

Yes, they usually mean to turn the other cheek when struck and to return charity for violence. They mean to avoid hatred and lust, and pursue reconciliation and good fellowship, and of course that is all to the good. But they do not go on to advocate the gouging out of eyes and the severing of limbs to improve one's likelihood of going to heaven (Mt. 5:29–30). Yet these admonitions are right in the midst of the other passages that are recommended to us with complete literalness, with no obvious literary indications that now we are dealing with hyperbole, not to be applied literally, while on either side of this passage we are dealing with straightforward ethical injunctions.

Furthermore, some of those ethical injunctions may not be as clear as has sometimes been alleged. Let us look particularly at the *locus classicus* on non-violence/non-resistance:

> You have heard that it was said, "An eye for an eye and a tooth for a tooth." But I say to you, Do not resist an evildoer. But if anyone strikes you on the right cheek, turn the other also; and if anyone wants to sue you and take your coat, give your cloak as well; and if anyone forces you to go one mile, go also the second mile. (Mt. 5:38–41)

I do not pretend to understand all of what Jesus means here in this notoriously difficult text—difficult hermeneutically, and then difficult practically. But I submit that he cannot mean that "do not resist an evildoer" is a blanket statement covering all instances. For example, he does not mean that parents should not resist evil in their children—else how could parents possibly fulfill their roles? It would be a bad parent who would refuse to prevent a child from hurting another child or endangering itself. Nor does it apply to church leaders, who are told by Christ's apostles in his inspired Word to exercise church discipline in order to resist the evildoer (e.g., I Cor. 5). So this injunction doesn't apply to at least two kinds of societies, families and churches. And these happen to be the only societies in which first-century Christians would have had freedom to fully realize their ideals. Thus I would argue that if following such a rule in this obvious sense would render impossible the proper functioning of Christian families and churches, a fortiori it would destroy larger and more pluralistic social units, such as cities and countries. So I cannot recommend that we "simply" obey it. And I cannot do so particularly as the church has not been uniformly sure even what this passage means from its earliest days, when some Christians continued to participate in the imperial armies, for example, while others taught that no Christian should do so.[20]

My sense is that many of the instructions of the Sermon on the Mount are meant indeed for us to take on straightforwardly and universally. But not all of them are. Jesus is a master of poetry and of parable, and we must be alert to his shifting genres. And if it is true that some of the Sermon is taught through hyperbolic imagery, as I think everyone must concede, then everyone is engaged in the same hermeneutical task of sorting out just what Jesus meant for us to believe and to do in this or that instance. No one can congratulate himself or herself for occupying the high and holy place in which "*we* just obey whatever Jesus said, unlike *you* sophists, casuists, and compromisers."

Second, this clear and radical position is incoherent with the Christian Story. For it fails to see that while Jesus is announcing the Kingdom of God, he alone lives totally within it. His disciples don't—whether while he is around or afterward once he is gone. The Kingdom has not yet fully come, even though wonderful elements of it, and its fundamental ethos, are already here, to be enjoyed by the

---

20. Harold Mattingly, *Christianity in the Roman Empire* (New York: Norton, 1967), 49. Richard Hays, who defends a pacifist view, demonstrates considerable integrity as he lists the several New Testament references to Christian soldiers and remarks that none of those verses indicate that the soldiers should leave the military. Indeed, Hays allows, "these narratives about soldiers provide the one possible legitimate basis for arguing that Christian discipleship does not necessarily preclude the exercise of violence in defense of social order or justice" (Richard B. Hays, *The Moral Vision of the New Testament: A Contemporary Introduction to New Testament Ethics* [San Francisco: HarperSanFrancisco, 1996], 335–36). Hays's discussion of the Sermon on the Mount in particular is a judicious counterpart to the interpretative line I follow here (317–46).

church and to be shared with all others.[21] So since the Kingdom is "already, but not yet" come, we should not be trying to act as if it has already and fully come, even as we strive to yield more and more to the impulse of those values that draw us forward and upward from "the age to come." Jesus' harder sayings point to this fact, as do some of his more spectacular miracles: a morality, a spirituality, a dominion over nature, a control over death itself that is typical of the wondrous world to come, but that only flashes out in brief signs in our era. Not everyone is healed, not all the storms are stilled.

Third, this clear and radical position *has never been instantiated in two thousand years of subsequent Christian history*. Not once. No congregation, much less denomination or territorial church, much less the whole extant church, for even one day, has succeeded in following this standard—not even close. No individual has lived up to these standards, short of Jesus Christ himself. This clear and radical hermeneutic might have been plausible as an ideal in the first century, because not yet fully attempted, but how plausible is it twenty centuries later? Have all of the churches and individual Christians since then been manifestly disobedient to the call of God?

Well, yes, we have been. But that fact doesn't mean that we should all just try harder to live out this clear and radical ethic. For one might suppose that if Christ did mean for us to live in this way, then the Holy Spirit of God would have empowered at least *some* Christians to do so. And I maintain that history shows that he has not. Therefore, one can ask, what makes the ethicist today who advocates this radical ethic think that here and now things will be so different from every preceding episode of church history such that the Sermon on the Mount will be fully obeyed by this community, or even this individual?

Such an argument, of course, does not *prove* that Jesus is not in fact grossly displeased with his church after he apparently was so clear to us about what he wanted for, and from, us. And I trust I am understood as not making a facile case from history as if "what is, is right." I am appealing to the reader's sense of probability and likelihood of explanation, to his or her sense of what is the most cogent of the available interpretations of the record.

Thus I suggest that two thousand years of church history tilts the burden of proof onto those who do think that indeed Jesus is just that disappointed. I suggest that a better way to construe the gospels, the Christian Story, and Christian

---

21. Mark Allan Powell reminds us that "people do not have to die and go to heaven to live in a realm of power ruled by God. Already, in this life, Jesus says, God is ready and willing to rule our lives. And this, he adds, is 'good news' (Mark 1:14–15)" (*Giving to God: The Bible's Good News About Living a Generous Life* [Grand Rapids, MI: Eerdmans, 2006], 37).

history instead is to posit an ethic by which the Holy Spirit has been rather more successfully guiding the church all along. This ethic has been both illuminated by these signs of the Kingdom of God and (as Reinhold Niebuhr and Dietrich Bonhoeffer suggested) judged by these standards of the Kingdom of God. Yet it allows that God does not expect us, nor does he command us, to "be perfect, as your heavenly Father is perfect" (Mt. 5:48)—that is, if "perfection" is understood as our direct and immediate practice of a literalistic understanding of all clauses of the Sermon on the Mount. This standard abides to inspire us, challenge us, and condemn us should we flout it. But God recognizes both our sinfulness and the topsy-turvy world in which we live, within which context sometimes we must do what normally ought not to be done, as I shall detail in chapters to come.

I realize, therefore, that I can sound like I am contradicting Jesus, but I am con-tradicting some *alternative interpretations* of Jesus. I agree with Oliver O'Donovan and others who suggest that the main point of Matthew 5, culminating in this counsel of perfection, is both the call and the promise to be complete and mature, with inner attitudes and private actions as well as outward, public performances matching the goodness of God. The perfection to which Jesus refers is that to which God is leading us: we are to be perfect, complete, mature *someday*, and Christ calls us *toward* this destiny now.[22]

I do not want to deflect or diminish Jesus' call to us. Instead, I am trying to under-stand, obey, and love Jesus, as all Christians have sought to do since Jesus took his leave on the Mount of Olives. And if the clear and radical version of Christian obedi-ence is the one we ought to have been following all of these years since the ascension, then we have been both badly mistaken and badly disappointing to God. I main-tain instead, however, that we have *not* always been either. And that's what the rest of this book will set out: an understanding of Christian ethics that neither ignores Jesus' example and teaching as irrelevant nor adopts them as a direct template.

Since the rest of this book concerns the life of the church between Jesus' first coming and his second, let's complete our brief survey of the Christian Story by considering the consummation of the ages in the return of Christ.

The history of Christian art shows us the common Christian aspiration for a return to the garden of Eden, a "peaceable kingdom" of rustic tranquility. Yet this vision is typical of nomadic peoples, and is central to the vision of Islam. It is the Qur'an that speaks of heaven in terms a Bedouin especially would appreci-ate: tall trees providing cool shade, endless water, lovely fruits, soothing greenery, and the like.

---

22. O'Donovan, *Desire of the Nations,* 100–13.

To be sure, the imagery of returning to Eden is importantly truer to the Bible than the even more common imagery in the West of our residing in celestial spiritual heights, with the expected accoutrements of robes, harps, and haloes. It is vital that this "church myth" be exposed as the horrible quasi-Platonic vision it is—a hyper-spiritual vision that not only promises everlasting boredom in the next life but nicely diverts Christian concern from matters of this one such as justice, compassion, and environmental responsibility. It renders us literally too heavenly-minded to be of any earthly good. Wendell Berry is scathing on this point:

> Despite protests to the contrary, modern Christianity has become willy-nilly the religion of the state and the economic status quo. Because it has been so exclusively dedicated to incanting anemic souls into Heaven, it has been made the tool of much earthly villainy. It has, for the most part, stood silently by while a predatory economy has ravaged the world, destroyed its natural beauty and health, divided and plundered its human communities and household. It has flown the flag and chanted the slogans of empire. It has assumed with the econ-omists that "economic forces" automatically work for good and has assumed with the industrialists and militarists that technology determines history. It has assumed with almost everybody that "progress" is good.[23]

(Lest this discussion be dismissed as an anti-capitalist screed, I daresay that what Berry writes can be applied to misplaced confidence in every economic sys-tem we humans have devised, including modern ones as diverse as mercantilism, authoritarian "managed" economies, socialism, and communism.)

We are not going to heaven. In Scripture, heaven is the abode of God, far above the earth in a spiritual realm reserved for spiritual beings (such as his angels as well). We are of the earth, and the earth is our home, upon which God has been graciously pleased to dwell with us.[24] The apocalyptic vision in both Testaments is decidedly earthy and earthly: a kingdom, with its capital in Jerusalem, that unites all the peoples of the earth around the worship of God. It is an astonishingly rich vision of purification, judgment, health, security, harmony, plenty, celebration,

---

23. Wendell Berry, "Christianity and the Survival of Creation," in *Sex, Economy, Freedom, and Community* (New York: Pantheon, 1992); quoted in Walsh and Keesmaat, *Colossians Remixed*, 168.

24. Paul Marshall, *Heaven Is Not My Home: Living in the Now of God's Creation* (Nashville, TN: Word, 1998). See also Richard J. Mouw's excellent exposition of Isaiah along these lines: *When the Kings Come Marching In: Isaiah and the New Jerusalem* (Grand Rapids, MI: Eerdmans, 1983).

diversity, and fellowship. We do not go back to the garden, and we do not go up to heaven. We go forward to the garden city of the New Jerusalem:

Then I saw a new heaven and a new earth; for the first heaven and the first earth had passed away, and the sea was no more.

And I saw the holy city, the new Jerusalem, coming down out of heaven from God, prepared as a bride adorned for her husband. And I heard a loud voice from the throne saying, "See, the home of God is among mortals. He will dwell with them as their God; they will be his peoples, and God himself will be with them; he will wipe every tear from their eyes. Death will be no more; mourning and crying and pain will be no more, for the first things have passed away."

And the one who was seated on the throne said, "See, I am making all things new." Also he said, "Write this, for these words are trustworthy and true."

Then he said to me, "It is done! I am the Alpha and the Omega, the beginning and the end. To the thirsty I will give water as a gift from the spring of the water of life. Those who conquer will inherit these things, and I will be their God and they will be my children. But as for the cowardly, the faithless, the polluted, the murderers, the fornicators, the sorcerers, the idolaters, and all liars, their place will be in the lake that burns with fire and sulfur, which is the second death."

Then one of the seven angels who had the seven bowls full of the seven last plagues came and said to me, "Come, I will show you the bride, the wife of the Lamb."

And in the spirit he carried me away to a great, high mountain and showed me the holy city Jerusalem coming down out of heaven from God. It has the glory of God and a radiance like a very rare jewel, like jasper, clear as crystal. It has a great, high wall with twelve gates, and at the gates twelve angels, and on the gates are inscribed the names of the twelve tribes of the Israelites; on the east three gates, on the north three gates, on the south three gates, and on the west three gates. And the wall of the city has twelve foundations, and on them are the twelve names of the twelve apostles of the Lamb.

The angel who talked to me had a measuring rod of gold to measure the city and its gates and walls. The city lies foursquare, its length the same as its width; and he measured the city with his rod, fifteen hundred miles; its length and width and height are equal. He also measured its wall, one hundred forty-four cubits by human measurement, which the angel was using.

The wall is built of jasper, while the city is pure gold, clear as glass. The foundations of the wall of the city are adorned with every jewel; the first was jasper, the second sapphire, the third agate, the fourth emerald, the fifth onyx, the sixth carnelian, the seventh chrysolite, the eighth beryl, the ninth topaz, the tenth chrysoprase, the eleventh jacinth, the twelfth amethyst. And the twelve gates are twelve pearls, each of the gates is a single pearl, and the street of the city is pure gold, transparent as glass.

I saw no temple in the city, for its temple is the Lord God the Almighty and the Lamb. And the city has no need of sun or moon to shine on it, for the glory of God is its light, and its lamp is the Lamb. The nations will walk by its light, and the kings of the earth will bring their glory into it. Its gates will never be shut by day—and there will be no night there. People will bring into it the glory and the honor of the nations. But nothing unclean will enter it, nor anyone who practices abomination or falsehood, but only those who are written in the Lamb's book of life.

Then the angel showed me the river of the water of life, bright as crystal, flowing from the throne of God and of the Lamb through the middle of the street of the city. On either side of the river is the tree of life with its twelve kinds of fruit, producing its fruit each month; and the leaves of the tree are for the healing of the nations. Nothing accursed will be found there any more. But the throne of God and of the Lamb will be in it, and his servants will worship him; they will see his face, and his name will be on their foreheads. And there will be no more night; they need no light of lamp or sun, for the Lord God will be their light, and they will reign forever and ever. (Rev. 21:1–22:5)

The earth suffers throughout the Book of Revelation. But, like its human inhabitants who also suffer, it is renewed and made fit for this final, eternal cohabitation of God, humanity, and the rest of earthly creation. We must note that it is not brand-new, just as its human lords are not brand-new: there is no *creatio ex nihilo*. God doesn't start all over again. Instead, he resurrects humanity and, so to speak, resurrects the earth as well into a resplendent ecology of vitality and beauty in which all live in mutually beneficial relationship with each other.

Oliver O'Donovan speaks of the church-become-city in Revelation 21:

No destiny can possibly be conceived in the world, or even out of it, other than that of a city. It is the last word of the Gospel, as it is of the New Testament: a city that is the heart of a world, a focus of international peace; a city that is itself a temple rather than possessing a temple, itself a natural environment rather than possessing a natural environment; a city that has overcome the antinomies of nature and culture, worship and politics, under an all-directing regime that needs no mediation; a city that has the universe within it, and yet has an "outside"—not in the sense of an autonomous alternative, but of having all alternatives excluded, a city with a Valley of Hinnom [O'Donovan means "hell"], which does not, therefore, have to carry within it the cheapness and tawdriness that have made all other cities mean.[25]

This vision is our "imagined future," without a clear sense of which no one can resist the relentless conformist pressures of our culture and strive for something different and better.[26] This vision is the hope of *shalom,* the rich Hebrew word that goes far beyond the cessation of hostility and disruption to encompass flourishing: each element (human, animal, plant, and so on) flourishing as itself, enjoying flourishing relationships with everything else, and joining with all creation in flourishing relationship with God.[27] Richard Bauckham writes about blessing as God's fundamental mode of relating to his creation, the mode of bringing *shalom,* and a mode we are to imitate as his image:

> Blessing in the Bible refers to God's characteristically generous and abundant giving of all good to his creatures and his continual renewal of the abundance of created life.... God's blessing of people overflows in their blessing of others and those who experience blessing from God in turn bless God, which means that they give all that creatures really can give to God: thanksgiving and praise.
>
> ...It is in the most comprehensive sense God's purpose for his creation. Wherever human life enjoys the good things of creation and produces the good fruits of human activity, God is pouring out his blessing.[28]

This vision thus implies vital principles for Christian ethics, among which are the following:

1. The individual matters, and so does the social. Individuality is maintained in the world to come, as is society—and as is the distinction between each of these and God (versus any sort of "blending," "melding," or other mystical

---

25. O'Donovan, *Desire of the Nations,* 285.

26. Anna Fels, *Necessary Dreams: Ambition in Women's Changing Lives* (New York: Pantheon, 2004); see also Barry A. Harvey, "What We've Got Here Is a Failure to Imagine: The Church-Based University in the Tournament of Competing Visions," *Christian Scholar's Review* 34 (Winter 2005): 201–15.

27. Among the best descriptions I have encountered of *shalom* is the one provided by Nicholas Wolterstorff in *Until Justice and Peace Embrace* (Grand Rapids, MI: Eerdmans, 1983), 69–72.

28. Bauckham, *Bible and Mission,* 34.

union that includes ontological loss of these distinctions). Thus we must not champion only the individual (as if one's own spiritual development is all that matters, as many people seem to think), nor only society (as if the welfare of the group—whether the church or society at large—is the sum of the faith).

2. The physical matters, and so does the spiritual. The New Jerusalem is depicted as truly physical, from what I call its architecture of superabundance that uses the most precious materials of this age as construction materials, with its mind-boggling dimensions (a cubic city, fifteen hundred miles on a side), to the river and garden that wind through it—a phenomenon ancient Jews had seen only in the imperial centers of Egypt and Mesopotamia. And this New Jerusalem enjoys the light of God's presence—reminiscent of the *shekinah* of God in the Old Testament, but now suffusing the entire city.

3. Unity matters, and so does diversity. It is one city, with one Lord, the capital of a single world. But the nations enter as such, in their evident differences, bringing the best of their cultures in tribute to the one King of all and in contribution to the mutual benefit of all. This is a vision of multicultural-ism that causes us to exclaim, "*This* is what we long for in all of our disap-pointed well-meaning here and now!"

4. The world to come is in continuity with this world, and fulfills the noble aspirations of this world, even as it clearly transcends this world. Again, the use of gold as paving material and gigantic precious stones as masonry sym-bolizes that the very best of this world corresponds with the very bottom of the next, just as our earthly bodies resemble and are the seeds of the glorious resurrection bodies to which we look forward; just as our current fellow-ship in the church and in human society more generally shows flashes of that joyful, easy, and loving companionship of that new era; and just as our periodic worship of God blossoms into constant enjoyment and praise of him as we dwell together in unity forever.

   The extravagant language of the vision also reminds us, as does the very image of a city descending from heaven to earth, that the New Jerusalem is fundamentally and finally God's gift from above, not our accomplishment from below. It is the fulfillment of our work, yes, but fulfilled by the sur-passing power, wisdom, creativity, and generosity of the God.

5. Implicit in this vision of the New Jerusalem and fundamental to the Chris-tian ethos is what I call the principle of "win-win-win." *Shalom* is an all-embracing life of mutual contribution and benefit. Within it, individuals and groups are never finally in a situation of choosing whether to benefit themselves or others, never finally in a situation of choosing to honor God

over their own well-being. Much Christian piety and preaching, I daresay, has been importantly misguided and misleading on this account, so let's expand on this theme.

Frequently in Christian ethics, a doctrine of "unselfishness" has been commended. Often this rather negative virtue is connected with the positive virtue of *agapē* as the highest and best form of love and defined as utterly other-focused self-giving. A related theme, particularly in Lutheran and Calvinist circles, has been "the glory of God," as if the pinnacle of piety is to seek God's glory at the expense of one's own utter loss.

The amazing paradox of Christian teaching here, however, is that losing one's life is the way to save it (Mt. 16:24–27). Spending one's goods on others is the way to pile up treasures of much greater value that will last forever (Mt. 19:21). Altruism is in one's own interest—including God's own interest. I need to say this carefully, so I will hew closely to the words of Scripture: Jesus suffered and sacrificed himself on the cross "for the joy set before him" (Heb. 12:2), not in a zero-sum game in which he simply had to lose so that we would gain. Yes, of course that is partly true also: "by his poverty you have become rich" (II Cor. 8:9). But it was a *temporary* sacrifice, a *temporary* poverty. It was an expenditure that was truly costly—may I not be misunderstood as denigrating the grace of God in Christ—but it was spent so as to bring joy to God, as well as to bring salvation to us. It is never one or the other.

For that is the nature of love: God's joy is bound up in our well-being.[29] As Irenaeus put it, "The glory of God is a man fully alive!" and the Westminster Shorter Catechism responds, "Man's chief end is to glorify God, and to enjoy him forever."[30] Our joy, when we are properly oriented to the world, is bound up in the well-being of everything else. The shepherd exerts himself to find the lost sheep because he cares about the sheep, yes, and his worry about the sheep makes him anxious and sad. So both the sheep and the shepherd return to the fold with joy (Mt. 18:12–14). It is ridiculous to try to pull apart what is, in the nature of the case, a seamless unit: my well-being depends upon the well-being of the beloved. Therefore it is bad ethics to urge people to care for others at their own expense in any ultimate sense. No, the

---

29. Daniel W. Hardy speaks of the "correlative well-being" of God and his creation, such that "God is…constituted by a concentration of well-being in relationship which is inseparable from the extending of this relationship with his people in the world, and from the expression of his well-being in that relationship" (*God's Ways with the World: Thinking and Practising Christian Faith* [Edinburgh: T. & T. Clark, 1996], 22, 29).

30. Irenaeus, *Against Heresies,* IV.20.vii (my translation); Philip Schaff and David S. Schaff, eds., *The Creeds of Christendom,* 6th ed. (Grand Rapids, MI: Baker, 1931), 676.

Christian view of love is *shalom:* when you win, I win and God wins. When God wins, you win and I win. And so on, endlessly around the circle of love.

The Christian gospel, therefore, does not ask the impossible and the irresponsible: "Give up your own self-interest for others."[31] Our self-interest is precisely that to which the gospel properly appeals: Here is how to be saved! Here is how to have life, and have it abundantly! Here is how to prepare for the everlasting joy to come! We are all in this together. Thus we work hard, truly self-sacrificially and even to the death, for everyone's benefit: God's, the world's, and mine. No zero-sum, but abundant life forever and for all.

To that work, then, we now turn.

MISSION: THE FOUR COMMANDMENTS

It is a commonplace in modern discussions of mission to link our mission with the *missio dei,* the "mission of God." There is an immediate paradox in the idea of the mission of God, however, for the word "mission" entails sending, and who sends God? Yet it is God who sends himself; God who cares for the world as Father, Son, and Holy Spirit; God who expends himself on the task he sets for himself: the redemption of the world he made, sustains, and loves.

As followers of Jesus, furthermore, and as those who have been adopted as children by the Father and who are indwelt, empowered, and directed by the Spirit, we are "co-missioned" by God to work with him in his global task.

The Bible bursts with insight, instruction, and illustration regarding our mission. But we can begin to attend to this welter of revelation by attending to four commandments of God, four mandates for our life and work in the world. These four can be grouped into two sets, what I will call "creation commandments" and "redemption commandments."

The Creation Commandments

THE CULTURAL MANDATE

Then God said, "Let us make humankind in our image, according to our likeness; and let them have dominion over the fish of the sea, and over the birds of

---

31. Jonathan Edwards is particularly helpful on this question, finding, as he does, that "a man's loving what is grateful [agreeable] or pleasing to him, and being averse to what is disagreeable... is the same thing as a man's having a faculty of will" (*The Nature of True Virtue,* in *Jonathan Edwards: Ethical Writings,* ed. Paul Ramsey [New Haven, CT: Yale University Press, 1989], 575–76).

the air, and over the cattle, and over all the wild animals of the earth, and over every creeping thing that creeps upon the earth."

So God created humankind in his image, in the image of God he created them; male and female he created them. God blessed them, and God said to them, "Be fruitful and multiply, and fill the earth and subdue it; and have dominion over the fish of the sea and over the birds of the air and over every living thing that moves upon the earth." (Gen. 1:26–28)

We have discussed this commandment already. Having created everything else, God then creates human beings specifically in his "image" and "likeness"— the exact words the author of Genesis uses to describe Seth, the child of Adam and Eve (Gen. 5:3). Whatever else we may say about the *imago dei* (and this term has been given a wider range of meanings than perhaps any other in the history of theology), we can say this: we human beings were created to resemble God, to be like God, and we are to be God-like particularly in a special role, namely, that of exercising lordship or dominion over everything else on the planet.

In order to accomplish this task (this mission) of dominion, God tells the first humans to spread out over the face of the planet: "be fruitful and multiply, and fill the earth"—three mentions of reproduction. And why do so? With the purpose of bringing the whole earth under cultivation: "and subdue it; and have dominion." The burgeoning human family is to move out from the initial garden, planted by God (Gen. 2:8–15), to make a garden of the whole planet as "little lords," as deputies of God, doing his kind of work and in obedience to his commandment. Thus God calls us to procreate in order to co-create.

At least three fundamental implications follow from this commandment. First, caring for the earth and making the best of it is our primary duty under God. I do not mean by this to diminish the fundamental importance of love of God or of neighbor: I take those for granted in the present discussion and will discuss the great commandments below. Nonetheless, whatever else we are to be and to do, in the Bible's account we literally are gardeners first. God has never rescinded this commandment. Furthermore, it will be our task, and our glory, to carry on this mission of dominion in the immediate presence of our Lord Jesus: "If we endure," Paul promises, "we will reign with him" (II Tim. 2:12). And in the Revelation to John, the Christian faithful several times are described as reigning with Christ (Rev. 5:10; 20:6; 22:5). Over what or whom is there for resurrected humanity to reign with Christ, all of his enemies having been removed from the scene forever? The answer is this: a renewed earth, as we continue to be and to function as the "image of God." Dallas Willard writes,

We will not sit around looking at one another or at God for eternity but will join the eternal Logos, "reign with him," in the endlessly ongoing creative work of God....

Thus, our faithfulness over a "few things" in the present phase of our life develops the kind of character that can be entrusted with "many things."...His plan is for us to develop, as apprentices to Jesus, to the point where we can take our place in the ongoing creativity of the universe.[32]

And how wonderful it will be to engage in work in that context: with the consequences of the Fall removed, with everyone fully cooperating, including nature itself, and in constant communion with God. We can scarcely imagine what scholarship would be like in that mode, or engineering, or music, or architecture, or cuisine...

It perhaps is worth mentioning here that, contrary to what has sometimes been affirmed on this question, the Incarnation of our Lord was not, in fact, necessary to "sanctify the ordinary" or otherwise to validate our everyday work. Jesus comes as the Son of Man, reminding us, as well as showing us flawlessly, of what God had already revealed to us at creation of the dignity of human being and of our divinely commissioned work in his world.

The second fundamental affirmation here is that all of our fellow human beings share the dignity and responsibility of this commandment. Those who obey it, whether they intend to honor God or not, are doing his will, and God continues to bless humanity with both a degree of correct orientation to this task and resources to undertake it.[33] We Christians (along with the Jews) have this Scripture to show us that fact. And inasmuch as any of our neighbors are indeed

---

32. Dallas Willard, *The Divine Conspiracy: Rediscovering Our Hidden Life in God* (San Francisco: Harper, 1998), 378.

33. I am not going to engage in a discussion of "natural law," "common grace," and so on, since I have not yet found the long-standing debates around them to have delivered solid, useful categories for the present project. I will say that I do think that the extremes in this discussion are unhelpful—making too little or too much of God's gifts to humanity and humanity's capacity to use them properly after the Fall. So I do not follow pessimists about human capacity, such as Barth or Ellul or Hauerwas, nor optimists such as Roman Catholic thinkers in the train of Thomas Aquinas. On the one hand, even John Calvin believed that the image of God was not totally effaced (*Institutes*, I.xv.4) and that God had blessed non-Christians with genuine knowledge and insight into the world (II.ii.15). On the other hand, no one should underplay the requirement for divine grace in order for us to have enjoyed even the degree of goodness our societies have enjoyed since Cain founded the first city, let alone the divine intervention necessary to bring us to the New Jerusalem. I will also remark

cultivating the earth in whatever might be their work, art, leisure, and so on, we can recognize it, approve it, and cooperate with it—again, whether or not the name of God or of Jesus is invoked in the enterprise.[34]

The dark side of this awareness of the creation mandate is that those whose work is *not* contributing to the welfare of the earth in some way, those whose efforts do not result in a measure of *shalom,* are recognized and judged. It is not enough to claim harmlessness; we are to accomplish positive good, and those who do not are wasting God's resources.

There is a danger here, to be sure, of seeing this matter through too narrow a sense of *shalom* and therefore too narrow a sense of what can count as worthy work, art, and so on. Advertising, cosmetics, and fashion, for example, are pursuits that are easily written off by Christians (and others) for their obvious excesses and evils, while we usually fail to credit their virtues: that advertising can help us make good decisions amid the welter of choices we must make in a wealthy society; that cosmetics can beautify the body in the same way in which we ingenuously beautify our homes or churches; and that fashion can reflect both our creativity and our limitations, as we cannot and do not think of design possibilities all at once, but formulate, elaborate, and enjoy them only seriatim. Yet

---

that Bonhoeffer's reflections on "the natural," briefly described above, have yet to be noticed sufficiently in these discussions. Finally, I find Carl Braaten's painstaking attempt to both rehabilitate and qualify "natural law" in terms of his Lutheran orientation poignantly to raise the question of whether the game is worth the candle—and I don't think it is: Carl E. Braaten, "Natural Law in Theology and Ethics," *The Two Cities of God: The Church's Responsibility for the Earthly City* (Grand Rapids, MI: Eerdmans, 1997), 42–58.

34. This is just one of many places in which I could signal, as I do now, both my frequent confusion about what Stanley Hauerwas is saying in his many writings, and my likely disagreement with him on some (but by no means all) key points. For instance, he writes: "Any attempt to provide an account of how Christian theological claims can tell us the way things are requires a correlative politics. In theological terms, such a politics is called 'church'" (*With the Grain of the Universe: The Church's Witness and Natural Theology* [Grand Rapids, MI: Brazos, 2001], 39). This unclear sentence he offers as a summary of his argument in his Gifford Lectures, so it is obviously important to understand his project.

Now, if Hauerwas means that properly making Christian truth claims requires instantiation in an actual community and that community is the church, then I am obviously in agreement, and just wish he would say that more clearly. But if he means that the articulation of Christian theology as a description of reality has political implications that are confined to the church—which is how I think Hauerwas frequently *sounds,* as he seems to relinquish responsibility for running society to non-Christians, at least in society's coercive institutions—then we do disagree. Christian theology addresses the politics of *everyone* in a positive way via the creation commandments, and in a negative way via the doctrine of sin.

Indeed, given Brother Hauerwas's current prominence, I must confess that I find him—despite his oft-praised penchant for the exciting phrase—so frequently obscure, as well as so frequently implausible, that I have focused my attention herein on the more intelligible and provocative work of his mentor, John Howard Yoder.

a properly broad understanding of *shalom* can then help us condemn harmful advertising, vain cosmetics, and stupid fashion, even as it helps us sort through other issues in culture: what *is* worth doing, and what should be discarded as in fact vain/worthless/empty, let alone positively evil?

Third, we must not let ourselves be driven to bad consciences, let alone self-loathing, by ecological extremists who are so unhappy about how we have harmed the earth that they condemn human dominion, if not humanity itself, as a curse. Of course we must bewail the mistakes we have made in our stewardship of creation. Of course we must repent of mistreatment of our fellow creatures. But we must do so as responsible lords who have acted irresponsibly and who now intend to make things right, not as usurpers who ought to slink away from the throne room and leave the world to fend for itself. God made us to bless the earth by exercising dominion. God did not want us to leave as few footprints as possible, leaving the earth alone as much as we can. He commanded us instead to spread out, over the whole globe, and bring it all under our influence, to subdue it for its own good, to make it even more fruitful, beautiful, and sustainable, under God's guidance and by the power he invested in it. We dare not be cowed into relinquishing this role out of shame that we have performed it badly heretofore. We must take it up afresh, do the best we can, and look forward to the *shalom* that our administration will bring, in concert with Christ's rule, in the world to come.

THE GREAT COMMANDMENTS

When the Pharisees heard that he had silenced the Sadducees, they gathered together, and one of them, a lawyer, asked him a question to test him. "Teacher, which commandment in the law is the greatest?"

He said to him, "'You shall love the Lord your God with all your heart, and with all your soul, and with all your mind.' This is the greatest and first commandment. And a second is like it: 'You shall love your neighbor as yourself.' On these two commandments hang all the law and the prophets." (Mt. 22:34–40)

This story comes from the life of Jesus, but Jesus quotes not something new and surprising but something old and familiar—old as the Torah and familiar as the Ten Commandments: love God thoroughly and above all others, and love your neighbor as yourself. Any Jewish kid with a decent religious education would have been able to cite these verses from the Book of Moses (Deut. 6:5; Lev. 19:18).

Yet, as usual, there is more than one level to Jesus' retort, more than a clever humbling of the scholar by making him recite his ethical ABCs. Jesus draws together these commandments from different parts of the Torah, welds them together, and then sets them down in front of Israel and, indeed, the whole world. Everything else God has to say, he says, hangs on these two commandments.

I suggest, then, that these two commandments form a unit that I am calling the second of the creation commandments. For surely these commandments do not begin to operate only in the giving of the Law to Moses, but from the creation of Adam and Eve. Implicit in the Garden of Eden is the expectation that the first humans will love God above all else—obeying him particularly in his command not to eat of the forbidden fruit—and will love each other as himself or herself, a commandment that is particularly graphic given Eve's origin out of Adam's body in Genesis 2 and their marriage that symbolically reunites them into that "one flesh" of primordial humanity.

We can draw similar implications from these commandments. First, we are to love God and love our neighbors as ourselves. There is nothing we can justify doing if it means not loving God above all else and with all that we are. There is nothing we can justify doing if it means not loving our neighbors as ourselves. Whatever other factors may obtain in an ethical choice, these two abide as the framework on which everything else hangs.

We as Christians have the wonderful privilege of recognizing, however, the win-win-win situation of God's economy. So we recognize that as we love God and our neighbors, we also do what is best for ourselves. That is the way God has made the world, and to try to wrench ourselves free of that order so that we may concentrate on what we think is our own welfare is to pull away precisely from the matrix of mutual blessing in which our own interest truly lies. So we, more than anyone, should embrace this dual commandment.

Second, the command is positive: "love." It is not negative: "avoid sin." This difference emerges in Jesus' disputes with the Pharisees, the most scrupulous of the Jewish sects of his day. Mark Buchanan writes:

> The Pharisees had an ethic of avoidance, and Jesus had an ethic of involvement. The Pharisee's question was not "How can I glorify God?" It was "How can I avoid bringing disgrace to God?" This degenerated into a concern not with God, but with self—with image, reputation, procedure. They didn't ask, "How can I make others clean?" They asked, "How can I keep myself from getting dirty?" They did not seek to rescue sinners, only to avoid sinning.[35]

---

35. Mark Buchanan, *Your God Is Too Safe: Rediscovering the Wonder of a God You Can't Control* (Portland, OR: Multnomah, 2001), 108–9. I recognize that E. P. Sanders and others have rehabilitated some Christian stereotypes regarding the Pharisees, but I think Buchanan's

Our mission is to get things done, not to avoid getting dirty, or bloody, in the process—and, to restate a theme in this ethic, we must recognize that loving God and one's neighbor in this troubled and troubling world often entails dirt and blood. Faithfulness can rarely oblige fastidiousness. David Martin broadens our view thus:

> Those who obey that [Christian] vision move from special privilege to special responsibility, from keeping themselves apart to welcoming the stranger within the gate, from the multiplication of Abraham's physical seed to the scattering abroad of a spiritual seed, from a Jerusalem jealously guarded as the citadel of an ethnic faith with a divine land grant, to new Jerusalems which offer a light to the Gentiles and envisage a free city in the spirit, the "mother of us all."[36]

It is worth pausing a moment over this command to love our neighbors, for frequently in discussions about Christian Realism the point is made that love is expected of individuals, while the lesser standard of justice is applied to governments and other secular institutions. Interestingly, both those who defend Christian Realism and those who oppose it in the name of an evangelical or Anabaptist or liberal alternative typically make this distinction. I suggest that both sides are mistaken on this crucial point.

As even Reinhold Niebuhr came to aver in his later writings, love is required of states, of governments at every level, of institutions such as hospitals and universities, of businesses, and of every other human group—not just of individuals. Love is crucial to the God-given task of cultivating the world, of making the best of it. Mere justice will not suffice to secure the greatest possible *shalom,* which is our calling. So love must function here, too.[37]

---

characterization stands—especially given the way Jesus addresses them, and the issues over which they contend with him.

36. Martin, *Christian Language,* 185.

37. Having already drafted this section, I belatedly find that Miroslav Volf has made a similar point (*Work in the Spirit: Toward a Theology of Work* [New York: Oxford University Press, 1991], 82–83):

> The concept of new creation implies certain principles that cannot be set aside if justice is to prevail. This we might call the "ethical minimum." But the new creation also implies principles that point beyond the way of justice to the way of love, which we might call the "ethical maximum."...
>
> The ethical maximum may not be zealously transmuted from regulative ideal to sacrosanct criterion. As one uses the ethical maximum to optimize structures, one must take soberly into account what is practically realizable.... At the same time it is crucial not to set love aside as useless in social ethics.... The practice of justice alone will not be sufficient to create a humane society. For without love, there is no *shalom.*

Let us be careful not to stumble at this point over the definition of "love." I do not mean a sentiment, a personal affection for another, and the like. Some ethicists believe that love can be shared only by individuals and not by groups, and so to call on states to "love" is to confuse categories. But to say so is to misunderstand the nature of love in this context. I mean by "love" the act of going beyond the strict requirements of justice, beyond satisfying some standard of correct behavior, to seeking the welfare of the other, to acting so as to benefit the other beyond his or her just deserts. Businesses, schools, hospitals, and governments, among other collectivities, can indeed love in this sense.

Consider the outcomes of the First and Second World Wars, and the difference between the punitive terms of the Treaty of Versailles and the effect on Germany, and Europe in general, of the Marshall Plan. Versailles certainly could be criticized for being less than just, but no one would characterize the Marshall Plan as mere justice. In fact, many contemporary critics of the Marshall Plan advocated strict justice instead: better to let Germany lie in the wretched bed it had made. Yet it was *not* better to do so—not better for Germany, but also not better for the United States or even the European nations who had been victimized by Germany. The Marshall Plan, going well beyond justice to what I would not hesitate to call love, made for peace—*shalom*—in Europe, as did similar efforts in postwar Japan.

One might retort that the Marshall Plan was mere geopolitical calculation, a shrewd move to secure America's own interests. But in a win-win-win scheme, this cynical view is not the only plausible one. Yes, it was truly in America's interests to make peace in Europe and to restore health to war-ravaged societies. So what? To benefit from an act of love doesn't make it less loving or less *shalom*-producing. The same goes for the more recent case of American armed forces providing major assistance to areas devastated by the Indian Ocean tsunami in 2004—scoring points with Muslims from Indonesia to Africa who otherwise were inclined to fear and hate America because of its violent involvement in Iraq and Afghanistan.[38]

The great Orthodox thinker Vladimir Soloviev discusses these themes also in his *Critique of Abstract Principles;* for an introduction to his thought on these and related matters, see Paul Valliere, "Vladimir Soloviev (1853–1900)," in *The Teachings of Modern Christianity on Law, Politics, and Human Nature,* ed. John Witte Jr. and Frank S. Alexander (New York: Columbia University Press, 2006), 1:533–575.

38. There is even evidence that Christian values can assist in a matter that gets as close to realpolitik as can be imagined, namely, the interrogation of prisoners. United States Marine Major Sherwood F. Moran applied techniques of care and respect for his subjects during World War II and was much more successful than anyone else at his job. The counterintuitive story of his interrogation manual is told in Stephen Budiansky, "Truth Extraction," *Atlantic Monthly,* June 2005, 32–35.

The way of love, which both includes and supersedes justice, is in everybody's interest.[39]

To be sure, this kind of love is framed and measured by realism. "Aha!" might come the reply. "God's love isn't like that. God's love is unmeasured, boundless, free. It is that kind of love that is required of individuals, and obviously cannot be expected of states."

Yet this characterization of God's love is sentimental and extravagant. God's love is vast, to be sure, but God does in fact measure it out to us according to his purposes. He does not make everything lovely. He does not make every day Christmas Day. Instead, as a wise Lord and wise Parent, he loves us in ways we don't like, and may even fear, according to the actual need of the situation and our capacity to respond well in it. The love that God expects of us—corporately and individually—is not unlike the love he shows us.

Thus we are to love our neighbors realistically—according to their need, according to their capacity to receive what we have to offer, and according to our resources, which are not limitless. Any wise parent refuses to simply shower his child with presents, much as he would like to do so, because the child would not benefit from this extravagance, nor would the parent. The same is true of any good supervisor, or executive, or owner, or governor. The truly loving thing to do is not strict distributive justice, but it is not a blizzard of indulgence, either.

We can now revisit the Sermon on the Mount and its call to "turn the other cheek," go the extra mile, and so on. These instances Jesus cites are instances of what I am calling in this context *love*. It is going beyond what is strictly necessary in the situation, to demonstrate the abundant life of the Kingdom, the generosity of God even to sinners. Note that none of Jesus' examples are life-and-death situations or even situations of grave harm—bodily, financial, or otherwise. Nor are they examples of people who have power to fundamentally change the situation—to bring the miscreant to justice or to prevent such oppression in the first place. I think it is a mistake, therefore, to generalize from these instances either to situations of extreme danger to oneself or others or to situations of political and police action. The examples are vivid instances about typical dealings with people who dislike you and do not seek your best interest—such as a Roman soldier mistreating a Jew.

---

39. To be sure, sometimes, if all too rarely, we human beings are capable of genuine self-sacrifice in the interests of justice and the welfare of others. Rodney Stark sums up the research of many others to observe that the abolition of slavery was advanced in America, Britain, and France to the immediate, lasting, and considerable cost of individuals and of those societies in general (*For the Glory of God: How Monotheism Led to Reformations, Science, Witch-Hunts, and the End of Slavery* [Princeton, NJ: Princeton University Press, 2003], 358–59).

Properly understood, then, these examples do not have to be understood as setting some terribly high standard—*pace* both Niebuhr and Yoder. Instead, this teaching of returning good for evil—"even if someone strikes you, let alone insults you or inconveniences you," I think it is fair to interpret what Jesus says—directs us in our particular circumstances to demonstrate the extravagant patience and (more than mere endurance) love of God. When someone cuts you off in traffic and then, down the road, wants to be let into your lane, what then? When someone steals your idea at work and then comes to you for help in implementing it, what then? When a neighbor annoys you with loud music late into the night, and then wakes you early one morning, unrepentant, seeking a boost for his dead car battery, what then?

Jesus' words are the ever-living, ever-relevant Word of God. Thus they guide us both when we are victims with little power, empowering us to go beyond mere compliance to a counterintuitive generosity as a mark of the Kingdom, and also when we do have power: we still show love. It is love, it is concern and care for the other, in fact, that is the common element in the ethics of weakness and oppression in this passage in the Sermon on the Mount and also in the ethics of power and responsibility I am articulating here from other Scriptures—from Genesis 1 forward.

The divine call, then, is to love our neighbors as we love ourselves, to treat them the way we would want to be treated, with the guidance and example of God ever before us. Let us go on to realize, moreover, what ought to be obvious in a globalized world of massive and increasing connections: everyone is our neighbor now, whether we like it or not. Thus compassion and concern are not pleasant and occasional additions to the responsibility of a state or a business, but are wisely commanded by God—for everyone's benefit. Let us have no more false dichotomies between justice and love.[40]

Third, we must recognize that inasmuch as our neighbors are loving God and loving their neighbors, they are doing the will of God. And, having recognized this goodness, we can approve and cooperate with it. The same caveat, furthermore, applies here just as it did in the previous commandment. If our conception

---

40. Ronald J. Sider combines these virtues in his presentation of "Seven Short Principles for a Political Philosophy," namely, "Everybody should have power, not just a few"; "The poor deserve special care"; "Every person should have the capital to earn a decent living"; "Maintain the balance between freedom and justice"; "Always think globally"; "Protect the separation of church and state"; and "Understand the limits of politics" (*Living Like Jesus: Eleven Essentials for Growing a Genuine Faith* [Grand Rapids, MI: Baker, 1996], 130–37). For a very different list that nonetheless combines realpolitik with justice and gives more than a nod to compassion, see Robert D. Kaplan, "Supremacy by Stealth: Ten Rules for Managing the World," *Atlantic Monthly,* July 2003, 66–83.

of what it means to love God or our neighbor is too narrow, then we will errone-
ously condemn as evil what is in truth good. A major question in our pluralistic
times, therefore, is to discern what is genuine love for God and love for the neighbor in the sometimes bewildering and even disquieting forms in which people
claim to be engaged in such love. We must be careful, at least, not to condemn
too quickly what is meant as good. At the same time, we have been given divine
revelation, divine guidance by the Holy Spirit, and the divinely oriented Christian community to assist us in such discernment, so we increase *shalom* when false
loves are exposed and resisted as such. Indeed, part of exercising dominion over
the world is to engage in such discernment, for we are responsible to cultivate the
good and weed out the bad as best we can.

We therefore have these creation commandments to love God and our neighbors
as ourselves as we cultivate the world. It is these commandments that guide Christians, as they ought to guide, and someday will guide, all people, in our work.[41]

---

41. These divine commands must be taken into account by such as Yoder, who speaks instead
of "what later Protestant social ethicists…call 'the ethic of vocation,' whereby what it
means to do the proper thing in one's given social setting is determined by the inherent
quasi-autonomous law of that setting, whose demands can be both known and fulfilled
independently of any particular relation to the rootage of Christian faith" (*Priestly Kingdom*,
83). My point is that to rule well is a generically human calling, ordained and ordered by
God, and does not in itself require a specifically Christian content—if that is what Yoder
means by the unclear phrase "independently of any particular relation to the rootage of the
Christian faith." There is one Lord, Jesus Christ, under whose authority all rulers rule and
according to whose order (logos) all rule, however (dis)obediently—whether they know
anything about Christianity or not. Thus the apocryphal saying attributed to Luther: "Better
to be ruled by a good Turk than a bad Christian."

To be blunt, I would turn the tables on Brother Yoder and say that it is people of his
persuasion, not people of my outlook, who are not fully obeying the Lord. It is he who tells
Christians to avoid certain functions of government, particularly involving "the sword," in
the name of following Jesus—even as, to his credit, he refuses to advocate a simple retreat
from the world and various other forms of cultural involvement and service. (This qualification is a key aspect of Yoder's thought, which must be given its due. Stanley Hauerwas makes
a similar qualification: "Christians must withdraw their support from a 'civic republicanism'
only when that form (as well as any other form) of government and society resorts to violence
in order to maintain internal order and external security. At that point and that point alone
Christians must withhold their involvement with the state" ["Why the 'Sectarian Temptation' Is a Misrepresentation: A Response to James Gustafson," in *The Hauerwas Reader*, ed.
John Berkman and Michael Cartwright (Durham, NC: Duke University Press, 2001), 105].)
But I reply that to obey the creation commandments in the current situation—post-Fall, pre-
Parousia—means to wield "the sword" indeed, and to leave those functions to others is, in
fact, to disobey Jesus—who is, with the Father and the Son, one God, and the Author of the
(whole) Bible. When I think of Yoder, and especially of Hauerwas, I am reminded of Oliver
O'Donovan's vivid phrasing: "The prophet is not allowed the luxury of perpetual subver-
sion. After Ahab, Elijah must anoint some Hazael, some Jehu" (*Desire of the Nations*, 12).

In the paragraph previous to the one cited, Yoder writes of Christian lords, after Constantine, who essentially disregard (Yoder uses the sarcastic locution "create some tension

Yet we do not dwell in Eden. Our situation has changed, and drastically. Thus our mission is altered also, as God redeems the world and draws it back into line with his original purposes.

The Redemption Commandments

THE NEW COMMANDMENT

I give you a new commandment, that you love one another. Just as I have loved you, you also should love one another. By this everyone will know that you are my disciples, if you have love for one another. (Jn. 13:34–35)

In this part of John's gospel, Jesus is preparing his disciples explicitly for the end of his earthly mission and the extension of theirs—really, of his, too, through them. As part of this mission, then, he gives them what seems at first to be an odd, if not offensive, mandate: to love each other. This is not a simple reiteration of the Great Commandment to love your neighbor, but a *new* commandment to love Christians in particular. It seems, in truth, a most un-Christlike injunction. This Jesus had spent much of his public career opening up doors in walls people had erected between one kind of human being and another: between Jews and Gentiles, between rich and poor, between men and women, between adults and children, and between "the righteous" and "sinners." Why did this Jesus then, at the end of his career and to his innermost circle, command this "scandal of particularity"? Why did he place this priority on loving fellow Christians in a way somehow distinct from the love given to neighbors in general?

Jesus gives the reason: "By this everyone will know that you are my disciples, if you have love for one another." The Jewish context of Jesus' ministry can help us here, as we consider a parallel to ancient Israel. Israel was singled out by God in the Old Testament as a nation through which God would demonstrate his

---

with") "what the later prophets and Jesus taught about domination, wealth, and violence" (82). So let me go on more generally to address the fact that "servant leadership" is typically portrayed by many Christians—with disproportionate emphasis on a particular view of servanthood—on the basis of Jesus' supposed example. Yet few of these portraits include such "leaderly" features of Jesus' career as his exercise of power over nature, the demonic powers, and human beings; his acceptance of worship; his commands to his disciples and his expectation of both fealty and obedience; his repeated warnings of impending divine judgment that he, as the Son of Man coming with the clouds of heaven, would mete out; and the like. Jesus does provide good material for consideration of leadership, particularly if *all* of it is taken into that consideration and if it is applied properly to mere human lords who, while they are not owed such deference, are yet properly to exercise authority—and who in doing so truly serve their fellows.

power and love to all nations, and thus through which he would call all nations to himself. Israel, when it was functioning properly (that is, according to the Torah) would stand as a beacon amid the murk of other ancient civilizations. It would exemplify order, security, prosperity, community, justice, and holiness—in short, *shalom*. Richard Bauckham puts this point sharply: "In order for the nations to be blessed Israel need only be faithful to YHWH. Her life with YHWH will itself draw the nations to YHWH so that they too may experience his blessing."[42]

This pattern characterizes the whole Bible, as Bauckham observes: "a kind of movement from the particular to the universal."[43] Thus also in the New Community of the New Testament, its life in the world would shine as a city on a hill. Thus the love of Christians for each other would be practical, of course: a bonding that would strengthen them for their redemptive work in the teeth of resistance from the world, the flesh, and the devil. But the reason Jesus gives in this gospel passage for this special love of Christian for Christian was that such love would be a testimony to the *shalom* at the heart of the gospel. Such love—love in the same Spirit as Christ's love for them—would image Christ to the world and show the world what happens when Christ is in a community and a community is in Christ (so John 15, later in this discourse). The paradox of the new commandment to the church, therefore, is in line with the paradox of Israel's entire existence: a special case that seems exclusive, but is in fact a special case whose purpose is globally inclusive, a particular that functions to bless the whole world.[44] While this "in-group" loves each other, it keeps its doors wide open and invites everyone else inside.

THE GREAT COMMISSION

And Jesus came and said to them, "All authority in heaven and on earth has been given to me. Go therefore and make disciples of all nations, baptizing them in the name of the Father and of the Son and of the Holy Spirit, and teaching them to obey everything that I have commanded you. And remember, I am with you always, to the end of the age." (Mt. 28:18–20)

---

42. Bauckham, *Bible and Mission,* 31.

43. Ibid., 11.

44. Thus it is that Jesus' own mission to Israel is the connection, again, between the Old and New Testaments, as Jesus calls Israel to become again a light to the nations in the restoration of the true worship of God, and then sends out the church to continue that work and to call the rest of the nations to that true worship as well. Indeed, as many New Testament scholars remind us, Jesus himself takes the role of Israel as light to the nations/light of the world, and calls his church to play that role also.

The risen Jesus, about to ascend into heaven as the crowning display of his divine authority, yes, but also as his hard-won authority as head of the church, the firstborn of many siblings (Rom. 8:29), the Son of Man as well as the Son of God—this Jesus tells his disciples to do one thing in particular that is remarkably parallel to the cultural mandate: in paraphrase, spread out through all the *oikoumenē* (the inhabited world) and discipline it. That is, "Go therefore and make disciples of all nations." What is fundamentally wrong with the world is the human worship of something other than God. So go and bring them back to the worship of God as disciples of Jesus, the true image of God (Col. 1:15), who have been inaugurated into this new/original life via baptism in the name of that one true God, now revealed as triune.

One recalls Paul's reflections that

> the creation waits with eager longing for the revealing of the children of God; for the creation was subjected to futility, not of its own will but by the will of the one who subjected it, in hope that the creation itself will be set free from its bondage to decay and will obtain the freedom of the glory of the children of God. We know that the whole creation has been groaning in labor pains until now; and not only the creation, but we ourselves, who have the first fruits of the Spirit, groan inwardly while we wait for adoption, the redemption of our bodies. (Rom. 8:21–23)

As creation's lords go, so goes creation. As we fell into sin and its consequences, so did we curse the earth. (God's pronouncements to Adam and Eve after the Fall in Genesis 3 have often been understood as God cursing the earth, but *we* somehow did that, and God's words acknowledge and warn us of that fact.) Thus just as the new commandment focuses on the church for the benefit of all humankind, now the great commission focuses on the redemption of humankind for the benefit of all creation. We see here, then, what has often been remarked as the centripetal and centrifugal movements in Biblical mission: drawing the nations in via the attraction of the worship of God, and going out to the nations to encourage them to turn away from false gods and come in to the center.

We also see that the redemption commandments serve the larger purpose of the creation commandments. They are emergency measures for an emergency situation. The world is fallen and needs redemption in order that it may resume its proper function as manifest at the creation.

The redemption commandments therefore are temporary, and direct us only in this particular phase of the story. In the New Jerusalem, there will be no need for the new commandment, no need for the great commission, and no need for the church. For there will be no one other than the church to whom the conspicuous love of Christian for Christian will serve as an example, since all will be one in the worship of Christ and love of each other. And there will be no one to be made a disciple, for all who survive the Last Judgment will be, ipso facto, following Christ. The creation commandments, by contrast, are God's abiding will for humanity and the creation under our care—apposite in Eden, apposite after the Fall, apposite in our day, and apposite in the world to come. The redemption commandments were given, therefore, not to supersede the creation commandments, but to serve them.[45]

To obey fully the creation commandments is to live in the Kingdom of God. Thus Jesus' proclamation of the arrival of the Kingdom is the proclamation that God is setting things right, with himself properly in the center and everyone and everything else accordingly being put in its proper place. To live in the light of the Kingdom is to live in *shalom*, and to seek the Kingdom is to seek a world in which the creation commandments are once again honored by everyone, every moment, in everything.

It is this relationship of the redemption commandments to the creation commandments that I think best explains why the New Testament is preoccupied with the former. It is because the New Testament presumes the Old: the creation commandments are never revoked, but rather assumed to be still in full sway. Thus the New Testament focuses upon the distinctive calling of the church and the project of redemption. The Old Testament—and, indeed, the apocalyptic in the New—remains as testimony to God's original, abiding, and final concern that all human beings garden the earth and thus promote and enjoy *shalom*.

In this light, then, we must not restrict Christian ethics to the project of redemption and thus to its particular vocabulary of self-sacrifice and non-coercive invitation. Yes, redemption is all about these things. But redemption is not all that we're about. To say so would be to misunderstand the New as being cut off from and uninformed by the Old—and by its own eschatology. Rather, we must see the

---

45. Tom Wright comments: "We only discover what the shape and the inner life of the church ought to be when we look first at the church's mission, and … we only discover what the church's mission is when we look first at God's purpose for the entire world, as indicated in, for instance, Genesis 1–2, Genesis 12, Isaiah 40–55, Romans 8, I Corinthians 15, Ephesians 1 and Revelation 21–22" (N. T. Wright, *Scripture and the Authority of God* [London: Society for Promoting Christian Knowledge, 2005], 84).

redemptive project and vocabulary as relating to the distinctive (but not the total) work of the church, which is nested within and indeed contributive to the generic mission of all human beings to cultivate the world.[46]

In the next chapter we will see further how the redemption commandments relate properly to the creation commandments as we consider the idea of vocation, of the calling of all humanity by God, and not just the church, to participate with him in his great work on earth.

---

46. David Martin notes this kind of restriction in the New Testament: "The New Testament gives us a language in which to understand and speak of redemptive sacrificial love but it has no language for just war, let alone mere warfare, unless we grossly misuse its metaphors of the sword of the spirit and the helmet of salvation. What then are we to do?" (*Christian Language,* 80). What we are to do is to access the whole Bible, see the Redemption Commandments in the light of the Creation Commandments, and trace out the implications for Christians who are called to obey them all—a project that I trust Martin himself would affirm (118).

SEVEN

VOCATION

The word "vocation" comes from the Latin word *vocare,* and thus means "calling." In Christian history, however, this word has become bound up with the category of "work," albeit in three different ways.

First, some Christians have understood that work *is* vocation. Especially in Roman Catholic and Orthodox Christianity, the term "vocation" means the call to a religious career and, indeed, life pattern: monks, nuns, priests, and so on are said to have a calling or a vocation. This use of "vocation" has been secularized in its application to other traditional professions—to what some would call "secular priesthoods"—so that one still hears of a calling to medicine, law, or education.

Second, other Christians have understood vocation to be the call of Christ to every Christian, not just the full-time clergy. But this call is to particular, Christian activities, not to a full-time job, much less to an entire life pattern. Thus work *is not* vocation. Our jobs provide for our physical needs, and are thus a necessity in the world as it is, but they are not actually part of our divine calling. Instead, the call of Christ is to evangelism, or charity, or some other work that goes beyond the regular work—indeed, beyond the regular life—of any normal human being.

This is the view in which I was raised. The only guidance my sectarian tradition offered me about most of my waking and working day was to do two things: avoid sin (such as lying or gossiping at work, stealing office supplies, cheating on taxes, and so on) and evangelize co-workers and customers as often as possible. It is perhaps surprising that in a different tradition, and at a much higher level of sophistication, the famous Christian legal expert and sociologist Jacques Ellul has also taught this sort of bifurcation. According to Vernard Eller, one of his exponents,

> Ellul...proposes that the Christian find his vocation outside of his occupation—as Amos did his prophesying and Paul his apostleship. "On his own time" and in the situation where the Christian *can* exercise a bit of freedom, let

him find activity that truly can witness to the age that is coming, that truly can be done in response to the call of God, that truly can be seen as a free service in behalf of God and the neighbor. Ellul cites his own volunteer work in a club for juvenile delinquents as an example of such vocation; his writing of Christian books would qualify as well.[1]

A third view is the one I commend, namely, that work *is part of* vocation. In most religions, there seems to be an inclination to distinguish between what we might call "heroes" and "ordinaries," or between "religious" and "secular" individuals. Buddhist monks hope to achieve nirvana through their rigors, while the vast majority of Buddhists live much less demanding lives. They support the monks in their superior labors and otherwise try to live properly according to their station in life. They do so in the hope of acquiring sufficient positive karma so as to be reincarnated as a superior sort of person who might, in fact, take up monasticism and thus achieve nirvana. Christianity in its various forms also has manifested this two-tiered system through the ages, although different traditions have lionized different elites. We might somewhat irreverently summarize the upper tier as, progressively, martyrs, monks, mystics, magisteria, missionaries— and megachurch leaders.

One of the key revisions of Christian life that emerged from the sixteenth-century Protestant Reformation was that of vocation. In this view, there are no "super-Christians" and "regular Christians," there are just Christians. There are not some people who are saints and others who are non-saints. All of us are saints, since the root of that word is "to be set apart for special use," and each of us is set apart by God for his service.

With this eradication of the two-tiered system in the Reformation, then, came two positive teachings: all (legitimate) work is blessed by God, and vocation is more than work. Vocation is the divine calling to be a Christian in every mode of life, public as well as private, religious as well as secular, adult as well as juvenile, corporate as well as individual, female as well as male. Thus to be a Christian in every mode of life is to show something of what it means to be a (redeemed and renewed) human being as well.

From these basic considerations, let us proceed to analyze vocation in nine sub-categories: two sets of three, and then a third trio that affects the first two.

---

1. Vernard Eller, "A Voice on Vocation: The Contribution of Jacques Ellul," *The Reformed Journal* 29 (May 1979): 20.

HUMAN

All

All human beings are called by God to fulfill the creation commandments, as we have seen. We are to worship God, seek each other's best interests, and care for the rest of creation. There is no one who is exempt from these commandments, nor are there activities that are legitimate beyond these commandments. Thus the Bible not only condemns sins as either acting wrongly or refusing to act rightly but also condemns "empty" or "wasteful" words and activities. There are no "neutral" actions (Mt. 13:48; Eph. 4:29 NASB). One is either making a contribution toward *shalom* or one is not.

To assess whether one is contributing to *shalom* requires, of course, a theology adequate to the task, one broad enough to encompass all that contributes to the flourishing of creation and the pleasure of God, and fine enough to see how particular tasks contribute to the whole.

The world since Genesis 3, however, is generally a tough place in which to make a living. Thorns and thistles are everywhere, resisting and retarding our efforts. Indeed, it is a proverb of vocational realism that every task, every job, every profession or trade, even every effort at leisure, has a certain irreducible quotient of what we might sum up as *crap*: absurdity, waste, vulnerability, uncertainty, disappointment, frustration, exploitation, and the like. Almost everything is harder than it should be. We also must have the realism to acknowledge that some work is truly alienating: turning screws on an assembly line or stitching endless piecework in a sweatshop is demeaning and the very definition of "unfulfilling."[2]

Human societies, furthermore, have developed evil patterns that privilege some and oppress others. The patterns change, and sometimes the cast—although women, children, the disabled, and ethnic minorities rarely enjoy privilege. But just as it is obvious that we are not in Eden, so it is obvious that we do not all share in the same post-Eden situation: some are much better off than others. There are lots of reasons for these disparities, and some of them are more acceptable, even proper, than others. ("If a man does not work, neither should he eat"; II Thes. 3:10.) At the same time, however, we recognize that some of those reasons are evil: unfair advantage, exploitation, collusion, and ruthlessness. Within such a world, then, human beings have to make their way as best they can, and that often means

---

2. The best Christian treatment of alienating work I know of is Miroslav Volf, *Work in the Spirit: Toward a Theology of Work* (Oxford: Oxford University Press, 1991), ch. 6.

making the best of an unfairly bad situation, including faithfully enduring a very bad time.[3]

What else does it mean, however, to truly make the best of it? A Christian ethic that encourages everyone always to remain in their "station," to accept the status quo as divinely ordered, to work away diligently in hopes of "pie in the sky by and by" can be an ethic that refuses to acknowledge God's redemptive purposes within history as well as at the end of (this phase of) history. It can be a slothful ethic (as we have seen in our discussion of Reinhold Niebuhr) that refuses the responsibility to seek as much *shalom* as possible—including the rearrangement of entire social structures not just by those who have been given the authority to do so but also by each of us, wherever we are in the hierarchy, all the way down to one's own daily decisions, either to press for improvement or simply to acquiesce in evil. Nicholas Wolterstorff writes,

> A Yes and a No is what must be spoken. Can we *entirely* alter what we do, so that here and now we practice the occupations of heaven? Of course not. Can we *somewhat* alter what we do, so that our occupations come closer to becoming our God-issued vocations? Usually, Yes.[4]

There is no defense being offered here, then, for a kind of capitulative work ethic that nicely reinforces the economic and political order. In fact, from our Christian understanding of creation and Fall we can take as given that every economic and political order, however good, is also corrupt to some extent and therefore can be improved. Aware of our place in God's plan of redemption and energized by a vision of a new heavens and new earth, Christians must be in the vanguard of efforts at improvement, keeping a relentless pressure on the powers to be transformed as much as possible according to gospel values.[5] Like the seeds

---

3. To be sure, we are in deep waters here. Suffering is evil, and normally we ought to resist it, but God often uses it to accomplish good that can be accomplished no easier way. Furthermore, he does so often in ways that are not perceptible to those in the midst of that bad situation. Sometimes, then, the way of discipleship is the way of acceptance of suffering. Glenn Tinder writes, "Suffering is so essential to the destiny underlying hope that, in our temporal hopes, we have to be wary of hoping for a cessation of suffering. In many cases, it is surely legitimate to hope that suffering will be greatly alleviated. Yet [in the fellowship of Christ's sufferings] we come down from the Cross only when we die" (Glenn Tinder, *The Fabric of Hope: An Essay* [Atlanta: Scholars Press, 1999], 68). For extended reflections on this subject, please see my *Can God Be Trusted? Faith and the Challenge of Evil* (New York: Oxford University Press, 1998).

4. Nicholas Wolterstorff, "More on Vocation," *The Reformed Journal* 29 (May 1979): 23.

5. David Martin: "We are not talking about stasis, therefore, but about tension as icons of fairness, reversal, infinite human worth and peaceability constantly exercise pressure against things as they are" (*Christian Language and Its Mutations* [Aldershot, UK: Ashgate, 2002], 27).

and leaven of Jesus' parables that are diffused and then influence all around them, Christians must quietly, steadily, and sometimes dramatically effect change—as Christians have, whether in the development of constitutional government, the rise of science, the abolition of slavery, the empowerment of women, the recognition of universal human rights, and more. It is true that Christians have resisted some or all of these improvements. But the historical record is clear that Christian principles and Christian people have also been crucial to the success of these campaigns for justice and compassion.[6] Therefore, appropriately informed and skilled Christians can bring insight to even the largest systems of interaction—so large we often take them for granted as just "the world we live in," whether the market or globalization or geopolitics or the environment—such that they do not escape analysis and both critical and creative suggestion.[7]

The fundamental Christian encouragement, therefore, is that one can do any legitimate job to the glory of God (as opposed to, say, helping to assemble illegal weapons), even as we regret also that the world has fallen so far as to produce an economy that requires corrupt and corrupting work of human beings who are capable of so much more. Paul encourages even slaves to do their work "unto the Lord," in the hope that the Lord will repay us far beyond our deserts with an eternal inheritance (Col. 3:23–24). "It is the Lord Christ whom you serve," he reminds us all—the Lord of the church, yes, but also the Lord of creation, to whose flourishing we contribute, and in whose flourishing we participate as best we can.

Craig Gay writes pastorally in this regard,

> Of course, we know that while we are in the world our "worth" will inevitably be judged on the basis of objective measures, and this will be a source of pain. Such, after all, is the way of the world. But we are not called to judge ourselves in this harsh fashion. Rather, we are called to mitigate the impact of the world's harsh objective assessment by continually reminding each other that what the world calls success God calls foolishness, and that what is of little value in the world is of great value to God (cf. I Cor. 1:20).[8]

---

6. See the historical-cum-apologetical opus of Rodney Stark, beginning with *One True God: Historical Consequences of Monotheism* (Princeton: Princeton University Press, 2001).

7. As one with no training in the relevant fields of economics, politics, international relations, and the like, I can only gesture at what needs to be done at such levels. But it must be done, and many are doing it.

8. Craig M. Gay, *The Way of the (Modern) World, or, Why It's Tempting to Live as If God Doesn't Exist* (Grand Rapids, MI: Eerdmans, 1998). Gay has a good passage on Christian vocation as a response to a dehumanizing, collectivizing culture in this book; see 175–79. See also Douglas Schuurman's fine discussion in *Vocation: Discerning Our Callings in Life* (Grand Rapids, MI: Eerdmans, 2004).

We must appreciate work, therefore, as a part of God's original blessing and calling of humanity, not as an evil introduced by the Fall that will be done away in the New Jerusalem. Thus we undertake work gratefully and joyfully. It is a dignified thing to be allowed to contribute to the goodness of the world. "God loveth adverbs," Bishop Joseph Hall has said, and thus Paul exhorts those Christian slaves, and all of us, to do our work—however mean, however mechanical— "heartily" (Col. 3:23).[9]

Indeed, there is work to be done by every person, short of those incapacitated by disease or injury. Churches and Christian businesspeople, therefore, need to be in the lead in finding ways of *letting* people work, not just putting them to work, much less saving them from work. And we must do all we can to provide and engage in creative and useful work that blesses the worker as well as the recipient of his or her labor.

Among those social improvements necessary in our time is space for rest and recreation—increasingly jeopardized, despite rosy predictions of a generation ago about a leisured society, by globalizing economic pressure, telecommunications that make us "available" at any time and anywhere, and a corporate ethos that rarely looks past the next financial quarter or two. The heat is on, and a new Christian defense of a reasonable workweek—and a correspondingly reasonable workday and work year—has become, as it was in the early modern period in the West, a crucial social issue, not only among the poor stuck in factories and on farms but also among financially prosperous but emotionally and socially ragged white-collar workers from Manhattan to Hong Kong to Mumbai.

Beyond work, then, lies the territory of other generic human activities that deserve Christian affirmation. We need a theological understanding of art, for example, as a worthy pursuit—from profound works that offer us new ways of perceiving, feeling, thinking, and acting to design that increases our enjoyment of a room, a front yard, or a person's appearance. We need a theological understanding of sport as a worthy pursuit—in its formation of character, in its symbolism (fair play, honest effort, clear rules, penalties for infractions, unequivocal outcomes), in its contribution to physical and mental health, and so on. We need a theological understanding of play in which enjoyment is sufficient rationale, rather than play being justified in terms of recreation in order to improve productivity at work or in terms of shared activity in order to improve familial, ecclesiastical, or corporate relations—however much these benefits also might accrue.

---

9. Quoted without further reference in John Drury, *Painting the Word: Christian Pictures and Their Meaning* (New Haven, CT: Yale University Press, 1999), 176.

To be sure, art, sport, and play can be loved inordinately, as can anything else, as Augustine warns us throughout his *Confessions*. My point is that it is also possible to regard them too lightly, and to emphasize only work and "religious" activities as deserving our sanction and providing the frame within which everything else must be justified. God is interested in more than productivity and spirituality. He made the whole world, he is redeeming the whole world, and he expects us to garden and reclaim the whole world with him. Part of cultivating the world is cultivating *ourselves* within it to become the best possible version of ourselves. And that means all that humanity can be, including art, sport, and play of all legitimate kinds.

Some Groups

In this category we recognize that various sorts of human societies have distinctive roles to play, particular callings to fulfill. Empires, states, nations, subcultures, municipalities, families, marriages, and friendships; professions, trades, guilds, corporations, shops, stock exchanges, banks, and insurers; transportation media, communication media, information media, schools, and museums; studios, galleries, performance halls, theaters, troupes, orchestras, bands, and ensembles; arenas, stadiums, teams, and leagues; nonprofits, charities, and cooperatives—all of these and many more are ways in which human beings have organized themselves in order to pursue some form of flourishing. It is not enough to say, as some theologians have said, that institutions have been given to us by God merely to restrain evil. I think it is abundantly evident that they have produced positive goods, and of many sorts. One of the blessed ironies of God's providence, in fact, is that sometimes even manifestly evil institutions—and what institution or group is not manifestly evil, made up as it is of clearly flawed human beings?—benefit others, whether it is splendid art and architecture left behind as the empire withdraws, or infrastructure that enables others to build better lives once the hegemony has receded (such as roads, schools, hospitals, or a lingua franca), and so on.

In the Bible, different nations play various roles, as do different professions and trades within Israel, as do different tribes and even families. Differentiation on a wide scale may be characteristic of modernity, but it has always been a part of God's ordering of the world to some extent. We do well to recognize and to receive gratefully what God has granted us in these various groupings. At the same time, we do well also to recognize and resist the common selfishness of groups, the chauvinism and imperialism that so frequently mark them. We do not have to agree with the early Reinhold Niebuhr of *Moral Man and Immoral Society* that societies are always collectively worse than the individuals that comprise them to recognize that there is nothing necessarily and automatically benign about community per se.[10]

One of the great useless emphases of our time, to reiterate, is the championing of community over individualism, as if the former is good and the latter bad—indeed, as if the former is a kind of cure for the latter. Surely the testimony of the last century or so, with its parade of "communities" of nationalists, imperialists, communists, fascists, Nazis, cultists, and terrorists, provokes us to see that community can be dreadful. Instead, we should conclude simply that individuality and community are both basic to human life, and in our present era, which follows the Fall and precedes the Second Coming, they display both benign and malign characteristics.

In this light, we can also lay to rest the perennial issue of whether society will best be improved by the conversion of individuals or by the conversion of social structures (a debate that notoriously involved Reinhold Niebuhr and Billy Graham in a previous generation). The correct answer, of course, is, *both*. Some of us are gifted and called to work with individuals. Others of us are suited to working with organizations and perhaps whole societies. And for good reason: The widespread conversion of individuals can have significant social consequences, as has been the case, for example, in Latin America's experience of evangelicalism, but individual attitudes can also be shaped by new social expectations and forms, such as the delegitimization of racism and sexism in North America.[11] It must also be acknowledged, however (and these examples serve here as well), that neither approach ushers in the Kingdom of God. Latin America and North America cannot yet pass for the New Jerusalem. Still, they are better in these respects than they used to be, and not only is change at both the individual and corporate levels important, but changes at those levels continue in dialectical fashion in constant social evolution.

The fundamental ethical question for groups, then, is precisely how they are contributing to *shalom*. It is not enough to ask of such groups whether they break any laws or commit any positive harm while maximizing return to their

---

10. Malcolm Gladwell takes another look at the notorious case of the 1964 murder of New York City Kitty Genovese and discovers an unusual aspect of this question. Citing the study of two university psychologists, he concludes that the presence of others can reduce the individual's sense of moral responsibility as "responsibility for acting is diffused": other people are around and *they* could do something, thus the imperative for *me* to do something is perceived to be diminished. Community therefore can be worse than individualism without any intentional wrong being done. See Malcolm Gladwell, *The Tipping Point: How Little Things Can Make a Big Difference* (Boston: Little, Brown, 2000), 28.

11. David Martin, *Tongues of Fire: The Explosion of Protestantism in Latin America* (Oxford: Blackwell, 1993); David Martin, *Pentecostalism: The World Their Parish* (Oxford: Blackwell, 2002).

shareholders, the electorate, or whoever may be their primary constituencies. What must be asked instead is whether groups are improving the world and whether they are improving it as well as they could.

What it means to improve the world, again, will depend on the theological framework in which the Christian makes her judgment, so we need to provide her with a theology adequate to that task. What exactly, then, does an insurance company do, and what *should* it do—with due regard not only for its clients but also for its shareholders, its competitors, its suppliers, the companies in which it invests, and so on? What does a rock band do, and what should it do—with due regard not only for its audiences but also for its songwriters, other bands that it can help or hurt, its backers, and so on? What does a magazine do—with due regard not only for its readers but also for its advertisers, its publishers, its influence on particular conversations and subjects, and so on? Is the world better because of this group? Is this group contributing as much as it can to *shalom*?

Such a question ought to both energize and direct a group, neither asking of it an impossible ideal nor releasing it to ethical complacency and thus to either stagnation or rapacity. It is this question that is asked too rarely—the truly *ethical* question—even in discussions of business ethics, medical ethics, and the like. And it is this question that Christians particularly—although not uniquely—are poised to ask of every group, starting with those that claim themselves to be Christian.

A second set of questions that must be asked, and asked constantly, is this: What is the particular purpose of this group? What is its characteristic way of increasing *shalom,* and what are ways in which it typically is distracted from its work? Is this group still fulfilling that purpose? If not, can the group improve its function, or has its time of usefulness passed (in which case it ought to be disbanded and its assets donated to groups that are doing that work better)?

Groups, like individuals, can get confused and lose their focus on their true *telos*. They can get slothful and settle for routine and "5 percent better than last year." They can pridefully take on too much, whether too lofty a goal or too broad an agenda or too great a portfolio of responsibility. And groups can fight for survival, even as the need for that particular group has passed.

There will always, in this age, be need for government, of course, and also for families, businesses, and other general forms of cooperation and authority. But not only do we recognize that this whole system eventually will give way to the direct governance and provision of Christ in the New Jerusalem, but even now particular governors come and go, particular families blossom and fade, particular businesses contribute and then impede. Change and limitation are realities that affect groups as they affect individuals. A proper ethic takes into account that what was true and good and beautiful yesterday may or may not be such today; what was a valuable contribution to the commonweal may not be such anymore; what was a fruitful organization is now in need of pruning or even liquidation and supersession. Christians properly venerate tradition and honor the work of the past. But Christians do not properly indulge in sentimentality and nostalgia. The Bible is full of reminders of the temporality of human life, and that includes groups as well as individuals. A realistic Christian ethic casts a clear, as well as compassionate, eye over all groups to ensure that they serve the great purpose of *shalom,* not merely their own interests.[12]

Furthermore, a Christian ethic recognizes that governments are not families, and governments and families are not businesses, and businesses are not charities or families, and so on. It is a mark of ethical confusion in our time—in the sense not of immorality (that narrow definition of "ethical") but of confusion over character or ethos—that hospitals are being run as businesses, universities are being run as businesses, governments are being run as businesses, and even churches are being run as businesses. With the loss of the sense of community experienced in previous generations in extended families, churches, and neighborhoods, furthermore, now we find that nonprofit organizations, charities, and even businesses are being characterized as "families"—which gives rise to the rueful (and confused) protests that you don't fire your family members or refuse to help them if they're in any trouble. Yet it is not only all right for businesses to fire people but essential that they do so. It is not only all right for hospitals to put patient care above fiscal efficiency but essential that they do so. It is not only all right for charities to refuse to help certain kinds of people or to help them in some respects but not others but essential that they do so. Differentiation, and thus ethical clarity, is essential for the proper functioning of each kind of group.

What keeps this appropriate differentiation from devolving into sheer fragmentation, however, and even a kind of low-grade civil war of various sectors and groups encroaching on each other's turf (churches wielding power like political parties, or civic groups offering a sort of "community substitute" for churches),

---

12. Oliver O'Donovan comments in regard to Jesus' relationship to Caesar and the other powers of his day: "His attitude to them was neither secularist nor zealot: since he did not concede that they had any future, he gave them neither dutiful obedience within their supposed sphere of competence nor the inverted respect of angry defiance. He did not recognize a permanently twofold locus of authority. He recognized only a transitory duality which belonged to the climax of Israel's history, a duality between the coming and the passing order.... The Two Cities [of Jerusalem and Babylon], with their concomitant Two Rules expressing Israel's alienation from its calling, gave way to the Two Eras. The coming era of God's rule held the passing era in suspension" (*The Desire of the Nations: Rediscovering the Roots of Political Thought* [Cambridge, UK: Cambridge University Press, 1996], 93).

is the underlying purpose of the cultural mandate. Each sector of society, and the groups and individuals within those sectors—whether education, health care, government, business, or the arts—maintains a central concern to improve the earth, to garden the world, to increase *shalom*—and will therefore welcome and cooperate with others who have the same concern.

Visions of *shalom* will vary, of course, and sometimes conflict. But it is not trivial to observe that businesses that clearly do not intend to contribute to the common good, but only to the good of, say, their shareholders and executives, can be judged as deficient. "'Deficient' by whose standards?" comes the retort. And the reply by the Christian is, "By our standards, which we believe are at least an approximation of the standards of the One who made the world, who sustains it, and who will bring it to judgment—and thus the standards of reality." Businesses that abuse their customers, suppliers, and competitors will not ultimately succeed: That is the Christian testimony. Yes, they might well acquire wealth and power for a while. History shows us that some of the wicked do prosper for a while. But we should observe first that many, in fact, do not. They are pushing against the grain of the original, good universe, and many bad businesses, as well as bad governments, bad schools, and other bad organizations, do fail. Furthermore, those who lead groups that do not seek *shalom,* as well as those who serve in them, usually pay a terrific toll in other parts of their lives, whether in romantic and family relationships, friendships, and physical and spiritual health. And however happily they experience and then exit this life, after that comes the inevitable judgment of history, let alone of whatever lies beyond. "My name is Ozymandias, King of kings [or the Third Reich, or Enron]: Look on my works, ye mighty, and despair!"—as their successes sink, broken and impotent, into the sands of time.[13]

Christians therefore call groups to function as their best selves, according to the clear purpose of serving *shalom* in their most characteristic fashion. Thus Christians can make genuine contributions to manufacturing, journalism, politics, art, advertising, education, medicine, and every other field as they help organizations in those fields stay faithful to their highest and truest ethos.

Individuals

Each individual is called by God to play a particular role in the gardening of the world. No one is useless, no one is free of responsibility, and each is called to contribute to the generic human task of contributing to *shalom*.

---

13. Percy Bysshe Shelley, "Ozymandias."

Even within oppressive social structures that tend to reduce individuals to machine parts—whether almost literally on assembly lines or metaphorically in large professional and financial firms—the individual human being matters and he or she is called by God to play a part that matters in the great garden of the world. Each of us does have a sphere of responsibility, and a considerable sphere it is: the total complex of our families, our friendships, our neighborhoods, our workplaces, our playgrounds, our political involvements, and so on. Again, we remember Paul's encouragement even to slaves that they do choose whether to do their work "heartily" or not, whether they advance God's concerns or not, whether they serve the Lord Christ or not (Col. 3:23–24). The world is importantly better or worse depending on how each of us lives in it.

This calling is also, therefore, a blessing. It sanctifies our work, makes it holy, as something God accepts from us with pleasure. One needs to remember that truth when changing the sixth diaper of the day, when putting out yet one more fire at the office, when struggling to pass one more badly phrased quiz, or when dealing with one more angry customer. To persist in a truly awful job is an act of faith. It shows not only that we trust God for our future but also that we believe he is not wasting us now. We have faith that he can bring good out of the most menial and even oppressive situations.

Furthermore, as we recall from a passage previously quoted from C. S. Lewis, not only do we ourselves matter as individuals, but so do the individuals whom we influence each day:

It may be possible for each to think too much of his own potential glory hereafter; it is hardly possible for him to think too often or too deeply about that of his neighbour. The load, or weight, or burden of my neighbour's glory should be laid daily on my back, a load so heavy that only humility can carry it, and the backs of the proud will be broken. It is a serious thing to live in a society of possible gods and goddesses, to remember that the dullest and most uninteresting person you talk to may one day be a creature which, if you saw it now, you would be strongly tempted to worship, or else a horror and a corruption such as you now meet, if at all, only in a nightmare. All day long we are, in some degree, helping each other to one or other of these destinations. It is in the light of these overwhelming possibilities, it is with the awe and circumspection proper to them that we should conduct all our dealings with one another, all friendships, all loves, all play, all politics. There are no *ordinary* people. You have never talked to a mere mortal. Nations, cultures, arts, civilizations—these are mortal, and their life is to ours as the life of a gnat. But it is immortals whom we joke with, work with, marry, snub, and exploit—immortal horrors or everlasting splendours.[14]

At the same time as we are encouraged by these affirmations, we recognize that we are limited in our abilities and, indeed, in our interests. Not only can we not do everything, but we don't even want to try. Is that bad?

There is a sense in which it would be swell to be interested in everything. But let us consider rejoicing in our limitations. I write this page in an office on the campus of a large university. I am a reasonably curious fellow and a lifelong academician, but there are great reaches of scholarship on that campus that do not interest me much: accounting, chemical engineering, plant biochemistry, the history of dance, Indian epic poetry. All of these are fields that fascinate many, many people, and yet I can barely glimpse the magic therein. Those subjects are not dull; *I* am dull to them. Yet this deficiency is also a blessing and an equipment for my service in the world. For I already experience frustration in trying to pay the attention I should like to pay to the things in which I am already quite interested. If all parts of the full panoply of human inquiry were equally compelling to me, my frustration is all that would increase. So I actually am glad for whole areas of human investigation that I can happily leave alone, since I never have all the time I should like to study what already intrigues me. The same principle holds for various leisure activities, various foods and beverages, and so on: God has endowed the world with a superabundance of goodness such that it is a positive mercy that we do not even *want* to enjoy it all.

We each therefore should seek to understand ourselves as thoroughly as possible in order to become the best version of ourselves that we can and make the best contribution we can. This self-awareness, again, is to be sought not in order to indulge ourselves or to take advantage of others, but in order to participate in the win-win-win of the Kingdom of God, in which everyone benefits by everyone contributing to *shalom*. Thus there is here no convenient rationale for picking the most lucrative, prestigious, and secure job of those available: "Since every legitimate job is valid, I'll opt for the cushiest." That is the Reformation doctrine of vocation run to seed. The imperative always is to do what most increases *shalom*. And we each should look forward to the world to come in which there will be no incompetent or repressive authority, no stupid or harmful work, no inane or degrading entertainment, and no boring or corrupting conversation. We will enjoy ourselves, each other, and God to the full.

---

14. C. S. Lewis, *The Weight of Glory and Other Addresses* (Grand Rapids, MI: Eerdmans, 1949), 14–15.

CHRISTIAN

All

When Christ took his leave of the disciples, he gave them one particular task: to bear witness of him (Lk. 24:48; Acts 1:8) and to make disciples of him (Mt. 28:19–20) throughout the world. This is the distinctive Christian mission. It does not replace the call of God upon all human beings, the creation commandments. But, as we have seen, it is a task made necessary by the Fall, and it is the task that only Christians can perform. We are the *ekklēsia*—literally, the ones "called out" to do this extraordinary work.

Why is it exclusive to Christians? It is not because Christians are intrinsically more spiritual or wise or holy than others. I acknowledge that by virtue of the Holy Spirit, who indwells and empowers us beyond our own qualities, we do become more spiritually aware, more wise (beginning with the fear of Yhwh; Prov. 1:7), and more holy (as "saints," set apart for divine service and becoming more and more conformed to the image of Christ). But we have not been assigned this distinct and distinctive task because we merit such an honor. Instead, it is assigned to us in the nature of the case. Christians are the only people in the world whose religion is named for Christ. We are the only people in the world who put Jesus in the center, where he belongs. We are the only people in the world who proclaim, "Jesus is Lord." Therefore we are the only people in the world who *can* bear witness to Jesus, who can invite others to repent and believe this good news, and who can teach people how to become disciples of Jesus. And we do simply invite them, as Richard Bauckham says: "Witnesses are not expected, like lawyers, to persuade by the rhetorical power of their speeches, but simply to testify to the truth for which they are qualified to give evidence."[15]

Everything else we are and do particularly as Christians connects with this mission. That is not to say that mission is the sole activity of the church—*contra* much of the evangelical tradition and some of the Missional Church movement of our day.[16] To say so is to substitute what Christians *distinctly* are to do for *all* that Christians are to do. Again, the creation commandments have priority: we are humans first and last, and "Christians" only temporarily. Thus the church engages in worship of God because that is the correct and healthful human response to God, to

---

15. Richard Bauckham, *Bible and Mission: Christian Witness in a Postmodern World* (Grand Rapids, MI: Eerdmans, 2003), 99.

16. Darrell L. Guder, ed., *Missional Church: A Vision for the Sending of the Church in North America* (Grand Rapids, MI: Eerdmans, 1998).

love God with all one's heart, soul, mind, and strength—not merely because worship helps the church perform its particular mission better, although it does. The church also cares for its own in fellowship because that is what people do when they are rightly related in *shalom* and love each other as themselves—not merely because fellowship strengthens the Body of Christ for service to others, although it does. In particular, it just isn't true, despite its frequent repetition in some circles, that "the church is the one society that exists for the benefit of its non-members." That's cute but not correct. Nor is Kierkegaard's image of the church as performers in worship with God as the audience: worship is a dialogue between God and ourselves, and he blesses us far more than we bless him, even as he gives us gifts with which to bless each other as well. The church exists in the win-win-win dynamic of the Kingdom of God: to love God, to love our neighbor, and to benefit ourselves simultaneously.

We can appropriate Bonhoeffer's brief suggestion of the "secret discipline" of the church in this way, referring as he does to the ancient church practice of refusing admission to the Lord's Supper to all but baptized members.[17] Such a practice seems repellent to our contemporary sensibilities of inclusion, hospitality, and anti-elitism. But the church maintains its integrity—literally, its integration around God in worship and with each other in fellowship—both for the intrinsic importance of authentic worship and fellowship and for the benefit of the world. For the world will be much more richly blessed by a strong, good, clear, warm church than by one that has compromised its worship and fellowship to the fads of popular culture, or even the lowest common denominator of those who happen to show up. Worship that is shorn of all terminology and ritual that is not immediately intelligible to the unchurched visitor; preaching that is restricted to the vocabulary, categories, and concerns of the occasional attender; spiritual conversation that never probes beneath the manicured surfaces of conventional propriety—none of these can grow a mature church that then can turn to offer the world a vigorous, definite, wise, and truly alternative society and mode of life.

The church is the depository of the Christian symbol set, narrative, experience, and practice—the keeper of the repertoire of ideas and actions that define us, motivate us, and guide us over against the scripts and agendas of other powers and interests. It is also the community that aspires to bring forth the best possible array of these treasures according to the need of the moment, helping each other individually and helping ourselves corporately to believe, feel, and act as God wants us to do in the current situation. Only a regular return to connect again

---

17. Dietrich Bonhoeffer, *Letters and Papers from Prison,* ed. Eberhard Bethge, trans. Reginald Fuller, Frank Clarke, and John Bowden (New York: Macmillan, 1962 [1953]), 286.

and again with this trove and this fellowship can keep us properly oriented and passionately inspired in our mission.

Furthermore, just as the Christian church in the medieval West posed an alternative structure, headed by a pope, to the normal hierarchies of power, headed by kings, and then as the Anabaptists emphasized the voluntary nature of church membership against the automatic package of Christianity-and-citizenship assumed in both Catholic and Protestant realms in the early modern period, so the Christian church always offers an identity and community more basic than those that are normally taken to be primary and ultimate. David Martin puts the point starkly:

> If I wanted to dramatize it I would point out that Mohammed was a warrior and a family man whereas Jesus was neither. Again notice that Islam sanctifies a holy city and is about territory whereas primitive Christianity is not. Indeed, for the early Christians Jerusalem was abandoned to desolation. The connection which underpins these differences is the link between the blood tie as realized in the family and land, possessions and violence. Christianity rejects the social logic embodied in genealogy, biological reproduction, and land, and attempts to set up spiritual and non-violent brotherhoods and sisterhoods outside that powerful nexus.[18]

To be sure, Martin can be misunderstood as overdrawing the distinction. For early Christians did value blood ties: "whoever does not provide for relatives, and especially for family members, has denied the faith and is worse than an unbeliever" (I Tim. 5:8). And the vision that inspired them was that of a New Jerusalem, a city come down from heaven to a new earth, which they would enjoy in resurrected bodies. But Martin is right to emphasize that the Christian community relativizes all other commitments, just as the Christian confession ("Jesus is Lord") relativizes all other loyalties. Therefore, as individuals become healthiest and also most helpful to others when they maintain a dialectic of solitude and community, so does the church as it alternates between times and modes of focus upon its Lord and its own development, and then times and modes of focus upon the world in service.

Yet the church is in fact missional in its distinctive task of witnessing to Jesus Christ and making disciples. All that it does, including worship and fellowship, contributes to that task, even as we must be careful not to subsume all that it does

---

18. Martin, *Christian Language*, 24–25.

under that task.[19] Before we proceed to discuss the church's mission, we need to pause to dispute with those who suggest that God's entire redemptive project focuses upon the church as both means and end—as if the world, both in the sense of the natural order and of global humanity, exists only as the "raw materials out of which God creates his church."[20] To identify the church as the sole locus of God's redemptive concern is badly to misunderstand the scheme of salvation. Indeed, it is to invert it. God wants *the whole world* back, not just a selection of human beings. And he wants it back not to bask in the eternal adoration of the redeemed saints, as per the vision offered at the end of Dante's *Paradiso* and in countless lesser depictions of heaven, but to enjoy the give-and-take of *shalom* with all his creatures and among them as well. To repeat, therefore: the church performs its distinctive redemptive calling within, and in the service of, the general call of God upon humanity to be stewards of the whole earth God loves.

In at least three respects, then, the church is engaged in mission: as witness, yes, but in two other modes as well.

As witness, the church experiences something and relates that experience to others. The central experience of the Christian church is Christ—not religious feeling or spirituality in general, not God or the divine in general, not faith or religion in general, but Jesus Christ. Inasmuch as the church witnesses to Jesus Christ—in its reception of his revelation, its baptism in his Holy Spirit, its enjoyment of his church, its work with him in the world—then the church performs its distinctive task and adds immeasurably to *shalom*. Inasmuch as the church speaks more generally and

---

19. John Webster offers these pertinent reflections: "The holiness of the saints is not a mere turning inwards; if it were, then it would all too quickly become mere sectarian hostility towards a profane world. If this kind of dynamic of withdrawal is questionable, it is not only because it tends to assume that the line between sin and achieved holiness coincides with the line between the Church and the world. It is also because strategies of withdrawal almost inevitably transpose the divine movement of election and consecration into social exclusivity, and so make the Church's holiness into a clean sphere over against a polluted world.... There is, unquestionably, a radical separation ... and that separation is visible as 'abstinence,' the Church's refusal to give itself to 'the passions of the flesh.' But the end of all this is 'that you may declare': holiness is to be maintained 'among the Gentiles' not simply to prevent the pollution of the Church, but with the end that 'they may see your good works and glorify God' (I Pet. 2:12; cf. Mt. 5:16; Phil. 2:15)" (John Webster, *Holiness* [Grand Rapids, MI: Eerdmans, 2003], 74–75).

20. The phrase is Robert Jenson's, from his "The Church's Responsibility for the World," in *The Two Cities of God: The Church's Responsibility for the Earthly City,* ed. Carl E. Braaten and Robert W. Jenson (Grand Rapids, MI: Eerdmans, 1997), 4. Jenson's essay proceeds from the premise that the point of creation is to produce "a community of redeemed sinful creatures." I shall not debate it point by point here, since the whole thrust of this book is against such opinions. For a more recent articulation of this view that the point of creation and redemption is the church, see Simon Chan, *Liturgical Theology: The Church as Worshiping Community* (Downers Grove, IL: InterVarsity, 2006).

less particularly about Christ, it might still add to *shalom*. But now it does so as just one among many agencies of social reform, charity, moral uplift, spiritual experience, and the like—and often not the most effective or inspiring of such agencies.

Again, let us be clear that worship and fellowship are not solely *for* mission. But genuine worship of Christ, corporately and individually, and genuine fellowship with other Christians provide regular occasions for encounter with Christ and thus give the church something to witness and thus to bear witness to others.

This honor of bearing witness to Christ would be glory enough, but Christ also calls the church to be an example. Christians are to live in the light of the Kingdom of God, however imperfectly we perceive it and however inconstantly we practice its principles. We are called, that is, not merely to witness to something over there and long ago, although what has happened is certainly crucial to our testimony: "God was in Christ reconciling the world to himself" (II Cor. 5:19). Nor are we merely to witness to something that is happening here and now and among us. But what is happening can be witnessed, in fact, by others who observe us. Albeit with the grace of the Holy Spirit, without whose ministry no truly spiritual thing can be apprehended (I Cor. 2:13–15), Kingdom life can be seen and interpreted for what it is, as we act out at least an approximation of the Kingdom of God in our individual lives, yes, but especially in our churches, families, and other Christian organizations. For the "eternal life" we are promised in the gospel (e.g., John 3) as our present experience as well as our future hope is *zoē aiōnios,* literally, "the life of the age to come."[21]

So we care for the poor—both the financially poor, as we defy the power of Mammon by giving away our money with liberality and faith that God will always provide what we truly need, and the poor in spirit, the depressed, the lonely, the unloved, the misfits and "losers" that society scorns and hurries past. So we rejoice with each other, rather than offering grudging congratulations through teeth grinding in envy, since we know that in God's economy of abundance there will be plenty of success and honor to go around. So we put ourselves at each other's service, making the most of our talents, skills, and resources to the maximal benefit of all. So we celebrate the arts, play sports and games, cook good food, and otherwise declare that the world is yet a gift from God and that he is a

---

21. Robert L. Wilken cites Michael Buckley, *At the Origins of Modern Atheism,* to remark that "to defend the existence of God, Christian thinkers in early modern times excluded all appeals to Christian behavior or practices, the very things that give Christianity its power and have been its most compelling testimony to the reality of God" (*Remembering the Christian Past* [Grand Rapids, MI: Eerdmans, 1995], 52). For further reflection on the ways in which Christians can exemplify the faith, please see my *Humble Apologetics: Defending the Faith Today* (New York: Oxford University Press, 2002), ch. 11.

generous Lord who enjoys our enjoyment.[22] So we pray for the day when suffering, sin, and absurdity are gone and all is light, goodness, and flourishing. And so we do whatever little bit we can to honor God, bless others, and fulfill ourselves.[23] The church is the new humanity, and as we live life as humans and not just as some peculiar, narrowly "religious" sect, we exemplify precisely the heart of our religion: faithfulness to the God of creation and redemption.

Third, Christ calls us beyond the roles of witness and example to be actual agents of his mission. Among the most extraordinary commands of the Bible is, in fact, the great commission: "go...and make disciples." Strictly speaking, of course, this is nonsense. We cannot make even ourselves into disciples, no matter how we instruct ourselves, remonstrate with ourselves, and pray for ourselves. The *imitatio Christi* model goes only so far. We must be born again by the Spirit. Christ must form himself in us. So how can Christ thus command us to make disciples of others?

This last, great command of Jesus' earthly ministry comes with the promise of the Holy Spirit (Acts 1:8). We are called to do what is truly divine work, the hardest work in the world: changing people's *loves*. And there is no way we could do this work unless the heart-transforming power of the Holy Spirit is coursing within us. But he *is* within us, and therefore "greater works than these" are commanded of us. We are to play an actual part in the drawing of men and women, boys and girls, to the Savior and help them respond to him as Lord.

Having surveyed these three great modes of our distinctive calling as Christians, then, we note several synergistic qualities of our work.

First, we see the win-win-win dialectic again in that as we care for others, such ministry redounds to our sanctification, which redounds to God's pleasure.

---

22. John Calvin, no one's idea of an aesthete or epicure, remarks at length on the creative generosity of God, who endows food with pleasant taste as well as nutrients, trees and animals with beauty beyond natural necessity, precious stones and metals strictly for ornament and art, and concludes: "Away, then, with that inhuman philosophy which, while conceding only a necessary use of creatures, not only malignantly deprives us of the lawful fruit of God's beneficence but cannot be practiced unless it robs a man of all his senses and degrades him to a block" (*Institutes of the Christian Religion,* ed. John T. McNeill, trans. Ford Lewis Battles [Philadelphia: Westminster, 1960], I:726–27 (III.x.2–3). I am grateful to Nicholas Wolterstorff for quoting this at the conclusion of a longer quoted passage in *Until Justice and Peace Embrace* (Grand Rapids, MI: Eerdmans, 1983), 131–32.

23. And while we rejoice in this great privilege, we can marvel at the humility of God, as a desperately hungry protagonist does in one of Lawrence Dorr's superb short stories, while he receives food from a nun: "Christ had died for him, died in real agony a real death. He was cramming the bread into his mouth, crying and chewing at the same time, overcome by a terrible sadness, pity for God, who chose him and relied on him to be a bearer and announcer of the divine revelation" (Lawrence Dorr, "A Bearer of Divine Revelation," in *A Bearer of Divine Revelation: New and Selected Stories* [Grand Rapids, MI: Eerdmans, 2003], 97).

As we become more holy, we become more faithful and more effective in our mission, which adds to God's pleasure. And we can count on God to be pleased to grant us all that we need to become both better people and more effective in his service.

Second, we see that our obedience to the creation commandments forms a vital part of our obedience to the redemption commandments. For we will be better witnesses of God's work in Christ and the Kingdom he brings as we experience that Kingdom life. We will be better examples of Kingdom life as we practice it in its fullness. And we will be more effective agents as our neighbors see the Kingdom life we live and are drawn, with the help of the Holy Spirit, to its impressive goodness.

Put negatively, it is a dark irony that Christian individuals and groups who narrow their understanding and practice of mission to evangelism end up less effective in that evangelism precisely because they are witnessing to, exemplifying, and acting on the basis of a truncated gospel, an important but thin slice of Kingdom life. Oliver O'Donovan offers a helpful warning in the particular sector of politics:

> Theology must be political if it is to be evangelical [by which he means, I think, both "of the gospel" and "evangelistic"]. Rule out the political questions and you cut short the proclamation of God's saving power; you leave people enslaved where they ought to be set free from sin—their own sin and others'.[24]

Proclamation is an essential part of both Christian mission and Christian life in general, but it not the totality of either. When it becomes predominant, the very message being proclaimed becomes less attractive because less true and less evident in those proclaiming it. We will be better evangelists precisely inasmuch as we do not concentrate all of our energies on evangelism.

Art, for example, is often dismissed or even more frequently ignored in Christian circles. Churches are constructed according to efficiency—maximum seating, lowest heating or cooling costs, best price—or evangelistic efficacy ("Will this impress those we hope to convert?"), not according to grandeur, or intimacy, or any other spiritual-aesthetic principle. In such circles art is, at best, mere decoration or device, and any more than a modest interest in architecture, interior design, clothing, or cosmetics is suspected of sheer worldliness. For does not the Bible itself warn against such things?

---

24. O'Donovan, *Desire of the Nations*, 3.

I desire, then, that in every place the men should pray, lifting up holy hands without anger or argument; also that the women should dress themselves modestly and decently in suitable clothing, not with their hair braided, or with gold, pearls, or expensive clothes, but with good works, as is proper for women who profess reverence for God. (I Tim. 2:8–10)

May I suggest that Paul is warning against extravagance here, not against beauty? He wants the focus in worship to be upon God, not upon oneself and particularly not on one's bodily adornment. For the God upon whom we are to focus is a God who loves beauty—the inner beauty of the spiritual, yes, but also the external beauty of the physical. For this is the God who lavishes beauty upon even the flowers of the field (Mt. 6:28–30), and who actually expects some effort on our part to provide beauty even in worship. This God, as the rabbi Paul knew well, required considerable outlay of materials and skill in the construction of the Tabernacle and the garments of the priests (Ex. 25–27, 35–39). God required perfumed incense in his worship, and the sacrifices on Israel's altars themselves were to offer a pleasant aroma to God (Ex. 29:18, 25; 30:34–37; Lev. 1–2). God later blessed Solomon's temple in all its magnificence (I Kgs. 6–8). God's prophets chided Israel for mediocre offerings that would offend even an earthly governor (Mal. 1:8). And we have seen already that he himself intends to construct the New Jerusalem in breathtaking splendor.

The appearance of Christian churches, Christian homes, and Christian bodies communicates our values. We are known by our art. If we keep our churches, homes, and bodies bereft of art, or bereft of *good* art, we are saying something about what we hold to be Kingdom values—and what we are saying is heretical, namely, that God doesn't care about the aesthetic.[25]

But aren't we in an emergency situation? So why paint pictures while the *Titanic* is sinking? This powerful metaphor is common, but also wrong, and we need to discard it once and for all. The world is in trouble, true, but in a kind of trouble not very much like a rapidly sinking ship. Instead, it is like what the New

---

25. One might make a similar case for so-called pure research, construing scholarship that investigates the world God made as a form of worship, of taking so seriously and appreciatively what he has done, and what his creatures have done, that we devote time and money to tracing it out. I assert, that is, that not all research has to "pay off" in some way, in some clear practical application in improving human life or the life of other creatures. "This research grant could have been sold and the money given to the poor."

Or perhaps such research yet does "pay off." For research that opens up God's work and ways, and helps us to see his creation better, is "paying off" indeed: "in wonder, love, and praise." Any version of Christianity that fails to support such God-honoring work is a truncated one.

Testament describes it: a garden, a city, a war, a planet—all long-term and complex systems. So we must not oversimplify the question.

Furthermore, we serve a God of abundant power and resources, and he has furnished this planet, and us, with abundance also. We are not in a situation of scarcity, but in a situation of badly distributed and badly used abundance. So it is simply not right to tell the artist to leave off his work, sell his art supplies, and get busy with evangelism or poor relief. Those Christians whom God has called both to support and to engage in evangelism and poor relief—*they* are the ones who are responsible for those tasks, and they are the ones to be blamed if the tasks languish.

It makes no sense to make bad missionaries out of good artists. The world suffers the loss of the good artistic work that would have been done by such people. More particularly, the salt and light they would have brought to the artistic community never penetrate. And many who would be attracted to investigate the Christian church will be repelled upon encountering such an aesthetic desert, no matter how eloquent our preaching and excellent our morals. Thus, again, our evangelism ironically is restricted precisely by an excessive focus on evangelism. The redemption commandments must be properly related to the creation commandments, or they will all be compromised.[26]

Some

All Christians, and all Christian groups, share a responsibility to proclaim Christ as Lord, to live as disciples, and to welcome others to become disciples as well. Throughout history, furthermore, various Christian groups have been formed to accomplish particular tasks: missionary societies, medical organizations, relief and development agencies, fellowships of various kinds of professionals, and so on. We can see also that particular congregations and denominations have been given both gifts and opportunities from God to do distinctive work, most obviously in the sense of ministering within particular locales (the church in Jerusalem and the church in Philippi) and thus to particular kinds of people (Jews in Jerusalem and Gentiles in Philippi).

Characteristic of modern societies is differentiation of social sectors and thus of social organizations, and the modern church has become differentiated as well. Particularly since the mid-twentieth century, special-purpose groups have proliferated

---

26. For some helpful reflections on a Christian appreciation of art, see Leland Ryken, *Culture in Christian Perspective: A Door to Understanding and Enjoying the Arts* (Portland, OR: Multnomah, 1986); and Nicholas Wolterstorff, *Art in Action* (Grand Rapids, MI: Eerdmans, 1980).

both within congregations (support groups for divorced people, youth groups of various levels, men's and women's fellowships, and the like) and beyond—indeed, *especially* beyond, in what are sometimes, and mistakenly, called "parachurch organizations," such as InterVarsity Christian Fellowship, World Vision, Wheaton College, Women's Aglow, Pioneer Girls, Neighborhood Bible Studies, Fellowship of Christian Athletes, and many, many more.[27] These groups, I say, are called "parachurch" mistakenly because they are not, in fact, beside the church, but are the church of Jesus Christ deployed in particular modes to accomplish particular purposes. Yes, they are not congregations, and in that (important) sense are not churches. But they are not, as "parachurch" can imply, stopgap devices to make up for some kind of deficiency in the work of congregations. Most of them do work that no congregation or denomination can do, or can do as well, precisely because they are so focused and because they are ecumenical to at least some degree.

For example, evangelical organizations on university campuses have blessed several generations of students by offering them age- and context-appropriate Christian education in an evangelically ecumenical environment that has introduced their members both to other traditions and to the evangelical consensus that binds them together. This experience is unlikely to happen in any other way. A Baptist or Pentecostal or Presbyterian campus group may well offer particular benefits to its members, but not these crucial benefits. Furthermore, groups such as the Navigators and InterVarsity can achieve a critical mass of members, drawing from across denominational lines, to accomplish certain things on campus that an array of disassociated denominational groups never would. Such is not always the case, of course, but my point is that there are important limitations to denominational divisions here, no matter how lively the denominations, that can be overcome by such ecumenical special purpose groups—or what I call *paracongregational* ministries.

Certainly there are attendant dangers to such organizations. They can spring up on the basis of some initial charisma of leadership and urgency of need and can then flail about, bereft of the wisdom and stability that a more mature organization could bring to such work. They can easily go astray under leaders whose entrepreneurship is not matched by managerial ability or spiritual maturity. And they can diffuse resources among several similar organizations that would be better spent on one just one. They also, however, can emerge more quickly and with innovative ideas and forms unlikely to emerge from established groups. And they (sometimes) can fade away more easily, and properly, when the moment of their

---

27. Robert Wuthnow, *The Restructuring of American Religion: Society and Faith Since World War II* (Princeton, NJ: Princeton University Press, 1988), chap. 6.

usefulness is past, rather than being propped up indefinitely by large congregations or denominations that refuse to prune them back.[28]

Furthermore, particular denominational traditions have particular qualities to offer to the world, and to other traditions. There is a great opportunity that has largely been missed to date in any ecumenical movement—whether that which normally bears the name, dating from the Edinburgh Missionary Conference of 1910 and now institutionalized in the World Council of Churches, or in the various evangelical ecumenical organizations, most notably the World Evangelical Alliance. That opportunity is to learn from each other, and particularly from each other's differences.

John Howard Yoder has been trenchantly critical of a particular version of ecumenical embrace of diversity:

> We see here at work the ordinary ethos of liberal Western ecumenism. One assumes that it is proper for each denominational community to have "their thing," perhaps thought of as their "gift" in analogy to the language of 1 Corinthians 12, or as their "talent." One assumes that each denomination's particularity is somehow "true," in that others should listen to it respectfully rather than calling it heretical as they used to. At the same time, one assumes that the kind of "truths" which the others hold is not overpowering, since that "respectful listening" does not obligate one to agree with them, or even to weigh seriously the reasons *they* give for their views.... Thus the price of this good-mannered ecumenical openness to hear one another at our points of distinctiveness is a pluralism that may replace the truth question with a kind of uncritical celebration of diversity.[29]

Yoder is quite right: a shallow relativism leads to a shallow engagement with the other, ending with, as Paul Griffiths writes about interreligious dialogue more generally, "a discourse that is pallid, platitudinous, and degutted. Its products are intellectual pacifiers for the immature: pleasant to suck on but not very nourishing."[30]

---

28. I have said more about parachurch organizations, both in affirmation and in warning, in "The Parachurch: Promise and Peril," in *Evangelical Landscapes: Facing Critical Issues of the Day* (Grand Rapids, MI: Baker Academic, 2002), 25–36.

29. John Howard Yoder, *The Priestly Kingdom: Social Ethics as Gospel* (Notre Dame, IN: University of Notre Dame Press, 1985), 81.

30. Paul Griffiths, *An Apology for Apologetics: A Study in the Logic of Interreligious Dialogue* (Maryknoll, NY: Orbis, 1991), xi–xii. Allan Bloom was just the most prominent of many pundits who have argued that serious conversation in the whole of modern culture is endangered by such attitudes; see his *The Closing of the American Mind: How Higher Education Has Failed Democracy and Impoverished the Souls of Today's Students* (New York: Simon and Schuster, 1987).

My recommendation instead, however, is that we do not surrender questions of value, whether absolute matters of truth, goodness, and beauty or relative judgment of more or less truth, goodness, and beauty. With those questions to the fore, in fact, we can interrogate various other traditions and truly learn something that can improve our own. Perhaps the Presbyterians really do know more than we do about due process in church government. Perhaps the Orthodox really do know some things we do not about iconography. Perhaps the Mennonites really can teach us the meaning of "enough." Perhaps the Pentecostals can help liberate us from dull and disembodied worship. Baptists who have learned to improve their procedures from Presbyterians, their art from the Orthodox, their finances from the Mennonites, and their worship from the Pentecostals do not therefore become worse Baptists but better ones. And so around the ecumenical circle, no?

I suspect that God has not vouchsafed to any denomination a pure and comprehensive tradition precisely in order to humble us and to draw us together in mutual regard, mutual edification, and mutual service. Ecumenical encounter that does not result in change all round is worse than useless: it confirms in each participant a smug self-containment that reinforces each tradition's inbred weaknesses as well as its strengths.

Our differences can serve God's purposes in yet another way. Again, I would like not to run afoul of Yoder's helpful warning about ostensible mutual affirmation stemming from a woolly relativism and thus the abandonment of any hope of improvement via the recognition of truly "better" and "worse" alternatives, or even more basic judgments of "right" and "wrong." So I offer the following proposal with some trepidation. Still, I offer it, so I shall do so by way of illustration precisely in a zone well trodden by Yoder himself as well as by a host of other Christian ethicists, namely, the legitimation of war.

The pacifist tradition and similar traditions that oppose any use of force (which is usually simply equated with violence) characteristically claim that Jesus shows us an alternative way to deal with the world's violence. Jesus does not fight fire with fire, but rather submits to immolation, so to speak, only to emerge triumphant from the ashes on the other side of death. We, too, must not resist evil, but instead must sacrifice ourselves in faith in the God who has overcome death and all other enemies in Christ's cross and promises resurrection for all who will follow this path.

Who can deny that this is a plausible reading of much of the New Testament? Yet I have found it difficult to square with the whole Bible as the Word of God. The Old Testament presents a God who resorts frequently to violence to accomplish his purposes and who calls his people to do the same—not always, but often. And what about the New Testament? Well, what *is* one to make of the cleansing of the Temple in Jesus' earthly ministry, an act of violence by any serious reading? What is one to make of God telling the church to obey and pray for those who wield the sword in the interest of justice (Rom. 13:1–7; I Pet. 2:13–14)? What is one to make of the apocalyptic Jesus riding in triumph over his enemies on a field of blood? Jesus is both the Lamb of God and the Lion of Judah, bringing Old and New Testaments together. He is the Prince of Peace, who makes peace "by the blood of his cross" but also by the strength of his right hand, the sword that proceeds from his mouth, and so on. Are such martial images best explained in pacifistic ways?

I cannot claim to resolve fully these deep matters. And that is my present point. It is not obvious to me how any one theology, nor any one Christian tradition or group, can articulate and exemplify our peace-loving God who sometimes resorts to violence to restore peace to a violent world. And I think it is a mistake of a pretty basic order to suggest that because Jesus in his earthly ministry did not resort to violence (except during the Temple cleansing), we are to eschew all force ourselves—particularly when we do see (at least most Christians do) this same Jesus forcibly subduing his enemies in the Apocalypse. Since we live neither in the era of Jesus' earthly ministry nor in the era of the Last Judgment, I suggest it is in fact an open question as to how Christians are to engage the challenges of this world, whether on the individual level of a thief or murderer entering one's home or a thieving and murderous horde entering one's village or nation.

I am inclined—in line with C. S. Lewis, Reinhold Niebuhr, and Dietrich Bonhoeffer—to conclude that Christians are to join with others, and with God, in using force to resist evil and promote good via police forces, judicial systems, armies, and diplomacy. I also testify that this violence is an ugly, regrettable, and temporary expedient that will be done away in the world to come precisely by the imperial power of the returning Christ who loves peace and comes quickly to bring it to our war-torn world. How, then, can Christians possibly bear witness to such a complicated understanding of violence, justice, and *shalom*? Perhaps, I reiterate, by a majority of Christians joining with others in the forceful restraint of evil and promotion of good, and simultaneously by a minority of Christians testifying to the regrettable evil inherent in such force, to the need to resort to violence only when all other means of resolution have failed, to the requirement that violence be contained as much as possible, to the recognition that this life and our place in it is not the highest good, and to the anomalous place that force has in God's economy. This latter testimony therefore does not delegitimize violence entirely, but it delegitimizes it absolutely, so to speak, as a terrible necessity that in the Kingdom of God will have no lasting place.[31]

---

31. I have argued mildly here about being open to the possibility of apparently contradictory positions being advocated by Christians in the same situation. I sincerely want to make room

Let us retreat from this awful subject to one that perhaps will make my larger point more agreeably. In terms of the conduct of corporate worship, it makes sense to say that some forms of worship are better than others. Those that neglect preaching, for example, or the eucharist, or prayer; those that discourage participation by the laity; those that do not call participants to their best efforts—all of these are simply deficient. But there is no order of service one can construct that encompasses the strengths of a Roman Catholic mass, a charismatic revival, and a Quaker meeting. A hybrid that incorporates elements of each is simply a fourth alternative with its own deficiencies relative to the others. Must we therefore say that one style is categorically better than the others? I suggest instead that no single worship form can help all people everywhere meet and celebrate God equally well, nor can any single worship form express the richness of God and the variety of his blessings on his widely variegated people. Therefore we can affirm multiple worship forms as genuine and good without feeling obligated to rank them. Again, we can see (as we have seen in terms of denominations generally) that each worship tradition might well benefit from learning from the strengths of other styles and thus become better versions of itself, and not feel obliged to abandon its distinctiveness for some putative norm of amalgamation.

Such a dialectic, then, brings together a willingness to recognize what is better and what is worse in other traditions so as to improve one's own ministry and perhaps to remonstrate with the others for their benefit. Such a dialectic also affirms that to articulate the whole counsel of God exceeds the capacity of any one theological, liturgical, devotional, or ecclesiastical tradition. This

---

for positions with which I disagree in situations in which I can see that those positions are plausible construals of God's Word. (I do not, that is, want to bless just any position, since I maintain that heresy is what the church has always understood it to be: dangerous and serious.)

Again, however, I would turn the tables on Yoder, Hauerwas, and company to ask how we can profess to "love our neighbor," and particularly the weak among our neighbors who are victimized, but also those who ought to receive their just due for their crimes *and no more,* if we wish to remove Christians generally from the (necessarily coercive) police, judicial, military, and political systems. (One advance reader tells me that Yoder allows for "discerning participation in these processes," but I don't see it. And even if that is so, the level of participation that Yoder's principles could allow must be tightly circumscribed indeed.) I am not implying that non-Christians will be uncharitable or unjust. I am saying instead that since we Christians recognize the divine commandments to care for creation and love our neighbors, we ought to see that in this time and place, wielding the sword is part of obeying those commandments.

I allow that it might be God's will for Yoder and others to argue for nonviolence and maintain a peace witness in their distinctive way. I wish in turn they would not declare that those who maintain a different Christian posture are necessarily theologically and ethically selective and defective, particularly when a counter-case for some such postures can be readily made.

attitude thus avoids both chauvinism and relativism and ought to result in both the strengthening of each particular group and a greater fellowship of mutual edification among groups. Without such an attitude, furthermore, ecumenism will remain in its current form, which is in fact formally the same whether one looks at liberal or conservative varieties: lowest-common-denominator theological and liturgical affirmations of little import and a certain amount of cooperation in basic, albeit often important, Christian ministry, whether social action, evangelism, or whatever.

John Howard Yoder offers a series of complementary observations about the positive role of minority traditions:

> Minority groups can also exercise pioneering creativity in places where no one is threatened. They can do jobs nobody else is interested in doing, and thereby gradually draw attention to some realm of social need for which it would have been impossible to find an imposed solution.... The presence on the stage of a very different position, even if not a possible model to be imposed as official policy by a majority, or even to be negotiated by a sizable minority in a coalition situation, still does change the total spectrum of positions, and thereby moves the balance point of the system.[32]

A final point about vocational diversity can be made about the particular call of Christ on particular groups, namely, congregations. It ought to be obvious that every congregation worthy of the name demonstrates certain traits and performs certain practices, even as Christians might disagree about whether other items belong on the list. A congregation that never prayed, read Scripture, or cared for the poor would fail anyone's definition of a genuine Christian church. Yet beyond these generic qualities and actions, each congregation is also called by Christ to particular work. As I suggested earlier, this should be obvious by its geographical location and cultural makeup. Yet many churches fail to take such fundamental realities thoroughly into account.

Many congregational leaders have never analyzed their own individual geographical and cultural particulars, nor have they analyzed their own congregations. They know very little about the ethnic makeup, the spending patterns, the leisure preferences, the educational backgrounds, the religious heritages, the networks of kinship and affinity, and other basic social realities of those whom

---

32. Yodes, The Priestly Kingdom, 97.

they are attempting to serve and serve with. Census, survey, and poll data that help advertisers, banks, and politicians influence communities are ignored by church leaders, who lead instead on the basis of their collective impressions—perhaps accurate, but impossible to verify or falsify objectively.

Therefore, many congregations have never asked a fundamental question: "What can and should we try to do for ourselves and those God has called us to serve?" They certainly have never asked the corollary question, "What shall we deliberately not do, or at least not do very much of, in order to faithfully execute God's particular plan for our ministry?" Churches all too often attempt to do a little bit of everything, and end up with mediocrity and ineffectiveness on every front.

Again, I am not advocating too narrow a focus here, as if a church ought to target, say, fun-loving teens and thus ruthlessly pare away everything that isn't amusing and avoid every demographic except teenagers. (I am not making up this example.) All churches everywhere are meant to include much more in their activity and membership than that. Nor am I giving comfort to churches that firmly insist every member be of a particular race, class, or political outlook. A degree of heterogeneity is assumed in New Testament churches so that each congregation experiences and exemplifies the expansive, welcoming love of God that breaks down walls of division.

A church that is located in a working-class area, however, is not obviously obliged to set up an advanced program in adult education in a way that a university church is so obliged—although it should have an *appropriate* adult education program. A church that is located among recent immigrants would normally focus on meeting the peculiar needs of those people rather than attempting to maintain some sort of generic and artificial balance of "all things to all people." Thus a particular congregation ought to free itself from any guilt feelings that it does not have this or that ministry to this or that group, as does the church down the street or across town. Instead, Congregation A might well refer prospective members to Congregation B precisely because Congregation B is good at serving such people, and Congregation B can reciprocate.

It is easy to imagine abuses of such principles, of course. Congregation A can send all of the people it deems troublesome or discomfiting to good-hearted Congregation B. Congregation B, in turn, can congratulate itself on its spiritual superiority to Congregation A. I trust, however, that no one will mistake my point. I suggest instead that congregations work hard to see themselves as clearly as possible for the distinct group of people that Jesus Christ has called to this place at this time, and then trace out the healthy implications of their distinctiveness for ministry, while blessing others who are different and thus called to different work.

Individuals

Since we are convinced that God loves the whole world and is calling it back to himself, and since we are convinced that God has called Christians to go out everywhere to work with him in this mission of redemption, then we can expect that God seeks to deploy Christians as his witnesses, examples, and agents everywhere. This syllogism will not startle anyone. But it contains significant implications.

One implication is that God has called particular individuals *in our particularity* to work with him. Yet some today seem to be distinctly uncomfortable with talk about individuals. In the contemporary reaction against individualism, many have embraced community. But this is to substitute an excessive emphasis on one pole of an ellipse for excessive emphasis on the other. For human beings are both created as individuals and enveloped by communities. It is not good that we are alone, and yet we always remain persons with individual dignity. In the Old Testament, we see the importance of many individual lives (Adam and Eve, Enoch, Noah, Abram, Sarah, Rebekah, Joseph, Rahab, Ruth, Hannah, David, Hosea, Jeremiah, Daniel, Esther, and Nehemiah, to name a variegated lot) even as God also deals with the people of Israel. Indeed, the Old Testament oscillates between emphases on corporate and individual responsibilities and consequences. The New Testament goes on to depict the people of God as a family or nation, an *ethnos,* and yet also as a voluntary society. It is thus a peculiar family or nation: one is invited to join by God, and one freely joins by faith and continues to enjoy by faithfulness. The New Testament thus again fulfills the Old: true Israel is constituted by individuals who *act* like true Israel—and therefore so is the church made up of those who trust God and declare that Jesus is Lord.

God wants his people to be in every walk of life, in every social stratum, in every ethnic group, in every location precisely to maximize his influence and draw the world most effectively to himself. Thus he strategically deploys individuals. There is a kind of circular logic here that is nonetheless important. I am situated where I am, and I am the person I am, precisely to do what only a person such as I can do: namely, to witness to, to exemplify, and to effect the gospel in my particular social matrix. Only I have these relatives, these friends, these co-workers, these enemies, these neighbors, and so on, and only I am in this set of relationships, and only I am this sort of person, therefore only I can exert the particular benign influence that only I can exert. This sounds nonsensical, of course, but I don't think it is. Instead, such a statement is vital to the realization that God has not made mistakes in making us who we are and placing us where he has in order to get done what he wants to get done.

Let me illustrate this point by referring to one of the great accomplishments of contemporary cinema, the James Bond series. These movies have starred such actors as Sean Connery, Roger Moore, Timothy Dalton, Pierce Brosnan, and Daniel Craig—and, indeed, George Lazenby. Now, among the less plausible features of this entirely implausible series are the striking good looks of these men. When Sean Connery or Pierce Brosnan enters a room, everyone notices. Thus it is ridiculous to suppose that James Bond, looking like *that,* could be a secret agent for longer than about two seconds. I, on the other hand, routinely enter, dawdle in, and exit rooms without anyone paying the slightest attention. I could be an excellent secret agent. "The name is Stackhouse: *John* Stackhouse."

To put this lightly (and I promise to resume a serious theological tone in a moment), we ought to give thanks to God that we are not more gorgeous than we are—or more intelligent, or more creative, or more rich—because if we were much more gifted, we could not function the same way in our particular roles. People might write off our testimony with "Well, that's easy for *you* to say." Or they might never feel they could identify with us, and so never confide in us. Or they might try to push into the Kingdom of God for the wrong reasons, to enjoy the trappings rather than the substance of the gospel of renewal. One day, thank God, we will be more beautiful and talented than we are today. But for now we are "under cover," playing the roles we have been given in order to achieve key mission objectives that could not be achieved were we to drop our disguises and appear in the glory that God has prepared for us (II Cor. 3:18; 4:17; I Jn. 3:2). Thus we are properly *resigned* to our situation because we trust that we have been *assigned* to it.

Perhaps I can add a more speculative idea on this theme. I have long wondered why God did not more quickly and thoroughly sanctify some people, straightening out their tangled theology, or ethics, or lifestyle, or whatever. Of course some people resist God's work in their lives: indeed, we all do to some extent. But what about the apparently quite sincere, serious, and spiritual people for whom I could personally vouch? Why did God let them persist in odd beliefs, attitudes, or behaviors? Take one acquaintance, a Bible scholar of international reputation who maintains views of the Scriptures that I find disconcertingly liberal, while his piety is warmly evangelical. Take another acquaintance, someone who swears frequently, drinks heavily, and smokes a pack a day, and is a brilliant and effective evangelist. I have come to surmise that God might not be hurrying along their sanctification in these respects—partly because they don't matter as much as the "weightier matters of the law" (Mt. 23:23), to be sure, but also because the former friend never would have been appointed to his position of influence in a major university had his views been more conservative, while the latter friend never would have gained and retained the audiences she has among the religiously alienated if she were straitlaced. These brothers and sisters thus function as "bridge people," whose combination of the genuinely good and the apparently not-so-good equips them for their distinctive task of connecting Christianity with those far from it. And aren't we *all* "bridge people" in one way or another? God paradoxically and pragmatically thus can use all sorts of things about us to achieve his purposes.

From these reflections on limitations and deficiencies, we turn to the positive issues of spiritual gifts and membership in the Body of Christ. Really, these two issues go together: each of us is gifted by the Holy Spirit in order to participate in the Body of Christ, whether in edifying each other or in furthering our work of mission in the world:

> Now there are varieties of gifts, but the same Spirit; and there are varieties of services, but the same Lord; and there are varieties of activities, but it is the same God who activates all of them in everyone. To each is given the manifestation of the Spirit for the common good. To one is given through the Spirit the utterance of wisdom, and to another the utterance of knowledge according to the same Spirit, to another faith by the same Spirit, to another gifts of healing by the one Spirit, to another the working of miracles, to another prophecy, to another the discernment of spirits, to another various kinds of tongues, to another the interpretation of tongues. All these are activated by one and the same Spirit, who allots to each one individually just as the Spirit chooses. (I Cor. 12:4–11)

However much our spiritual gifts draw upon the natural talents we possess—again, by the gift of God—they are special in that they are focused on the church's own life and its particular mission in the world. Most of them are special also in that they evidence supernatural power, demonstrating a Spirit at work beyond normal human ability and motivation—whether in healing and prophecy, or in giving and compassion (Rom. 12:8). Indeed, in some cases our spiritual gifts will *not* be directly related to our workweek skills: the high-powered executive might delight to serve others by preparing and pouring coffee after worship on Sunday; the stay-at-home parent might brilliantly direct a Sunday school or soup kitchen. Everyone is gifted, everyone is called. Good church leaders will help people identify those gifts and callings, and put them to work where they are best suited.

(May I point out that putting people's spiritual gifts to work does not necessarily entail putting them to work in the local church? They might well be better suited to serving in paracongregational ministries, or perhaps their spiritual gifts—such as evangelism or hospitality—will be best used outside explicitly Christian organizations entirely.)

There are no useless Christians, because there are no useless members of the Body of Christ. The living Spirit flows through each of us and gives us good work to do. Paul continues:

> For just as the body is one and has many members, and all the members of the body, though many, are one body, so it is with Christ. For in the one Spirit we were all baptized into one body—Jews or Greeks, slaves or free—and we were all made to drink of one Spirit. Indeed, the body does not consist of one member but of many. If the foot would say, "Because I am not a hand, I do not belong to the body," that would not make it any less a part of the body. And if the ear would say, "Because I am not an eye, I do not belong to the body," that would not make it any less a part of the body. If the whole body were an eye, where would the hearing be? If the whole body were hearing, where would the sense of smell be? But as it is, God arranged the members in the body, each one of them, as he chose. If all were a single member, where would the body be? (I Cor. 12:12–19)

A crucial axiom here is that each of us is a *member,* not a microcosm. We have particular gifts of ability and opportunity, and corresponding limitations. So we must not strive to be "well-rounded" in the sense of performing every kind of ministry with equal success. Nor must we try to be self-contained, needing no one else. Of course it is good to be as useful as possible. Of course it is good to avoid sloth that improperly burdens others. But we must see that we are called and equipped by Christ to be *members* that perform only a restricted range of service and that require the help of other members not only to accomplish the larger goals of the Body, but also to grow up ourselves into health and maturity. The Bible tells us to "bear one another's burdens" (Gal. 6:2). Such a situation is not pathological, as if the church is a sad bunch of cripples desperately leaning on each other for support—although in some important senses it *is* just that. But the ideal is not a Stoic or Nietzschean individual independence. The Biblical ideal, we recall again, is *shalom:* a healthful interdependence of strong, growing creatures who both recognize and rejoice in their need for, and service to, each other, God, and the rest of creation.

Thus we must avoid any improper individualism. Furthermore, while we should delight in our own particular ministry, we must honor the ministry of others that differs from our own. Just because we are enthusiastic about what we are doing—or perhaps because we are *not* enjoying what we are doing—we must not begrudge others their particular service and chide them for not joining us in ours.

At the same time, we must not feel guilty because we do not take on their ministry, however impressive it is, but instead must commend them to God and then stick to the particular work God has given each of us to do. I heard of a faculty meeting at a Christian college in which one professor announced his impending resignation in order to pursue a calling among the poor of that city. It was a moving address, and afterward little knots of conversation formed in faculty offices. In one such conversation, a distinguished senior professor was overcome by such admiration for his younger colleague's ministry that he openly doubted the worth of his own career. Yet, as a friend pointed out, this senior colleague had blessed the Body of Christ with decades of fruitful Biblical scholarship, while the younger professor leaving to work with the poor had not been inclined to that form of edification for the Body. Serving the poor is good and teaching the Scripture is good (cf. Acts 6:2–5). Few can do both. We should be content to be mere members of a Body that collectively does many things.

Paul's classic passage about spiritual gifts continues further, and we should observe at least one more point he makes:

> As it is, there are many members, yet one body. The eye cannot say to the hand, "I have no need of you," nor again the head to the feet, "I have no need of you." On the contrary, the members of the body that seem to be weaker are indispensable, and those members of the body that we think less honorable we clothe with greater honor, and our less respectable members are treated with greater respect; whereas our more respectable members do not need this. But God has so arranged the body, giving the greater honor to the inferior member, that there may be no dissension within the body, but the members may have the same care for one another. If one member suffers, all suffer together with it; if one member is honored, all rejoice together with it. Now you are the body of Christ and individually members of it. (I Cor. 12:20–27)

This part of the teaching on spiritual gifts tends not to be exposited as thoroughly as the rest, and I wonder if it is because the teaching becomes progressively more radical as we near the end of chapter 12 and head into chapter 13, the famous passage on love. For in most of our churches we do precisely the opposite of what the Holy Spirit commands us to do via Paul in this text. We lavish honor on those who are already conspicuous and we take for granted those who do the hidden, even repellent, but necessary work of the church. I say this as a preacher and a musician myself: Don't people gifted in these ways routinely get lots of attention and honor? What about those involved in less respectable work? I think Paul might be indulging in a little irony here, calling "less respectable" those ministries that the proud, worldly Corinthians would be inclined to ignore or demean. Yet consider these ministries: caring for babies in the church nursery; playing games with and teaching the junior high kids; preparing and taking meals to shut-ins; shoveling the snow off the church sidewalk early on a freezing Sunday morning; poring over the church accounts to make sure they are in order. Where are the audiences? Where is the applause, or at least the fervent amens, for these members of the body—the sort of encouragement that speakers and singers enjoy so routinely? A mark of the church functioning properly surely must be the practice of inverting the normal hierarchy of honor and making sure that every member receives the recognition that he or she deserves according to the values of the Kingdom of God. And such recognition, Paul says, will bear the splendid fruit of both compassion and celebration.

For Paul's teaching on spiritual gifts proceeds to unfold into his paean to Christian love in I Corinthians 13, the "greatest" of all gifts and ministries, and one that any member and all members can and must manifest as the supreme mark of the Christian church. Yet, again, we love each other, we love God, and we love the rest of creation both as individuals and as congregations. Thus we see both a duality and a dialectic brilliantly depicted in the inspired imagery of members of a body.

TIME

Always—Sometimes—Now

A crucial dimension of vocational discernment is the temporal. What is it that Christ calls us to do all the time? What does he call us to do some of the time? And what does he call us to do now?

Human beings are always supposed to love God, love our neighbors, and care for the rest of creation. Christians are always supposed to be bearing witness and making disciples in a posture of worship and a community of conspicuous love.

Within this constancy are rhythms or progressions in which some actions are appropriate and others are not. Such patterns come in a wide range: work, leisure, and rest; waking and sleeping; creating, criticizing, and revising; friendship, courtship, marriage; beginning, middle, and end:

For everything there is a season, and a time for every matter under heaven: a time to be born, and a time to die; a time to plant, and a time to pluck up what is planted; a time to kill, and a time to heal; a time to break down, and a time to build up; a time to weep, and a time to laugh; a time to mourn, and a time to dance; a time to throw away stones, and a time to gather stones together; a time to embrace, and a time to refrain from embracing; a time to seek, and a time to lose; a time to keep, and a time to throw away; a time to tear, and a time to sew; a time to keep silence, and a time to speak; a time to love, and a time to hate; a time for war, and a time for peace. (Eccl. 3:1–8)

In this list, the Preacher includes both one-time events (birth and death) and continual rounds (planting and harvesting). This is the nature of our lives and, while the Preacher seems generally dour about it all, the Christian sees it as providential (Mt. 5:45; I Cor. 3:5–6).

Furthermore, there are indeed special episodes in life in which something must be done that will not be asked of us again. Childhood is such an episode. Marriage is such an episode for many. The parenting of small children and the parenting of teenagers can be usefully seen as distinct episodes. Student days, starting a business or professional practice, retirement, caring for elderly parents or handicapped relatives—all of these pose special challenges, opportunities, and limitations.

A young journalist once interviewed an older woman in a Canadian city. The up-and-coming broadcaster sat for hours and became steadily more amazed at the septuagenarian, whom she at first had been inclined to pity as just "old" and therefore "uninteresting." But it turned out that her interview subject had married, loved, and buried two husbands, raised four children, and was enjoying twelve grandchildren. She also had earned three university degrees, and upon the completion of her Ph.D. began an academic career that resulted in two landmark studies of aboriginal peoples. She had served churches, civic boards, and charities. And now she was learning her sixth language.

"How did you possibly accomplish all that?" exclaimed the interviewer, her professional poise now shattered under the impress of the other woman's résumé.

"I have had the great blessing," came the reply, "of getting to do everything I wanted to do in life. I just never tried to do it all at once." For, as it turned out, she had not begun her second degree until her family had been raised, and did not complete her doctorate until she was nearing sixty. She got her university post, turned out those two books, and retired ten years after beginning. To everything in her life, there was a season.

God does not promise all of us such a life, of course. But we do well to accept God's pace, looking around particularly for what can be done only at this particular time of life and in these particular circumstances, and not letting its special opportunities slip away as we complain about its special limitations.

Jesus himself offers us a striking picture of timeliness, of living at a divinely ordered tempo. He did not hurry into the public part of his ministry. Then when he did begin it, as Mark Buchanan observes, he

> did it in an attitude of nearly unbroken serenity, almost leisureliness. He never seemed to be watching the clock. He could get tired, but He had no qualms about falling asleep just about anywhere... or having luxurious dinners out. He could be wonderfully responsive to the demands of others—a gruff centurion, a panicked father, a desperate widow—but never got caught up in their anxiety. Just as often, He could without a twinge of guilt walk away from demands and expectations. When the disciples interrupted His prayers because "everyone is looking for you," He responded by saying, "Let's go somewhere else" (Mk. 1:37–38). Or when news reached Him in Capernaum that His friend Lazarus was dying in Bethany, he stalled.... Even after He "set His face like flint" to go to His death in Jerusalem, He meandered.[33]

Jesus lived this way, with such preternatural *poise*, because he had a clear vocation and a constant relationship with his Father in the Spirit. He died without the normal marks of success—marriage, family, wealth, fame—and yet could say, "It is finished," and commend his spirit assuredly into the hands of his Father. This astonishing clarity and companionship is offered to the rest of us in the way of discipleship. François Fénelon gave this advice to himself:

> [Cheered] by the presence of God, I will do at each moment, without anxiety, according to the strength which he shall give me, the work that his Providence assigns. I will leave the rest without concern; it is not my affair.... I ought to consider the duty to which I am called each day, as the work God has given me to do, and to apply myself to it in a manner worthy of his glory, that is to say *with exactness and in peace*.[34]

Time is therefore no enemy, but a resource we can expend and a medium we can negotiate with confidence because we do so according to the express will of God.

---

33. Mark Buchanan, *Your God Is Too Safe: Rediscovering the Wonder of a God You Can't Control* (Portland, OR: Multnomah, 2001), 101–2.

34. Quoted without reference in David Martin, *Christian Language in the Secular City* (Aldershot, UK: Ashgate, 2002), 141.

MISSION AND VOCATION

Over the last century or so, there have emerged three, or perhaps four, typical conceptions of Christian mission. Evangelicalism and certain strands of Roman Catholicism have emphasized personal evangelism: saving souls. Their exemplar might be evangelist D. L. Moody, who once proclaimed, "God has given me a lifeboat and said to me, 'Moody, save all you can.'"[35] Liberal Christianity, both Protestant and Catholic, has taken up another form of gospel service and tried to save society. Nowadays, the religious right in various countries, and especially in the United States, has brought the spiritual and the social back together, but in a decidedly limited agenda of saving souls (and not whole persons) and saving society in narrow terms of sexual morality without attending to other social dimensions at all, whether capitalism's excesses, globalization's dark sides, or nationalism, consumerism, and other blights on the social landscape—let alone literal blights on the literal landscape of ecological degradation. Finally, of course, there is the perennial view of mission all too evident in all too many pews and pulpits, namely, that God's purpose is to provide for one's constant and ever-increasing happiness.

God, however, aims much higher and broader than any of these blinkered concerns. He aims to rescue, revolutionize, and renew all of creation toward its maturation in *shalom*. Jesus came preaching the Kingdom of God (Mk. 1:14), yes, but everything he did and said demonstrated Kingdom values. His miracles were signs, pointing to the truth about God and what God intends for the world. But Jesus attended weddings and dinner parties, blessed little children and old people, prayed alone and taught others to pray, rebuked errant disciples and warned vicious enemies, cherished friends and honored his mother—all of these actions also demonstrated God's way for us in the world.

Those Kingdom values then help us refine the Reformation doctrine of vocation that moved Christianity out of the two-tiered system to validate all Christian living. Those values help us go beyond this general validation to choose the best among extant choices. Given that a range of options in a given case can seem legitimate in Kingdom terms, we do not simply pick our favorite, but ask: What will do the *most* for the Kingdom? What job will make the most of my gifts, make the most impact, make for the most *shalom*? What leisure activity will bring the most creativity, recreation, joy, playfulness, or rest—whatever is most important at that

---

35. Quoted in George Marsden, *Fundamentalism and American Culture: The Shaping of Twentieth-Century Evangelicalism, 1870–1925* (New York: Oxford University Press, 1980), 38.

time? What relationships, among the many I do have or might have, should be cultivated, and in what directions—and what relationships should perhaps be pruned back or dropped altogether?

Bonhoeffer is right that we must avoid a religious mania that consciously asks for God's explicit will every moment we make a decision. God has provided us with reason, tradition, experience, and Scripture; with community wisdom; and with freedom he expects us to exercise. We shouldn't have to pray to ask him to tell us to avoid certain options and select others. We should, and we do, already know what is right, and we might instead pray simply for the moral strength to do what we know we ought to do. As W. H. Auden puts it, "We can only / do what it seems to us we were made for, look at / this world with a happy eye, / but from a sober perspective."[36]

Most of us, however, are very far from compulsive praying. Instead, we tend toward a pattern of practical atheism, acting as if we believe God does not exist. So we might do well to cultivate the regular asking of the question "What is the best way to honor God and advance the Kingdom in what I am doing and what I plan to do next?" The next time one is choosing a DVD, the next time one is choosing a date, the next time one is choosing a book, the next time one is choosing a job, this question ought to be asked. For if it is not asked, and asked frequently, then other values will in fact be determining our choices.

When someone asks, therefore, "What are you doing for the Kingdom?" we might well reply with any of the following:

- I'm mowing the lawn.
- I'm washing the dishes.
- I'm making a puzzle with my three-year-old.
- I'm paying the bills.
- I'm composing a poem.
- I'm talking with my mother on the phone.
- I'm teaching a neighbor child how to throw a ball.
- I'm writing the mayor.
- I'm preaching.

Everything. Everywhere. Every moment. That is the scope of God's call on our lives, and that is the dignity our lives enjoy.

---

36. Epigraph to Alan Jacobs, *A Visit to Vanity Fair: Moral Essays on the Present Age* (Grand Rapids, MI: Brazos, 2001).

EIGHT

PRINCIPLES OF A NEW REALISM

How, then, do we fulfill our calling within the global mission of God and in our particular place in the Christian Story? This chapter sets out a series of principles by which we may construe that vocation and then construct our participation in it.[1]

A MIXED FIELD, MIXED MOTIVES, AND MIXED RESULTS

Jesus once described the Kingdom of God in this unexpected way:

> The kingdom of heaven may be compared to someone who sowed good seed in his field; but while everybody was asleep, an enemy came and sowed weeds among the wheat, and then went away. So when the plants came up and bore grain, then the weeds appeared as well.
>
> And the slaves of the householder came and said to him, "Master, did you not sow good seed in your field? Where, then, did these weeds come from?"
>
> He answered, "An enemy has done this."
>
> The slaves said to him, "Then do you want us to go and gather them?"
>
> But he replied, "No; for in gathering the weeds you would uproot the wheat along with them. Let both of them grow together until the harvest; and at harvest time I will tell the reapers, Collect the weeds first and bind them in bundles to be burned, but gather the wheat into my barn." (Mt. 13:24–30)

---

1. Along with sources mentioned below, I recommend Robert Benne's teaching from an American Lutheran perspective. For an introduction to his thought that goes well beyond the "economic life" of the title, see his "The Calling of the Church in Economic Life," in *The Two Cities of God: The Church's Responsibility for the Earthly City,* ed. Carl E. Braaten and Robert W. Jenson (Grand Rapids, MI: Eerdmans, 1997), 95–116. Then see his *The Paradoxical Vision: A Public Theology for the Twenty-First Century* (Minneapolis: Fortress, 1995).

This parable comes between two more familiar parables in Matthew's Gospel, the parable of the sower and the parable of the mustard seed growing large. Those parables seem relatively straightforward compared to this one, and perhaps get more attention as a result. But this one opens up a vital perspective for us on the world as it is. Jesus explains:

> The one who sows the good seed is the Son of Man; the field is the world, and the good seed are the children of the kingdom; the weeds are the children of the evil one, and the enemy who sowed them is the devil; the harvest is the end of the age, and the reapers are angels. Just as the weeds are collected and burned up with fire, so will it be at the end of the age. The Son of Man will send his angels, and they will collect out of his kingdom all causes of sin and all evildoers, and they will throw them into the furnace of fire, where there will be weeping and gnashing of teeth. Then the righteous will shine like the sun in the kingdom of their Father. Let anyone with ears listen! (Mt. 13:37–43)

"The field is the world," Jesus teaches, and that field is mixed indeed, populated by the children of God and the children of the devil—two constituencies that could hardly be more different. Yet those two populations are so intertwined that somehow uprooting the latter would also damage or destroy the former. The economy of the world as it is, therefore, somehow requires that these two sets of inhabitants, these neighbors, be allowed to become fully themselves, maturing until the time of harvest, when all is uprooted, judged, and rewarded with blessing or curse. As Augustine warned, now is not the time for apocalyptic confrontation with the enemies of Christ, who might yet become his friends before the end of the age.[2]

With the world itself already corrupted by the effects of the Fall, and with the enemy inspiring human agents to divert the earth's resources to their useless endeavors, to mar it by their ugliness, and to impede those who are being inspired by God to pursue *shalom*—in short, to act like "weeds"—what should we expect of life today?

---

2. The phrasing is Oliver O'Donovan's (*The Desire of the Nations: Rediscovering the Roots of Political Thought* [Cambridge, UK: Cambridge University Press, 1996], 202; citing Epistle 189). For a brief and bemusing account of Augustine maintaining this language against the binary language of the Donatists of a simply evil world, see Garry Wills, *Saint Augustine* (New York: Penguin, 1999), 107–8.

We should expect sin. We should expect some politicians to engage in graft, and some officials to accept bribes.[3] We should expect some executives to sell out their companies, shareholders, and customers for personal gain. We should expect drunk driving, drug pushing, cartels, sexual assault, stock manipulation, terrorism, and a hundred other evils. Expecting sin does not mean accepting it, much less ignoring it. Expecting sin means something practical: planning for it. It means refusing to live as if we were in Eden or the New Jerusalem, and instead intentionally structuring our lives, individually and corporately, with the expectation of evil.

Beyond sin, we should expect waste. It should not shock us that governments, armies, and corporations waste money. It should not shock us that schools, hospitals, and charities waste money. It should not shock us that institutions waste people's time, people's talents, and the earth's resources. For Genesis 3 tells us that work will be harder to do than it should be, that "thorns and thistles" are everywhere, that the field is full of weeds. Indeed, beyond sin and waste, we should expect stupidity and absurdity, vanity and promiscuity.

Over and within this landscape of evil, there hangs obscurity, such that weeds can look like wheat and vice versa, such that the way forward is not immediately evident, and such that results are hard or impossible to discern. The field presents not only evil to us but ambiguity as well. Many Christians have not taken the reality of ambiguity seriously enough to actually expect it and thus to plan for it. Whether the Christians are liberal or conservative doesn't matter: each sort tends to see the world in stark polarities of good and evil, even as they differ as to what gets which label. But the field is mixed, and ambiguity is a factor with which we must reckon.

To be sure, not all is unclear. Indeed, most of this book has dealt in categories and commands that I have tried to depict as clear. Now, however, we confront the application of these clarities to the murky terrain we must traverse on the way to the city where the shadows disperse and "the righteous will shine like the sun in the kingdom of their Father."

---

3. We perhaps should expect this especially from politicians and even more especially from our most elevated leaders, as Glenn Tinder remarks (in an echo of Lord Acton's dictum): "Steeped in violence and power, the state is morally impure at its best. And it is never at its best. State power is rarely in the hands of people who are morally very good. This is partly because few such people exist. And it is partly because high positions in the state are nearly irresistible incitements to pride. The leaders of states enjoy privileges, pleasures, and adulation to a degree that can leave only the most extraordinary personalities undefiled" (Glenn Tinder, *The Fabric of Hope: An Essay* [Atlanta: Scholars Press, 1999], 168).

As we peer into such fog, we must also peer inward to admit the haze of our own ambivalence. For not only is the world out there mixed, but we ourselves are mixed as well with motives great and small, good and evil. We perceive that we do in fact hate our enemies; we do in fact crave luxury, power, and fame; we do in fact turn away from the light and prefer the darkness—at least at times and, paradoxically, at least a little all the time. The line distinguishing good and evil does not, as Solzhenitsyn warned us, run between countries or peoples or classes, but within our own hearts.

We must reckon, then, not only with what is bad out there, but also with what is bad in here: in our individual selves and in our most sacred institutions, whether families, churches, or other Christian organizations. And reckoning with those things means structuring and conducting our lives so as to restrain the evil within us and the evil without us as best we can, and to respond properly when those restraints give way, as they so often do. Such reckoning also means that we do not wait until our motives have resolved into perfect purity before we attempt to do God's work, since few of us consider ourselves entirely sanctified as of yet. Furthermore, such reckoning means that we not only are not shocked by impure motives in others but that we *presume* impure motives in others. Doing so, we yet will decide sometimes to support them, cooperate with them, and praise them for their successes, since we do not demand of them an unrealistic purity.

We can extend this issue of expectations further. We ought to expect politicians and parties to engage in crass practices, repellent compromises, and strange alliances. We will always wish it were otherwise, and we will demand legality at least and high principle at best, but we will not merely wring our hands and despair of politics until a truly good political option appears. For we will then have to wait for Jesus' return and remain useless politically in the meanwhile (except perhaps contributing the limited blessing of chiding everyone else for failing to be as good as he or she ought to be). We will expect our leaders—in government, commerce, the professions, and also the church—to be tempted by power, money, and fame. So we then will construct the healthiest possible hierarchies, which will both help them resist temptation and protect the rest of us from their *expected* failures to do so. We will expect school boards to be assailed by widely and wildly conflicting agendas, families to be riven by various interests, courts to be perverted by various forms of social engineering, universities to parrot the views of the powerful, and corporations to seek financial success over community service.

Let me give one example of what I mean by living in the light of such expectations. One of the oddities of so much American evangelicalism is its simultaneous commitment to American political institutions and to an ecclesiastical culture of populism. To reverse the order, American evangelicals typically lionize the entrepreneurial spiritual leader who boldly leads an institution by force of character, vision, and talent: a Billy Graham, a James Dobson, a Charles Colson, a T. D. Jakes, or a Bill Hybels. (I deliberately select examples from the mainstream; more extreme examples can be easily adduced from megachurches, religious broadcasting, and parachurch missions.) These same Christians typically also revere the Declaration of Independence and the Constitution. Yet these latter documents articulate a vision of leadership that is profoundly at odds with the paradigm of the populist leader wielding great personal command and responsible only to his followers. For the Founding Fathers—despite their general, if not universal, lack of Christian orthodoxy—shared a much stronger expectation of sin among the powerful and feared above all the concentration of power that would enable tyranny. They therefore built the distinctive American system of checks and balances with this expectation and fear in mind. Yet these evangelical leaders typically head organizations with precious few such curbs on their authority. And scandal after scandal thereby results, to the ever-renewed shock of evangelical constituents whose notoriously dark theology of sin is not put to work in a prophylactic way in their own organizations.

All of these negative expectations, however, arise not out of despair, which enervates and immobilizes, but out of both clear-eyed empirical analysis and our own theology, which illuminate and motivate. Our theology, which contains a robust doctrine of sin, includes also robust doctrines of both providence and redemption. God set up institutions to bless us, despite their corruption, and he continues to work through them. God also rules history, and aids those who press for greater *shalom* in those institutions. God is not discouraged by the evil evident in ourselves and our world. He is sad about it, angry at it, and grieved by it, but not discouraged. He works away at it, knowing that his labor is certain to produce fruit. And he has called us to do the same, as human beings and as Christians.[4]

God's expectations do indeed include fruit, but they also include weeds. We disciples of the one who told this parable, then, must also develop appropriate expectations. Realism requires that we expect good results: Jesus is Lord. But until his Kingdom comes in glory, we do not expect perfect results, and we are not surprised or discouraged by bad results. The combination of evil, ambiguity, and

---

4. Daniel Hardy writes, "Cultures are not fixed and self-enclosed; they are dynamic and intertwined with others. And yet within this intertwining, there is a braiding in which God himself may be present. And the question before us is *how*, in that intertwining, God in Christ is present, and how, by recognizing the presence of God in Christ, we may further effect the consequences of this presence" (*God's Ways with the World: Thinking and Practising Christian Faith* [Edinburgh: T. & T. Clark, 1996], 32).

our own ambivalence tempers our expectations from the utopian and conforms them better to what Jesus told us to expect: persecutions and progressions, sins and successes, accidents and accomplishments, resistance and renewal.

The Old Testament exemplifies this realism. The Law does not mandate total righteousness, or anything close to it—as law never properly does. Law sets out, instead, minimal standards of goodness, fairness, and prudence. The Torah (the word also means "instruction") nonetheless lifted Israel above its ancient Near Eastern neighbors. No other legislation that we know of is so generous to the needy and vulnerable, so concerned for individual and family welfare against the concentration of wealth, and so rich with joyful celebration of its deity. But this legislation also allows for slavery, differences in the treatment of women and men that most of us moderns find repellent, and so on. The Law deals with the actual people in that actual context and, as instruction, calls them to walk forward and upward. It doesn't require them impossibly to leap straight up into perfection.

With this realism guiding us, we will not always hold out for all-or-nothing resolutions—in government, on school boards, in our workplaces, and in our homes. True, sometimes one has to draw a line and say yes or no. Some decisions—such as whether to confess the faith, whether to preach the gospel, whether to support fellow Christians in need, and whether to care for the poor— are simply binary. Yet even in these categories there is a need for prudence. How do we confess the faith and preach the gospel in this context? What means do we use to support fellow Christians in need or to care for the poor? Must we advertise what we do as loudly as possible? Perhaps, but also perhaps not—as Jesus and the apostles sometimes "went public" and sometimes stayed private. Must we be as confrontational as possible? Again, perhaps (Jesus and the apostles sometimes were directly confrontational to their enemies: Mt. 23; Acts 4–5), but also perhaps not (as the Jesus and the apostles sometimes were not: Mt. 26–27; Acts 24–26). A good cause does not justify just any choice of action—although those inclined toward what they like to think of as "the prophetic" tend to feel this way, alas, and leave wreckage in their wakes. Instead, Christians ought to select means carefully, according to the intelligence, intuition, and inspiration we are given, in order to do the most good possible—to maximize *shalom*. And that will mean to think politically in a fundamental sense, for politics is "the art of the possible."

Many Christians refuse to think in terms of "half a loaf is better than none," "pick your battles," "live to fight another day," and the like. They see such compromises as derogatory toward the holiness of God and faithless toward the power of the Spirit. Only total victory will do. And such Christians are right—but they are right about the ultimate outcome in the Second Coming of Christ. They are not right about the penultimate stage in which we currently serve God. In this era, we live in a mixed field still growing, not at the harvest.

In the midst of this mixed field, then, what does the normal Christian life look like? Can we hope for more? And what happens when the normal recedes into the darkness of the borderline situation?

THE NORMAL ... AND BEYOND

Steering Societies, Converting Communities, Improving Individuals

In a culture saturated with information—indeed, in a culture in which media compete for our attention—issues usually come to the surface in the form of crises. A crisis, let us recall, is not necessarily a bad thing, but it is an urgent thing, a moment in which a choice must be made (from the Greek *krisis*, "decision"). At such moments, sometimes a single action or individual, sometimes a small group, can tip the balance. So we alert the troops, marshal the resources, and plunge into the fray. But we also need to pull back to gain an adequately large view of such events. If we don't, if we remain in perpetual close-up, then we will be stuck in perpetual crisis mode, reacting to what suddenly appears on our screens, jumping to conclusions, and forever taking emergency measures. If we are going to participate intelligently and effectively in cultural struggles, we need to keep several principles in mind.

First, we have to realize that crises emerge out of processes, not out of nowhere. Recognizing process has at least two ramifications. For one, processes usually take a while. So those who wish to influence them must appreciate the metaphors of inertia and momentum. Steering a society is more like steering an ocean liner than a speedboat. Ocean liners have tremendous inertia, so they are hard to get going and, once they are going, they require the application of sustained and substantial force, and thus great patience, to steer. An iceberg comes into view, and the ocean liner had better start changing course a long distance away. What is true of steering societies, furthermore, is usually true of changing smaller communities (such as businesses or charities or churches). They, too, have considerable inertia and tend to run the way they are running now, to be corrected only with considerable force and patience. And what is true of them is, frankly, true of most individuals. Self-help books tell us—at least the wise ones do—that breaking habits is hard, and establishing new habits, whether in diet, exercise, parenting, or praying, is long, slow work.

Another ramification of recognizing process is that those who control the process thereby exercise considerable control over the crisis. For the process generally sets the terms of the crisis—how the situation now appears (compared with how it looked a while ago), what is being considered (and what is now out of view as irrelevant), and what options are available (and what no longer are). The process therefore can set up the crisis so that it is most likely to break a certain way. That is the benefit of controlling momentum. If the ocean liner has been heading steadily for the rocks because of a drunken pilot, when the alarms are finally sounded, the much more skilled captain can awaken at the last minute, correctly appraise the situation, and take exactly the right action—and yet the ship will still crash. Control of the process often entails control of the crisis, no matter who enters the picture once the crisis emerges. Any good politician knows that. Any Christians who want to affect the real world need to know it, too.

A second major principle to bear in mind is that cultural processes are not often, and rarely completely, controllable because history is not made up of straight lines—nor is it made up of circles. Yet many people think in one image or the other, thus thinking that they can predict historical outcomes either by the extrapolation of current trends or by the expectation that things will come round to the way they used to be. To be sure, sometimes history does proceed for a while in reasonably continuous ways, whether fairly flat lines (as in the typical life of a peasant throughout much of the Middle Ages) or fairly steep ones (the economic rise of the Western working class after World War II, particularly in America). And there are cyclical patterns in history, whether the overextension and collapse of empires, the rise and fall of tyrants, or the business cycles on which so much of our current economic stability depends. Yet these lines are not ever quite straight, nor are they ever quite circular. For the Middle Ages did see technological and political changes that disrupted and sometimes improved the lives of peasants. Not everyone in the Western working classes enjoyed upward mobility—certainly not those whose livelihoods were replaced by mechanization, economies of scale, and outsourcing or "offshoring." Empires and tyrants do not, *pace* Spengler or Toynbee, rise and fall the same way, and our current business cycles are still prone to great unpredictability, as the dot-com bubble and NASDAQ meltdown at the turn of the millennium reminded us.

History is made up of multiple lines with multiple curves with very limited predictability. This is both a hopeful reality and a cautionary one. It is hopeful because when some levels of history seem to be moving in a bad direction, often others are moving in a good one. Many Christians today are convinced that modern society—North American, European, or whatever—is morally far worse than it was, say, a hundred years ago. And if one consults certain cultural indicators— such as the incidence of divorce and abortion, the decline of church attendance, the statistics on violent crime—such a conclusion is justified (although even then,

American church attendance is actually higher than it was a century ago, versus the general pattern of decline in the British Commonwealth). Yet consider today versus a hundred years ago: if you had to be poor, would you rather live now or then? What if you had to belong to a racial, ethnic, or religious minority? Be handicapped? Female? A child? I suggest that the less you look and sound like me—a middle-class, middle-aged, white man—the better it is for you today. So we must beware of the jeremiads that damn everything in sight and be grateful for what God is doing—for he is the source of all good, including all good social trends (Jas. 1:17).

There is also, however, a cautionary side to appreciating the multiplicity of historical developments. We do not have a comprehensive grasp of the past. We do not have a comprehensive grasp of the present. And even if we had the past and the present clearly in view, history does not proceed in nicely predictable lines, not least because much of history is made by free human beings whose behavior is not, shall we say, entirely predictable, even by themselves. We therefore do not have anything approaching even a sure glimpse, much less a comprehensive grasp, of the future.[5]

To live, therefore, as if tomorrow will be just like today, next year just like this year, and the latter decades of my life like the earlier decades is to ignore reality. We must eschew simplistic claims of "what has happened" and "what must be done." (That caution alone would shut the mouths of many a pundit, including Christian preachers, broadcasters, and, yes, professors.) We must beware even of sophisticated analyses that can only ever offer us more or less educated guesses— no matter how many charts and graphs from our favorite futurist might bedazzle us. Who saw World War I coming, or World War II? Who predicted the founding of the State of Israel? Who foresaw the Vietnam War, Watergate, the Iranian Revolution, the fall of the Berlin Wall, the end of apartheid, Bosnia, Rwanda, 9/11, or Darfur? Who anticipated transistors, microchips, the Internet, fiber optics, or the Walkman and its iPod progeny? Who predicted the rise to world significance of Riyadh, Shanghai, or Bangalore? Who prophesied the global force of Pentecostal and charismatic varieties of Christianity?

---

5. I confess that as a graduate of the University of Chicago's Divinity School, I have been bemused over the last two decades to read in my alumni magazine of University of Chicago economists winning prizes, and not a few Nobels, for modeling that takes into account the startling idea that human beings do not always conform to rational-choice theories and often make decisions that are not obviously in their rationally calculated economic self-interest. We div school grads might have helped our B-school colleagues take all that into account some time ago....

What is normal, what is predictable, in fact, is both a degree of continuity—else we would be utterly unable to conduct our lives—and a degree of discontinuity, for which we can only try to prepare and then encounter with resilience. Whether change is good or bad, it is a fundamental part of life now, and increasingly so in both scope and degree. Realistic Christian living in the world requires that we stop thinking in straight, simple, and single lines, or round, simple, and single circles. It also requires that we do what we can to direct the lines of history toward good outcomes, in full recognition that our efforts may be thwarted or even have unintended and undesired effects. We must do our best, under God, for ourselves and for the world. We strive for *shalom,* and that means all the time: in the processes, as well as the crises, of life.

Does such an attitude, however, bespeak a lack of faith in God's power? Does it settle for a kind of procedural worldliness and low horizon of possibility in which God no longer does great things, and nor do we? Let us turn, then, to the question of the normal and the wonderfully not-normal.

The Normal and the Miraculous

Jesus promised his disciples that they would do "greater works than these" after his ascension and their reception of the Holy Spirit at Pentecost. I see no compelling reason to doubt that he included miracles among those works, particularly as the Book of Acts depicts the disciples in fact healing the sick, flinging away venomous snakes, and predicting the future. A miracle, basically defined, is an event that does not arise out of the normal course of things—what we usually call "nature" in this discourse—and thus a miracle by definition is "supernatural." A miracle arises out of a sort of addition to the system, a boost that enables wonderful things to happen that ordinarily do not and cannot happen given the normal functioning of the world.[6]

The greatest and most important of these events in our experience is the conversion of human beings from spiritual death to spiritual rebirth and eternal life. But subsidiary miracles are expected and reported in the New Testament as well, as we have noted. I am not convinced of cessationist arguments that authentic miracles were supposed to mark only the apostolic period; rather, I believe that the church should expect a miracle, so to speak, when a miracle is required.

---

6. C. S. Lewis's discussion of this subject has not been bettered: *Miracles* (San Francisco: HarperSanFrancisco, 2001 [1947]).

God normally works in normal ways through normal means—that is why they are normal. We must be clear about that axiom. Otherwise, we will hunger for miracles as if they are to be normal, and there is no indication in Scripture that they are. The apostles themselves seem busy with just the sort of activities we would expect any such people to undertake: preaching the gospel, setting up churches, counseling individuals, training leaders, writing instructions, enjoying fellowship, engaging in worship, and the like. The miracles serve to underline in their work what they underlined in the work of Jesus himself: the gospel of the Kingdom of God come in Christ and the consequent mission of making disciples. Wherever miracles are necessary for such emphasis today, we should pray for them and, indeed, expect them.

For most of the history of the church, however, God has worked through the normal means of non-spectacular work. I do not say "non-supernatural," for, again, the work of the Holy Spirit in convicting people of sin and convincing them of the Lordship of Christ is both his regular work and the greatest miracle he does. There is otherwise never enough energy in the system, so to speak, to produce the New Birth. But the Spirit tends to channel this energy through conversation, preaching, reading, charity, and other normal means.

One must speak carefully here. To emphasize these normal means can sound like one or both of two kinds of mistake. The first mistake would be to treat as normative what has been merely the history of the Western church, as if our experience has been "just right" and therefore should stand as the measure of all other Christian experience. Yet the modern Western church manifestly has been compromised by false beliefs, lack of faith, and worldliness, so we must not say to our brothers and sisters in Africa or South America or Asia, "Settle down, stop all of this spectacle, put on the proper robes, and get back to the (Western) liturgy." Our siblings in the Two-Thirds World might well be having experiences of God's power that would inspire and inform us if we would be open to them.

The second mistake, therefore, would be to sound as if we ought not to seek such miracles in our own day and time, as if such events were abnormal in the pejorative sense. Again, I do not doubt that the modern Western church badly needs a lot of things, one of them being more confidence that God is working powerfully among us and wants to do more than we have been willing to do in his service. Spectacular miracles, both as signs of God's power at other levels (such as evangelism and social reform) and as significant accomplishments of his purposes in themselves, can and should always be prayed for. They might do us a world of good in certain circumstances.

Having said that, however, in genuine hope and what is, I trust, a measure of genuine humility on behalf of my particular Christian community, it remains evident in both the pages of the New Testament and the history of the global church that spectacular miracles are indeed rare and are not to be the normal fare on which the church's faith is nurtured. Nor are they to be the normal mode in which the church's work is accomplished.

The teaching of the gospels and the epistles focuses on holiness of character, integrity of life, purity of witness, and persistence in service. I reiterate that these are themselves miraculous in the sense that they require the Holy Spirit's power. They cannot be effected by human power alone. Yet the New Testament does not focus on exorcism, healing, resurrection, prophecy, or other obviously supernatural events. Nor does the history of the church. Nor should we.

We need to steer, then, between two evangelical catchphrases: "Expect a miracle" and "Pray as if it all depended upon God; work as if it all depended on you."[7] Whatever "it" is, we must not work as if it all depended on us, which is a sure route to exhaustion and self-pity. Rather, we must do our part heartily—in the power of the Holy Spirit, to be sure—and also expect God to do his part, whether through other Christians, other people, events elsewhere in creation, or direct intervention. Trusting God to work does not entail expecting a miracle in the sense of divine activity beyond God's normal modes of operation (namely, through the power he has already vested in creation and through the Spirit he has vested in the church) because God evidently chooses to use miracles rarely.

This principle applies on a broad landscape—indeed, to all of the Christian life. Yes, we can and should pray for healing, whether from a cold or from a cancer. God might use the normal means of healing (via the body's own devices or via medicine), or he might directly intervene, or he might do neither. But we are expected to pray and also to do our part: to look after the sick person as best we can, recognizing our dependence on Providence for any sort of healing. Yes, we can and should pray for the success of an evangelistic campaign by our church. God might use the normal means of persuasion (friendship, family relations, preaching, charity), directly intervening if they are to succeed (for only he can convert a person)—or he might not. But we are expected to pray for his help and also to do our part: to care for our neighbors as best we can, including proclaiming the gospel to them as best we can, while recognizing our dependence on Providence for any evangelistic success.

Likewise, we can and should pray for just and compassionate legislation from our governments, for wholesome entertainment from our media, for wise and informative education from our schools. Here, too, however, we need to see that God normally works through normal means. The Holy Spirit normally flows over

---

7. This aphorism has been variously attributed.

the extant contours of the sociological landscape, pouring in where openings have been made, moving around obstacles in his path, smoothing rough places, and usually surging most powerfully in channels that have been cut. All of this means that we must work with God to fashion that landscape as best we can and not to expect many flash floods of Holy Spirit power that sweep down and carry everything before them. That sort of miracle can happen, and perhaps it would happen more often if we would pray that it would. But, again, the Biblical and historical evidence would lead us to think that the normal mode of the Spirit's work in social matters is to work with what is there, ameliorating what is bad, strengthening what is good, and sometimes helping press recalcitrant features into new and better shapes.

David Martin is especially perspicuous on such matters. He writes about how to relate realistic analysis of processes to the good intentions of actors within them:

> No doubt this query arises from the ordinary, ancient, and everyday observation that we cannot do what we like and that we nearly always achieve something other than what we intended. But the systematic exposure of cramps and costs sharpens the query very considerably. If, for example, sociological analysis shows that the conflict of Catholics and Protestants in Ulster is a particular instance in a class of conflicts, so that given the coordinates A to n ... C and P are bound to clash, then ecumenical breast-beating becomes a rather otiose activity. Furthermore, if sociological analysis suggests that mediators or intermediate conciliatory groups are likely to be impotent or even to exacerbate the situation, then the search for a mediating role becomes morally very problematic. The moral problem is not solved nor put on one side by such an analysis, but it is set in sharpened perspective. At any rate, the ordinary liberal and (intermittently) Christian assumption that the solution is basically a matter of goodwill is undermined. The situation may at certain previous junctures have been willed, but it is now determined and goodwill cannot be relied upon to mend it.
>
> No doubt goodwill is required, but the simple willing of the good cannot overcome the structural constraints within which people seek evil. Of course, if everyone were to will the good simultaneously then the structural constraints might be ameliorated or even abolished, since everyone would simultaneously desire not only peace and harmony but also justice. But one knows on good sociological grounds, let alone on good theological grounds, that an immediate and universal desire for peace and justice is not humanly or statistically likely.[8]

---

8. David Martin, *Reflections on Sociology and Theology* (Oxford: Clarendon, 1997), 62–63. The previous paragraph of mine is inspired by Martin's use of geological and hydrological metaphors throughout his work.

Indeed, we might say, such an event would be a miracle.

If we take the previous points together, then, we would see that God has equipped us to negotiate the world, and to negotiate *with* the world, so that good things happen and bad things don't. We can ask God for sensitivity, skill, and wisdom, we can attend to processes, we can apply our resources to them, and we can try to steer any crisis to a good resolution. We are not to stand on the sidelines, wringing our hands over situations in which we have refused to invest ourselves and invoking God's miraculous power to achieve what our disobedience has not. To practice this sort of piety—a sort of perpetual oscillation between indolence and crisis-mode begging of God to perform what are in fact political, psychological, and sociological miracles—is not to glorify him. It is to dishonor the means he has put at our disposal and to disregard the commandments he has clearly given for human life in general and Christian service in particular. Living without miracles is conceited—"Father, I don't need you anymore and I can handle it myself"—but living in reliance on constant miracles is juvenile: "Daddy, it's too hard! *You* do it."

Sometimes, however, normal life gives way to extraordinary and even excruciating circumstances. What do we do then, in the borderline situations?

The Normal and the Borderline

The most common example of an ethical dilemma is so often used that its horror can recede into a sort of dark cartoon: the SS pounding at the door of the Dutch house at midnight, the frantic hiding of Jews in attics or basements, and the officer demanding, "Are there Jews here?"

The intruder in one's home who threatens one's family, the terrorist in custody who might be tortured to reveal information that would prevent a disaster, the use of nuclear weapons to end an otherwise even costlier war—everyone has their favorite instance of a borderline situation when normal ethics might have to be compromised in the interest of the greater good.

It is a maxim of jurisprudence that extreme cases make bad laws. I think that the extremity of these hypothetical or historical examples, however, literally doesn't matter. For the choices available to the conscientious, responsible, realistic Christian are just two, no matter how high or how low the stakes. The first is to refuse always to do something that is forbidden somewhere in Scripture (or perhaps, by extension, in Christian tradition), no matter what the intention or expected consequence. One commits the matter to God, who will do what is right, according to his sometimes mysterious plans, but who never requires the believer to do what is evil in order that good may come. The second choice is to do whatever will be truest to the revelation of the will of God, taken as a whole, recognizing that in a topsy-turvy world sometimes one must do what one would never do in Eden or the New Jerusalem, something that is objectively impure but that nonetheless is the best of the available options and will produce the most *shalom* in the situation. These two options sometimes are mapped onto the classic ethical categories of "deontological" (according to duty, no matter the consequences) and "consequentialist" (one's moral duty is, in fact, to produce the best possible consequences). I prefer, however, to see the second view as combining these two ethical types: one's duty *is* to produce the best possible consequences. Seeking to maximize *shalom* is a crucial component of the attempt to ascertain the will of God.

"Duty" proponents typically chide "consequence" proponents on two counts: that they open up a dark door to a casuistical calculus that arrogantly presumes to judge what really is best in a situation, despite the manifest proscriptions of Scripture, and that they dangerously expose Christians to rationalized self-interest in their decision making. Those who hold to the second view chide holders of the first view on two counts also: that their view is incoherent, for there is no way to love your neighbor by telling the Nazis where that neighbor is hidden, or even by remaining silent (not lying), which would signal to them the same thing; and that it avers a childish expectation that God will deliver them from all ethical difficulty and never require that they trouble their consciences. I propose to acknowledge these mutual charges and then to leave them behind, since I think both sides have their retorts (this exchange has a long history) and neither side persuades the other. Instead, to reiterate, the approach I offer combines regard for both duty and consequence, seeing our duty as in fact involving consideration of consequence.

So now I will deploy some principles already established in this discussion and draw in some further theological material that ought to be stipulated by anyone in this conversation. We'll see how far we get.

The first consideration is to observe where we are in the Christian Story. We are not Jesus, and we are not in the time of Jesus. We are downstream of Pentecost and the Book of Acts. We are also not in the New Jerusalem. Instead, most of the readers of this book are in countries in which adult Christians enjoy citizenship in democracies, in more or less open economic systems, and in more or less free arenas of ideological exchange and contest—none of which were the conditions of Jesus or the apostles. We also do not expect the Lord to return, and the present system to end, within our lifetimes, as the early Christians apparently did—although we hope and pray that this will happen.

With these greater freedoms and this responsibility to live for the long haul, then, has come the question of responsibility. If we can vote, should we? If we can run for office, serve in the police department, or join the military, should we? If we can work in corporations, investment houses, movie studios, or news organizations, should we? If we can teach in public universities, sit on public school boards, or write books for public consumption, should we? These are all questions that simply do not occur in the New Testament, because the choices did not occur in that culture. Either the doors were closed to such participation, or one had no choice in the matter (such as being pressed into military service), or one expected it all to be irrelevant in the light of the Lord's imminent return.

It seems to me, then, to indulge in a weird kind of "second naïveté" (Ricoeur) to continue to advocate an ethic that depends on the strong expectation of the imminent coming of the Lord—as Yoder conspicuously does.[9] To encourage Christians generally to keep away from government—indeed, to encourage Christians to keep themselves disentangled from any compromise with any social structures of coercion—because the old order is passing away and Christ is soon to return is to willfully ignore the passage of two thousand years. Since Christ's ascension, Christians have had many opportunities to shape government—and other social institutions and relations—for the better. Let me make clear that I believe Christ really could return at any moment, and I pray that it will be soon. But it may well *not* be soon, so to act as if one knows it will be is, literally, presumptuous and thus irresponsible.

It is also to get church history exactly backward to sneer at Christendom as a fall from grace, as if the church sold its soul under Constantine and has gotten it back only here and there, in small sects and marginal prophets, ever since. Oliver O'Donovan remarks that

> it is not, as is often suggested, that Christian political order is a *project* of the church's mission, either as an end in itself or as a means to the further missionary end. The church's one project is to witness to the Kingdom of God.

---

9. John Howard Yoder, *The Politics of Jesus: Vicit Agnus Noster* (Grand Rapids, MI: Eerdmans, 1972), ch. 9. A particular instance of this sort of mentality is telling. Yoder writes, in a discussion of Romans 13, that "the instructions to the Romans are to be subject to a government in whose administration they had no voice. The text cannot mean that Christians are called to do military or police service" (205). He means that "subjection" does not mean complying with conscription—a very live issue for him, as he was writing in the United States during the Vietnam War. Yet the argument seems obviously to be workable the other way. Precisely when Christians *do* have a voice in a government, what are they then to do? Yoder never seems to address this question directly.

Christendom is a *response* to mission, as such a sign that God has blessed it. It is constituted not by the church's seizing alien power, but by alien power's becoming attentive to the church.[10]

The emergence of Christendom, that is, should be construed not as a grotesque deviation from authentic Christian mission but as a natural result—with all of its attending challenges—of missionary effectiveness.[11] Over the three centuries preceding Constantine, the church had spread not only broadly throughout the nations of the Roman Empire, but also up and down the social scale. In fact, at the time of the Great Persecution at the turn of the fourth century, two of the emperors responsible, Diocletian and Galerius, were married to women who were disposed favorably to Christianity, and perhaps even Christians themselves.[12] Thus for the succeeding emperor to embrace Christianity (however slowly and piecemeal Constantine did embrace it) might have seemed like a dramatic reversal, but it was also really just the last social domino to fall, the last social stratum to be penetrated.

The Christian responsibility in, and for, the world thus looks quite different in such circumstances—circumstances not of despicable capitulation but of evangelistic success. To be sure, the emergence of Christendom did pose a new set of threats to the church as well as opportunities for it—particularly the threat of relaxing the church's missionary zeal, softening its demands of sanctity, and contenting itself with the status quo as if it were the Kingdom of God. Wherever such attitudes ruled, and wherever they persist today, they do need to be confronted and the gospel standards proclaimed afresh. Such confrontation and proclamation, however, ought to be conducted with appreciation for the good that has attended Christendom and, indeed, for the missionary success that bore it in the first place.

Therefore, to say that we are now in a situation different from what Jesus and the apostles faced (as we are also in a situation different from that of Constantine and his court, to be sure) is not to disregard Jesus and the apostles. It is instead to

---

10. O'Donovan, *Desire of the Nations,* 195.

11. I say "with all of its attending challenges" to distinguish my view sharply from the effusions of Eusebius of Caesarea, notorious celebrant of Constantine (see particularly the "panegyric" in his *Ecclesiastical History*, Book X, chapter 4). For a classic account of the early challenges, see Charles Norris Cochrane, *Christianity and Classical Culture: A Study of Thought and Action from Augustus to Augustine,* rev. ed. (Oxford: Oxford University Press, 1980 [1940, 1944]).

12. Kenneth Scott Latourette, *A History of the Expansion of Christianity,* vol. 1: *The First Five Centuries* (New York: Harper and Brothers, 1937), 154.

say merely that it is at least worth considering whether anything ought to change in the Christian ethos when the opportunities to obey the commandments of God change quite radically.[13] To these commandments again, then, we now turn.

The second consideration therefore is to recall the creation commandments and the redemption commandments, and their relation to each other. Some Christians have opted to obey the redemption commandments and to leave the rest of creation to the care of non-Christians and God. Serving in the justice system, for example, requires both compromise and coercion, so Christians avoid both by avoiding the system itself, trusting God to run it as best he can through non-Christians.

I reiterate in reply that God has not set aside the creation commandments—for Christians or for anyone else. So any ethic that implies otherwise is immediately suspect. If the only way to honor God by avoiding apparently evil actions is to withdraw from doing our best to promote *shalom,* then we have not avoided contradiction—and sin—after all.

Yet, comes the rejoinder, the church does its best for *shalom* by refusing to join with the worldly powers in the coercive work of government, the justice system, the military, and so on. By maintaining an alternative community, the church bears witness to greater ideals than individual or national self-interest, greater than expediency and efficiency, and greater than the zero-sum logic of secularism that always requires the sacrifice of some for the benefit of more.

I have always respected this radical viewpoint—impressively detailed by John Howard Yoder and defended beyond Anabaptist circles by Stanley Hauerwas, William Willimon, and others. And, as I have suggested earlier and will affirm again, I'm not persuaded that such Christians shouldn't continue to maintain this witness, powerful as it is precisely in its almost typological purity. At the same time, however, I will honor Brother Yoder by refusing to retreat into the relativism he so hated and say instead that I think it is wrong for *all* Christians to hold

---

13. Again, O'Donovan is helpful on this matter: "It was the missionary imperative that compelled the church to take the conversion of the empire seriously and to seize the opportunities it offered. These were not merely opportunities for 'power.' They were opportunities for preaching the Gospel, baptizing believers, curbing the violence and cruelty of empire and, perhaps most important of all, forgiving their former persecutors" (*Desire of the Nations,* 212). Robert Wilken echoes this point as he discusses the matter from Augustine's point of view: "For Christians who lived during the first three centuries the task of running the cities and the empire seemed to be someone else's responsibility....By Augustine's time, however, Christians did not enjoy such luxury. Without the participation of Christians the cities would lack qualified people to serve as magistrates, judges, civic officials, teachers, and soldiers" (Robert L. Wilken, "Augustine's City of God Today," in *The Two Cities of God: The Church's Responsibility for the Earthly City,* ed. Carl E. Braaten and Robert W. Jenson [Grand Rapids, MI: Eerdmans, 1997], 35).

to this view. Indeed, I think it is best that *most* Christians take another, more participatory, and thus more morally dangerous and ambiguous stance. I say so on the basis of two further considerations, each of which recurs to one of the previous two.

The third consideration, then, is to return to the Christian Story to witness God involved in violence, deception, and other contraventions of "normal" morality. The Old Testament depicts God as killing individuals, nations, and once even the whole inhabited earth in the Flood. God deceives his enemies, causing some to panic before an imaginary threat he supervises (Judg. 6–8). God uses nations against other nations (Habakkuk), and other creatures against humans (as in the storm and the great fish of the Book of Jonah). God even allows Satan to work mischief on his favorites, whether Job or the apostle Paul (II Cor. 12:7–10). And in the New Testament, Jesus warns of the Day of the Lord in which God will judge all, punish the wicked, and eradicate all of his opponents from the earth in a global spectacle that results not only in the joy of the blessed but also in the "weeping and gnashing of teeth" of the damned (Mt. 13).

Furthermore, God's people achieve his purposes by killing others, whether in assassination, as in the story of Ehud (Judg. 3), or in attacks on whole peoples, as in the conquest of Canaan (Deut. 20:17).[14] God brings salvation through liars, such as the Hebrew midwives (Ex. 2:15–20) and the prostitute Rahab (Josh. 2–6). God puts his prophets through agonies both physical (Ezekiel) and marital (Hosea). He calls other prophets to take up arms and kill his enemies—prophets as admirable as Samuel and Elijah.[15] And in the New Testament, God sends both his Son to the Cross and his witnesses (literally martyrs) to their deaths.

---

14. This is not the place for a full apologetic on behalf of divinely mandated genocide, particularly since it is an open question in biblical studies as to just how extensive—or how hyperbolic— these commands really were. But I do not find this command of God immediately implausible, as many of my contemporaries do. A society that has become so evil that it sacrifices its own children to its gods, as the Canaanites were known to do, could well be a culture that is irretrievably wicked and harmful—indeed, lethally harmful even to its own children. The eradication of such a society might well have been in everyone's interest, particularly from a Christian point of view that takes resurrection seriously and believes in a merciful God who would be generous in the next life to any innocents killed in such a way. All I want to say here is that such Old Testament accounts should not be immediately set aside as unworthy of God, but read as Scripture in the hopes of understanding God and his ways better.

15. One advance reader of this book, who prefers the Yoder-Hauerwas take on things to mine, asked, "Who are 'God's people' today who would receive these commands?" The answer to me is, I have to say, obvious: those Christian police officers and soldiers whose duty it is to use deadly force on those engaged in evil actions. The answer would also include those in politically extreme situations, as Dietrich Bonhoeffer was, who must resort to violence to overthrow an intolerable, illegitimate government.

(I recognize that God seems not to call the apostles to any ethically ambiguous action. But in the brief sketches we have of them in the New Testament, we must recognize also they simply are never depicted as facing an ethical dilemma, so we have no analogies to the Nazis pounding on the door asking for hidden Jews. Nor are they ever in a position of social and political authority in which they have the opportunity to wield such power on behalf of others or of the gospel. So the strongest argument from the apostolic practice against what I am saying is, at the end, only silence. I acknowledge, then, that the apostles do not say and do the sorts of things I am discussing here. But I point out also that they are never shown to be in positions to make such decisions.)

I have tried hard in the foregoing to avoid exaggerated or inflammatory language. I think God did just those things I have listed, and so did his people under his command. So the case against Christians being involved in anything coercive or anything else that would normally be seen as evil (such as consigning an innocent carpenter-cum-rabbi to crucifixion) cannot be made on the basis of some putative holiness of God that excludes such things.[16] The holiness of God somehow includes all of these actions.[17] Instead, the case must be made on the basis of a fourth consideration.

This fourth consideration is the distinction between God's work and ours, between what is proper only to him and what we are to do in resemblance to, and in cooperation with, him. Since we were created in the image of God to engage in godly work in the world—namely, caring for the rest of creation—and since we are always to love God and our neighbors as ourselves, then we must continue to obey those commandments. Finding refuge from them in the redemption commandments will not do, as we have seen in other contexts. Indeed, in this context we can say that as Christians refuse to work for justice in coercive ways, as well

---

16. Mark 6:3 describes Jesus as a carpenter, and that is the traditional understanding of his occupation previous to his preaching ministry. But Lucien Legrand makes a persuasive case that the word rendered "carpenter" is better rendered "house builder" (some say "artisan"), which makes better sense of Jesus' repertoire of parables and other illustrations: see Lucien Legrand, *The Bible on Culture: Belonging or Dissenting?* (Maryknoll, NY: Orbis, 2000), 107–8.

17. In this regard, I am taking the Bible in the orthodox way, reading the Old Testament as rather straightforwardly revealing something of God's character, even as I appreciate that it does so in the progress of revelation through the Testaments. I find it perplexing in this regard that some Christian realists would prefer to distance themselves from such a reading of the Old Testament, whether Reinhold Niebuhr's espousal of "myth" or David Martin's sense that the New Testament not only fulfills, but also subverts as it transforms, the image of God depicted in the Old. Christian realism becomes more plausible by taking both Testaments more literally than by downgrading the Old Testament—which move actually seems to contribute better to the pacifist agenda.

as in non-coercive ways, we could be implying that coercion is always wrong, when in fact we believe in a God who finally will coerce the whole universe back into line.[18] To be sure, there are Christians today who believe, as some Christians have believed in the past, in a non-coercive God who merely woos or lures or suggests. But this is not orthodox, Biblical teaching, whether it is couched in terms of process thought, New Age syncretism, or liberal sentimentality. No, the only recourse is to distinguish between God's work and ours in such a way that helps us avoid ethical dilemmas.

Perhaps there are grounds for such a distinction.[19] I myself have insisted on the uniqueness of Jesus' role in salvation. He alone is Savior and Lord. So what might be good for Jesus to do (such as judge the world) is not proper for us to do. Along this line, Paul quotes the Old Testament to instruct the church not to retaliate when mistreated: "'Vengeance is mine, I will repay,' says the Lord" (Rom. 12:19; Heb. 10:30). Human beings cannot be entrusted with the prosecution of vengeance, which requires both more data and more intellectual and moral refinement than we can produce for the task.

I myself oppose capital punishment, in fact, on similar grounds. Our justice systems—including international courts and war crimes tribunals—are so porous, so fallible, so amenable to improper influence, that we cannot risk putting innocent people to death, as we manifestly have done. I recognize that there are cases that seem utterly obvious (Hitler, Stalin, Mao, Pol Pot). But I cannot think of a way to draw a clear line between them and, say, their lieutenants, and then *their* lieutenants, and so on in an infinite regress. Since we believe in a God who will

---

18. A related semantic muddle afflicts this discourse regarding the word "power." Some of the transformationist type enjoy the idea of power rather too much: their own cleverly and industriously marshaled power to accomplish their agendas, and especially the invocation of divine power to overcome all resistance. Others, however, suggest that power is simply bad; instead, weakness is good. Yet being "for" or "against" power is like being for or against light, or fire, or momentum—all, not coincidentally, forms of power. The question is not about the intrinsic morality of power, as if there is such a thing. The question is always a *set* of questions about such matters as who is exercising power, of what sort, in what circumstances, according to what motives, to achieve what result, and so on. Thus even those who glory in weakness always end up extolling the power of the Cross, the power of the Holy Spirit, the power of love, and so on.

One advance reader of this book asked me whether by "coerce the whole universe back into line" I am defending universalism. I am not. But whether by universal salvation or by the salvation of some and the condemnation of others, the world is made right again by the power of God: that is the Christian hope here.

19. It is important to defend Yoder and company against a common charge, here articulated by Glenn Tinder: "To forsake the state in order to safeguard a moral purity that is lost by those implicated in the use of power and violence is to build a wall between moral conduct

repay each according to his deeds, and since our society can afford to protect itself from dangerous people through incarceration, we simply do not need to practice capital punishment; we can let God make up in the next life whatever is truly due a person. Indeed, we hopeful and compassionate Christians can work for prison systems that provide the best possible context for repentance and amendment of life of all convicts, even these who have transgressed the most. At least we can campaign, as Christians historically have done, for humane conditions for our fellow human beings, including the worst murderers—not because they clearly deserve it, but because God loves them and wants us to do the same.

Yet society does need to be protected, and to be protected by violence—legal, authorized, monitored, and minimal violence, but violence nonetheless. Some people distinguish between "coercion," which might be modified by the adjectives in the previous sentence, and "violence," which would not be. I recognize this distinction, but I do not want to be seen as disguising the true nature of my proposal. Whether it's called coercion or legitimate and proportionate violence, somebody has to exercise it in the divinely instituted capacity of government.[20] Why would God's own people not play a part in such a system?

God's own people, in fact, did play parts, and sometimes key parts, in precisely such systems of worldly government. Indeed, some of the most familiar Bible heroes devoted their talents to helping pagan, even oppressive empires. Joseph was made prime minister of Egypt. Moses was an adopted grandson of Pharaoh and doubtless later a courtier. Daniel was a leading administrator of *two*

---

and human beings on earth.... One does not achieve moral goodness by abandoning the earth and the human race, even though the circumstances of earthly existence inevitably involve one in evil" (Glenn Tinder, *The Political Meaning of Christianity: An Interpretation* [Baton Rouge: Louisiana State University Press, 1989], 143). I agree with Tinder that this abandonment is the de facto implication of Yoder's position, but I daresay Yoder would respond that Christians of his viewpoint are "abandoning" the world *to God's providence*, and that one must obey what God has called one to do, and trust God to deal rightly with spheres (such as government and warfare) to which God has not called Christians. Indeed, one stands with the victims of oppression in solidarity with their suffering and in testimony against injustice. The question, then, is exactly one of mission and vocation: What is it to which God has called us?

20. Yoder makes a different distinction in his exposition of Romans 13: "The function of bearing the sword to which Christians are called to be subject [note: not "to wield"] is the judicial and police function; it does not refer to the death penalty or to war" (*The Politics of Jesus*, 205). But this distinction rests on his conviction that no war is ever fought according to the strictures of "just war theory"—which makes one wonder how many courts and police forces meet Yoder's standards.

This is one place among many in which I can point readers to the important reflections on these matters in Hans Boersma, *Violence, Hospitality, and the Cross: Reappropriating the Atonement Tradition* (Grand Rapids, MI: Baker Academic, 2004).

empires, the Babylonian and then the Medo-Persian. And Mordecai, Esther, and Nehemiah were leading figures in the latter empire as well. Jeremiah was given a prophecy to explain such paradoxical callings, callings that reflect the embeddedness of all of us in the world:

> Thus says the LORD of hosts, the God of Israel, to all the exiles whom I have sent into exile from Jerusalem to Babylon: Build houses and live in them; plant gardens and eat what they produce. Take wives and have sons and daughters; take wives for your sons, and give your daughters in marriage, that they may bear sons and daughters; multiply there, and do not decrease. But seek the welfare of the city where I have sent you into exile, and pray to the LORD on its behalf, for in its welfare you will find your welfare. (Jer. 29:4–7)

I have suggested earlier that a Christian community that tries to engage in evangelism by leaving off participation in other activities that instantiate Kingdom values (such as art, commerce, and political renewal) will thereby compromise its very evangelism. I suggest now that a Christian community that tries to witness to the world by leaving off participation in other activities that instantiate Kingdom values (such as order, justice, security, and freedom) will also thereby compromise its very witness. This fact is deeply ironic because such communities typically see it in the exactly opposite way. They fear that involvement in these activities will compromise their witness. But I suggest that the contrary is true. God is the God of the land of milk and honey, the God of the peaceable kingdom, the God of the New Jerusalem. But along the way, and precisely in order to get there from here, God is not ashamed to be the God of the Conquest, the God of the destruction of Jerusalem, and the God of Armageddon. It is not enough to say that God gives himself up on the Cross and so we should never promote violence upon others for righteousness's sake. God also visits violence on his enemies in this life, as well as in the life to come, and he called many of his people to visit his violence on his enemies as well. All of this is part of the testimony of the church, and however unpleasant or even terrifying it is—for it is a terrifying thing to fall into the hands of the living God (Heb. 10:31)—it is true.

What, then, of the borderline situations?

> "You shall love the Lord your God with all your heart, and with all your soul, and with all your mind." This is the greatest and first commandment. And a second is like it: "You shall love your neighbor as yourself." On these two commandments hang all the law and the prophets. (Mt. 22:37–40)

The Bible is a rich resource to help us understand what it means to love God and love our neighbors as ourselves. We are not to glibly deploy either a shallow love ethic or a ruthless justice ethic or even a well-intentioned *shalom* ethic, with all of their vulnerability to oversimplification and rationalization along whatever lines suit our interests and sensibilities. We are not, that is, simply to try to maximize *shalom* in defiance of explicit teachings of God's Word, nor in simplistic deference to a few verses or principles we think we have adduced from Scripture as applied to our best take on the scene before us. The Bible not only tells us to seek *shalom* but also gives us considerable detail as to the definition of *shalom*—and of love, justice, and other key terms. We are not free to simply snatch these words from the Bible, write them on a banner, and then fly that banner over whatever we would like to do. We are to heed the *whole* Bible, bearing in mind the wisdom of the Christian tradition, the deliverances of reason, and the impressions of experience. We are to consult our fellows in the church, seeking to profit from their various perspectives. And throughout this deliberation we are to trust the Holy Spirit of God to guide us to the action that makes the most sense of all of these resources in the interest of maximizing *shalom*. We do not wait until all of the pieces of the puzzle nicely fall into place and the way forward opens up before us utterly clear and bright. We walk by faith, not by sight. But we also do not precipitously charge forward on the basis of our favorite simplistic principle and a superficial reading of the situation. Instead, we do our part, our cognitive part, as responsibly as we can, and we trust God to supervise that process such that it will bring Christ's command to us in the here and now.[21]

If we do engage in such thorough study and reflection, we will see that we live in a world in which God himself does not nicely avoid difficult decisions that result in violence against his own ultimate ideals. We live in a world instead into

---

21. One is reminded of Bonhoeffer's warning of the primeval temptation in Eden to critique God's express Word ("Do not eat") by what the serpent presents to Adam and Eve as a superior principle, a higher knowledge, a better view of things than God's literal command—"instead of simply listening to it and doing it" (Dietrich Bonhoeffer, *Creation and Fall: A Theological Exposition of Genesis 1–3*, ed. John W. de Gruchy, trans. Douglas Stephen Bax (Minneapolis: Fortress, 1997), 108. An intriguing parallel warning against even a pious version of this mistake comes from Oswald Chambers's English devotional classic *My Utmost for His Highest* (New York: Dodd, Mead, 1935): "It is never right to think that my obedience to a word of God will bring dishonour to Jesus. The only thing that will bring dishonour is not obeying Him. To put my view of His honour in place of what He is plainly impelling me to do is never right, although it may arise from a real desire to prevent Him being put to open shame....Many of us are loyal to our notions of Jesus Christ, but how many of us are loyal to *Him*?" (88, emphasis added).

which God has thrust us to do his work of cultivation and redemption, and the way he does it sometimes involves dirt and blood.[22]

Let us consider Bonhoeffer and the plot against Hitler in this light. It is unpleasant to say, but the plot *did* fail, and Bonhoeffer himself was executed because of his involvement in that plot—scant days before the Allied forces liberated his prison. Had he remained out of the fray, he might well have survived the war and brought us another thirty or more years of theological fruitfulness. So the consequences of his actions do not obviously justify them.[23]

Yet it also remains true that Hitler fell because lots of other Christians, among others, were flying planes, driving tanks, and piloting ships against the Third Reich. Maybe Hitler would have eventually fallen as a result of the German people coming to their senses, repenting, and resisting him, or by some other means besides war. But we do not know that (though we may try to infer it from certain pacifistic convictions, to be sure). What we do know is that armed resistance *was* effective and liberated many from a demonic regime. The decision to bomb Hiroshima and Nagasaki made a similar, awful sense to those charged with that decision: the apparent choice was to opt for a bloodbath as Japan roused its citizen militia to fight to the death for the emperor (although, again, who can say when God might have prompted the Japanese people to stop fighting?) or to opt for what was hoped to be a horrific warning by way of the extinction of one city, and then another—which *did* end the fighting.

Some Christians have suggested that no price is too great to pay to maintain ethical purity, and if God allows carnage as a result of our refusal to exercise coercion, then that is, bluntly, his responsibility. It is not effectiveness that is their concern, they say, but faithfulness. I will deal with the question of effectiveness versus faithfulness below. Right now I want to acknowledge again that this view does have a powerful logic, and the question simply remains this: *is* it God's will that Christians eschew the use of force? The use of force has proved effective at

---

22. Richard Bauckham offers some provocative reflections on the story of Noah—the paradigm case of the "conservationist" and "gardener"—and on the Noahic covenant of Genesis 9, in which God pragmatically and redemptively accommodates the realities of violence and sin (*The Bible in Politics,* 135–36).

23. Ironically enough, the failed attempt on Hitler's life in 1944 perhaps strengthened his megalomania. Traudl Junge, Hitler's former secretary, told a reporter that Hitler was convinced that he enjoyed divine protection and that this conviction grew after surviving the bomb. "After the July 1944 attack," she said, "I believe he felt himself to be an instrument of providence, and believed he had a mission to fulfill"—hardly terms on which Hitler would have considered a negotiated end to the war (Timothy W. Ryback, "Hitler's Forgotten Library: The Man, His Books, and His Search for God," *Atlantic Monthly,* May 2003, 85).

least sometimes in restraining evil and promoting good, however many times we can easily show that it has done the opposite. And restraining evil and promoting good are the call of God to *all* humanity in the creation commandments. To eschew the use of force and then leave it entirely up to God and non-Christians requires a very strong confidence in one's interpretation of the Bible on these matters—and not in the comfort of a classroom or library or pulpit, of course, but in the situation room, in the trenches, and in the living room at midnight as one stares into the eyes of a marauder.

It also means that one must think that Bonhoeffer was wrong—and so were the citizens of Le Chambon-sur-Lignon, and Raoul Wallenberg, and Oskar Schindler, who used repeated and systematic deception to rescue Jews from the Nazis. One must think that they should have trusted God to rescue the Jews without their having to lie—in the face of what one might (generously) call God's apparent lack of miraculous rescuing of Jews all around them. Or does anyone want to defend the idea that God *wanted* all of the Jews to be rounded up by the Nazis, and so Bonhoeffer, Wallenberg, and the others were actually resisting the will of God? There seem to be no pure choices in this real-world boundary situation, and it would be good to know what the opponents of Christian Realism think ought to have been done in these cases.[24]

Bonhoeffer's chief legacy on this question is his ethical reflection that led to his actions, but his actions of deceiving the Gestapo and aiding the intended tyrannicide are important to consider as well. His thought and his example have prompted subsequent decades of sober consideration of the possibility that God may well call us onto the borderline, to do something that is in fact consistent with Scripture and yet at the same time something that normally would not be done and one day will never have to be done again. I myself have come to the awful conclusion that Bonhoeffer was right to participate in the plot against Hitler, and I submit it here with trembling.

---

24. I am going to put the following ad hominem comment in this footnote rather than the main text, because it is not essential to the argument I am making. But I confess to wondering how someone in the Two-Thirds World, groaning under one or another form of tyranny, would hear North American or British ethicists telling them to eschew violence and rebellion in the cause of justice. Given the British legacy of imperialism and mercantilism, which profited Great Britain at the expense of peoples around the globe, and given the American tradition of violent self-assertion, going back to the subjugation of native populations, the American Revolution itself (which, to these Canadian Loyalist eyes, looks like a violent overreaction to the non-tyranny of George III), and the consequent, largely profitable wars with France, Spain, Germany, Japan, and more—isn't it just a trifle suspect for those of us who enjoy positions of safety and prosperity won through violence to tell others not to use it?

Again, one must not see here a carte blanche for whatever seems merely advantageous, let alone personally or corporately convenient. Maximizing *shalom* can never properly be reduced to maximizing profits or maximizing my personal welfare or maximizing our political position.

Furthermore, of course one ought to practice straightforward goodness as the norm, expecting in turn both recognition and praise from some and incomprehension and resistance from others. Christians must not underestimate the importance and the power of what David Ford calls "prophetic gentleness or patience."[25] Normally we know what to do and must do it, especially because our estimates of consequences are so limited and distorted. Bonhoeffer did what he did because he could not believe that any other action/inaction would result in something better—that's how extreme the situation was. So being open to this possibility does not mean license to disobey God's clear instruction whenever we think we might be able to achieve a little more *shalom* another way.[26]

One must elect to do the normally wrong thing only after pleading with God for another, easier, clearer way to act, and then proceed only after imposing every anticipatable limitation on the evil to ensue. The ethically paradoxical choice must be the last resort. And if one is to engage in such ethical improvisation, so to speak, it must be what all good improvisation is: first mastering the normal (and complex) rules and patterns and only then transcending them (which is thus not merely breaking them) to effect something clearly better than would have been produced by routinely following them.

---

25. David F. Ford, *The Shape of Living* (London: HarperCollins, 1997), 69.

26. I thus am responding, in part, to Yoder's version of the epigram attributed to Chesterton: "Christianity has not been attempted and found wanting; it has been found difficult, and therefore not attempted." Here is one instance of Yoder's challenge (from his *The Priestly Kingdom: Social Ethics as Gospel* [Notre Dame, IN: University of Notre Dame Press, 1984], 115):

How do we know that violence will be effective toward the ends which are posited? Has a long enough time frame been allowed? Has there been attention to the possibility that social changes imposed by superior forces are less stable, or that the people living under unfreedom are less productive than when social change is achieved without violence? Has really serious legal process or really serious social science analysis been invested in testing whether the violence one is ready to resort to is really the last resort, and whether there would be no nonviolent alternatives offering a comparable percentage of probability of achieving comparable results?

Yoder's point is important at least as a part of deliberations regarding a "just war": violence should be a last resort, employed only when no nonviolent means can be prudently expected to obtain equal or better results. Yoder's challenge thus is a perennial one for those of my outlook, as well as of his.

Sometimes, then, some of us must improvise. As Bonhoeffer reminds us, in certain extreme situations we cannot settle for living "correctly" according to some neat ethical calculus we have devised and congratulating ourselves for our integrity while blaming God for whatever happens next. We are responsible to care for the earth and to love our neighbor as best we can, and if we think we can do that better in an unusual way that leaves us vulnerable to second-guessing and maybe even to error, we nonetheless should do it. For what is the alternative? It is to shrink back from this possibility and settle for the safety of the rule book, the comfort of the clear but circumscribed conscience.

Most of the time, then, we know what to do and must simply do it. Sometimes, however, the politician has to hold his nose and make a deal. The chaplain has to encourage his fellow soldiers in a war he deeply regrets. The professor has to teach fairly a theory or philosophy she doesn't think is true. The police officer has to subdue a criminal with deadly force. We are on a slippery slope indeed—and one shrouded in darkness, with the ground not only slippery but shifting under our feet. So we hold on to God's hand, and each other's, and make the best of it.

FAITH AND FAITHFULNESS

Faith in God's Providence

The Christian life is one of faith: trusting in God for salvation—of oneself, one's neighbors, and the world. A vital aspect of that faith is trusting the work of God *in* oneself, *in* one's neighbors, and *in* the world. Another is trusting the work of God *through* oneself, *through* one's neighbors, and *through* the world.

The concerned Christian person can forget to trust God in these ways and take on herself the burden of converting her husband to Christ, keeping her teenagers

---

Where we differ is in our answer to these rhetorical questions. He presumes, I think, that the answer will be that nonviolence can be shown to be at least as effective as violence, although he doesn't actually attempt any such demonstration himself. I presume that two thousand years of Christian history indicate that sometimes, at least, violence has been the best of the bad choices—a case which, to be sure, I have not demonstrated, either.

Those who share my presumption nonetheless can profit from Yoder's challenge to consider how well warranted from actual evidence our presumption is. His point thus stands as, again, an appropriate reminder to Christian realists to be true to their own principles. In particular, it means to be true to the empirical data, as both Niebuhr and Bonhoeffer remind us to be, in our prescriptions and policies. More particularly, we must not resort to violence unless we have strong warrant, including empirical warrant, for our conclusion that it is the best choice in a given instance.

away from fornication, or persuading her father to give up drinking. She can try to convince the school board to pick different books for the library, or the city council to rezone her neighborhood to remove pornography stores. She forgets that only God can convert people in regard to this fundamental choice or that lifelong habit. She also forgets that God uses a variety of means to effect his purposes, and what she does is only part of his plan. Such forgetting usually has the bitterly ironic result of actually interfering with God's work. She becomes a pest to her husband, a nag to her children, a harpy to her father. The school board and the city council ignore her as that odd, strident woman who shows up at meetings with no supporters and seems to speak only for herself. She overplays her hand, arrogates to herself the work that God wants others to do, fails to even consider building alliances, and so remains frustrated.

Christian groups also can "work as if it all depended on them." They can be suspicious of other Christian groups in the same arena, perhaps because they are from a different denominational tradition, perhaps because they have a different style of engagement, or perhaps because their political philosophy is somewhat different. So such groups fail to cooperate and achieve together what they cannot achieve alone.

Yet other Christian groups can be willing to band together with other Christians, at least of certain acceptable sorts, but then refuse to make common cause with non-Christians. They fail to see that, at least for *this* issue and on *this* occasion, Muslims or Mormons or Marxists might share the same goals and support the same plan.

Increasingly in our day we have seen Christians set aside such individualistic or chauvinistic attitudes to form alliances of various sorts to try to accomplish various goods. And Christians have needed to be warned about the quid pro quo of politics, the strings that may be attached to promises, the trade-offs that are usually expected in order to maintain access to power. Sectors of American fundamentalism in particular have veered from one extreme to another in just the last generation or so.

So we need a new Christian Realism that trusts God to work through the various means he has shown that he is pleased to use—brave, persevering individuals, yes, but also families, churches, groups of other kinds, alliances of various sorts, rulers, and even whole nations. And the Bible shows us that he is willing to use those who do not believe and honor him, as well as those who do. At the same time, we attempt to discern what God is doing in the world and to cooperate with that mission with our theology of sin ready to hand, prompting us to look hard for what motives may be in play, what traps are set, what consequences may ensue, and what price must be paid.

Some Christians, of course, will recoil from all such considerations, retreating into Christian communities of what they hope will be purity of heart and cleanness of hand. Such communities may well play a useful role in reminding us of the ultimate holiness of the Kingdom of God and in undermining the convenient temptation to believe that all that we do is somehow both shrewd and good. Still, such communities in the nature of the case will do only a little to affect political life. I do not mean to dismiss the efficacy of their witness nor of their prayers. But in the world as God has seemed to ordain it, and from the pages of scriptural history in which God is shown to act politically, it appears that the secular adage is true: Political decisions, at least most of them, are made by those who show up.

I trust it is understood, furthermore, that by "political" decisions I mean far more than just party politics and the various levels of government. I mean the decisions made by corporations, professional guilds and practices, schools, courts, hospitals, and so on throughout our society. God is working through all of these institutions and through all of their constituents—Christian or not—to promote *shalom*. And I appreciate that many of my pacifist brothers and sisters will be working alongside the rest of us in many of these institutions, if not all of them. The question for us is whether we will discern and cooperate with that work of God, in faith that God is doing such work and will help us join in it.

Irony, Paradox, Integrity, and Effectiveness

The apostle Paul warns us against congratulating ourselves on the outcomes of our labors:

> I planted, Apollos watered, but God gave the growth. So neither the one who plants nor the one who waters is anything, but only God who gives the growth. (I Cor. 3:6–7)

Given what we have observed about the mixed field in which we live and work, we should expect the outcome of our labors often to be at least somewhat obscure. Mark Buchanan puts it trenchantly: "To pray well is to cultivate holy patience and perseverance. It is to practice holy waiting, which means often to keep on praying in spite of the poor results."[27] For who can say what the central,

---

27. Mark Buchanan, *Your God Is Too Safe: Rediscovering the Wonder of a God You Can't Control* (Portland, OR: Multnomah, 2001), 228.

let alone the total, impact of one's work might be in any given instance, let alone over a whole lifetime? Frank Capra's film *It's a Wonderful Life* is a cinematic parable that reminds us how interwoven our lives are with those of others, and that a small action here can affect great matters down the line.

Furthermore, we recognize that our actions can have consequences quite other than we intend. Ironies abound in the fallen ecology in which we make our way. Welfare programs can encourage sloth, while workfare programs can crush the innocent. In seeking to protect their children from danger, parents may render them so soft and naive as to be incapable of coping with the world. Teachers try to bolster their students' self-esteem through constant praise, and in the process they so obscure the connection between industriousness and achievement that the students' falsely based self-esteem shatters against the hard demands of reality. Labor-saving devices make it easier for employers to demand more output but no less labor. Low-fat snack foods encourage binging and greater obesity. And desperate evangelistic confrontations can rupture relationships so that no further communication is possible.

As replete in ironies as is our world, we must not throw up our hands and retreat into quietistic prayer. We have faith in the God of paradoxes who, on the jumbled landscape of our broken world, draws straight with crooked lines. We trust that the God who specializes in bringing good out of evil will make something beautiful out of our efforts to love him and our neighbors in creation. Indeed, God often brings good out of our failures, and even our sins.[28] For in the aftermath of such events, we sometimes learn humility, and faith, and other vital lessons as we would learn them no other way. Furthermore, sometimes others can receive our gifts better from meek hands and chastened voices. At the heart of our religion, after all, stands a Cross, the supreme paradox of human history: shame/glory, suffering/joy, wrath/love, horror/gratitude, death/life, end/beginning. The Cross shows us that we won't always win. And it shows us that we always, finally, *do* win—through the Cross, and through our crosses.

As we take up our crosses to follow Christ, therefore, we are encouraged by Paul's affirmation:

For by grace you have been saved through faith, and this is not your own doing; it is the gift of God—not the result of works, so that no one may boast. For we

---

28. Thus Frederick Buechner asks, "What about sin itself as a means of grace?" (*The Sacred Journey: A Memoir of Early Days* [San Francisco: HarperSanFrancisco, 1982], 3).

are what he has made us, created in Christ Jesus for good works, which God prepared beforehand to be our way of life. (Eph. 2:8–10)

"Our way of life" is to be performing good works, so we need not be paralyzed by our inability to discern with certainty what to do in a difficult situation or to foresee all of the consequences of our actions. We trust that God will show us what he wants to show us in order for us to respond as he wants us to respond. He promises to guide us, so we trust that promise and carry on with good works.

Those good works, furthermore, are good in two ways. The first way is the way of integrity: doing what the Spirit prompts us to do out of obedience to the Lordship of Christ and out of faith that God is good and what he commands therefore is good. Faithfulness, then, means doing our duty.

Many individual Christians, however, and also churches and other groups of Christians, congratulate themselves on their faithfulness over against any consideration of effectiveness. "Our job is not to be effective—that's God's business—but to be faithful." How convenient it is for such Christians to fly the flag of faithfulness as their numbers dwindle, their evangelism remains fruitless, and their social ministry stands unwelcomed by others: "We're small, and uninfluential, and disparaged by others, but that's just because we are so true to the gospel." I grew up hearing this from conservative Christians, but nowadays one hears such rationalization also from those on the religious left as they reassure themselves about what they are pleased to call their prophetic fidelity.

Such Christians do not have a full definition of Christian faithfulness, however. Hear again this familiar parable:

For [the Kingdom of heaven] is as if a man, going on a journey, summoned his slaves and entrusted his property to them; to one he gave five talents, to another two, to another one, to each according to his ability. Then he went away.

The one who had received the five talents went off at once and traded with them, and made five more talents. In the same way, the one who had the two talents made two more talents. But the one who had received the one talent went off and dug a hole in the ground and hid his master's money.

After a long time the master of those slaves came and settled accounts with them. Then the one who had received the five talents came forward, bringing five more talents, saying, "Master, you handed over to me five talents; see, I have made five more talents."

His master said to him, "Well done, good and faithful slave; you have been faithful in a few things, I will put you in charge of many things; enter into the joy of your master."

And the one with the two talents also came forward, saying, "Master, you handed over to me two talents; see, I have made two more talents."

His master said to him, "Well done, good and faithful slave; you have been faithful in a few things, I will put you in charge of many things; enter into the joy of your master."

Then the one who had received the one talent also came forward, saying, "Master, I knew that you were a harsh man, reaping where you did not sow, and gathering where you did not scatter seed; so I was afraid, and I went and hid your talent in the ground. Here you have what is yours."

But his master replied, "You wicked and lazy slave! You knew, did you, that I reap where I did not sow, and gather where I did not scatter? Then you ought to have invested my money with the bankers, and on my return I would have received what was my own with interest. So take the talent from him, and give it to the one with the ten talents. For to all those who have, more will be given, and they will have an abundance; but from those who have nothing, even what they have will be taken away. As for this worthless slave, throw him into the outer darkness, where there will be weeping and gnashing of teeth." (Mt. 25:14–30)[29]

The definition of faithfulness here is results. It is effectiveness—and not just effort, either, as some would prefer to view the story. The first two slaves double their master's investment in them. That's what the master cares about; he does not inquire as to how they did it or how hard they worked at it.

The third slave does not make any money at all, but rather retains his master's original investment in him and hands it over upon the master's return. This slave is the very picture of integrity without effectiveness. He carefully guards what the master gives him, as many Christians guard their faith, their purity, their witness. And when the master returns, they have not compromised. The original investment is returned in full integrity: it's all there, intact and complete. But the master is furious. He gifted the slave with the talent not in order to have it preserved but to have it multiplied. And he punishes the slave as a total failure, as "worthless" and thus fit only for removal as so much trash.

The four commandments of God all entail performance, accomplishment, effectiveness: cultivate the earth, love God and your neighbor, love each other in the church, and make disciples of all nations. Notice particularly this last one. If one confines oneself to Luke's accounts of Jesus' last words to his disciples, one can be forgiven for understanding the mandate to be simply to "bear witness," whether anyone listens or

---

29. I altered NRSV's "trustworthy" to the traditional, synonymous "faithful."

not (Lk. 24 and Acts 1). But Matthew's account makes it quite clear: the command is to "make disciples," not merely to drop the gospel at the world's feet like a brick and then turn away, satisfied with another job well done. We must engage the world and stay with the world until the world—or, at least, lots of the world—has joined Jesus' band.

Faithfulness, therefore, requires consideration of both integrity and effectiveness. Indeed, they work together. Keeping integrity in full view will caution us against inappropriate methods of attracting and retaining the world's attention, against minimizing the scandal of the Cross, against growing churches—or businesses—by any means possible. Keeping effectiveness in equally full view will caution us against self-righteousness, insularity, and sloth. A church must have integrity to be effective in the genuine work of disciple making, and a business must have integrity to be effective in serving the world. Likewise, a church concerned for true effectiveness is a church alive to the gospel and its possibilities, just as a business concerned for true effectiveness generally enjoys a fresh sense of its identity and key values as they are put to work.

Finally, a concern for faithfulness will mean assessing situations as carefully as possible and then expending our resources wisely for maximum effect. Since our resources are always finite, furthermore, we will not attempt to solve every problem at once, react to every threat with full force, or jump at every opportunity. God himself does not try to teach us everything at once, make us perfect immediately, and solve the world's problems at a stroke.

Thus we will need to exercise a holy shrewdness, a spiritual prudence about what—in a world bristling with problems and crying with needs—we should do. We need to keep our minds on the big picture, recognizing all the while that such awareness often entails interrupting our plans to care for the wounded stranger by the side of the road. We must be true to our vocations and be wise in their fulfillment. We will remember that we are not called to root up all the weeds. We thus will need to abide in Christ (John 15), to know thereby what his will is for us in this moment and to trust him for all that he is *not* calling us to do. And we will be willing to overlook minor issues to focus on major ones and to sacrifice lesser goods for greater ones—a principle that is very hard to accept for certain binary-minded Christians, those who think that compromise always involves tolerating a certain amount of evil (which it usually does) and therefore must always be avoided (which is the way to get very little accomplished in the real world).[30]

---

30. David Martin comments: "Too much Christian comment has retired to an apocalyptic view that conceives the 'World,' and especially the West, as a domain of political sin, and of pollution and violence, without trying to understand how it and all the other extant political systems actually work.... The missing category between the peace of the Gospel and the

Again, God tolerates a certain amount of evil and does not try to fix everything at once. We should therefore be more godly and less fastidious. And we can do so because we hope in the God who one day will make all things new.

Hope

The Christian hope comes from believing and living in the Christian Story as disciples of Jesus. We are in that Story, and we are "in Christ," as Paul enjoys repeating. Thus we look ahead to the New Jerusalem with eager sureness. We know the Lord of history, and he has told us how the Story will turn out. Our hope is sure—as certain as anything can be for us, since God's faithfulness is as certain as anything can be for us. We thus undertake our work in the world without despair and without desperation (both of which conditions entail, literally, being without hope), but instead with confidence—literally, with faith (*con fide*)—in the One who is entirely faith-worthy.[31]

Glenn Tinder chides us:

Christians who are very anxious about the fate of God's truth must have forgotten the doctrine of the Holy Spirit, which implies that God does not send his truth into history like a ship that is launched and then forgotten. He is the source at once of the truth human beings face and of the inspiration that enables them to recognize it as the truth and, in a measure, to understand it. ... Need Christians, then, fear that God's voice will be drowned out by human error?[32]

'principalities and powers' has to be the Aristotelian notion of practical wisdom" (*Does Christianity Cause War?* [Oxford: Clarendon, 1997], 107). One would add only that the Bible itself is replete with practical wisdom, and not confined to that of the so-called Wisdom Books (Proverbs, Ecclesiastes, and so on), as the mediating category Martin seeks.

31. Rex Murphy, Canadian pundit extraordinaire and himself a Newfoundlander, speaks in *Points of View* (Toronto: McClelland & Stewart, 2003), xiv, of what happens to a people who have lost hope, and particularly in politics:

I think that Newfoundlanders begin their understanding of politics with a presumption that all politics is futile, a deceit and a vanity, and that all politicians, until ever-so-rarely proven otherwise, are weathercocks of their own miserable ambitions and nothing more. This is as much a defensive attitude as a streak of genetic cynicism. Disappointed so often over their long, tormented, devious history, Newfoundlanders are deeply chary of investing hope in the promise of electoral actors. ... I think it is the Irish strand of the Newfoundland imagination, that strain of hard humour put up as a shield against large or overwhelming realities, or at least to deflect or contain their operation, that has converted politics into a game.

Christians are among those peoples that run the risk of similarly distancing themselves from politics in sad, fearful dismay.

32. Tinder, *The Political Meaning of Christianity*, 131.

In the meanwhile, therefore, we live out the penultimate, as Bonhoeffer says, with the ultimate, our hope, ever in view. Here, then, is another dialectic with practical implications. Because the ultimate is what finally and forever counts, we ought to sacrifice whatever is necessary in the penultimate in its cause. Yet we ought not to be reckless with or indifferent to the penultimate. Instead, we ought to value it highly. Because the ultimate is the consummation of, and not merely the successor to, the penultimate, the ultimate validates the penultimate as worthy of our respect and care. In short, we take the present world seriously—and not too seriously.

It is time, however, to confront an apparent contradiction from Scripture that threatens this happy scheme:

> But by the same word the present heavens and earth have been reserved for fire, being kept until the day of judgment and destruction of the godless.... But the day of the Lord will come like a thief, and then the heavens will pass away with a loud noise, and the elements will be dissolved with fire, and the earth and everything that is done on it will be disclosed. Since all these things are to be dissolved in this way, what sort of persons ought you to be in leading lives of holiness and godliness, waiting for and hastening the coming of the day of God, because of which the heavens will be set ablaze and dissolved, and the elements will melt with fire? But, in accordance with his promise, we wait for new heavens and a new earth, where righteousness is at home. (II Pet. 3:7, 10–13)

To many Christian ears, this passage has sounded like annihilation. The lesson then drawn for us is to focus our entire energies and resources upon evangelism. Since it's all going to burn anyhow, why bother with art, sport, business, or anything other than full-time evangelism?

The first thing to say is that the author of the epistle himself doesn't draw the conclusion from his own eschatology that we should engage in nothing but evangelism. The implication for him is that we should lead "lives of holiness and godliness, waiting for and hastening the coming of the day of God"—with which general description of Christian living no Christian of any stripe should disagree.

Second, the imagery of fire here is parallel to the image of water, which immediately precedes this passage: "the world of that time [Noah's day] was deluged with water and perished" (II Pet. 3:6). The "world of that time" was judged by God, purged by the Flood, and renewed by way of Noah, his family, and the animals on the ark. So there was great discontinuity with the world as it was, but also great continuity. God did not create a new world ex nihilo, but cleansed the world of what was evil, preserved what was good, and brought it into a new era. I suggest that the same pattern is in view in this passage in II Peter, except via fire instead of water. (Indeed, it is an open question whether this passage depicts literal fire with which God will purge and rearrange things, or whether this fiery language is symbolic of purgation and renewal by other means.) The fundamental idea, therefore, is not total destruction but judgment through which what is good will be preserved to enjoy a better context in a new order—"where righteousness is at home."

Third, even if annihilation *is* in view, then I reiterate my earlier paradoxical assertion that our evangelism is better if we do not restrict ourselves to it. Even if it *is* all going to burn, furthermore, we ourselves will undergo a better process of sanctification to fit us for the life to come if we do not restrict ourselves to a single activity, evangelism, that will be entirely unnecessary in the world to come.

Finally, we must appreciate that this passage must be integrated with the many other apocalyptic passages in the Bible, the vast majority of which do not speak in such apparently totalistic language. Yes, fire and destruction are usually in view, but those are images consistent with what we would expect as God removes what is bad and purifies what remains for the glorious and total *shalom* to come. To be sure, however, I have suggested here that even II Peter is better understood as not speaking in terms of total destruction and a brand-new restart.

The Christian hope, therefore, is of renewal, of course, but renewal as in purgation, healing, and vitality so as to enable the maturation of the seeds already planted, the life already begun, the patterns already established, the Kingdom that has already come and will yet come in fullness. Thus the Christian hope also teaches us to wait on God, to take the time to listen for the voice of guidance we expect and to receive the equipment we know he will provide. Precisely because we hope *in God*, we can act with confidence. But also precisely because we *hope* in God, we do not perpetually rush forward into the next thing with our ready-made programs and provisions, but rather cultivate the humility that awaits *his* direction and supply.[33]

LIBERTY AND COOPERATION

Liberty: Our Own

In our discussion so far we have touched on zones of freedom in Christ. We are free, first, from sin and death. No longer must we obey sin and fear death. We are free to choose the good in the hope of eternal life.

---

33. On this theme, see ibid. and Tinder, *The Fabric of Hope*.

Out of his experience of wrestling with sin, fearing death, and longing for a good God, Martin Luther rejoiced to affirm that the Christian is free from worrying about his destiny, is therefore free from egocentricity, and so is free truly to love God and his neighbor.[34] We can extend this insight to affirm that the Christian is thus free to tend the earth without selfishness. And, according to the redemption commandments, the Christian loves his fellow Christians and serves the rest of the world in genuine regard for the other, rather than out of concern for his own gain.

Yet we have gone beyond Luther's point in the win-win-win concept. For if I know my destiny is secure in Christ, I might be capable now of genuine altruism to my family and friends, but why would I bother caring for others whom I dislike, or even who oppose me? I do so not only out of grateful regard for God's preferences—and he has commanded me to love such people—but also because God promises to reward my obedience (Mt. 6:3–6,17–21). So I do not have to try to summon up a pure *agapē* that will never arise. I can instead cheerfully love God in the multiple (not mixed) motives of benefiting everyone involved in the reinforcing complex of *shalom*.

Liberty, furthermore, is mine both to enjoy the world and to exploit opportunities for service to God and neighbor. The Christian is not to live merely by a set of rules, not merely by conformity to a new law (whether the Sermon on the Mount or the whole New Testament). To be sure, it is not that the Christian is antinomian, either, living free from all guidelines or commands. For the commands of God remain upon her, as we have seen. But these commands are part of what we might consider her human operating system. They articulate for her what automatically causes her to flourish and to contribute to the flourishing of others. They describe the way things actually are, and she observes them to her everlasting benefit:

> The law of the LORD is perfect, reviving the soul; the decrees of the LORD are sure, making wise the simple; the precepts of the LORD are right, rejoicing the heart; the commandment of the LORD is clear, enlightening the eyes; the fear of the LORD is pure, enduring forever; the ordinances of the LORD are true and righteous altogether. More to be desired are they than gold, even much fine gold; sweeter also than honey, and drippings of the honeycomb. Moreover by them is your servant warned; in keeping them there is great reward. (Ps. 19:7–11)

---

34. Martin Luther, "The Freedom of a Christian," anthologized in *Martin Luther: Selections from His Writings,* ed. John Dillenberger (Garden City, NY: Anchor, 1961), 52–85.

Furthermore, the particular commands of God upon her life as an individual, her particular vocation, are merely the clarifications of her true essence, purpose, and destiny. Within those statements of the identity and meaning of her life, God then expects her to exercise the freedom both to consult with him as necessary (via prayer, Bible study, attention to preaching, conversation with other Christians and so on) and to make good decisions based on the resources he has provided her to decide and act. God does not want us to be volitional invalids who need him to decide everything, to walk around in a mystical cloud in which we consciously experience his guidance every moment on every particular. That isn't faith; that is religious mania. Yes, we should enjoy "practicing the presence of God," to "pray without ceasing," to cultivate an attitude of responsiveness to him and his will. And as we do so, we are free to play chess, to drive our kids to school, to research a report, and to order new stock, because these actions are the sorts of things that are consistent with what God has shown us in our vocation. We don't have to keep checking with him, so to speak, before we do them: they are part of what Bonhoeffer calls "the natural." God wants us to be both responsibly and dependently free, yes, but free as spiritual adults who have taken the time necessary to discern God's will and who then get on with doing it.

The Christian remains terribly free, moreover, to disregard the call of Christ, the voice of the Holy Spirit, the teaching of the church, and the law in her heart. She can still indulge in sin. The burden of freedom is ours, then, both positively to take up our cross, fulfill our vocation, and live as free adults, and also negatively to live as slothful, shirking juveniles who refuse the responsibility entailed by such glorious and dangerous liberty.

With these principles of freedom in view, we turn to the important fact that the New Testament emphasis is on freedom *for the other*. Indeed, the most discussion about Christian liberty occurs in Paul's writings, and his main theme is a paradoxical freedom to refuse to use one's freedom in order to bless other Christians:

> For you were called to freedom, brothers and sisters; only do not use your freedom as an opportunity for self-indulgence, but through love become slaves to one another. For the whole law is summed up in a single commandment, "You shall love your neighbor as yourself." (Gal. 5:13–14)

> But when you thus sin against members of your family, and wound their conscience when it is weak, you sin against Christ. Therefore, if food is a cause of their falling, I will never eat meat, so that I may not cause one of them to fall. (I Cor. 8:12–13)

"All things are lawful," but not all things are beneficial. "All things are lawful," but not all things build up. Do not seek your own advantage, but that of the other. (I Cor. 10:23–24; cf. I Pet. 2:16)

Let's be clear that the actions in question are not sinful. If they were, they would simply be forbidden. Paul's point is that they are generally legitimate in themselves, but they become illegitimate if enjoying them will somehow impede the supreme cause of the spread of the gospel and the edification of the Christian community. Good things, then, are to be foregone in the interest of *better* things, in a benign inversion of the "lesser of two evils" principle to the "greater of two goods." One sacrifices something one is legitimately free to undertake and enjoy in order that others will benefit.

Paul's example of eating meat that has been offered to idols (vegetarianism is not in view here) needs translation, of course. We might think of Christians who feel free to drink alcohol, watch movies with controversial content, or socialize in a nightclub. Such Christians will consider the example they set for younger or weaker believers who may lack their perspective and self-control and so follow their lead into a situation in which they will flounder. Less typically, perhaps, we might think of Christians who will take clever tax deductions, drive hard bargains, and assume high risks in investments or loans. Again, such Christians will be careful of the encouragement they may appear to be giving to less sophisticated Christians who will then take the liberty to cheat, exploit, and gamble. Liberty is a precious and dangerous thing, and the apostle urges us to recognize that while freedom is part of our ultimate destiny, penultimately it is an instrument that we freely take up or lay down, so to speak, as the need requires.

Liberty: Others'

The issue then arises of granting others liberty as well. The principle of granting and respecting freedom is fundamental to Christian faith. God creates humanity and immediately commands us. Despite its implication of authority, "commanding" also implies the freedom to obey or disobey. One doesn't command a fork, a flower, or a flood.

To be sure, our freedom is not absolute. The commandments of God guide us to the best paths, to the highest vocations, to our fundamental purpose and ultimate destiny. Disobeying those commands is to enjoy the freedom only to harm and finally to destroy oneself. The passenger on a ship crossing the Pacific is free to jump overboard, free to swim in the ocean for a while, and then free only to drown. For it is not his nature to have that degree of independence. Thus his freedom is curtailed by his limitations in other respects.

Among those other respects, furthermore, is the freedom of others. One must not act as if one is the only passenger aboard, eating all of the food, monopolizing the swimming pool, and so on. One hurts others by abusing one's freedom, and one also hurts oneself: one loses one's health by gluttony, one's friendships by selfishness, and so on. So it is to one's own advantage, as well as to the advantage of others—whom one is commanded by God to love as one loves oneself—to observe proper limits to one's freedom. And what is true of individuals in relation to others is usually true, and in very similar respects, to families, tribes, corporations, churches, and states.

As God has granted each of us freedom, furthermore, so we must grant each other freedom. This is a difficult principle for Christians to understand and practice, as it is for any others who are highly confident of the universal applicability of their own ethic. It is a natural impulse to insist on beliefs and behaviors that appear to one to be simply *right*, whether according to a particular Christian tradition (e.g., Roman Catholic, Orthodox, Puritan, or evangelical), a particular variety of Islamic *shari'a* (from Wahhabi to Isma'ili), a particular variety of Communism (Leninist, Maoist, or what have you), or a particular version of democracy and capitalism (whether Burke or Smith or Keynes or Rawls). Those who are convinced of the rightness—yea, the righteousness—of their cause find hegemony a highly attractive, even automatic, political mode, whether in a family, a church, an organization, or a state.

Yet confidence in one's religion and hope for the future can lead in the opposite direction: toward patient, hopeful tolerance of others based on belief that God is in control and will bring his good purposes to pass.[35] The Bible reminds us that God grants us the liberty to refuse to honor him, to refuse to care for each other, and (thus) to refuse even what is in our own best interests. For love and community cannot grow out of coercion—a truism that in our day perhaps deserves emphasis: *love and community cannot grow out of coercion.*

---

35. Irshad Manji inquires into her own Islamic tradition to investigate why some Islamic regimes have been tolerant, even welcoming, of "others." She attributes this openness partly to "the concept of a future," to an Islamic confidence that all is unfolding as God wants it to do: "Accumulating military victories meant that Arabs felt they had an appreciable and secured future. Which, in turn, meant that Islam didn't need to be thoroughly rigid or in-your-face.... When Arab Muslims lost their empire, they also forfeited the balance between past and future, tribalism and tolerance" (*The Trouble with Islam: A Wake-Up Call for Honesty and Change* [Toronto: Random House Canada, 2003], 157). Those Christians who believe that Jesus is Lord, that the Kingdom of God is here and expanding, and that Christ will come again—that is, all Christians worthy of the name—ought to be especially willing to accommodate others and to cooperate with the often non-linear, apparently meandering, and usually pluriform providence of God.

God does not always free us from the consequences of our liberty, to be sure, although he graciously offers to forgive us our sins, ameliorate and help us deal best with what we might call the temporal consequences of our sins, and to bring us to eternal life in the world to come. We may refuse that package, however, and thus be left with the full and final consequences of our freedom.

As those created in God's image and directed to do godly work in the world, according to the creation commandments, we are to grant each other a measure of freedom as well. Yes, we have to insist on a certain degree of conformity and a certain measure of enforcement in order to enjoy the benefits of society. Families agree on mealtimes if they want to enjoy the blessing of table conversation; churches agree on meeting hours, regular practices, and proper discipline if they want to enjoy worship, fellowship, and mission; businesses agree on hierarchies, teams, hours of operation, and the like in order to maximize their work; and so on. In Western societies in which unbridled individualistic liberty seems the supreme value, in fact, we must make these points about cooperation and curtailment more frequently and insistently.

Still, we ought to grant as much freedom as we can to individuals and to groups to pursue their vocations as particularly as possible—and, indeed, to refuse or to fail at that pursuit. We must beware of an overbearing attitude toward others, a condescension that too easily issues in control. True, we must eschew also a different kind of condescension that pretends that all is well and therefore requires no effort from me on behalf of another. Instead, we ought to maintain a neighborly, respectful compassion for our neighbors. We must remember that good parents, good teachers, good spouses, and good friends offer both accepting love and transforming love: I love you as you are, and I respect your difference and freedom; I am also dedicated to helping you to overcome your problems and to flourish in whatever way I can, in whatever way will be truly helpful, and in whatever way you will accept.[36]

We must beware also, of course, of the much less benign motivations of some of those who seek greater state control over individuals and intermediate institutions such as families, churches, and nongovernmental organizations. And we especially need to seek liberty for everyone to exercise his or her God-given freedom to choose about ultimate things, and particularly about God himself.

---

36. The terms "accepting love" and "transforming love" are attributed to William F. May in Michael J. Sandel, "The Case Against Perfection: What's Wrong with Designer Children, Bionic Athletes, and Genetic Engineering," *Atlantic Monthly,* April 2004, 57.

Glenn Tinder is especially helpful on this theme:

On Christian principles, affirming liberty expresses trust in God and mistrust of human beings, particularly human beings as organized in society and the state. Human beings do not know how to create faith or eradicate sin. Christians believe that God does. Individuals are left free in order for them to be fully accessible to God. It cannot be denied that many Christians have despised or attacked liberty from a concern for faith and virtue. But did they not, in that way, manifest a confidence in state officials that might more appropriately, at least for Christians have been placed in God?[37]

These are the main grounds for the Christian support of liberal democracy. It is not only the least bad of the available alternatives, but it manifests positive and crucial Christian values such as justice, the dignity of all people, due process, transparency, honesty, liberty, responsibility, love of one's neighbor, and the humility to recognize the fallibility of both individuals and systems, including the state itself. Of course it is a far cry from the *shalom* of God's direct rule in the New Jerusalem. Of course it is corrupt in every real-world instance. Of course it cannot guarantee the perfect outworking of its own values, which often collide in particular cases. Christians rightly witness against any presumption or pretension, let alone the typical self-congratulation, of any political system or particular regime, including democratic ones. Yet Christians also recognize the roots of liberal democracy in the soil of our own religion, and we properly commend and defend it as the only form of government we know of that even attempts to include all of these values.

Recognizing and granting liberty to others, finally, stands in tension with granting liberty to harm themselves or third parties. Within a liberal democratic state, John Howard Yoder writes, Christians must face up to some political and moral realities:

There are sins which it is not possible or desirable to treat as crimes, even if one had the kind of majority status that would permit making the laws. One major American experience in this respect was with prohibition. There are also voices today [this article was published in 1984] suggesting that drug abuse, like adult homosexuality and heterosexual adultery, like most of the

---

37. Tinder, *The Political Meaning of Christianity*, 106. Tinder has much to say on this theme of liberty; see the chapter by that name in ibid., 101–49; and also his *Liberty: Rethinking an Imperiled Ideal* (Grand Rapids, MI: Eerdmans, 2007).

other deadly sins (gluttony, sloth, avarice, pride …) could not properly be dealt with in the courts even if there were a majority to declare them worthy of civil punishment.[38]

I agree here, again, with Yoder: Christians must do all we can to bring as much *shalom* as possible without trying to construct the New Jerusalem by ourselves. It is not enough to counter the false claim "You can't legislate morality" with the half-truth "Law is always legislated morality," much less with the might-makes-right attitude "Oh, yes, we can!" Yet these are the typical responses of many Christians today, frantic to wield what cultural power they have left to conform their societies to their values as much as possible. We need to think about what law can do well and cannot do well in a liberal, pluralized, democratic situation in which we participate as disciples of Jesus and as neighbors to many fellow citizens who are not. Law is a minimum, not an ideal, which orders our life together.

Yet law is not merely restrictive, not simply a necessary negative. Law is encoded, enforced discipline, and through discipline—properly devised and observed, of course—we learn how to live. In that light parents discipline children, teachers discipline students, coaches discipline teams, and society disciplines its members. It is both regulative and pedagogical—indeed, it is regulative partly in order to be pedagogical. (Again, the Torah itself is both "law" and "instruction.") One learns beautiful improvisation only once one has learned the basics, through discipline. Law can provide us with a framework out of which we learn how to live freely and well. Of course many laws in the real world are made badly, just as parents make mistakes, teachers are not equally talented or motivated, coaches can be incompetent or corrupt, and so on. And no law, just like no leader, will always do well. But for lack of perfection we hardly need to slide into despair and see law—or any other discipline—solely as a grim restraint upon evil and something that, oddly, is itself a bad thing.[39]

We must seek law that is as consonant as possible with how God has shown himself to prefer to work in the world—and that way, in this era, seems to entail law that both provides as much justice and compassion as possible and as much social stability as is necessary, along with the least possible curtailment of the freedom of individuals and groups to live as they believe is best. Some might see such

---

38. Yoder, *The Priestly Kingdom*, 100–1.

39. On this point see George Weigel, *The Cube and the Cathedral* (New York: Basic, 2005), 78–86. And, of course, see Heb. 12 and its discussion of the Law and discipline, blending images of the Old and New Testaments.

a statement as capitulating to secular modernity. I maintain, however, that the combination and the tension of each element with the others—justice, compassion, stability, and liberty—is Biblical. It is the way God works, and the way God wants us to work, this side of the New Jerusalem. In this tension we will recognize, as Tinder warns us, that "respecting and defending the liberty of others means working for conditions in which one's own physical and spiritual being are in peril."[40] Such is the "opportunity cost" of liberty in a fallen world.

On the international scene, we must ask whether wealthy countries have any moral obligation to help poorer countries improve their self-destructive economic practices. Before I answer, let me simply signal that I do not believe that poorer countries are poor only because, or even primarily because, they have such practices. I am not trained in economics, nor do I have substantial knowledge of business life or of nations outside North America, so I am not competent to say anything specific on this matter. I am raising the hypothetical to put the issue at least on the table as an example.

The International Monetary Fund and the World Bank do offer help both financial and prudential—the former usually depending on compliance with the latter. Many critics of these organizations see the IMF and the World Bank as simply perpetuating a cycle of wealth for the minority and poverty for the majority. But those same critics usually suggest ways in which such organizations could provide better assistance of both sorts. They don't usually suggest the IMF and World Bank just go away. Still, few suggest that the IMF and the World Bank simply take over particular national economies, tempting as I expect it is for some in those organizations who are convinced of the rightness of their recommendations. We generally acknowledge that nations, like individuals, are entitled to choose their own path, even a path of self-harm—even as they should be offered assistance to make the best of their situations.

At the same time, we recognize that a nation is not simply a bloc. Nations and states are decidedly complex, with elites normally running the show and many, many people remaining poor both economically and politically. What, then, of any obligation on the part of the powerful elsewhere to intercede and intervene on behalf of the poor within another nation? In the modern era, we have considered a small spectrum of options: diplomatic remonstrances with the leaders of another state; offers of financial and other assistance; offers of assistance tied to changes in policy or leadership; threats of political and economic harm if there

---

40. Tinder, *The Political Meaning of Christianity,* 112–13.

are no changes in policy or leadership; escalating political and economic coercion; and armed intervention.

In each of these cases, the balancing is done among various principles: the sovereignty of a state (and, by analogy, we can consider the sovereignty of each family, or corporation, or municipality when it comes to the question of intervention); the self-interest of others, legitimate or otherwise; our own interests; and then also a sense among at least some of us of an overarching morality that requires loving one's neighbor and particularly the needy and vulnerable neighbor, both to benefit and to protect—of which the Universal Declaration of Human Rights is but one articulation. Again, belief in the latter sort of principle cannot automatically and easily trump the others, although it may indeed trump them in a given case. One can imagine a case in which all interests can nicely be pursued. Alas, however, one can also easily imagine cases that require the compromise or even simply the abrogation of one of them.

To pick the most unpleasant case, those of us with power have to decide how often, how much, and in what way to wield it on behalf of those who lack full human rights. Do we diffuse our limited resources everywhere at once? Do we pick a few places and leave the others to languish? It is simply untrue to the facts to say, "Do the right thing, full out and everywhere, and trust God to make it all come out right." The world we live in, under the mysterious providence of God and affected deeply by our sin, is a world of limits, ironies, paradoxes, and opportunities. To find a way through requires political wisdom informed by the highest principles and the best information. But that way is never guaranteed to be right, nor without its compromises and disappointments. Christian ethics does not always provide a convenient sword simply to cut the Gordian knot of geopolitics—or of relating to an obnoxious neighbor or difficult family member. Sometimes Christian ethics requires a patient picking away at issues with the intent of accomplishing as much as one can on a given occasion, and with the resolve to return to work away at it again as a new occasion arises.

We have glanced here at enormous issues of deep complexity with the simple recognition of tensions that we must acknowledge in all of our dealings with others—at home, in traffic, at school or work, at play, in politics, in church, and everywhere. Freedom is a complicated matter, and no simple, single slogan will suffice for our understanding of it and of our negotiating the world in the light of it. As we shall now see, freedom is no less complicated when we turn to the church itself.

Unity and Diversity in the Church

Traditionally, the question of unity and diversity in the church has been resolved either by asserting that one form is correct and the others are more or less correct as they resemble and relate to that norm or by asserting a "mere Christianity" that is then fleshed out according to different historical circumstances: fifth-century Mar Thoma churches in India, eleventh-century Orthodox churches in Russia, seventeenth-century Roman Catholic churches in New France, twenty-first-century house churches in China, and so on. Another possibility is the idea that on some themes and in at least some particulars there is no way for a single form of Christianity to image all the richness available, whether in matters of social ethics (thus our discussion of some Christians waging war while others advocate nonviolence) or worship (an African-American Baptist service versus a Greek Orthodox service versus a Taiwanese Presbyterian service).[41]

We do not have to choose just one of these options to govern our understanding of unity and diversity in the church. We might well believe simultaneously that our denomination is the best of the extant choices, that it yet shares a more fundamental "mere Christianity" with lots of other groups, and that at least some of those other groups might have a better way of dealing with this or that question or challenge than we do. One can relativize this even further, without lapsing into sheer relativism, by affirming that one's denomination is the best for me, or for me to belong to in this context, or for anyone to belong to in this context, while maintaining the other considerations as well.

Furthermore, having made this introductory point, we move on to recognize that denominational diversity is not the same as different stances toward culture. Every major Christian tradition in the world has had to deal with the experience of disestablishment in the United States, Canada, Australia, and elsewhere. And traditions that were originally minorities have experienced the challenge of wielding cultural power in various situations, whether Puritans in early modern England and New England, Mennonites in southern Manitoban villages, Baptists in most of the American South, Mormons in Utah, and so on. Richard Niebuhr's types now define various modes that various churches and individual Christians can adopt depending on their situation, rather than being locked into a mode

---

41. Richard Mouw affirms this viewpoint in *He Shines in All That's Fair: Culture and Common Grace* (Grand Rapids, MI: Eerdmans, 2001), 79–80.

that used to define them in a quite different cultural context. Therefore history shows us Catholics and Orthodox sometimes being "against" culture, Calvinists and Lutherans sometimes being "of culture," Baptists sometimes being "above" culture, and so on.

Recognition of these varying responses to varying historical vicissitudes should have at least three salutary implications. First, an individual Christian or a group of Christians should be open to considering a stance different from what they have maintained heretofore in the name of tradition, if the cultural situation has changed importantly. The sectarianism that made sense under persecution five centuries ago might make no sense in a free country today, while the hegemony that seemed to work well in the Middle Ages or in a colonial situation can't work in the modern era. Second, we should find grounds for ecumenical cooperation among those adopting the same stance. Many Christians are finding such grounds today, as they have in the past. Many more could do so. And third, we should be willing to at least consider affirming others in stances different from ours, even at apparent cross-purposes to ours, as we recognize that Christ may have called them to this apparently contradictory, but perhaps also complementary, stance. We will be more willing to affirm them if we realize that our own tradition might end up "there" someday, or perhaps even has already been "there" in the past. To be sure, we might *not* affirm others in certain other stances if we believe the circumstances do not justify it: I do not endorse either relativism or sentimentality. But we should be at least open to the possibility that our way is not identical with, and completely comprehensive of, all that God wants to do and show and say through all Christians in this situation.

Beyond all of this ecumenical openness, however, we recall that John Howard Yoder boldly affirmed that there was, in fact, one best model for considering the questions of church and culture. I think he is right that there is, but clearly I disagree with him on what particular model is best. To this last, comprehensive question, therefore, and to more of its implications, we turn in the final chapter.

CONCLUSION

Making the Best of It

Dietrich Bonhoeffer posed the ultimate question: "Who is Jesus Christ, for us, today?" The Christian religion centers on Jesus Christ: knowing him, proclaiming him, serving him, and enjoying him and all his blessings. Furthermore, he is not only Lord of the church and Lord in general, but also Lord of this Christian individual or that Christian community here and now. And since we cannot hope to comprehend all of who Christ is and does, our priority is to learn what we need to know of him, of his work, and of his call to us in order to grow in love for him and to do his will in the world.

I have then posed the complementary question: *Who are we, for Jesus Christ, today?* What sort of person am I, and what sort am I to be, for Jesus Christ, today? What sort of family, or congregation, or organization are we Christians, and what sort are we to be, for Jesus Christ, today?

In the light of what we have seen regarding mission and vocation, I have advocated a renewed Christian Realism. This realism is not cynical, jaded, clever, arrogant, manipulative, messianic, or self-serving—all of which, it must be admitted, realism can be. Instead, it is a realism that tries to be true to the nature of things, to *reality:* true to the nature of the world, to the nature of God's revelation in Scripture, to the nature of the experience of God's people through several millennia, and especially to the nature of Jesus Christ as we know him, and hear his call, today.

This new Christian Realism poses a crucial alternative to the two options most often offered to modern Christians today: (1) withdrawal from certain worldly institutions, or at least from coercive sectors of those institutions, into holy communities that bear witness to the world of the alternative ethic of the Kingdom of God, and (2) wielding all the power available in the name of Christ to draw the world under the rule of the Kingdom of God. I certainly can see that there might be a circumstance so extremely dark that the church must essentially adopt a "Christ against culture" stance. There are terrible societies in the world today, as there have been in every age. I also recognize that there might be a circumstance so promising that the church might well be tempted to think in terms of "Christ transforming culture." But is there any culture so bereft of the light of God such that Christians must be entirely against it? And is there any culture so open to the light of God that it can be conformed utterly to the way of Christ? I doubt it. Thus I think we need a more realistic model of how to make our way in at least most parts of the world today.

To return briefly to H. Richard Niebuhr's typology, let us consider the phrase now common in consideration of the Kingdom of God: "already, but not yet." It seems to me that we can see two of Niebuhr's types as various versions of an "already" motif: "Christ of culture" and "Christ above culture." We can also see "not yet" as characteristic of "Christ against culture." Niebuhr's fifth type, "Christ transforming culture" does conform to the tension of "already, but not yet." But only Niebuhr's fourth type, "Christ in paradox with culture," retains the full tension of "already, but not yet"—itself literally a paradox.

Let us turn, then, to a lingering issue that must be clarified before we can conclude. I have cited John Yoder a number of times in this essay, largely because I think his will be, for many readers, the most attractive and provocative alternative voice to the model I offer. I trust that it is now obvious that I disagree with Yoder in a number of respects, even as I agree with him in others. It is now time to state the heart of our agreement and disagreement.

I return to a passage I quoted early on:

> Some elements of culture the church categorically rejects (pornography, tyranny, cultic idolatry). Other dimensions of culture it accepts within clear limits (economic production, commerce, the graphic arts, paying taxes for peacetime civil government). To still other dimensions of culture Christian faith gives a new motivation and coherence (agriculture, family life, literacy, conflict resolution, empowerment). Still others it strips of their claims to possess autonomous truth and value, and uses them as vehicles of communication (philosophy, language, Old Testament ritual, music). Still other forms of culture are *created* by the Christian churches (hospitals, service of the poor, generalized education, egalitarianism, abolitionism, feminism).[1]

---

1. John Howard Yoder, "How H. Richard Niebuhr Reasoned: A Critique of *Christ and Culture*," in *Authentic Transformation: A New Vision of Christ and Culture*, ed. Glenn H. Stassen, D. M. Yeager, and John Howard Yoder (Nashville, TN: Abingdon, 1996), 69. Martin E. Marty offers a similar observation from his Lutheran vantage point: "Calvin and his cohorts embody 'Christ Transforming Culture' impulses in respect to politics. Luther meanwhile needs to post

It must be clear that I recognize that Yoder does not advocate a simplistic "Christ against culture" model—nor do his latter-day epigones, such as Stanley Hauerwas, William Willimon, and others. They are too intelligent and too Christian for that. Thus I agree strongly with this passage of Yoder's. It is an excellent start at making the sorts of distinctions we all must make in terms of this or that element of culture, this or that pattern in culture, this or that institution of culture, and this or that opportunity or threat posed by culture.

The fundamental disagreement has to do with the cultural opportunities and, indeed, threats posed by societies whose dominant institutions are open to Christian participation. To be sure, *all* societies are open to Christians participating in their dominant institutions as long as those Christians leave their distinctive convictions aside while they assist those societies toward their autonomous goals. But of course I mean an openness to Christians participating *as Christians,* with their convictions properly and fully operative in what they think, say, and do. The Roman Empire in many respects was not open to such Christian participation, and that is the cultural context of the New Testament. But what happens when the emperor not only opens a door to Christians but welcomes them in, as Constantine did? Those of Yoder's stripe see this occasion as the Great Disaster, the co-optation of the church by the world, which they never tire of identifying as the root of all sorts of evil. But what if, as we have remarked already, we see the new era inaugurated by Constantine as an evangelistic success story, as simply the logical working out of the mission of God in the Roman Empire—with full recognition of all of the ambiguities, limitations, failures, *and blessings* that attend the mission of God being accomplished via human beings in the world?

It is obvious that few of us live in anything like "Christendom" today. Yet we still have far more opportunity to participate in the life of our culture than did the first Christians—including participation in every institution of society. What, then, are Christians supposed to do in this context? Keep acting like a repressed minority, when we are no longer repressed and no longer a minority? Yoder and his ilk do seem to suggest that it would have been entirely salutary for Christians to have retained that mentality.[2] And he, as always, makes an attractive case,

---

a dualism, 'two kingdoms.' One of them always displays the way 'the demonic pervades the structures of existence.' However, when it comes to affirming images in church building, the arts, and music, it is Luther who is the culture-affirmer....He minimizes the dualism there and sees possibility in converting at least some aspects of the culture" (foreword to H. Richard Niebuhr, *Christ and Culture,* expanded ed. with a new foreword by Martin E. Marty and a new preface by James M. Gustafson [San Francisco: Harper, 2001 (1951)], xviii).

2. John Howard Yoder, "The Kingdom as Social Ethic," in *The Priestly Kingdom: Social Ethics as Gospel* (Notre Dame, IN: University of Notre Dame Press, 1984), 80–101.

particularly as we stand many centuries downstream of the Constantinian era and rue the entanglements of Christianity and culture that have occurred since then.

Examples lie ready to hand. One tours the papal palace at Avignon and hears a guide tell of medieval popes presenting that year's favorite prince with a golden rose at Christmas and granting the privileges of kissing the pope's toe and then reading the third lesson of the mass. One listens to generation after generation of American politicians claiming God for their side, ignoring the great wisdom of Abraham Lincoln, who grimly recognized that God might be judging *both* sides in the Civil War. One reads of widespread abuse of Native Canadian children in the mandatory residential schools established by federal governments and run by the major Christian denominations. Clerical blessing of colonial oppression of peasants and natives throughout the Americas, Christian support for the African slave trade and later for apartheid, repression of women's civil rights in the name of Christian order—all of these and more can be listed as implications of Christian participation in the governing institutions of the world.

As attractive as the option always is to eschew power and glorify weakness, maintain one's sanctity without compromise, and denounce both worldly institutions and one's fellow Christians who participate in them, we must return to these questions: When we are now members of the royal court, so to speak—indeed, when some of us are members of the royal family—who are we, for Jesus Christ, today? When we have the opportunity not only to purchase goods or services from a company, but to influence or even run that company by working in it or buying shares in it—who are we, for Jesus Christ, today? When we have the opportunity to vote or even run in elections and to share in the governance of cities and states—who are we, for Jesus Christ, today? When new forms of dissemination arise, and audiences emerge, for art and entertainment shaped by Christian values—who are we, for Jesus Christ, today?

We are redeemed and reoriented human beings who heed God's primeval call to make the best of it, using the resources Providence has put to hand. That is how Christians reformed the excesses and debaucheries of the medieval church in both the Protestant and Catholic Reformations. That is how Abraham Lincoln did indeed provide saving—the adjective is not too strong—leadership to America in its greatest crisis. That is how Christians have sacrificed greatly to provide good schools, good farms, good water supplies, and many more charities around the world. That is how Christians have advocated for land reform, for the end of slavery and apartheid, for women's suffrage, and for universal human rights. Christians did all the things Yoder wanted them to do—pray, proclaim, form godly communities that modeled alternatives, serve society in various other positive respects—*and* they wielded power: the power of information media, the power of money, the power of politics, even (let us not be squeamish) the power of guns. And good things happened. Not unequivocally good things, as I have suggested we should not expect before Christ returns. But better things happened than were apparently going to occur without the use of these kinds of power.

That, then, is the point. Are Christians to work with others to wield power— not only spiritual power through prayer and worship, not only moral power through holy living and charity, not only persuasive power in evangelism and advice, crucial as these are—but also the power of coercion, whether financial, political, or military? Are Christians to make deals, even make compromises, in order to make the best of it? I believe that the cumulative testimony of the Bible—the *whole* Bible—and of church history is that yes, we sometimes should.

If we are to adopt this dangerous stance—and dangerous it certainly is, let me repeat, for lurking everywhere are snares of pride, greed, lust, self-righteousness, and self-deception—then we need a clear sense of mission and vocation, as I have tried to outline above. We need to shape our lives by gospel standards, and to respond with obedience to Christ in the face of the shaping of our lives by forces outside our control, in order to optimize our participation in the mission of God. In particular, we need to consider what we can do to engage fully in public life, as God grants us opportunity to do so. To these matters we now turn.

THE SHAPE OF OUR LIVES

We can look at the question of the shape of our lives in terms of what we do to shape them, which I will call *construction;* the situation in which we do that construction, which I will call *context;* and the intermittent, interrupting, and sometimes interesting surprises that occur, which I will call *contingencies*. And I will look at how we shape our lives in three modes: individual, home/family, and church.

Construction

It perhaps will seem truistic to say that the shape of our lives should reflect God's mission and Christ's particular call upon us. But because of evil in ourselves and in our surroundings, which is to say because of the confusion and enticement and oppression in ourselves and in our surroundings, our lives often do not reflect what we profess about the mission of God and the vocation Christ has given us.

What would our priorities appear to be in an analysis of our checkbooks, credit card statements, homes, closets, garages, e-mail files, browser caches, and PDAs? The Bible from first to last speaks of routines, disciplines, and habits that manifest inward conditions and produce distinctive results—"by their fruits ye shall know them" (Mt. 7:16). A basic commitment of discipleship is to shed whatever impedes it and acquire whatever improves it. One therefore could profitably spend time periodically assessing one's own life, one's home life, and one's church life to ask about each element and trait of those lives, "How does this help me be who I am supposed to be for Jesus Christ, today?" Families and churches can do the same: "How does this way of meeting, this schedule, this activity, this form of decision making, this hierarchy, or this budget help us to be who we are supposed to be for Jesus Christ, today?"

Such a basic activity is fundamentally theological, requiring as it does the most appropriate understanding of the mission of God and the call of Christ on us, here and now. Therefore it is crucial for individuals, families, and churches to educate themselves theologically on just these matters, and to keep these themes of mission and vocation in the foreground: "How does this subject matter—this book of the Bible, or this Christian text, or this historical survey, or this discussion of current controversy—help us be who we are supposed to be for Jesus Christ, today?" And "What do we need to learn in order to be who we are supposed to be for Jesus Christ, today?"

Sylvia Keesmaat and Brian Walsh highlight Paul's concern for knowledge—both experiential and theological, without obvious division—as a crucial component to Christian faith and resistance to the evil powers of this world. Their summary reflections on Colossians are worth citing at length:

> How do you sustain profound commitments and truth claims that tend to be rather exclusive…in the face of a monolithic empire that subsumes all spiritualities and religious options under one imperial cult?
>
> …It is clear that Paul knows that truth and knowledge are central issues for this young Christian community. He first describes the gospel they have received as a "word of truth"…(1:5). He then goes on to pray that the community might be filled with "the knowledge of God's will in *all* spiritual wisdom and understanding" (1:9). Such knowledge, like all true knowledge, will engender a praxis ("bear fruit in *every* good work") that itself results in further growth "in the knowledge of God" (1:10)….And he says his deepest hope for this community is that the word of God be "fully known" (1:25) in their midst….
>
> When Paul begins to describe what that maturity will look like, he remains focused on matters of wisdom and knowledge. He says that he longs for this community to have "assured understanding" and sure and secure "knowledge of God's mystery, that is, Christ himself, in whom are hidden *all* the treasures

of wisdom and knowledge" (2:2–3). Such secure knowledge is necessary lest the community be taken "captive through philosophy and empty deceit, according to human tradition" (2:8)....To conclude this quick survey of themes of knowledge and truth in this epistle, not that the "world of truth" we met in chapter one is said to "dwell...richly" in the lives of the Colossian believers as they "teach and admonish one another in *all* wisdom" (3:16) and seek to speak to outsiders with wisdom and grace (4:5–6).[3]

In a wide-ranging study of a number of major American denominations, the Search Institute of Minneapolis determined that the most important factor in producing a mature, well-balanced, and well-integrated Christian faith was not excellent preaching, worship, small-group fellowship, or anything else but adult Christian education.[4] And yet I daresay there is no element in contemporary church life that is more poorly undertaken in most churches. A sermon and a home Bible study each week cannot possibly suffice.

Consider this. A basic course in, say, New Testament survey taken in a North American college or seminary would take somewhere between 120 and 170 hours of time for most students to complete: lectures, discussions, reading, assignments, and examinations. At the pace of a thirty-minute sermon (in an era in which sermon length continues to diminish) plus a one-hour Bible discussion plus one hour of individual preparation per week, it will take a little over a year to put in the same time. Allowing that eight to ten courses of this sort would be the equivalent of a single year of theological education, one is looking at a decade or more to gain anything like that single year's worth of full-time study.

We have got to take time to read, and read well. We have got to find ourselves teachers—ideally, in person, whether every week at church or regularly at conferences and summer schools, but for many people in remote places or in under-resourced churches study will have to be online. We have got to make friends of Christians who are similarly serious about growing up into spiritual maturity and devote time to study together. We have to move on from milk to meat, as the New Testament exhorts us (I Cor. 3:1–3; Heb. 5:11–6:2).

Moreover, theological knowledge is crucial, but not itself sufficient:

---

3. Brian J. Walsh and Sylvia C. Keesmaat, *Colossians Remixed: Subverting the Empire* (Downers Grove, IL: InterVarsity, 2004), 97–98.

4. Eugene C. Roehlkepartain, "What Makes Faith Mature?" *The Christian Century,* May 9, 1990, 496–99; Peter L. Benson and Carolyn H. Eklin, *Effective Christian Education: A National Study of Protestant Congregations: A Summary Report on Faith, Loyalty, and Congregational Life* (Minneapolis, MN: Search Institute, 1990).

For this very reason, you must make every effort to support your faith with goodness, and goodness with knowledge, and knowledge with self-control, and self-control with endurance, and endurance with godliness, and godliness with mutual affection, and mutual affection with love. For if these things are yours and are increasing among you, they keep you from being ineffective and unfruitful in the knowledge of our Lord Jesus Christ. (II Pet. 1:5–8)

To this discipline of study, then, we must add the other holy habits of the normal Christian life, such as prayer, worship, charity, and the like. Our habits simply are the basic structures of our lives, so we need to scrutinize each one—our eating habits, our entertainment habits, our shopping habits, our thinking habits, our worrying habits, our friendship habits—to see, again, how it helps us participate in God's mission and fulfill our calling.

Furthermore, we must consider how we have arranged these units into the overall shape of our lives. Clearly, we must try to remove obvious contraries: reading elevating literature in the morning and debasing literature at night won't get us far, just as exercising in the morning and overeating at night won't make us healthy. But we also must arrange things according to the priorities of God's mission and our calling. Exercise is good, but most of us would be neglecting our divine calling if we undertook the rigors necessary to sculpt our bodies into athletic or aesthetic excellence. Bible study is good, too, of course. But I have known students so enthusiastic about their Bible study—alone and in groups—that they neglected their coursework and thus jeopardized the academic and professional careers to which God was calling them. Entertainment is good, but not at the expense of one's responsibilities at work or at home. And the opposites are true also, to be sure: family life and work must not crowd out the physical, spiritual, intellectual, aesthetic, emotional, social and—for want of a more ordinary word—ludic dimensions of our lives.

Is the goal, then, the perfectly balanced life? Many Christians think it is, and seek the correct ratio of Bible study to prayer to work to leisure to sleep to exercise to…No, the goal is to be whom we are meant to be in order to grow in love for God and do his work in the world. And, since the context keeps changing in at least some respects, so must the shape of our lives.

Context

Earlier I discussed the crucial category of time in regard to our vocation. "To everything there is a season," the Preacher reminds us, and each season of life includes its own limitations and opportunities. Just as it is foolish to try to educate a child at the level of a graduate student or to train a "weekend warrior" at the level of an elite athlete, so it is foolish to formulate a daily, weekly, or annual regimen for everyone to follow—or even for ourselves to follow in perpetuity. The classics of Christian spirituality routinely refer to ladders, mountains, and other metaphors of upward progress.

The progress, however, is not always simply upward. Sometimes we must move sideways, or even backward, in order to attend to parts of our selves and our lives that now properly can come to the foreground of our attention. Whereas we might have focused on certain activities, traits, and other "growth edges"— not exclusively, to be sure, since there are some things to which we always must attend—now the "curriculum" of our lives moves to something else. God respects the fact that we cannot make progress on everything at once, and the context of our lives under his providence shifts to provide us with a fresh set of stimuli, challenges, blessings, and limitations.

We must not, therefore, attempt to ignore our situation and try to maintain the same shape of life that worked well in the previous one. Some things, again, do need to carry on—prayer, Bible reading, fellowship, worship, mission, and so on—but even those will be properly reshaped by the environment of our lives now. Other things will be new: we studied then, we practice now; we were enthusiastic then, we persevere now; we were oblivious then, we comprehend now; we were childless then, we have children now; we were growing and healthy then, we are older and sicker now.

Realism is key here. We must take stock of the reality in which we are living now and shape our lives realistically. Christians living under a repressive regime, for example, must reshape their practices accordingly. They do not abandon meeting, except in the most extreme instances (Heb. 10:25); they do not abandon prayer, as Daniel did not (Dan. 6); they do not remain silent about the gospel, as the apostles did not (Acts 4–5). But they simply must take into account the lack of dedicated meeting spaces like those available to Christians in freer countries, the lack of Bibles and other Christian literature, the lack of freedom of conversation, the lack of economic and professional opportunities for those refusing to kowtow to the state, and so on. As the earliest Christians made their way as best they could under the frowns of both Jerusalem and Rome, so Christians make their way as best they can in difficult situations today.

And the difficulties come in different shapes. Christian businesspeople and professionals in Hong Kong, for example, must work longer hours than they might think is best for a healthy family and church life because there simply are no jobs that allow one to work less than long days Monday to Friday and some part of Saturdays as well. For such Christians to maintain a full-day Sabbath each week would require them simply to leave that society—which can hardly be the will of God for them all. Farmers, factory workers, and many others around the world (who certainly cannot opt out of their societies) also generally work very long hours. What shall Christian leaders recommend to them regarding an appropriate balance of family life, personal devotional time, recreation, and so on? It is so very easy, and so absurd, for those of us in North American professional comfort to prescribe the "normal Christian life" in terms that are utterly abnormal to the way most of the rest of the church must live.

Context, then, must be seen providentially. Yes, our contexts are shaped by evil: the evil in individual leaders at every level, the evil in institutions, the evil in traditions whose stamp remains operative down the generations, and so on. And Christianity encourages us to do what we can to resist evil and reshape these contexts toward *shalom*. But God rules above it all. And, paradoxically and dialectically, he works through and even sometimes in these elements to occasion opportunities for his people to serve his purposes and to themselves be blessed— even as those opportunities sometimes are attended by suffering and strain.

Indeed, God rules above, and works through and even in, the interruptions, surprises, and "emergent-cies" of life.

Contingencies

The Book of Acts is full of interruptions. Christians are going about their business, presumably fulfilling their callings, when something odd occurs. A beggar accosts them and asks for money. Peter and John have none to give, but they heal him instead (Acts 3). Members of the church are donating money for various worthy causes—what can be more routine than tithes and offerings?—but one couple lies to the church and also, as Peter makes clear, to the Holy Spirit, and they fall down dead (Acts 5). Preachers are arrested and jailed (a nasty kind of interruption) and then freed by divine intervention (a splendid kind of interruption) (Acts 12, 16).

Philip is a good man, a deacon, in fact, and an effective evangelist:

Philip went down to the city of Samaria and proclaimed the Messiah to them. The crowds with one accord listened eagerly to what was said by Philip, hearing and seeing the signs that he did, for unclean spirits, crying with loud shrieks, came out of many who were possessed; and many others who were paralyzed or lame were cured. So there was great joy in that city. (Acts 8:5–8)

Some confusion breaks out, and Peter and John come down from Jerusalem to sort it out. But when they leave, does Philip resume his apparently very successful ministry? No, he does not. Instead of continuing an already pretty extraordinary and profitable work, he is suddenly ordered by the Holy Spirit to a strange place to encounter a strange man doing a strange thing:

> Then an angel of the Lord said to Philip, "Get up and go toward the south to the road that goes down from Jerusalem to Gaza." (This is a wilderness road.) So he got up and went.
>
> Now there was an Ethiopian eunuch, a court official of the Candace, queen of the Ethiopians, in charge of her entire treasury. He had come to Jerusalem to worship and was returning home; seated in his chariot, he was reading the prophet Isaiah.
>
> Then the Spirit said to Philip, "Go over to this chariot and join it." So Philip ran up to it and heard him reading the prophet Isaiah. He asked, "Do you understand what you are reading?"
>
> He replied, "How can I, unless someone guides me?" And he invited Philip to get in and sit beside him.
>
> Now the passage of the scripture that he was reading was this: "Like a sheep he was led to the slaughter, and like a lamb silent before its shearer, so he does not open his mouth. In his humiliation justice was denied him. Who can describe his generation? For his life is taken away from the earth."
>
> The eunuch asked Philip, "About whom, may I ask you, does the prophet say this, about himself or about someone else?"
>
> Then Philip began to speak, and starting with this scripture, he proclaimed to him the good news about Jesus.
>
> As they were going along the road, they came to some water; and the eunuch said, "Look, here is water! What is to prevent me from being baptized?" He commanded the chariot to stop, and both of them, Philip and the eunuch, went down into the water, and Philip baptized him.
>
> When they came up out of the water, the Spirit of the Lord snatched Philip away; the eunuch saw him no more, and went on his way rejoicing. But Philip found himself at Azotus, and as he was passing through the region, he proclaimed the good news to all the towns until he came to Caesarea. (Acts 8:26–40)

There is an intermingling of the mind-bogglingly supernatural and the entirely pragmatic in this story that is characteristic of the Book of Acts. It is as if the Holy Spirit says, "Okay, we've got this Samaria thing sorted out; now I need an effective evangelist to talk with this Ethiopian who is about to leave the country. Philip, that's you. Go."

Philip goes, and is indeed the right man for the job. The Ethiopian official is converted and, according to tradition, is the beginning of the conversion of that entire nation—one of the two claimants (along with Armenia) to the title of first Christian nation in the world. It is an astonishingly strategic encounter, but it starts with the Holy Spirit telling Philip to go (how?) and Philip going—and then proceeds to depict Philip doing just what he always does, evangelizing, with wonderful results.

The story ends as strangely as it begins, with the Spirit snatching Philip away, redeploying him elsewhere until he comes to Caesarea—where the narrative leaves him for good, except for one small mention later in the Book of Acts: Philip the evangelist is residing in Caesarea now, with a Christian family (his four daughters are prophets), and hosting Paul, Luke, and others on their way to Jerusalem.

What is normal and what is supra-normal in this narrative? When Christians are living in the Spirit, there is no stark division between the one and the other. So must we shape our lives today to be open to the radical, and even instant, reshaping that arrives in the form of interruptions, crises, opportunities, and even disasters. For, again, Christ is Lord of all *now,* and under his guidance the church makes its way over the ever-shifting terrain of this troubled earth. Philip does not become someone he is not—it is precisely because he is an evangelist that he is moved from one place to another. But he could easily have misread these moves as distractions, as temptations, as removals from his true work. "Why leave Samaria, where crowds have been rejoicing, to stand by the side of this deserted road and talk to a single foreigner on a chariot heading home?"

To be sure, we must not see every interruption as a blessing in disguise to be seized at once. Particularly if we are not enjoying the work to which God has currently called us, we shall be quick indeed to interpret any opportunity to escape as the will of God. It is true that interruptions sometimes are temptations to abandon obedience, to prefer the trivial and easy to the important and hard. Christians therefore must be as Philip was: *in the Spirit,* able to discern the Spirit's voice and then willing to do what he asks, whether it is to travel here and there from one exciting evangelistic encounter to the next, to make this apparently preposterous journey to encounter the Ethiopian eunuch, or to settle down in Caesarea, raise a family, and perform the same ministry, but in this yet different mode.

In sum, we can retain the ideal of a balanced life, but now in a way radically qualified by our understanding of mission and vocation. Balance in this case is not the balance of a dancer raised on one foot, or even of a spinning top. It is much more dynamic: the balance of a runner traversing a broken-up and heaving landscape. To maintain the balance for this step and to prepare well for the next step, the runner might well have to lean way off center—to be deliberately off-balance in terms of a snapshot, but properly balanced in terms of a journey. This metaphor thus rules out both the idea of a detailed template in which every Christian life ought to be lived and also the utter confusion in which no option, no matter how extreme, can be judged as wrong. The proof is in the success of the journey. Missteps of either sort—trying to maintain a static, universal ideal or indulging in a capricious impulse—will result in a fall. The question is, does the runner keep going toward the goal?

Realism thus requires a constant renegotiation of changing contexts and contingencies. We both maintain the perpetual elements of any proper Christian living and adapt them to the features of this particular occasion. Such a challenge means that it is not always clear that we are, in fact, making the right choice. Ambiguity cannot be avoided here, either. Spiritual pride might compel some Hong Kong Christian businesspeople to attempt to live in defiance of economic realities and thus bring themselves, their families, and their churches to financial ruin with no obvious gain for the gospel. Sloth, however, might keep them from continually and effectively pressing that system for healthful change—as Christians have successfully pressed elsewhere for improvements in working conditions. What do we do? We make the best of it—in concert with our fellow Christians, in cooperation with our other neighbors, in the power of the Holy Spirit, and in discipleship to Jesus Christ, to the glory of God.

When we do have opportunity, then, as most readers of this book will have, to engage public life in the furtherance of *shalom,* what can we do and say?

BEHAVING IN PUBLIC

Grounds for Hope

It is easy for Christians in Europe, North America, Australia, and New Zealand to be discouraged about the future of Christianity in those countries. Many observers have tracked the decline of Christian influence over the last century or so—in the references to Christian values and themes in public discourse, in church attendance, in the role of clergy in public events, in the presence of Christian symbols in schools and other public places, and so on. Conversely, the trend toward greater secularity seems to proceed apace: Sundays treated as Saturdays in both commerce and recreation; liberalization of laws regarding sex, marriage, and family; religious people depicted in popular media as fanatics, buffoons, or hypocrites—the list goes on.

Yet, as we discussed earlier, history does not proceed in single, straight lines indefinitely, and the trajectory of secularization or "de-Christianization" is one such non-single, non-straight line. For one thing, as we observed above, many aspects of contemporary life are more in keeping with Christian values than ever, particularly in the treatment of those who are not moneyed, white, Christian, and male. For another, the modern world has seen the rise of various forms of religion alternative to the polite Christianity that dominated western Europe and its colonial offspring, from evangelical Protestantism of various stripes, to a manifold Islam, to Asian religions, to new religious movements that fuse elements of various traditions. For yet another, Christianity itself has not gone away. In the United States, church attendance since World War II has remained at the highest level in American history. Canadian religious interest and observance seems to have stopped declining and shows signs of reviving. Evangelical Christianity, conservative Catholicism, Islam, and other faiths are burgeoning in Britain and in some places on the Continent. All in all, it is not clear that religion is "over" even in these countries in which so many obituaries for religion have been recited. Indeed, Philip Jenkins speaks of a perennial paradox in church history:

> The best indicator that Christianity is about to experience a vast expansion is a widespread conviction that the religion is doomed or in its closing days. Arguably the worst single moment in the history of West European Christianity occurred around 1798, with the Catholic church under severe persecution in much of Europe and skeptical, deist, and Unitarian movements in the ascendant across the Atlantic world. That particular trough also turned into an excellent foundation, from which various groups built the great missionary movement of the 19th century, the second evangelical revival, and the Catholic devotional revolution. Nothing drives activists and reformers more powerfully than the sense that their faith is about to perish in their homelands, and that they urgently need to make up these losses further afield, whether outward (overseas) or downward (among the previously neglected lost sheep at home). Quite possibly, the current sense of doom surrounding European Christianity will drive a comparable movement in the near future. Resurrection is not just a fundamental doctrine of Christianity, it is a historical model that explains the religion's structure and development.[5]

---

5. Philip Jenkins, "Downward, Outward, Later," *Books and Culture* 12 (September 2006), 15. Jenkins is well aware, of course, that churches have also disappeared, whether in North Africa, the Near East, and elsewhere, and that the same destiny might indeed await European Christianity—as he notes on the same page from which this quotation comes.

Furthermore, as Martin Marty has observed about America (and the same is true of other countries), there is no easy "culture war" motif to sum up all that is going on.[6] The cultural landscape instead is crisscrossed with alliances traversing various religious and philosophical lines: over abortion, environmentalism, overseas wars, (de-)regulation of business, tax changes, welfare reform, and on and on. Today's enemy on this issue may be needed as tomorrow's friend on another one, so the battles are fought civilly, so to speak, relative to the shooting wars fought under religious banners elsewhere in the world and previously in history. Recognition of the propriety of making such political alliances has come slowly to some religious groups that previously saw the world in binary terms, and only the pure could stand with the pure. Here is the crucial significance of Jerry Falwell's Moral Majority in the 1970s and 1980s, and of the new religious right in the United States ever since: even fundamentalists could form alliances with other kinds of Christians and—*mirabile dictu*—people of other faiths in order to achieve as much as possible of their vision of *shalom* in their nation and the world.

The political and social question for those who hold to other religious or philosophical traditions, then, is whether their religions or philosophies can produce the resources necessary to equip them to participate in democracy in this way, or whether they are bound by those outlooks to persist in absolutist categories and strategies that will not rest short of total social domination. The question for the rest of us—Christians or otherwise—who are committed to liberal democracy, the Western legal tradition, and the like is how much anti-pluralist absolutism of various sorts we can welcome and accommodate in our society. As Charles Taylor warns, "Liberalism can't and shouldn't claim complete cultural neutrality. Liberalism is also a fighting creed. The hospitable variant I espouse, as well as the most rigid forms, has to draw the line."[7]

Our multicultural societies are only now realizing that we do need to draw such a line. At least since 9/11 we have begun to face the facts that we cannot tolerate, much less affirm, everything and everyone, and that we cannot continue to absorb heterogeneous and heteronomous elements into our various

---

6. Martin E. Marty makes this theme of shifting alliances a key category in his study of *Modern American Religion*, vol. 1: *The Irony of It All, 1893–1919* (Chicago: University of Chicago Press, 1986). For an introduction to this theme, see Martin E. Marty, "Cross-Multicultures in the Crossfire: The Humanities and Political Interests," in *Christianity and Culture in the Crossfire*, ed. David A. Hoekema and Bobby Fong (Grand Rapids, MI: Eerdmans, 1997), 15–27.

7. Charles Taylor, "The Politics of Recognition," in Charles Taylor et al., *Multiculturalism,* ed. Amy Gutmann (Princeton, NJ: Princeton University Press, 1984), 62.

societies indefinitely without peril. The next decades of political argument will deal largely with where we will draw the line and why.[8] We must not go back to the terrible old days that kept out everyone who was not "just like us," so that Jews were trapped within the Third Reich that was temporarily willing to expel them. In particular, we must maintain hospitality for as many of the world's needy as we can help. Yet we will have to move beyond merely celebrating pluralism as diversity to what Martin Marty calls pluralism as "a polity and a framework for action," "a way of organizing life and encouraging an ethos to develop."[9]

There are grounds, therefore, for caution, yes, but also for both gratitude and hope. Secularization is not an irresistible force. There are no sure evidences of an irreversible decline of Christianity in the West. As Jenkins has reminded us, it is too rarely acknowledged amid all the prognostications of spiritual doom that "un-Christian" and even "post-Christian" societies have been converted or revived time and again in Western history—whether during monastic revivals in the Middle Ages, the sixteenth-century Reformations, the Puritan and Pietist movements, the eighteenth-century evangelical revivals, the nineteenth-century renewal movements among Catholics and Protestants, and so on. There is no obvious reason why such societies cannot be significantly drawn to the Gospel in our own time.

Furthermore, even if our societies do not turn decisively to Christianity in our time, there are yet grounds for realistic engagement: for patience, strategy, compromise, and trust in God to work in and through our broken, but still useful, cultural institutions to produce a measure of *shalom* and a way for the Gospel to reach still more people—as he does through us, broken but still useful.

We also should pause to ask ourselves a fundamental question: is the imposition of a Christian regime in America, or Canada, or Britain, or elsewhere *desirable,* even if it were possible?

Let us recall instances from the modern past in which Christians did exercise comprehensive cultural control: the Christian "total cultures" of sixteenth-century Calvinist Geneva or Catholic Spain, of seventeenth-century Puritan England under Cromwell or Catholic France under the Sun King, eighteenth-century quasi-Puritan New England, the nineteenth-century American South or

---

8. Jürgen Habermas issues warnings precisely along these lines: "Struggles for Recognition in the Democratic Constitutional State," in Charles Taylor et al., *Multiculturalism,* ed. Amy Gutmann (Princeton, NJ: Princeton University Press, 1984), 125–42.

9. Martin E. Marty, *When Faiths Collide* (Oxford: Blackwell, 2005), 69–70.

Orthodox and czarist Russia, or twentieth-century South Africa and Rhodesia. Each of these cases ought to give us pause. As grateful as we should be for the blessings God has given the world through Christian civilization, the record also shows that we Christians—who are, in Luther's phrase, *simul justus et peccator* (at the same time justified and yet sinners)—are capable of just as much selfish mischief as almost anyone else when we wield unchecked power. We are, inevitably because of sin, *worldly* when we run the show.

Thus, I agree with Glenn Tinder's warning:

> The political meaning of Christianity, then, does not lie in the ideal of a Christian society for no such society can exist.... Society is the unity of human beings in subjection to one another and to the worldly necessities underlying custom, law, and governance. The terms *Christian* and *society* cannot logically be joined.[10]

Indeed, when we think we are acting simply and purely for the glory of God and doing simply and purely the will of God, we are never in more danger of rationalizing our particular, sinful agendas—as Reinhold Niebuhr reminds us constantly. Worse, in a situation in which Christians govern in the name of God, there are no obvious grounds on which substantial dissent can be raised on fundamental matters. Until Jesus returns to reign directly and unambiguously, we must recognize that anyone purporting to wield political power with divine authority according to revelation makes large-scale disagreement impossible, for how can arguing with God be countenanced? (We Christians already have plenty of examples of small-scale political pathologies in our families and churches that feature those in authority styling themselves representatives of God's will and thus brooking no dissent.)

I suggest that we consider seriously the idea that God wants us not simply to "take it over for Jesus" but instead to bring the goodness of Christian motivations, values, and insights to the God-ordained project of earthkeeping that we share with our non-Christian neighbors. Even as we believe that our Christianity, inasmuch as it is authentic, will improve any situation—and I do believe that—so we can affirm that God works through others to affirm justice and charity and

---

10. Glenn Tinder, *The Political Meaning of Christianity: An Interpretation* (Baton Rouge: Louisiana State University Press, 1989), 61. Tinder's point recalls the classic distinction between *Gemeinschaft* (community) and *Gesellschaft* (society) made in 1887 by Ferdinand Tönnies (*Community and Society*, trans. Charles P. Loomis [Mineola, NY: Dover, 2002]).

to keep our own sin, and especially the sin that proceeds under the cover of righteousness, in check.[11]

Those who write as I do sometimes are accused of endorsing allegiance to liberal democracy as prior to Christian commitment. And some might think I am somehow antipathetic to the happy circumstance in which a majority of citizens freely support Christian values in a given society. Both of these charges will not stand. I am simply registering a Christian suspicion of all majority power, much less unchecked power, whether wielded by Christians or anyone else short of the Lord Jesus himself. And I thus recommend pluralism to help us in this penultimate era, given the fallenness of everyone, including us, until God achieves his ultimate purposes and we enjoy the immediate reign of Christ.

Show

The multitude of Christian congregations, denominations, and other organizations in the world today is itself an example of modern plurality. So how are we doing in modeling successful cooperation even with other Christians? Can we give the idea of constructive pluralism some plausibility by our own actions? It's one thing to say, "Here's how we think it might work." It's a wonderfully different thing to say, "Here's how we do it."

Indeed, church leaders have been making this point for a long time. Franklin Littell half a century ago remarked on the dark irony that churches had sought to impose upon all citizens certain strictures, such as prohibition and resistance to evolution, that they had failed to elicit by theological and ecclesiastical means from their own members. His words echo down the decades to resonate powerfully today:

> Politicians in the churches attempted to secure by public legislation what they were unable to persuade many of their own members was either wise or

---

11. Oliver O'Donovan pushes beyond considerations of the modern individual state to rebuke any larger ideal of Christian political aspiration as well. He avers that the Old Testament stands against empire, even a righteous one, and that "divine providence is ready to protect other national traditions besides the sacred one" (*The Desire of the Nations: Rediscovering the Roots of Political Thought* [Cambridge, UK: Cambridge University Press, 1996], 73). He concludes that "Yhwh's world order was plurally constituted. World-empire was a bestial deformation.... *The appropriate unifying element in international order is law rather than government*" (72). And, finally, "the titanic temptation which besets collectives needs the check of a perpetual plurality at the universal level. There are always 'others,' those not of our fold whom we must respect and encounter" (73). These passages, by the way, show how facile it is to construe O'Donovan as merely an apologist for Christendom.

desirable....Lacking the authenticity of a genuinely disciplined witness, the Protestant reversion to political action was ultimately discredited, and the churches have not to this day recovered their authority in public life.[12]

At the most local level, then, how well do we handle diversity in our families, congregations, or denominations? How much do we in fact seek not only common ground for our life together, but also for the flourishing of our complementary differences for the enrichment of each individual and of each other? Societies must insist on a certain amount of conformity of belief and activity, of course, or nothing can be done together. But beyond what is necessary, our families and churches—like most groups—tend toward maximal conformity instead of maximal creativity. Let us not be romantic but realistic and acknowledge that cultivation of diversity is inefficient, or at least more costly in time, effort, and attention. But if we fail to provide places for different people to grow and to grow together, we will alienate both our own "non-standard" brothers and sisters and also, in the case of churches, all those outside our communion who might have wanted to join but now see that they would not be welcome *as themselves*. Those who remain thus become more and more themselves in a kind of sociological inbreeding that inevitably results in pathology. God has so arranged the world, that is, that we actually *need* a certain amount of diversity just to avoid going wrong, let alone to help us go more and more right.

We return to the metaphor of gardening. Are we deliberately planting diversity? Are we making room for it? Are we feeding it, nurturing it, inviting it? Or are we worried by it, fearful of it, and quick to discourage and uproot it? Leadership styles among parents or pastors are key here to setting the tone for everyone else, and it takes a convinced, secure, and capable parent or pastor to actually welcome diversity while also enlisting it in the common good.

Beyond the family or particular Christian tradition, how much effort do we make to consider what the Mennonites or the Episcopalians, the Baptists or the Pentecostals, the Methodists or the Presbyterians have to say to the rest of us out of their *differences,* as well as out of the affirmations in common with other Christians? As I suggested earlier, our patterns of ecumenicity tend to bracket out our differences rather than to celebrate and capitalize upon them. Finding common ground has been the necessary first step in ecumenical relations and activity. But the next step is

---

12. Franklin H. Littell, *From State Church to Pluralism* (New York: Doubleday Anchor, 1962), 120; quoted in John Howard Yoder, *The Politics of Jesus: Vicit Agnus Noster* (Grand Rapids, MI: Eerdmans, 1972), 154.

to acknowledge and enjoy what God has done elsewhere in the Body of Christ. And if at the congregational level we are willing to say, "I can't do everything myself, for I am an ear: I must consult with a hand or an eye on this matter," I suggest that we do the same among whole traditions. If we do not regularly and programmatically consult with each other, we are tacitly claiming that we have no need of each other, and that all the truth, beauty, and goodness we need has been vouchsafed to us by God already. Not only is such an attitude problematic in terms of our flourishing, as I have asserted, but in this context now we must recognize how useless a picture this presents to the rest of society. Baptists, Presbyterians, and Roman Catholics failing to celebrate diversity provide no positive examples to societies trying to understand how to celebrate diversity on larger scales.

At the same time, we can ask how well we are working out the implications of what we might call "excessive diversity," in which groups really are at odds with each other on fundamental values intrinsic to the life of the society. The Anglican Communion, for example, is currently in crisis on just this matter. It has prided itself on its vaunted capacity for inclusivity. But, like any other organization, it can tolerate only so much diversity—theological, ethical, and political—before it becomes simply a weird association of individuals and groups who have not only differences but opposing and mutually destructive ones. The same thing is true of a country such as Germany, the United States, or New Zealand: a society can absorb, tolerate, and profit from only a limited amount of diversity before it simply must disintegrate into warring factions. The church has a long tradition of insisting on regulating core beliefs and practices—indeed, formulating a "rule of faith" (*regula fidei*) in the early church and many statements and canons ever since. Yet it must be acknowledged that church discipline is in a sad state in the West today—it is usually lax, while occasionally domineering. So can the church be a light to the world in facing also this fundamental challenge?

Finally, in our dealings with other religious believers, and with all of our other neighbors, there is an opportunity to model a constructive and principled pluralism. In this pluralism there will be affirmation of common concerns and initiatives in our common task of cultivating *shalom*: in artistic organizations, charities, youth groups, sports clubs, environmental societies, and everything else that promotes the flourishing of human beings and the planet given to us to tend. Yes, there are the secondary or corollary benefits, so to speak, of making friends among those who are not yet Christian so that we might draw them toward the faith. But the activity is *good in itself* as obedience to the creation commandments of God, whether any direct evangelism takes place or not.

Beyond affirmation and participation, there will be tolerance of different modes of life, including some that we are convinced are unhealthy but must be granted in the name of the liberty God has already given us. "Tolerance" is a good word, not just a bad one. Of course, tolerating egregious evils is no virtue. But nowadays, while tolerance is sometimes derided as a grudging, grumpy thing, the real fault found in it is its intrinsic judgment: one tolerates what one does not, in fact, approve of. To which the answer is that there is much in contemporary society, as there is much in the church and even in myself, of which I do not approve. So what? I can either tolerate these things, out of respect for the humanity of the other and for the liberty God gives us all, and in the hope of their eventual improvement, or I can *not* tolerate them. What I cannot do, however, is what many voices nowadays tell us we must do in order to qualify as enlightened and commendable people: affirm everyone else's difference. The absurdity of such an attitude emerges immediately upon one's refusal to affirm this or that idea, behavior, or group with which one disagrees: one is then condemned (note: not affirmed). I fear that we simply have to wait out this current adolescent attitude of trying to affirm everyone while fiercely judging all who will not play the same game. Eventually, one hopes, an adult recognition of the necessity of tolerance as a civic virtue will (re-)emerge.[13]

In our pluralized societies there will be conflict over different means to the same end, and even over which ends are the best to pursue. Conflict is not to be feared as the great threat, however. It is to be expected and even welcomed as an occasion to consider important differences and to find a better way forward than we might have found in a homogeneous society.[14] It is with this sensibility that Christians participate in school boards, governments, and other forms of electoral politics, and also in the courts as the conflicts of the day are worked out in that mode. Yet civility ought to govern our participation in such conflicts—literally, an attitude of common citizenship, a solidarity that comes from recognizing that together we bear the image of God and share a common purpose in his service, whether all of our neighbors recognize that basis of civility or not (as, of course, many won't).

Finally, there will be opposition to those ideas, practices, individuals, and groups that threaten one's own community or individuals within it, and also to those that

---

13. Amy Gutmann helpfully distinguishes further between views that one can disagree with but respect, and views that one might tolerate but not respect, such as "misogyny, racial or ethnic hatred, or rationalizations of self-interest or group interest parading as historical or scientific knowledge." See her introduction to Charles Taylor et al., *Multiculturalism*, ed. Amy Gutmann (Princeton, NJ: Princeton University Press, 1984), 22.

14. John Feikens, "Conflict: Its Resolution and the Completion of Creation," in *Seeking Understanding: The Stob Lectures 1986–1998* (Grand Rapids, MI: Eerdmans, 2001), 343–71.

threaten the commonweal. But Christians ought to be especially determined to oppose threats that arise to *others,* and especially to those with less power to defend themselves. Are Christians conspicuously caring for their embattled neighbors, or are we just another interest group preserving our piece of the pie?[15]

The modern world needs good ideas and good examples. The challenge for the Christian church is indeed to be a bright city on a hill—a true city, a social organism of diversity in unity, of individuality and cooperation, of creativity and discipline, rather than an anarchy of self-centered and small-minded individuals and factions. The further challenge of our times is for Christians to model true civility within a world increasingly troubled—and also blessed—with the pluralization of societies that were once more comfortably homogeneous.

The Christian hope is that God will eventually in fact rule all nations. But he certainly ought to rule first in Christian individuals and institutions.

Tell

The most important message we have to tell, of course, is the gospel of Jesus Christ. That gospel, however, is nested within the great Story of all that God has done and said, and all that God wants for us. So we have much to say, of different sorts, in the public sphere today.

First, we ought to teach and maintain the values intrinsic to modern public life: democracy, the rule of law, human rights, self-worth, the worth of others, cooperation and competition, freedom and responsibility, and so on. These are values that are consonant with Christianity and with other worldviews—although not all—and they frame our common life in North America, Europe, and more and more of the rest of the world. It is easy to be cynical about democracy and

---

15. Some might think here of the lines of Bonhoeffer's famous colleague Martin Niemöller:

When the Nazis arrested the Communists,
I said nothing; after all, I was not a Communist.
When they locked up the Social Democrats,
I said nothing; after all, I was not a Social Democrat.
When they arrested the trade unionists,
I did not protest; after all, I was not a trade unionist.
When they arrested the Jews, I did not protest; after all, I was not a Jew.
When they arrested me, there was no one left to protest.

(This is my translation of the original German, found with variant translations at http://en.wikiquote.org/wiki/Martin_Niem%C3%B6ller, accessed 14 September 2006.)

Yet beyond the stark realism of Niemöller's words, Bonhoeffer's own example is much more commendable: he protected Jews simply because he thought that was right, not because he wanted to be sure that someone would be left to protect him if he were later arrested.

capitalism, and even law and government. But as disheartening as it is to witness waste, fraud, venality, and oppression, we must keep in view also the good things that emerge from these ideologies and systems, especially when compared not with the New Jerusalem but with other extant or likely alternatives. As I have maintained, the values of the Kingdom of God properly and helpfully judge all of our efforts and programs and values. We must never directly equate anything we do with the Kingdom, and we must instead conduct ourselves with the humility, faith, and openness to correction that such recognition entails. Yet we also must be realistic enough to make the best of what we have to work with. And we must not discourage ourselves *or others* (Mt. 18:6) by indulging in a perpetual round of grumbling, which serves only to foster an attitude of pseudo-prophetic superiority coupled with a delicious *Weltschmerz*. If better values and systems are actually on offer, by all means let us embrace and commend them. We must not settle slothfully merely for what is. Nor, however, must we abandon the defense of what good we have been able to attain and enjoy out of guilt for previous abuses and regret over evil results—moral, aesthetic, economic, agricultural, political, or whatever—we are not yet able to avoid.

Furthermore, we should hold our fellow citizens, our media, our public institutions, our courts, and our politicians to those values. We may do so when we are injured by our neighbors' failure to observe those values toward us, of course. But we should do so especially when our own interests are not at stake, and especially on behalf of others who need assistance, representation, and defense—such as children, the undereducated, the mentally retarded, the ill, and so on. Despite almost everyone's avowal of these values, we must see that they are constantly under threat in matters great and small. People constantly are treated as less than human, prejudice does run rampant, the strong perpetually oppress the weak—and Christians must vigilantly champion the values we all say we believe.

Second, we need to teach that not everyone "wins" in democracy. Not all "values" are equally valued in our common life, nor should they be. Most of us frown on vigilantism, abuse, fraud, treason, bestiality, necrophilia, and child molestation. We do not believe, in fact, that everyone and everything is entitled to equal affirmation or (and this is more controversial) even respect.

In a free society, we are entitled to disagree with each other on profound matters. Indeed, for a democratic society to work properly, there are often times in which we are positively *obliged* to argue with each other over such things, in order that the truth has a chance to emerge and be embraced by everyone, or at least by more people than previously recognized it. In some cases, we are obliged even to work to impose behaviors on all citizens in the name of one set of values over another. That's what governments, courts, and police properly do. As we have seen, toleration and even respect for each other do not entail agreement and affirmation—how could they?

Out of respect for you, as well as for your victim, I will not treat you as a mad dog or a virus, but as a human being thinking or doing something I think is harmful and wrong. Sometimes I will tolerate your different choices, as you will tolerate mine. And sometimes toleration must give way to intolerance on behalf of common life as we make hard choices that not everyone will like. Many people nowadays resist this grown-up idea, preferring a happy fantasy of everyone just leaving each other alone—or, better, everyone blessing everyone else with affirmation. But democracy is the best way we have yet found, short of the direct reign of God, to broker a common life together, to accommodate what minorities we can, and to leave the door open for further discussion. And in democracy, there are usually winners and losers. Not everybody wins, because when there are intractable and irreconcilable differences, there is no way for everyone to win. Christians need to join with others who are equally realistic to make this plain in the controversies of our day.

(One of the great things about democracy, to be sure, is that the way is always open for a defeated idea or party to make its case again. That, too, must be reaffirmed in the face of those who defend established positions very convenient to themselves with "We've already decided that" and "Let's move on.")

Third, Christians can speak up to teach the public what Christians actually believe and do, rather than what various members of the public might think we believe and do. We should correct misstatements and caricatures in the media with better information and more accurate interpretations. As upsetting as it might be to see oneself and one's spiritual family distorted in public, we can also rejoice in these opportunities to proclaim the gospel message—which opportunities rarely arise otherwise than in a controversy provoked by someone else's mistake or attack. The *New York Times* or CNN will never, in fact, ask someone to set out the gospel unless Christians are somehow under attack and a spokesperson is thus given the opportunity to reply with "Here's what we *do* believe...."

Fourth, we can resist any form of sectarianism, any ideological bullying, any teaching or (what is more common) assumption of any single religion or worldview as if it alone is entirely true and all other viewpoints are entirely false. Christians should be not proponents of a restrictive orthodoxy of belief in which all diversity and novelty are feared but defenders of genuine liberty in which ideas can emerge freely to then be tested.

For example, there is considerable confusion today about how to teach science. As Neil Postman points out, it is bad science education to present physics, chemistry, biology, or whatever as a collection of agreed facts and indubitable explanations.[16] The very nature of science is empirical, which directly entails that it is never certain—never closed to new information and ideas, never settled once for all. To teach evolution as a fact, therefore, is to confuse empirical observations of nature, such as "All of the red light waves we have measured are much longer than the blue waves we have measured" or "All life as we know it is carbon-based," with sociological observations of human beings, such as "Evolution is a theory that most scientists currently think is an explanatory scheme so helpful as to make an alternative seem highly implausible." It is a fact that most scientists do think this way, but that doesn't establish evolution itself as a fact. Most scientists used to think the same way about the existence of an "ether" and phlogiston, or the impossibility of a vacuum, which no one takes as fact today. Without us getting into technical philosophy or history of science, such a distinction (between fact and theory) is just basic to science, and for defenders of evolution to say otherwise is to be literally unscientific. (One suspects that when scientists get doctrinaire, something other than science is at stake.)[17]

Postman makes the provocative suggestion that so-called creation science (for which he has no sympathy at all) should be taught in the classrooms precisely to show students how science works, in the contention of competing theories.[18] Now, some years after his essay was published, we might see Intelligent Design as even more useful in this regard, as its proponents are much more circumspect about scientific protocols than creation science advocates generally have been, and it clearly is not just creation science "dressed up," as some pundits have it.

Whether one accepts Postman's pedagogical suggestion or not, however, his epistemological and political point remains. Science is precisely *not* the discourse in which teachers should speak as if what happens to be in the textbooks in this particular edition is "just plain true," or for science museum curators to mount exhibits with captions written as if everything they say was settled fact, or for science magazines to pooh-pooh anyone who is not entirely convinced of whatever consensus happens to

---

16. Neil Postman, "Scientism," in *Technopoly: The Surrender of Culture to Technology* (New York: Vintage, 1992), 144–63.

17. In a huge field, see the work of scientists-cum-theologians John Polkinghorne (e.g., *Belief in God in an Age of Science* [New Haven, CT: Yale University Press, 1998]) and Alister E. McGrath (e.g., *The Foundations of Dialogue in Science and Religion* [Oxford: Blackwell, 1998]). See also J. Wentzel van Huyssteen, *Duet or Duel? Theology and Science in a Postmodern World* (Harrisburg, PA: Trinity, 1998).

18. Neil Postman, *Conscientious Objections: Stirring Up Trouble About Language, Technology, and Education* (New York: Vintage, 1988), 128–35.

reign at the moment. This is not science but bullying, resorting to power to preclude any dissent. Christians provide a public service, increasing *shalom*, when we stand up against any oppression, including intellectual and cultural oppression, and particularly on behalf of the weak—in this case, children and the less informed.

To pick another example, Christians can help public discourse by resisting value judgments by public authorities and arbiters (such as schoolteachers, professors, and judges) that do not reflect the consensus of society, such as the depiction in history and anthropology of "good guys" and "bad guys" (e.g., good natives and bad missionaries, traders, and soldiers) or the affirmation of homosexuality by public officials. In fact, I suggest that Christians should oppose as well any educator, textbook, or judge who says the opposite: that natives are bad and missionaries are good, or that homosexuality is not normal but sinful. Properly circumspect social science tells us only what *is* the case and why. We must then turn to our religions and life philosophies to tell us whether what *is* is good or bad. That is the first distinction that tends to be forgotten. Some Christians resist all fact/value separation, but natural science, social science, and history rest on being able to do so in a disciplined—although, of course, never completely objective—way.

The second distinction to be made in these matters rests on the fact that it is ultimately necessary to make ethical judgments about events and characters in history, sexuality, and a host of other human issues. Yet because most such judgments are made according to values particular to individuals or groups, rather than according to the values that frame our common life (examples of the latter are "Legal due process is good" and "Slavery and racism are wrong"), they should not be made in public institutions such as schools, courts, or legislatures—which should reflect the state of society, including its dissension. Families, religious communities, and advocacy groups are among the places in which such judgments are properly rendered.

So teachers can report, accurately, that there were winners and losers in the story of Europeans coming to the New World, that promises were made and many were broken, that terror tactics were used by various groups in warfare, and so on. Such teachers do not have to render a comprehensive moral judgment, for such a judgment will depend very much on values that are not universally shared and on complicated matters of interpretation, such as the usefulness and genuineness of the missionary motive, the value to the native peoples of receiving modern technology willy-nilly, the relative difference in the treatment of natives by the Spanish, English, and French, and so on.

Likewise, teachers can report, accurately, that some people are attracted to members of the same sex such that they want to have romantic and even matrimonial relations with them. They can report that most of the world's religious traditions disagree with this behavior, and that nonetheless many people think otherwise and that it is perfectly legal for such people to pursue their chosen affections. Children won't grasp all of the nuances here—the difference, say, between what a society allows and what a society affirms—but the teachers are telling the truth now, and not adding an element of their individual take on an issue about which there is no public consensus. Furthermore, teaching this way can open up interesting and vital questions about pluralism, tolerance, respect, the law, and so on that are usually smothered by the well-intentioned blanket of affirmation, which renders these other issues moot.

Fifth, Christians can be in the vanguard of cultural change, instead of fighting rearguard battles to maintain our diminishing cultural privileges, in regard to any religious events and symbols in schools, legislatures, courts, and other public institutions. Christians properly can protest presentations of religion that move beyond information to encourage what amounts to liturgical participation, whether a Native Canadian troupe at a school assembly inviting the room to chant a prayer to a native god, a "winter festival" (formerly a "Christmas concert") that proceeds to offer songs to a round of deities, or a teacher of Transcendental Mediation or yoga who includes elements of *puja,* veneration of a Hindu spiritual worthy of some sort.

We can speak up about such things with integrity, of course, only as we cooperate in the removal of our own practices, such as saying the Lord's Prayer, reciting the Ten Commandments, and singing Christmas carols. Perhaps we can suggest even that Christian holy days should not be recognized above other holy days in the public calendar. (It is not at all clear to me, for example, why Good Friday still should be celebrated by the pluralistic public at large.)

Sixth, and related to this point, is the responsibility to practice a proper silence. In this discipline, we avoid and resist misuse of privilege, whether by Christians or by others, in regard to taking advantage of authority in order to proselytize: teachers and coaches, physicians and nurses, politicians and judges, and so on. We bring Christian values to bear on our functioning in such roles, yes, but as we have seen, those values are not restricted to evangelism. Those values include doing those jobs well for their own sakes, toward the cultivation of the world according to the creation commandments. And we expect other people to do their jobs the same way, for it is the human task as divinely ordained. It is vocationally unethical, then, to exploit authority in one role (teacher, physician, judge) to try to influence others in another—namely, as a religious advocate.

Seventh, Christians can watch our language in public. We will be simply unintelligible to our fellow citizens if we use too much "in-house," Christian jargon.

This sort of point is made often enough, however. Its complement must also be affirmed, namely, that we must resist the cultural pressure to leave our religious identities and vocabularies at the door when we want to engage in public conversation. This pressure is a secularizing pressure, a pressure to use only the language of secular rationality, sense experience, and the ever-changing conventions of the *au courant* intelligentsia.

The way forward, then, is not to relegate explicitly religious values and categories to our private lives. That would be to succumb to ideological bullying. Instead, we must get beyond the public/private distinction and look at what our Lord and the apostles did: they sought to be *persuasive*. If Peter was addressing Jews (Acts 2), he referred them to the Old Testament and their common experience of Jesus' recent ministry and execution. If Paul was addressing Greek philosophers (Acts 17), he used their own religious poetry and art. They made use of rhetorical materials that fit the task at hand.

In a democracy, public speakers ought to be free to refer to any source, any text, and any authority they like. If a speaker—whether a school board member, a legislator, a pundit, or a workmate in the cafeteria—wants to cite her favorite book, whether *The Communist Manifesto,* the *Qur'an,* or the *Bhagavad-Gita,* then she should be allowed to do so. The practical question that follows is simply that of what will persuade a majority to agree. If she wants not only to announce her opinion but also win support, then she must consider whether she can persuade the most people by referring to the authority of Adam Smith, or Martin Luther, or the Dalai Lama. Nothing should be ruled out of bounds a priori. So Christians should campaign for Christian concerns today using whatever rhetoric in public they believe will do the job they want done. For, as postmodernists never tire of reminding us, there is no generically human philosophy to which we ought to conform our language and our activity. There are only particular societies, cultures, and conversations, each with their own distinctive qualities and limitations and characters. As Yoder puts it well, "There is no 'public' that is not just another particular province."[19]

In light of this epistemological and political realism, therefore, we nonetheless have to follow the dominical advice to be as wise as serpents if we want to be heard on national networks or read in major periodicals. We will have to learn what will and what won't be acceptable to the producers and editors of such media, and that will mean picking both our language and our issues carefully—again, in order to do as much good as possible. This sort of compromise is simply realistic. Major media won't let us simply preach the gospel, but they will let us offer pithy

---

19. Yoder, *The Priestly Kingdom,* 40.

commentary on the day's events and issues if we can speak both intelligibly and attractively about them.[20]

To be sure, however, we may find that the filters are so thick against what we want to say that we will abandon some of these media, at least in particular instances. And the medium itself may be problematic. Television news in particular is so terribly compressed—a "major" story can get all of three minutes—that some issues simply cannot, and should not, be discussed in that medium. Television is much too limited to discuss, say, the providence of God in a natural disaster, the reasons for and against the legalization of homosexual marriage, or the various issues involved in churches offering sanctuary to refugees. And the pressure to entertain, even in the news, is widely recognized now as relentless and overwhelming. In the age of the Internet, desktop publishing, and other revolutions, Christians can recognize that there are lots of other media of public discussion in the world today that we can access, and we should make use of those that can do a particular job well.

When we do speak up, moreover, we should not apologize for being who we are as Christians, just as most of our neighbors don't expect Jews or homosexuals or feminists or native peoples to apologize for who they are and to adopt some kind of generic, neutral, and depersonalizing language just to be heard in public. Glenn Tinder observes,

> While Christians can sometimes put their understanding of things in secular terms..., they cannot do invariably. They cannot leave out distinctive Christian

---

20. This is perhaps the place to remark on a weird semantic struggle that crops up in public theology and philosophy between the use of the term "virtues" versus "values." This distinction is supposed to be rooted in the fact/value distinction so typical in modern philosophy. Some Christians seem to think that to use the word "values" is to concede entirely to relativism, as if "values" means simply subjective preferences while "virtues" means objective realities. Alas, this is a distinction not supported by any dictionary I consulted. Calling one's own values "virtues" in this context simply means that one considers one's values to be objectively grounded—to be true to the nature of things, to be *facts*. To think so is perfectly fine, of course, and not uncommon. But such nomenclature doesn't solve the rhetorical and political challenge of convincing other people to come round to one's point of view. Indeed, such usage might well be exposed for what it is, an implication that "*we* have virtues (we are right) while *you* have mere values (and thus are wrong)." And in this current political-cum-epistemological situation, to insist on using "virtues" in this way does seem to me like "wishing will make it so." If I keep calling my values "virtues," then my values will more likely be recognized by my auditors as objectively true than if I call them "values." Such a tactic makes no sense to me. I am all for arguing that some values are better than others and, indeed, that some values are much more in line with the universe and the Lord of the universe than others are. But insisting on "virtues" versus "values" gets us nowhere.

terms entirely and still speak as Christians. Hence to forbid Christians to use Christian terms in the public realm is tantamount to excluding them from the public realm.[21]

Yes, in some modern societies, or at least in some sectors of some societies, there is still a backlash against Christians in particular—the understandable, if regrettable, resentment that lingers in the wake of our former cultural hegemony over them. Commonly, it takes the form of a double standard, by which Christians are treated worse than any others. Let's recognize, however, that Christianity is treated differently than all other outlooks in the West because the position of Christianity in Western history is different from that of all other outlooks.[22] Such treatment is just to be expected, and we simply have to weather this storm until it abates. Increasingly, however, our neighbors are recognizing that we, too, deserve the same respect as anyone else in the name of multiculturalism, diversity, and the like. The very decline of Christianity has this silver lining: it has allowed many people—especially outside the United States, where the cultural influence of Christianity is still particularly strong—to lower their guard and let Christians say their particular things along with everyone else in the forum of public opinion.

Quite practically, then, I believe our preachers, teachers, writers, broadcasters, and activists especially need to learn true "public speaking" that will get them heard by the public at large, and by key publics such as the courts, the legislatures, the news media, the entertainment media, and the schools. And then they can model such discourse for the rest of us as we go about our vocations, seeking to speak a good word wherever and whenever we can.[23]

---

21. Glenn Tinder, *The Fabric of Hope: An Essay* (Atlanta: Scholars Press, 1999), 7.

22. Rodney Stark remarks: "Recently, the local media expressed approval when the chief of police of Seattle prohibited his officers from wearing their uniforms to take part in a 'March for Jesus.' The media were equally agreeable when, the *next day,* the chief wore his uniform to march in the 'Lesbian Gay Bisexual Transgender Parade.' In similar fashion, protest vigils against capital punishment held outside prisons when an execution is scheduled are invariably treated with respect, but vigils outside abortion clinics are not. When animal rights activists berate and abuse women in public for wearing furs, their media treatment is favorable in comparison to that given demonstrations against clubs featuring women wearing nothing.... Indeed, the media could not even report the death of Mother Teresa without providing 'balance' by soliciting nasty attacks on her sincerity and merit from various professional atheists" (Rodney Stark, *One True God: Historical Consequences of Monotheism* [Princeton, NJ: Princeton University Press, 2001], 251–52). Even allowing that Stark speaks of "the media" as a monolith, which they obviously aren't, his observations do ring true for many parts of North America today.

23. See my "Speaking in Tongues: Communicating the Gospel Today," chap. in *Evangelical Landscapes: Facing Critical Issues of the Day* (Grand Rapids, MI: Baker Academic, 2002), 185–204.

Eighth, our Christian theology can help us help society think through difficult questions and solve difficult problems by keeping together a combination of virtues and actions that, if isolated, result in mere vengeance or sentimentality. In attempting to resolve aboriginal land claims, for example, or the legacy of slavery and racism, or corporate misbehavior, we can agree with those who call for justice. But we will not stop there, as so many have stopped, with some disputes thus locked indefinitely in mutual accusation and fury. We can go on to forgiveness. Some issues cannot be resolved by trying to revert everything and everyone to "first position," nor is it always possible to calculate, let alone afford, full recompense for damage done. Forgiveness helps us cut the chains of history that perpetually hamper us from moving together into a good future.[24]

To be sure, Christians also will affirm that forgiveness entails naming what happened in its stark evil and in whatever moral ambiguity also attended it. Forgiveness does not mean hiding the past; quite the contrary. It means to be totally clear-eyed about what was done by whom to whom, and then having the offended party forgive. Furthermore, genuine forgiveness is not just exhorting people to "move on" and "get over it," which would be to victimize them a second time. Forgiveness ought to be rendered after the offenders—and those who have benefited from the offense—both own up to what happened and then do their part: confession of offense if appropriate, restitution if possible, and then whatever else is necessary to make things as right as can be. The realistic imperative here is to *make the best of it*. Otherwise the cycle of injustice and anger continues indefinitely.

Thus we can bring hopeful practicality to the table. We can remind those who need to hear it that disputes are often about more than mere money and power but about personal and spiritual matters as well. We can remind others that goodwill and wishful thinking are insufficient to remedy situations that do indeed have important economic and political dimensions. Christians have all of these categories in place in our theology, and we can help our societies think and behave in a way that pays proper tribute to each element of this complex of healing and renewal, however approximate it will always be.

Ninth, part of good telling is good *listening*. There is a place for arguing over things that matter. But argument need not, and must not, be our primary mode of conversation with our neighbors: conversation must be. And conversation involves

---

24. For reflections that bear the marks of the author's own Croatian experience, see Miroslav Volf, *Exclusion and Embrace: A Theological Exploration of Identity, Otherness, and Reconciliation* (Nashville, TN: Abingdon, 1996); and Miroslav Volf, *Free of Charge: Giving and Forgiving in a Culture Stripped of Grace* (Grand Rapids, MI: Zondervan, 2005).

listening, learning, and enjoying each other as much as possible, in the cooperative mode rather than the competitive or calculating. As Martin Marty puts it, "One does not hear claims such as 'I sure won *that* conversation!' And conversation is especially appealing because it invites in on equal terms host and guest, belonger and stranger, the committed and the less committed, the informed and the less informed."[25]

How can we really know who our neighbors are and how we can love them best if we do not spend considerable time and effort in listening to them—and particularly to those who are on the margins and who thus are not used to being listened to? For that matter, we can hardly be said to love our enemies if we listen to them only to immediately refute and defeat them, and never attend to the underlying fears and aspirations that motivate them—with which we might in fact have some sympathy, and with which we need at least to reckon.[26]

Finally, therefore, the image of conversation reminds us of the apostolic injunction to speak the truth *in love* (Eph. 4:15). This has both formal and material dimensions. Formally, we simply have to speak the truth in love because most of our neighbors will not listen with genuine openness to someone who doesn't convey care, who doesn't assure them that this message is coming with their best interests at heart. (And if we don't honestly love our neighbors, then we should keep quiet. As Francis Cardinal George reminds us, you cannot "evangelize what you don't love," and you cannot persuade people who suspect you do not, in fact, care about them.)[27]

Materially, we must speak the truth in love because, to put it starkly, God cares about people even more than he cares about mere principles or propositions—about "truth," in that restricted sense. To speak truth without caring about whether it actually touches and helps our audiences—as many do, especially when they are frightened and angry—is merely to indulge oneself, scoring points on one's own tally of duty and accomplishment but failing to please God at all.

Campaign

Finally, let's turn to the particular question of advocacy, of campaigning for what we think is right and good for the common life of our schools, neighborhoods,

---

25. Marty, *When Faiths Collide*, 91.

26. An admirable example of listening and responding, in this case to postmodernists, is J. Richard Middleton and Brian J. Walsh, *Truth Is Stranger than It Used to Be: Biblical Faith in a Postmodern Age* (Downers Grove, IL: InterVarsity, 1995).

27. Francis Cardinal George, presentation titled "Society and the Mission of the Laity," 9 May 1998; quoted without further reference in Jean Bethke Elshtain, *Who Are We? Critical Reflections and Hopeful Possibilities* (Grand Rapids, MI: Eerdmans, 2000), 155.

municipalities, regions, and countries. Let's consider, in turn, which Christians should do it, in what modes we should do it, and how we should do it.

Recalling our discussion of vocation, it follows that not everyone is responsible to take part in public advocacy in any major way, and some perhaps not at all—except to support those who do with prayer and perhaps also money or other logistical help. Some Christians clearly are gifted and called to various kinds of campaigning, equipped with wise speech, political authority, personal networks, technical expertise, and so on. Others may not feel so gifted, but providence thrusts them into advocacy through experience and therefore opportunity: Mothers Against Drunk Driving, for example. We recall that just because a particular form of service, in this case advocacy, is good doesn't entail that everyone should be involved in it. At the same time, precisely in an era of widespread disillusionment with public institutions, small numbers of well-positioned people can make a big difference. We must each keep considering whether this season and circumstance of life is one in which we are now called to service, whether to fight the incursion of gambling into our town, support refugees, resist rapacious development, or encourage civic beautification.

Pastors particularly must have a clear sense of what they can and cannot do well. It is Christian politicians and political scientists who usually will have the clearest and most helpful advice about politics; Christian educators, social scientists, and parents who will think most critically and creatively about schools; Christian physicians, nurses, other medical professionals, administrators, chaplains, and patients who will have the most to offer regarding health care; and so on. Pastors serve such Christians well in two modes: teaching them about the fundamental principles of Christian engagement (such as the nature of Christian mission, vocation, and the like) and exhorting them to pursue their particular callings. But it is the unusual pastor who has the genuine expertise, insight, and opportunity to enter another realm—such as politics, education, or health care— and do or say something better than his fellow Christians who already work in that realm. (Indeed, pastors and politicians work not only in different categories but also to a considerable extent in mutually exclusive ones. Pastors emphasize purity, loyalty, clarity, and totality, while politicians must work with mixedness, expedience, ambiguity, and compromise.) Furthermore, when pastors insist on speaking out of their depth, they risk undermining their credibility and usefulness in their primary calling, in what they *do* know. Finally, pastors who engage directly in party politics will be implicated in the sin and failure that inevitably attend every régime, and will thus forfeit their position as prophets to whoever is subsequently in charge. One can think of exceptions to these cautions, of course. In general, however, if pastors long for Christian voices to be raised and Christian hands to be employed in this or that cultural challenge, they must be clear that their particular calling is not to leap into it themselves but to "equip the saints for the work of ministry" (Eph. 4:12).

The Christian church can be deployed in a wide range of modes in order to accomplish a wide range of actions. We can act as an individual, as a family, as a congregation, as a denomination, as an ecumenical fellowship, as Christian special-purpose groups (such as World Vision or Focus on the Family), as inter-faith coalitions—and also in secular political parties and other secular channels: a neighborhood association, a charity, a labor union, or an advocacy group such as Amnesty International.

Again, pastors, congregations, denominations, and ecumenical fellowships—what we normally, and too narrowly, tend to call "the church"—need to consider what each individual and group can do well and what other individuals and groups can do better. On vexed issues, there is rarely a particular policy that is "just plain Christian," that simply flows directly out of the Bible and Christian tradition. Sometimes, to be sure, we do face such an issue: campaigns for the care of children or for the end of religious persecution can be such causes. Protecting the Jews was one such cause in Bonhoeffer's time, such that he could call such an issue a *status confessionis*—a basic matter of Christian conviction. But in most cases, people of equal fidelity and competence can disagree about just what is to be done in a given circumstance. Pastors, congregations, denominations, and ecumenical fellowships—those officers and organizations that represent what we might call "the church in general"—need to distinguish carefully between proclaiming prin-ciples to guide such decision making (which can be a vital ministry) and advocat-ing particular decisions themselves (which may serve only to confuse the situation and even impede the work of those Christians with more pertinent competence).

It would be far better, I submit, for pastors, congregations, denominations, and ecumenical fellowships to encourage each Christian to take his or her proper place in these other modes and to work with other Christians and with other citizens of goodwill as best he or she can. Yes, that will often mean that members of the same family or church or congregation will end up in different parties or otherwise advocate different recommendations as to what is to be done. Thus pastors, congregations, denominations, and ecumenical organizations can be very glad for Christian special-purpose groups that represent various outlooks, par-ticipate in various cultural sectors, and offer various solutions. These organiza-tions represent Christian diversity: they let us focus our energies in particular and diverse ways, as no single, unitive organization (such as a congregation or denom-ination) can do. Our congregations, denominations, and ecumenical fellowships then represent Christian unity as they "maintain the bonds of peace" among us around our common life in Christ: sacraments, preaching, liturgy, mutual service, and so on.

Therefore, when someone looks at a current controversy or area of need and asks, "Where is the church? Is it involved?" the answer is not to be couched solely in terms of the actions of clergy, congregations, denominations, and so on, as if Christ deploys his church only in these modes. The answer instead should be: "Here, and here, and here: indeed, everywhere there is significant, useful action by Christians on behalf of *shalom*."

Finally, a few words about how Christians ought to participate in public contention, reiterating themes I expect are now familiar to the reader. In the form of Christian Realism I suggest, Christian individuals and Christian organizations will do whatever they can that, in their view, will result in the most *shalom* that seems possible in the situation. Again, Christians can and should pray for miracles, for what does *not* seem possible in the situation. God may choose this particular time to intervene, and we will be glad. But God does not ask us to lay aside everything we have learned about how the world normally works and how to participate most effectively in that normal world so that instead we can just pray and he can do all the rest. That is not what God told us to do in the cultural mandate, nor in any of his other commandments. *Ora et labora,* as the medieval monastic motto had it: pray and work.

So we will form partnerships, compose strategies, make compromises, and otherwise do the best we can to cultivate the earth and make disciples. In doing so we will join with a changing cast of allies on this or that issue, and it is important to underscore that our allies will change depending on the issue. I thus do not believe it makes sense to say, as a number of religious conservatives have been saying, that the new line of division in society lies between "people of faith" and secularists. The Bible itself approves no such thing as "faith in general" or "people of faith." Moreover, many secularists are *particular kinds* of secularists, namely, secularized Christians or Jews, and thus they retain many values similar to ours. Many of them will agree with Christians about retaining monogamy as a societal norm, for instance, versus the preference for plural marriage among most Muslims and a small but conspicuous minority of Mormons—"people of faith" most definitely. To pick another example, one that actually separates Christians from each other, many Protestants—even evangelicals—will agree with secularists on strategies to deal with HIV/AIDS that will dismay their conservative Catholic neighbors (our allies in the pro-life struggle) because the latter want nothing to do with artificial contraception. Part of Christian Realism, then, is a willingness to cast about for the most and best allies possible in each particular campaign. It also means to beware easy, dangerous "culture war" categories of "us versus them," or "red versus blue," or "good versus evil," as if everyone and every issue sorts themselves nicely into one category or another and as if we ourselves are always both coherent and correct about everything.

As we campaign, then, we will also trust God to guide us along the way. If he prefers us to take a path we are not planning to choose, we will depend on him to tell us so, and we will joyfully, faithfully take it. But until he does direct us in such a clear way, we ought to act like the responsible adults God created us to be and simply make the best of it—in recognition of our finitude and fallibility; of the certainty that we will not accomplish everything good and that evil will accompany whatever good we do accomplish; of the likelihood of unintended consequences that we will then have to deal with; and so on. We seek half a loaf if a whole loaf seems unavailable; we will even abandon particular battles if the war can be fought better in doing so. We recall that God doesn't proceed on all fronts simultaneously with *us*. We remember that some things matter more than others. We keep our main ends in view, with due regard for the particular situation, with its constituent opportunities, limitations, and temptations. We think strategically, tactically, and logistically, trying to be faithfully effective. And then we act to make the best of it.

True, this recommendation is fraught with ambiguity, ambivalence, paradox, irony, and danger. How easy it will be to invoke this ethic to promote the merely convenient, let alone the positively self-serving. How tempting it will be to call this theology to the aid of one's self-deception and one's manipulation of others. I haven't said much about the devil in this book because I think the Bible basically tells us to trust and obey God, and Satan will be kept at bay. But here is where diabolical mischief lies closest to hand: in rationalization and ideology, in veiling both our ruthless voracity and our lazy conformity in the guise of "Christian Realism." So we must be vigilant against this constant peril.

Yet, as I have argued, the options of total purity or total conquest seem to be not only inconsistent with the (whole) Bible's teaching but also simply impossible short of the return of Jesus in power and glory. We live in the meanwhile, and we must be prepared to work as God works: glad for today's gains, however meager or magnificent; sad or even angry about today's setbacks, however great or small; certain of the ultimate end of perfect peace; and therefore persistently faithful in the tasks at hand.

The Fundamental Move

The fundamental move to make is quite simple: to turn the tables, to put the shoe on the other foot, to ask "How would you feel if it happened to you?" For instance, Christians must see more sympathetically the imposition of "bubble zones" against pro-life protesters at abortion clinics, as we may soon want antagonists kept away from the entrances to our churches. Christians must refrain from proselytizing in the workplace in any way that they would object to if a Jehovah's Witness or Muslim were doing the same thing.

It is in this light that I again question the retention of special public privileges by Christians. I have asked why our holy days should be celebrated as statutory holidays. Does it make sense for Easter Sunday to be a national holiday in countries in which only a minority of citizens attend church and can articulate even basically the doctrines behind the paschal celebration? More generally, why should God be invoked in national anthems (Canadian and British), or cited in the Pledge of Allegiance (American), or be prominent in other such national symbols? The word "God" is just specific enough to marginalize those citizens who are not monotheists while not being specific enough to indicate which deity is being referenced: Yhwh? The God and Father of our Lord Jesus Christ? Allah? Vishnu? If we require monotheism as a qualification of citizenship, then using "God" in this way makes sense. But since we do not, then we should not encode it in our national symbols.

It needs to be clearly understood in this discussion that simply because a majority believes in God does not mean we should be putting the word "God" in national symbols, for national symbols in the nature of the case are binary: here is who we are and are not. You can't be "mostly" British or "mostly" American. Therefore the opinions of majorities, no matter how large or passionate, must not determine such basic issues. Otherwise we have the farcical situation of citizens being conscience-bound to opt out of various clauses of national anthems and pledges, singing or saying two or three out of four lines—which is exactly the opposite of the intent of such unifying symbols.

Churches and other religious institutions do perform functions, I believe, that the contemporary pluralized state can recognize as worth supporting through tax breaks and other means. A case can be made for clergy in this respect as well. As I trust I have made quite clear by now, I do not intend by these remarks to encourage a secularist evacuation of all religious institutions, symbols, values, and personnel from public life—not at all. Instead, we Christians should be taking the initiative to surrender those privileges that no longer make sense in a post- or semi-Christian society and instead use our shrinking cultural power to establish new relations of religion/society and church/state that will benefit all participants, including religious communities and state institutions, without unjustly penalizing or privileging any. Indeed, we should use what influence we have left to help construct the sort of society in which we ourselves would like to live once our power to effect it has disappeared. And we can be guided in part by our experience of being a minority at our beginning, and in various societies ever since. How unseemly it is for Christians to fight in the courts and legislatures for what remains of the dubious honors and advantages of Christendom. There is no more prudent time to do unto others as we would have them do unto us.

Let us conclude this section with examples of Christian cultural participation in three illustrative jobs: teacher, chaplain, and politician.

As we have already noted, the Christian teacher in a public school must not see his job as primarily an opportunity for proselytizing his students or his colleagues. Nor must he see it primarily as an opportunity for impressing his pupils with his own particular values. Instead, he must see public education on its own terms as worthwhile from a Christian perspective and undertake it in that spirit. Thus he will count it a good day's work, or a good year's work, or a good career's work even if no child under his care and no colleague within his acquaintance ever professes a conversion experience because of his example or teaching. He will wish it were otherwise, of course, since he longs for every one of those children to be reconciled to God. Nonetheless, the task of public education must be viewed as worthwhile in itself.

To be sure, a Christian who teaches with passion, skill, sympathy, and prudence will shine out such that colleagues may well ask him to discuss his motivation and values, which might result in spiritual conversation. And as he naturally shares his life with students in the course of teaching, he will unselfconsciously drop clues (such as mentioning church, or prayer, or God) that will connect him with his religion and thus add luster to students' opinion of that religion. But two conclusions follow.

First, the success of the Christian teacher is to be measured by *teaching,* not by some other activity such as evangelism. Second, the Christian teacher must always remain just as circumspect about his faith as he would want the Mormon teacher in the next classroom and the Muslim teacher down the hall to be as well. None of them should hide who they are. None of them should be shy about answering the sorts of questions that anyone can be asked in the workplace. But none of them should take advantage of their teaching position to do something else—even something as wonderful as evangelism. For the will of God is for public education to be conducted well by everyone involved, just as it is the will of God for Christians to evangelize—without the two activities interfering with each other.

In the second case, the Christian chaplain—let's say in a hospital, but the same principles stand in a prison, the armed forces, or some other public institution—cannot be other than who she is (Christian), and no system should ask her to be other than that. In particular, she should not be expected to become "generically religious" or "spiritual," or to become a religious chameleon who can be Buddhist to Buddhists, Islamic to Muslims, and Wiccan to Wiccans. Such transformation is impossible, so no chaplain can properly be asked to perform it.

Instead, chaplains need to be clear about their role in such an institution. That may take some doing for, as in public school teaching, there is no unanimity about all that the institution should be trying to accomplish. But what *can* be done by chaplains is to offer a measure of care that takes spiritual things seriously in an environment (hospital, prison, military base) that otherwise rarely does so. And chaplains can offer that spiritual care to people in the measure and in the style in which they consent to be helped. To do so is to love your neighbor as you love yourself, and to do to others as you would have them do to you.

So a Jewish chaplain who naturally cannot pray with a Christian "in Jesus' name" can yet sit with that Christian while he prays that way, or find a Christian to pray with him, or listen to him discuss his spiritual concerns, or secure Christian books for him to read while he convalesces. The chaplain can also happily offer what wisdom and encouragement he can from his distinctive tradition. And the Christian chaplain can do the same for his non-Christian charges. Thus there is much that a chaplain can do for a broad public without being asked to compromise his distinctive faith commitments.

In the third case, the issue of personal faith and political decision making actually breaks out into two questions: should a politician take her faith into account when she is considering an issue, and should a politician make policy strictly according to the strictures of her religion?

In the first place, the answer is easy if we are true to the form of government we have. Canadians, Americans, and others around the world have chosen representative democracy over direct democracy. We elect people to represent us in political decisions: they are to gather the information, listen to all sides, and then decide on our behalf. They are, in short, to do this work for the rest of us who are too busy, uninformed, or unskilled to do the job ourselves. And if we are sufficiently unhappy with what they decide, we replace them in the next election. Our choice on election day, that is, is for people who will decide on our behalf, not people who will simply survey our collective opinions and then vote. That would be direct, not representative, democracy—the sort of politics that is meant when we complain of "government by polling" rather than "government by principle."

The confusion comes right in the word "representative." Are our legislators supposed to represent simply the current collective opinion in their ridings (54 percent in favor, 30 percent against, 16 percent undecided—at least until tomorrow's poll)? Or have they been elected by the majority to be entrusted with the task of thinking through the issues and then offering their best judgment as to what is right for the riding and the country? If we really want the former sort of decision making, then we don't need representatives at all anymore. Now we can govern the country via the Internet, and we can all log on every day and cast our own votes and make laws directly. Some days, granted, that option looks pretty good. But I doubt we really want that sort of mob rule. We have chosen instead to elect a small group of people to be equipped with staff and technologies and personal expertise to do our deciding for us.

Since we have so chosen, then we should be thinking hard about just whom we are sending to the legislature to decide for us. Such a person is, after all, a particular combination of upbringing, education, job experience, family life, and religious commitment—understanding "religious" in the broad sense of whatever is most basic to his or her philosophy of life. When our representative is deciding about an issue, why should she be expected to pretend she doesn't know something that she thinks she does know—such as what the Bible says as the Word of God on this matter? If we have elected a traditional Christian, we should expect her to decide as one. And if we elect someone else, say, a secular humanist or a liberal Muslim or an observant Jew, then we should expect him or her to decide accordingly.

So a Christian politician is both a Christian and a politician. She decides what she thinks is right according to her best, Christianity-informed judgment. She might, in considering the vexed issue of government recognition of same-sex marriage, agree that marriage really is best defined just the way traditional Christianity says it is. But that's not the end of the matter. She then should act as a politician, trying to broker the best arrangement for all concerned—and *that* is how she represents everyone in her constituency, on behalf of the common good. As she looks at the options available to her, she might well decide among various possibilities, not just automatically try to impose traditional Christian teaching about marriage on a very varied population. Thus she might vote for the state to call same-sex unions "marriages"—again, whatever her own views about marriage might be—while preserving the rights of religious groups to reserve their own marriage ceremonies only for those unions they can conscientiously bless. Or she might move to take the word "marriage" out of the state's vocabulary entirely and endorse "civil unions" or "registered domestic partnerships" instead. Or she might well decide that traditional Christian teaching about marriage is exactly what is needed in her society, and so she votes that way.

If her constituents don't like the way she makes up her mind about such things, they are free to replace her. But the crucial thing to note is that she has done her job properly in any of those three ways: She has voted according to what she felt was politically the most realistic way to secure the most *shalom* for her home constituency and her country—whatever the current polls show her constituents think about the issue. To be sure, she does not ignore polls, for she must remain in office to get certain things done. Sensitivity to her constituents' preferences is also a legitimate and important part of political office. It just is not the only one—else we don't need a representative at all.[28]

Some religious and philosophical outlooks, including some Christian ones, cannot accommodate such a view of politics. They know what is right and everything must be exactly their way or not at all, since their way is "God's way" and God brooks no compromise.[29] One observer ruefully lumped together Christian, Communist, and Islamist fanaticism in regard to Osama bin Laden's second in command, Ayman al-Zawahiri: "Like a good Marxist or Leninist, al-Zawahiri was interested in 'building the Kingdom of God on earth.' "[30] But I have been suggesting that as we Christians read our Bibles, we find God working in mysterious, patient, and piecemeal ways to bring his blessings—blessings that anticipate the final coming of the Kingdom that only he can bring. So we can commend good politicians also, of whatever stripe, for doing the best they can, step by step, to bring blessing as well.

Such, then, is a formal view of the work of such Christians in public settings. Before we leave them, let us say a word about the content of their participation. Beyond the generic concern for *shalom* making, at least two particular concerns

---

28. David Martin offers trenchant reflections for politicians—and for academicians—that have informed this discussion in his "The Christian, the Political, and the Academic," in *On Secularization: Towards a Revised General Theory* (Aldershot, UK: Ashgate, 2005), 185–99.

29. One advance reader asked me, "Are you not convinced by the argument that marriage *cannot* be subject to human construction?" I reply, first, that it is simply a matter of fact that marriage *has* been subject to human (re-)construction, notably in polygamy, in the taking of concubines and mistresses, in the serial monogamy typical of modern societies, in common-law marriages, and so on. Second, I think the reader means instead that, however we human beings have altered marriage to suit our wishes, marriage is in fact a divine institution, as per Genesis 2, and therefore has just one actual, legitimate form. With that, I agree. But the fact that I think so doesn't mean that I might not see, as a politician, that the best decision I can make in a given situation might be to cast a vote for the redefinition of the word "marriage" so as to preserve what can be preserved in the face of malign or confused social forces that otherwise would score an even bigger victory against what I believe to be the best—that is, divinely instituted—values of human relationship. The fact that I believe that there is only one proper understanding of marriage doesn't mean I could not vote for the legal accommodation of more than one in the law of a plural society, just as I might vote for the legal accommodation of more than one expression of sexuality, despite my traditional views to the contrary. It all depends on what political options happen to be available, among which I have to choose that which I trust will produce the most *shalom* in a situation deeply compromised by sin and confusion.

30. Thomas Friedman, quoting his friend Abdallah Schliefer, in *The World Is Flat: A Brief History of the Twenty-First Century* (New York: Farrar, Straus and Giroux, 2005), 396.

will be on their agendas. The first will be to preserve a sense of the importance of the spiritual and to resist the pressure to reduce matters to the merely economic, or psychological, or political. Believing teachers, chaplains, and politicians will model as well as espouse such a view of things that includes a dimension of transcendence, and will help others at least to respect their fellows who do so, so that important public matters do not get squeezed down under the low ceiling of secularism.

The second abiding concern will be to defend free space specifically for the Christian church. Not only the "spiritual in general" but the gospel in particular must be protected, else society loses a crucial voice—not only about the world to come but also about the here and now. The church is not the sole valuable voice of this sort, but Christian teachers, chaplains, politicians, and others in public life will be especially appreciative of the church's mission and will therefore do what they can to help others appreciate it and thus maintain its liberty. As governments and developers increasingly view church property through the lens of economic growth, as institutions find it increasingly inconvenient to oblige religious concerns in the workplace or in leisure activities, and as society at large increasingly wants the public schools to produce the next generation of compliant and productive citizens without any irksome religious oddity, let alone recalcitrance, Christians will work to maintain freedom for the church to bring its distinctive message and perform its distinctive service to the world. To be sure, "freedom" does not mean "privilege," and we must be clear about the difference or else we risk losing both—or gaining both at the cost of sacrificing any claim to altruism.

GOVERNING MOTIFS

Despite the themes of ambiguity and ambivalence that have recurred in this account of Christian ethics, many other themes—themes of the Christian Story, the mission of God, our vocation, and our hope—frame our ethos, give it firmness and direction, and help us make the critical daily decisions necessary to follow Jesus, to be and to do what he wills for us today. We thus must distinguish the concern for *shalom* making from mere utilitarianism, which is at best half right. Yes, we seek the greatest good possible, but not just for the greatest number. Moreover, what counts as "good" is not merely calculable along an axis of pleasure and pain, and certainly not merely the pleasure of the powerful (whether an elite or the majority) at the expense of others. Instead, what is good is defined for us by the Bible in a richly complicated way, which I have only begun to thematize in this volume. As we conclude, then, we can emphasize some motifs in this ethic by way of contrast with dangers that lurk around any careless, half-understood, or desultorily undertaken version of this way of being Christian.

Dialectic Without Capitulation

We engage our culture willy-nilly. I simply *am* a Canadian, an Anglo-Canadian, a Canadian who studied and taught in the United States, a Canadian from northern Ontario who has lived on the prairies and now lives on the West Coast. These are geographical statements, and in the nature of human life they are statements about who I am and about how the shape of the land and the shape of human societies on that land have shaped me. So, as Jesus prayed, we are given to him by the Father from the world and then we remain in the world, sent into it as Jesus was, in order to perform our calling here (John 17).

Therefore we engage in an ongoing conversation with the world, a give-and-take, a symbiosis, a dialectic. We were originally created this way, out of the very earth itself and yet also enlivened by the breath of God (Gen. 2). As we fell, we dragged the world down with us. So now we participate with God in redeeming the world, in dragging it up again here and there, in remaking what cannot be salvaged, in waiting for the restoration that only God can bring at the end of this time.

I did not define "we" or "world" in the foregoing, because I think whatever definition we attach—"we" as generically human or specifically Christian, or "world" as planet or as human community—the relationship and the vocation remains the same. We simply *are* in dialectic. There is no available option of either complete withdrawal or complete domination. So we make the best of it.

Making the best of it therefore means refusing to capitulate to the world. Again, this is not merely a Christian imperative, but a human one. We human beings were put in charge of the world to cultivate it—indeed, to subdue it. We are not to succumb to the lure of "natural rhythms," of letting things be, however beautiful they are and however ashamed we feel about our previous mismanagement. We are to garden the world, to take its potential and improve it. We are not to abandon our dignity and responsibility, however intimidating the task may seem and however unnerved we are by our recognition of past failures. We are to make *shalom*.

In this crucial sense, then, the Christian is not called to something fundamentally different from that to which anyone else is called. As I have tried to show, the redemption commandments are simply in the service of the creation commandments. As Christians live out all of these mandates, we truly witness to what it means to be generically human, not peculiarly Christian—for to be

Christian, in this fundamental sense, means to follow the Son of Man, the very image of God (Col. 1:15), in the work of generic humanity: loving God and one's neighbor as oneself and cultivating the earth. It is the destiny of the whole earth to follow that one Lord—the peculiarity of Christianity and its temporary redemption commandments will fade away as "every knee shall bow...and every tongue confess that Jesus Christ is Lord, to the glory of God the Father" (Phil. 2:10–11).

Of course, then, if no human being should capitulate to the "wild" of the natural world, the not-yet-cultivated spaces of it, a fortiori no Christian should capitulate to the limitations, much less the evil, of the current world system. We must beware—not categorically avoid, but beware—any alliance with the powers: powers of government, powers of commerce, powers of ideology, powers of entertainment. Such alliances always will tend to draw us away from the Lordship of Christ and toward idolatry. Ultimately, we cannot serve two masters, and we must be vigilant against any alluring inclination to think we can. We can cooperate with the powers as far as such cooperation produces *shalom* and avoids worse evil. But we must also simply expect "tribulation" in the world (Jn. 16:33) from those powers, since our loyalties are elsewhere and higher, and conflict is inevitable.

Our apologists throughout history have claimed that Christians make good citizens, good employees, and good neighbors. That claim is true. It is true, however, only until the powers demand from us what we will not give as disciples of Christ: whether the cessation of our evangelism, our complicity in wrongdoing, our silence in the face of injustice, and our basic allegiance above all. When that conflict comes, then we are to be, once again, the subversives we have always been when we have had our priorities straight. And the powers seem to know, better than sometimes we do ourselves, that we are such dangerous people—which is why the powers never stop suspecting the church and trying to keep it under control, one way or another.[31]

We also live in the dialectic of the responsible individual and the church. We love the church and esteem it as our primary group, our new "family" that tran-

---

31. Oliver O'Donovan indicates a crucial difference in the political realm between the Christian understanding of society versus rulers: "Society and rulers have different destinies: the former is to be transformed, shaped in conformity to God's purpose; the latter are to disappear, renouncing their sovereignty in the face of his....Christ has conquered the rulers from below, by drawing their subjects out from under their authority"—and, as I say above, I think many rulers, as well as other sorts of powers, sense that fact, fear it, and resent it (*The Desire of the Nations*, 193).

scends all other social allegiances. We recognize that the church one day will be the splendid community of peace depicted in Biblical prophecy. In the light of that prophecy, however, we recognize that the church today only approximates that golden future. We therefore will be alert to social forces in congregations, denominations, special purpose groups, and even home fellowships that compromise Christian ideals and harm the individuals involved. We will not be amazed at sin and stupidity in the church; rather, we will expect it, plan for it, deal with it, forgive it, and carry on. And we will also be grateful for the church's patience with each of us, as we sometimes dilatorily, sometimes dogmatically, and sometimes zealously participate in it.

Each of us belongs to society and to the church, and we participate in each as faithfully as we can as disciples of Jesus Christ——fully beholden neither to society nor to the church, but only to Christ, even as we long for that day in which the distinction between society and church forever disappears.

Living in dialectic—which entails patience, compromise, and persistence in the face of setback and only partial success—must never mean the sloth of capitulation. Nor can it mean the slothful resignation of "Oh, well, what can you do?" What you can do, what we all can do, is the will of God: to bring as much *shalom* as we can in every situation. Thus we will also maintain a crucial measure of "holy discontent" (John Stott) until the New Jerusalem descends.

Transformation Without Imperialism

This impetus to garden, and the specifically Christian impetus to recover and redeem, must be tempered by the recognition of our own limits and sinfulness. We may hope to reign with Christ someday; we dare not presume to reign *for* Christ now. One certainly can sympathize with Ian Frazier's rueful warning that "history may be useful to know, but when people start thinking of themselves in terms of history with a capital 'H,' look out."[32] We Christians, who *do* think of ourselves—and everyone else, and the whole planet—in terms of the Christian Story, are reminded by our own Story of how susceptible we ourselves are to the lure of power justified by self-righteousness.

Furthermore, any inclination to domination must be tempered also by the recognition of the genuine humanity of our neighbors and thus of the contribution that they, too, are making to the fundamental work of gardening the world. God has broadcast his blessings to further his purposes everywhere, so this worshiper

---

32. Ian Frazier, "Invaders," *New Yorker*, April 25, 2005, 54.

of a false God over here has an extraordinary gift of art, and this follower of a misdirected philosophy over there has an extraordinary gift of integrity, and this community of another faith has an extraordinary gift of technical ability, and so on. We can and must rejoice in goodness discovered anywhere, since all goodness comes from the same fountain (Calvin, *Institutes*, I.i.2; cf. Jas. 1:17). And we must be both humble and careful not to destroy the good that God has placed here or there in our rush to correct whatever errors we find with the gospel. "Transformation" rarely, if ever, ought to mean "total eradication and then rebuilding from the ground up," nor should it mean "our way is identical with God's way, so we shall brook no dissent nor compromise," although it has often meant exactly that in the history of Christian imperialism.[33]

Lesslie Newbigin is eloquent on this point:

> All human traditions, institutions, and structures are prone to evil—including religion and including Christianity and the Church. They are all part of this present age. They are all prone to make absolutist claims. They are all ambiguous. There are always good reasons for attacking them. But human life is impossible without them, and God in his mercy preserves them in order to give time for the Church to fulfill its calling to make manifest to them the wisdom of God.... We are not conservatives who regard the structures as part of the unalterable order of creation, as part of the world of what we call "hard facts" beyond the range of the gospel, and who therefore suppose that the gospel is only relevant to the issues of personal and private life. Nor are we anarchists who seek to destroy the structures. We are rather patient revolutionaries who know that the whole creation, with all its given structures, is groaning in the travail of a new birth, and that we share this groaning and travail, this struggling and wrestling, but do so in hope because we have already received, in the Spirit, the firstfruit of the new world (Rom. 8:19–25).[34]

---

33. Nicholas Wolterstorff refers to an anonymous "seventeenth-century English writer" who testified, "I had rather see coming toward me a whole regiment with drawn swords, than one lone Calvinist convinced that he is doing the will of God" (*Until Justice and Peace Embrace* [Grand Rapids, MI: Eerdmans, 1983], 9). Wolterstorff does so, I think, with playful approbation. But the quotation works the other way, too. The regiment might yet be reasoned with, bargained with, or even bought off, if necessary. But the "lone Calvinist" convinced of the identity of his cause with God's will, will be relentless and implacable—which will be entirely in order if the gospel itself is at stake, but not if just anything else is. Yet, in the context of Wolterstorff's discussion, *everything* else is at stake in "world-formative Christianity," as he calls it. Thus I resist what I see to be in fact an imperialistic mode of being Christian.

34. Lesslie Newbigin, *The Gospel in a Pluralist Society* (Grand Rapids, MI: Eerdmans, 1989), 209.

Plurality Without Relativism

Even as we recognize that our non-Christian neighbors contribute to the generic human program of earthkeeping, so we ought to recognize that our Christian siblings make distinctive contributions to the specifically Christian work of redemption. We thus should endorse a plurality of missional modes, each accomplishing something particular and good, and a plurality of missional messages, each articulating something particular and good. Such a principle is easy to articulate but sometimes hard to practice, particularly if one is passionate about one's own perspective on, and proposed solution to, a keenly felt problem. But humility about one's own limitations and gracious recognition of our siblings' dignity should open us up to the likelihood that they, too, have something good to contribute to this matter. We must go beyond a benign tolerance of such differences, a kind of "comity" arrangement that lets the Presbyterians do their thing there while we Methodists do things here, as happened in the history of missions, and lets the environmentalists do their thing there while we evangelists do our thing here. We must see how attending to our differences often can help us be better versions of ourselves: environmentalists suffused with the excitement of their work being truly evangelistic and evangelists rejoicing to proclaim a God who loves the whole earth, not just human souls. And we must allow that in complex situations, Christians may end up saying and doing not just different but even apparently contrary things, in a paradox of faithfulness the resolution of which is understood only by God.

Affirmation of plurality, however, does not mean surrender to relativism. Not all options advocated by just anyone claiming Christianity can be, or should be, affirmed or even tolerated. All sorts of horrors have been justified in the name of Christianity, from chattel slavery to genocide to cultural annihilation to spousal abuse to child molestation. If we have no qualms about simply pronouncing these things wrong, and I trust we have none, then we can be poised to flatly disagree with other options offered in the name of Christ. Humble openness to honor God and each other in the recognition of authentic plurality must remain in tension with the humble willingness to honor God and each other in the recognition of authentic error and sin. I have myself tried to listen to and learn from interlocutors mentioned in this book, and many more who have not been, without feeling obliged to affirm or agree with all they did or said—including Lewis, Niebuhr, and Bonhoeffer.

No one, to be sure, can be certain of striking a perfect balance here just because no one but God can be certain of perfect judgment on *anything*. So what I write today I might well want to modify or even retract tomorrow—indeed, I almost certainly will want to do so, since this book is not a finding rendered from some pinnacle of adjudication but rather a report from one pilgrim on the journey on which we all are embarked. Still, we each are called to make decisions—important decisions—and to do so we must strive to be as open as we can be to goodness, while also as resistant as we can be to all that is not good.

Conviction Without Hubris

We walk with confidence in Christ, therefore, because we have the conviction that he really is Lord, that he really has called us into his company, and that he really has assigned us a mission—the distinctive Christian mission of redemption—along with our "standing orders" of cultivating the earth. These are the convictions that shape and dignify everything we do, everywhere, at every moment. Thus we will be both patient and persistent. We will be patient because of our understanding of God's providence, even understanding that we yet do not understand so much of God's providence and can trust him anyway. And we will be persistent because we have heard God's call and strive to obey it as the very words of life. We walk by faith, not by sight—but we do walk, trusting God to guide us, equip us, correct us, forgive us, bless us, and use us.

Strong in these convictions, we yet strive to avoid hubris. We cannot succeed on our own. We need each other in our Christian communities, we need the support and wisdom of other Christian communities, we need the cooperation and gifts of other human beings, we need our fellow creatures, and we need God, ever, always, now. We also recognize that we might be wrong about much, and we are undoubtedly wrong about some things—unless we are claiming a degree of correctness and infallibility that neither the Scriptures nor church history can plausibly be understood to warrant. We further recognize that our best-intentioned, best-conceived, and best-executed work will not entirely succeed, nor result in only good consequences. And we go on to recognize that very little of our work meets even this standard, with the expectation that the rest is even more likely to issue in far less than optimal outcomes. Our speech, therefore, ought to be qualified by such humility, as should our actions, our relationships, and our self-esteem.

Humility, however, is not lukewarmness, pusillanimity, resignation, or confusion. Humility is, fundamentally, submitting gladly to God the Father and following joyfully his Son in the power of the Spirit. The world needs bold, enterprising, passionate, and persistent disciples of Christ who will see it for what it is, who will love it as God does, and who will care for it with creativity, realism, and hope. The whole world—God's world, our world—is at stake, and we must make the best of it.

INDEX

INDEX OF SCRIPTURAL
REFERENCES